Thank YOU

This book
purchased
with donations
made to the
GiveBIG
for Books
Campaign.

The
Seattle
Public
Library
Foundation

www.foundation.spl.org

SHIFTING SANDS

SHIFTING SANDS

The United States in the Middle East

Joel S. Migdal

Columbia University Press   New York

Columbia University Press

Publishers Since 1893

New York   Chichester, West Sussex

cup.columbia.edu

Copyright © 2014 Joel S. Migdal

All rights reserved

Library of Congress Cataloging-in-Publication Data

Migdal, Joel S.

   Shifting sands : the United States in the Middle East / Joel S. Migdal.

      pages cm

   Includes bibliographical references and index.

   ISBN 978-0-231-16672-0 (cloth : alk. paper)—ISBN 978-0-231-53634-9 (e-book)

   1. United States—Foreign relations—Middle East.   2. Middle East—Foreign relations—

United States.   3. United States—Foreign relations—1945–1989.   4. United States—Foreign

relations—1989–   5. Middle East—Politics and government—1945–   I. Title.

   DS63.2.U5M5327 2014

   327.73056—dc23

                                2013020256

Columbia University Press books are printed on permanent and durable acid-free paper.

This book is printed on paper with recycled content.

Printed in the United States of America

c 10 9 8 7 6 5 4 3 2 1

Jacket Image: © Rosa Isabel Vazquez / Gallery Stock

References to websites (URLs) were accurate at the time of writing. Neither the author nor
Columbia University Press is responsible for URLs that may have expired or changed since the
manuscript was prepared.

For Marcy, in loving memory

Contents

Preface

In *Shifting Sands*, I explore the ups and downs of the United States since World War II in what has become the most important and volatile region in the world, the Middle East. In explaining America's rollercoaster ride, I employ a novel approach, showing how U.S. officials from the close of World War II through the end of the twentieth century built a rigid strategic model atop the shifting sands of the region; even as the Mideast region underwent several cataclysmic changes, they employed a constant formula to guide their policies. That model was not unique to the Middle East. I argue that the United States had a universal model, derived from its postwar experience in Europe, that it applied in region after region around the world, with mixed success.

In the pages that follow, I have avoided the standard approach of treating the Middle East as a more-or-less self-enclosed entity and the United States as an external, often disruptive, force.[1] Such a view presents the "West" and specifically the United States in the last two-thirds of a century as throwing the region into disarray by disrupting its natural, or traditional, order. Underlying such a notion is a kind of nostalgia for a harmonious, socially equal precolonial past. This perspective robs Middle Easterners of their agency, of their important role in bringing about the changes that have swept across their region, and it transforms them from players into victims. And this approach portrays the United States as far more capable than it has actually been.

Instead, this book looks at the region as one in which the United States early on became an integral, everyday regional player. Since World War II, the United States has been highly integrated, for better or for worse, into the ongoing patterns of interaction (especially between governments and their populations), forms of cooperation, fault lines of conflict, and dominant ideology of the region—what I call "regional dynamics." The United States has had a profound effect on the Middle East, just as it, in turn, has been deeply affected by the region. But by no means has it been the only critical player, nor has it often been able to achieve its goals.

No single set of relations has characterized the region over the last two-thirds of a century. Instead, I have identified three major breakpoints that the Middle East experienced since World War II, each creating new patterns of regional and state-society relations in the various countries of the area. The first two of those upheavals each transformed the dynamics of the region, as well as the underlying relations between governments and their citizens, for a generation. The long-term regional patterns to emerge from the last upheaval are just now becoming evident.

The first shakeup occurred in 1948 through 1952, sparked by four monumental events: the fitful withdrawal of the European colonial powers from the Middle East, the entry of the United States and Soviet Union into the everyday affairs of the region as they squared off in the Cold War, the creation of Israel, and the breakthrough of Arab nationalism in the 1952 Free Officers Revolution. Those events helped establish a set of regional patterns that lasted through the 1950s, 1960s, and 1970s.

The second major disruption came in 1979, with two political bombshells within days of each other: the Iranian Islamic Revolution and the Egyptian-Israeli peace treaty. The period that followed saw Iran emerge as the dominant local power as Egypt receded in importance, the withdrawal of the Soviet Union as a day-to-day player, and the elevation of the United States as the sole global power in the region, more deeply involved than ever before. And, finally, the Middle East imploded again in this century, with the tumultuous events tied to the Green Movement in Iran in 2009 and, even more momentously, the Arab Spring starting in late 2010. The region is just now beginning to see patterns of relations stemming from this last wave of turbulence.

This book tackles a number of key questions. Why did U.S. presidents find it so challenging to achieve their goals in the region? Why did administration after administration experience such difficulty in building the kinds of coalitions and partnerships that could advance America's position there? What should and can the United States accomplish in today's tumultuous environment? Are past foreign-policy tools relevant to the post–Arab Spring era? If not, what should the United States now seek in the region, and which tools would help Washington achieve its goals?

The argument in the pages ahead, in schematic terms, is that for more than half a century following World War II, Washington applied a fixed strategy to a moving target. Faced with fundamentally changing regional relations and patterns of interactions between governments and citizens—the shifting sands of my title—the United States responded with a rigid strategic model. That model came out of America's post–World War II experience in Europe as the Cold War took shape. Indeed, that formula was applied by American officials around the world, with the Middle East being a prime example of how that uniform strategic vision was repeatedly used as the United States established its global preeminence and faced off against the Soviet Union.

Two motivating—and somewhat contradictory—forces drove the construction of the model: the felt need to project power in nearly every nook and cranny in the world to combat communism and the skyrocketing costs of being a truly global power. U.S. presidents from Roosevelt and Truman on looked for a formula to exert power around the world while still somehow limiting the outlay of American resources, not bankrupting the United States, as President Eisenhower put it. The model that emerged was fairly simple: find a regional strategic partner—some local power that could play a role, like Great Britain did in the European context. A strategic partner could do America's bidding in the region and share the burden and costs of exercising power. The model also looked to build, if possible, a security alliance along the lines of NATO. U.S. participation in the Middle East was based on this formula, especially the quest for a regional strategic partner, for the rest of the twentieth century, and this was abandoned only after 9/11.

This strategy certainly had elements to recommend it, but its success depended on applying it carefully, accounting for differences from region to region. Unfortunately, American policy makers did not do particularly well in responding to the particular regional order in the Middle East from the 1950s on or the major changes in that order starting in 1979. State-society relations in individual countries and regional relations often were overlooked as policy makers applied the formula, undermining

U.S. efforts. After 1948, the rapid rise of Arab nationalism, the growing dominance of Egypt and secondarily Iraq and Syria, and the intensity of the Arab-Israeli conflict all set in motion forces that repeatedly foiled the designs of American policy makers.

The United States fared much better in the 1970s and 1980s. But the upheaval in Iran in 1979, the decline of Arab nationalism, and the end of the Cold War created new challenging conditions, including the rise of political Islam and an Iranian-led bloc that stretched from the Persian Gulf to the Mediterranean.

The search for strategic partners during the decades after World War II yielded uneven results. But American strategy did succeed in tempering direct U.S. involvement in the Middle East. The United States successfully avoided a sustained, massive military presence in the region in the twentieth century, with the brief exception of the Gulf War in 1990 and 1991. The first decade of the twenty-first century, though, witnessed just such a sustained massive deployment of U.S. troops in this volatile area, with destructive consequences for both the region and the United States.

The chapters that follow analyze how the United States lost its way in the decade after 9/11. They point to three critical factors—the changing regional patterns after 1979, the failure of American officials to read those changes, and the abandonment by the George W. Bush administration of America's longstanding strategy of limiting costs by allying with a strategic partner in favor of another strategy entirely. The Bush administration's new approach saw the Middle East, generally, and Iraq, in particular, as keys to taming the global forces that most threatened the United States. Those threats, Bush officials believed, were located in an area I call the "Arc of Instability."

The approach and argument in *Shifting Sands* offer a novel and, I think, effective frame for understanding the checkered experience of the United States in the Middle East, especially the immense setbacks it suffered during the first decade of the twenty-first century. Exploring U.S. strategy in light of the particulars of Mideast regional relations and the changing patterns of relations between governments and their citizens provides a basis for assessing how the United States can pursue its interests and contribute positively to the region in the years to come. In the last three chapters, I look at how the Obama administration has attempted to change course after the mishaps of the previous decade, and I analyze whether and how the United States can establish an effectual, constructive role in today's Middle East.

The genesis for this book lies in a course at the University of Washington that I have given on a regular basis, "The Making of the Twenty-First Century." Students through the years have prodded me and doubted me as I tried to develop a coherent picture of the United States in the world and, in one big chunk of the course, in the Middle East. More tangibly the book began as a series of talks that I gave as the Iraq War drew down. In particular, the lectures I gave in the spring of 2009 at Tufts University and Wesleyan University, arranged by Leila Fawaz and Mary Alice Haddad, respectively, were instrumental in leading me to think that the lectures could form the basis of a book. Later talks at the University of Florida and Western Washington University also helped shape my thinking.

With another project on the docket, I hesitated to begin shaping my thoughts into a book. But my wife Marcy urged me to give it a try, and I spent much of the summer of 2009 in an Israeli café, starting the writing. I then felt ready to ask the Institute for Advanced Study in Princeton, where I would serve as a member in 2009–2010, if I could change from my proposed project (on the construction of public space in the United States) to one on the United States in the Middle East. Not only was the change generously accepted, but the institute proved to be a perfect haven for me. My wonderful colleagues there and the crack library team, led by Marcia Tucker, spurred me on and supported me as I completed much of the first draft of this book.

Later others read portions of what I had written and gave crucial advice, including Yüksel Sezgin, Ariela Migdal, Yoav Duman, Marcy Migdal, Penina Glazer, Myron Glazer, Ayala Rosen, Christian Novetzke, and Dov Waxman. My colleague Scott Radnitz organized a writing group in my home department, the Henry M. Jackson School of International Studies, and the comments I received in that group were invaluable to me. Those reading and commenting on the manuscript, besides Scott himself, were Daniel Chirot, Reşat Kasaba, Sabine Lang, Sunila Kale, Victor Menaldo, Mary Callahan, and Gad Barzilai. I received invaluable research assistance from Zeynep Aydoğan, Heather Guyton, Tim Rich, and Albana Dwonch. Mark Benjamin helped with the preparation of figures. I am also deeply indebted to the endowment set up by Robert F. Philip, which has supported my research for nearly twenty years. The biggest thanks go to my life partner, Marcy Migdal, for her strength and support right through the very end of the production of this book. It is to her blessed memory that I dedicate the book.

SHIFTING SANDS

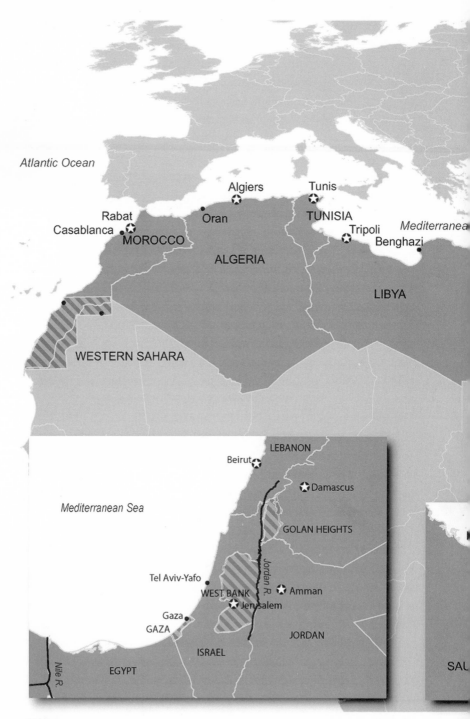

MAP 0.1

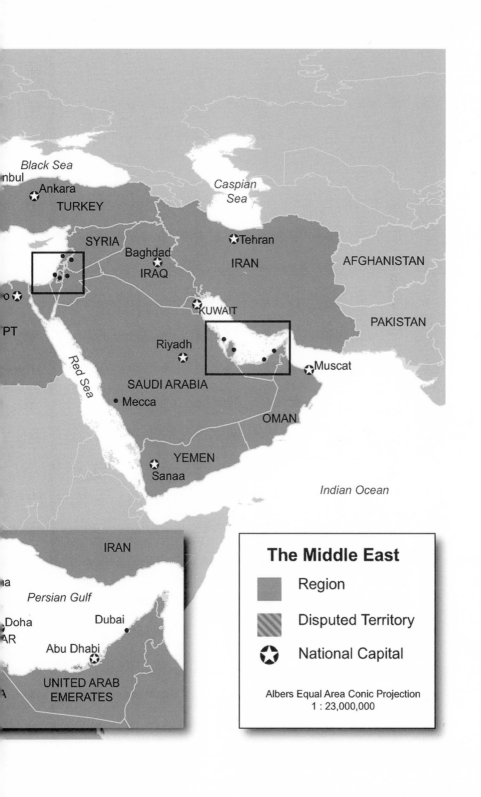

Black Sea

nbul

Ankara ✪

TURKEY

Caspian Sea

o ✪

PT

Red Sea

SYRIA

Baghdad
✪
IRAQ

Tehran ✪

IRAN

AFGHANISTAN

PAKISTAN

KUWAIT ✪

Muscat ✪

Riyadh ✪

SAUDI ARABIA

• Mecca

OMAN

YEMEN

Sanaa ✪

Indian Ocean

IRAN

Persian Gulf

a

Doha

AR

Dubai •

Abu Dhabi ✪

UNITED ARAB
EMERATES

A

The Middle East

Region

Disputed Territory

✪ National Capital

Albers Equal Area Conic Projection
1 : 23,000,000

PART I

Introduction

1   The Middle East in the Eye of the Global Storm

Three Mideast Transformations

During the final months of the Second World War, the United States made its first bid to be a permanent player in the Middle East. President Franklin Delano Roosevelt took a much publicized detour to the region in February 1945 on his way home from the famous Yalta Conference, only two months before his death. The immediate purpose of his trip was to meet with the king of Saudi Arabia, Abdul-Aziz ibn Saud, on the Great Bitter Lake along the Suez Canal in Egypt. FDR's circuitous (and risky) sailing route back to Washington, even when he was exhausted and already gravely ill, spoke to the importance his administration put on U.S. relations with not only Saudi Arabia but the entire Middle East as the war sputtered to an end.

Following on his declaration in 1943 that the defense of Saudi Arabia was vital to American security, Roosevelt took the first step, in his post-Yalta trip, in making the United States an ongoing actor in the region. He also instituted what would become a longstanding foreign-policy approach in the area, one grounded in leader-to-leader—president-to-autocrat—relations. From that moment of Roosevelt's journey until this day, the Middle East has remained a focal point of American foreign

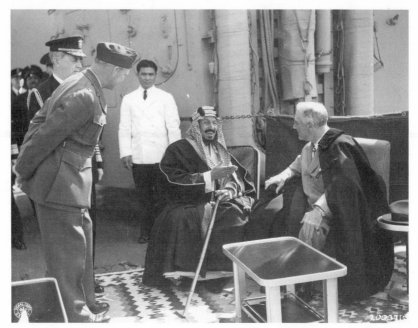

FIGURE 1.1   Franklin D. Roosevelt and King Ibn Saud of Saudi Arabia at the Great Bitter Lake in Egypt, February 14, 1945.
Source: Courtesy of Franklin D. Roosevelt Presidential Library and Museum.

concerns. For better or worse, every president since FDR has contributed to the abiding presence by the United States in this strategically crucial but troubled part of the world.

The same key regional factors that drew Roosevelt and his successor, Harry S. Truman, into the region's web in the first place have persisted over two-thirds of a century: access to oil, the Arab-Jewish conflict, the geographic centrality of the area, its key shipping lanes, the desire to block other powers from establishing a power base in the region, the threats the area held to global peace and stability, wars, more wars, violence, and more violence. Despite these seemingly unchanging issues and what appear to be timeless regional animosities, the Middle East actually has been a rapidly changing, fast-moving region (Korany 2010, 282). Leading powers, dominant ideologies, the basis of hostilities, the fault lines of conflict, and ongoing coalitions—what I call the *dynamics* of the region—have all shifted dramatically. The modern Middle East that FDR found had been fashioned in the latter stages of the First World War and its aftermath, and it has been substantially revamped several times since then.

In fact, almost like clockwork, a fundamental transformation of Mideast regional dynamics has occurred every three decades since 1918, when the Ottoman Empire collapsed and new indigenous states and European imperial rule came to dominate the region. By the time Truman followed up on Roosevelt's trip and made the bid for the United States to become a permanent player in the Middle East, in 1947–1948, the region was already on the cusp of another thoroughgoing change. The creation of Israel in 1948 and the breakthrough of Arab nationalism in the 1952 Egyptian Free Officers Revolution, along with the coming of the Cold War to the area, all worked to change the regional dynamics for a generation. Later, the United States would witness two additional fundamental transformations, one beginning in 1979, with the Iranian Revolution and the Egyptian-Israeli peace treaty, and another in 2009–2011, with the outbreak of major protests in Iran and those of the Arab Spring.

No single reason explains the odd fact that the Middle East has had a major upheaval about every thirty years. Each regional transformation had its own conditions and causes. Still, the pattern is not entirely coincidental. In each case, a new set of ideas, institutions, and leaders came on the scene with energy and excitement. But after a generation those ideas, institutions, and leaders had exhausted themselves. The ideas no longer spoke to the challenges that common people faced. The institutions were marked by cronyism and tired approaches to the problems of their countries and the region. The young leaders grew old in office, and the region had precious few states with effective modes of political succession: sons of rulers replaced their fathers and tended to stick with the same shopworn ideas and cronies. Ideas, institutions, and leaders that had arrived in a burst of innovation eventually strangled any new efforts at innovation. Even as Mideast societies changed rapidly, their politics remained stagnant, unable to cope with unfolding social change.

Each of these transformations, in 1918, 1948–1952, 1979, and 2009–2011, reordered the entire political and social dynamics of the area. The last three also complicated policy making for the United States, in its attempts to use its heft to influence those dynamics. This book follows the transformations in regional dynamics and traces the twisting path that Washington took as it insinuated itself as a day-in, day-out power in the Middle East.

The 1948–1952 Transformation: The Creation of Israel, the Free Officers Coup in Egypt, and Arab Nationalism

The Middle East that Roosevelt encountered was one that had been configured in great part by Great Britain and, secondarily, France. After nearly half a millennium of ups and downs, the Ottoman Empire, which had ruled the region—sometimes actually, sometimes nominally—collapsed entirely in 1918. In its place an array of territories appeared whose borders were carved out by the British and French as well as by local wars and political machinations. By the time of Roosevelt's trip, some of these territories housed real states exercising a credible degree of sovereign power; others contained states in name only, with imperial European powers hovering over them or with local tribal or other forces doing most of the actual governing; and still others were mandates ruled like colonies by the French and British.

When Roosevelt visited the region, though, the characteristics and dynamics of the post–World War I Middle East were already under great stress. The battering that the British and French took in World War II, the spread of anticolonial and nationalist thinking among the peoples of the region, the crystallization of conflict between Jews and Arabs in Palestine, and the burgeoning power of the Soviet Union to the north all pointed to the coming of a major transformation of the modern Middle East only thirty years after its birth.

Two local events set off the rush of regional changes. The first was the creation of Israel in 1948 and the first Arab-Israeli War. In that war, Arab armies unsuccessfully attempted to reverse the establishment of the Jewish state. Many of the familiar issues marking the region for the rest of the century and beyond were generated in the crucible of 1948. The global centrality of Israel, the Palestinian refugee crisis, the participation of Arab states and societies in the struggle against Israel, and the seeds of a Palestinian resistance movement all came out of the struggles of that year.

But a second event only four years later had just as important a role in establishing a new set of dynamics for the region. On July 23, 1952, a small group of junior army officers in Egypt calling themselves the Free Officers overthrew the Egyptian monarchy. A confluence of forces in the Middle East led up to the coup d'état, including the continuing heavy hand of European colonialism and imperialism despite the debilitation of the European powers by World War II; the shameful defeat of the Arab armies in the 1948 war with Israel; the growth of a powerful Arab nationalist ideology, especially in the 1940s, dedicated to the creation of a single, unified Arab state; and the corruption of the then ruling monarchies and their collaboration with foreign powers, particularly Great Britain.

The Free Officers coup and ensuing revolution jolted the entire Middle East like an electric charge. By 1958, three Arab nationalist regimes, led by Egypt and including Iraq and Syria, had set the tone for the entire region. For all Mideast players, including the United States, it was the Arab nationalists who lay at the heart of the region's dynamics. Those local dynamics took place in the context of the Cold War between the United States and the Soviet Union, which was itself taking shape just as the effects of the Free Officers coup rumbled through the Middle East. U.S. administrations from that of Truman on tried to shoehorn events in the area into the Cold War frame, but the region stubbornly had its own set of institutional configurations, lines of conflict, and axes of cooperation. The local dynamics were doubtless deeply influenced by the global U.S.-Soviet faceoff, but what actually occurred in the region stubbornly cleaved to locally generated factors.

What were these regional dynamics that marked the postcolonial, post-1952 Middle East? Four bitter struggles marked this period and shaped both the international and state-society relations in the region:

1. The ongoing battle between the new postcolonial nationalist Arab republics, with Egypt at the head, and Arab states clinging to older forms of governance, particularly monarchical rule
2. The triangular and often hostile relations among the principal new Arab nationalist republics, Egypt, Syria, and Iraq (and whomever they could line up on their sides)
3. The conflict between Israel and the Arab states, led, again, mostly by Egypt
4. Lines of division generated by the global bipolar division between the United States and the Soviet Union, especially as they acted through regional client states

If there was one country that as a single lever moved the entire area, it was Egypt. Under the leadership of the charismatic Gamal Abdul Nasser, it was the font of the ideology of Arab nationalism that deeply touched people's hearts, from the Persian Gulf all the way to the far reaches of northwestern Africa. The new Egypt drew key allies, even to the point of political unification with them. And it stood on one side of practically every war and serious conflict in the area. Egypt was a leader of the Non-Aligned Movement globally and was at the heart of U.S.-Soviet competition in the region, sometimes drawing close to one, other times to the other. For nearly thirty years after 1952, the ideas coming out of Egypt—secular republican rule, independent postcolonial states, Arab unity, socialism, and more—shaped the character and the conflicts of the Middle East.

Both the 1948 Arab-Israeli War and the 1952 Egyptian Revolution occurred as the Cold War between the United States and the Soviet Union took shape. Truman and his successors, along with the various leaders of the Soviet Union, interpreted the swirl of Mideast ideas, alliances, and fault lines primarily through the lens of the Cold War, which dominated their thinking. And while the distribution of power in the region certainly intersected time and again with the larger global power struggle, it was far from simply derivative of the Soviet-U.S. conflict.

The 1979 Transformation: The Iranian Revolution, Political Islam, and the Egypt-Israel Peace Treaty

Several factors contributed to the close of this Egypt-dominated era. Not least among them were the lingering effects of the humiliating defeat suffered by the Arab states, most notably Egypt, in the June 1967 war with Israel. But, similar to the first transformation of 1948–1952, it was just a couple of immediate occurrences that touched off a period of fundamental change and reconfigured the area's regional dynamics.

Within five days, two critical events took place in 1979. On March 26, Israel and Egypt formally signed a peace treaty, a phenomenon that was unthinkable only six years before, when the two, along with Syria, fought a ferocious war—the third Israeli-Egyptian War in six years. That treaty unofficially marked Egypt's abandonment of Nasser's Arab nationalist dream. It put an end to ideas of Arab political unity. The treaty also opened the door for a new, much more active diplomatic and political role for Israel in the entire Middle East, although it would take more than a decade for that to become obvious. Finally, the treaty was a godsend to

Washington, which underwrote it. It enabled subsequent U.S. administrations to ally both with Israel and the most powerful Arab state simultaneously, crowning America's rise as the single most important outside power in the region.

The second, even more momentous event occurred in Iran. After months of growing popular unrest, including massive demonstrations that carried through 1978 and into 1979, Iran's autocratic monarch, Shah Mohammad Reza Pahlavi, fled his country—to Egypt, ironically. The ousting of the shah led to the collapse of the regime, indeed, of the Iranian state itself. Islamic religious forces, led by the most notable figure in the Shiite sect and, perhaps, in all of Islam, Ayatollah Ruhollah Khomeini, guided the population through a national referendum that created the Islamic Republic of Iran on April 1, 1979.

Iran's revolution was a portent of major change for the entire Middle East. It provided an alternative model to the secular republics that had arisen in and dominated the region over the previous three decades. Iran demonstrated that a revived Islam could serve as the basis for rule in modern, republican Mideast states. This model, *political Islam*, called for a rededication and purification of personal religious practice, a change in the construction of public space, and the establishment of a state governed by Islamic law. Ayatollah Khomeini's theological justification of an Islamic republic was grounded in Shiite doctrine, but political Islam became a goal for Sunni Muslims as well, and its ideology displaced Arab nationalism in its ability to move Muslims deeply throughout the region.

Khomeini was not interested in revolutionary change in Iran alone; he was a true regional revisionist, just as Nasser had been a generation earlier. His aim was to export the Islamic revolution to other Muslim states, particularly in the Middle East. Slowed at first by a long, bloody war with Iraq, which lasted from 1980 until 1988, Iran emerged as the new lever for regional dynamics, replacing Egypt. Its increasing influence in the region coincided with the growing interest and power in the region by the Middle East's two other non-Arab powers, Turkey and Israel.

The region changed from one dominated by Arab states and ideas to one in which non-Arab states played the central roles and in which violent nonstate actors also became major players. Long-subservient Shiites now surged in power with the help of Iranian successes, material aid, and meddling. And various forms of political Islamic ideology became the dominant set of ideas in the region. And all this occurred as the global

Cold War, which framed so much of what had occurred in the region until the early 1980s, diminished in importance and then disappeared altogether with the collapse of the Soviet Union.

In the wake of the 1979 Iranian Revolution and the end of the Cold War, the regional dynamics changed markedly; they were now characterized by four different, sometimes overlapping fault lines:

1. The emergence of an Iran-led coalition—in part defined by anti-Americanism—that stretched westward across the entire expanse of the Middle East, from the Gulf to the Mediterranean, and its perceived threat to a heterogeneous group of other states and actors
2. Political Islam's push against existing regimes of nearly all stripes
3. Israel's conflict with the Palestinians and, secondarily, with Syria and Hezbollah in Lebanon
4. American imperial presence in the region, exercised principally in Iraq, and the deep opposition it engendered

If the fulcrum of regional dynamics for most of the period up to 1980 was Egypt and Arab nationalism, it subsequently became Iran and political Islam. And as the global context and the region changed, so did the role of and the challenges for the United States. After multiple successes in the 1970s, capped by the Egypt-Israel peace agreement, in the 1990s and 2000s Washington faced the growing animosity and power of Iran, along with the challenges posed by Saddam Hussein's Iraq. From the high perch it had achieved in the region in the 1970s, it descended into unending, draining wars after September 11, 2001.

The 2009–2011 Transformation: The Green Movement and the Arab Spring

The popular demonstrations that convulsed the Middle East during the last weeks of 2010 and through 2011—the Arab Spring—destabilized and upended what had seemed to be immovable dictatorships. The grassroots uprisings that shook the region actually did not begin in spring 2011 or even in the Arab world. They appeared first in a remarkable three months of street protests that shook Iran in 2009, sometimes called the Green Movement or the Persian Awakening. The demonstrations came after a national vote on June 12, 2009, that appeared to have been rigged by President Mahmoud Ahmadinejad, who was running for reelection. Ahmadinejad's security forces, including the Basij, a feared paramilitary force, brutally repressed protestors, killing dozens and arresting thousands of others.

The uprising and its eventual suppression riveted Middle East populations. The bloody events were often captured on cell-phone videos and were viewed by millions on YouTube; the Iranian regime had banned professional journalists. The pictures of Iranian authorities brutalizing their own population deeply affected people across the region. They undermined much of the popular support Iran had garnered in the region since its revolution, when it had stood up to the United States and offered a viable alternative to American-conceived democracy. And they served as an inspiration for the Arab populations that undertook social protests against their own governments a year and a half later.

The initial uprisings in the Arab world, beginning in Tunisia in December 2010 and then, during eighteen extraordinary days, in Egypt in January–February 2010, ousted both presidents, Zine El Abidine Ben Ali and Hosni Mubarak. Those dictators and other autocrats in the region had been in power for remarkably long periods—Ben Ali for twenty-three years, Mubarak for thirty, and some others going on half a century! They had survived for a variety of reasons, including their adroit manipulation of security forces, their ability to nip dissent in the bud, and their unrelenting suffocation of institutional innovation, which might create nodes of autonomous power, anywhere and everywhere in their societies.

Many lasted so long, too, because of their enduring, deep relations with the United States. Five American presidents, from Ronald Reagan to Barack Obama, had cultivated relations with the likes of Tunisia's Ben Ali. But their most intense and intimate ties were with two Egyptian presidents, first, Anwar Sadat in the 1970s, until his assassination in 1981, and then with Mubarak. One after another, American presidents from Richard M. Nixon to Obama had worked hand in glove with the Egyptian strongmen in executing U.S. policy throughout the region.

At the same time that Mubarak served as the most trusted confidante for American administrations and the strongman through whom U.S. policy in the region ran, he and his entire regime grew increasingly distant from their own constituents. I recall a telling moment in 2007, when I was in Egypt to deliver a lecture at the American University in Cairo. At the time, the university was in the center of Cairo, right off the heart of the city, in Tahrir Square (it has since moved to a spanking new campus far from the city center). As my hosts guided me to the lecture hall through the bustle of people in the side streets, I spotted a pack of fearsome men, aggressively shoving their way through the crowds. They wore grey galabiyehs, the traditional Egyptian robe, but they looked anything but traditional. I asked who they were. "Secret police," someone whispered in my ear, sent to break up a knot of perhaps twenty-five prodemocracy demonstrators in the square, hiding their identity behind the galabiyehs.

Little more than thugs, these barrel-chested men charged into the defenseless dissidents, who were protesting the next day's vote on constitutional amendments. The controversial amendments were intended to ensconce Mubarak even more firmly in the presidency, making it almost impossible for anyone not hand-chosen by his party to win the office. After the lecture, I saw that the square had been emptied of the protesters *and*, in fact, of all other ordinary citizens as well. The picketers had been driven into a building and beaten, and then police hauled them off to jail. Onlookers and simple passers-by had been pushed back into the surrounding streets.

In their place surrounding the vast naked square stood hundreds of uniformed security guards, positioned about six feet apart from one another. Each was in the ready position and held a rifle across his chest as he glowered out on the people in the streets. To me, the scene signified nothing less than a regime that deeply suspected and was terrified of the ordinary people. It was a scene of palpable fear and intimidation, and the fear ran both ways: the regime feared its own people as much as the people feared the regime.

The effect of the uprisings that ousted Mubarak four years later went well beyond Egypt. It undercut the existing dynamics of the region and rattled the foundations of U.S. foreign policy as well. The wildfire of protests in the Arab world, largely by swarms of peaceful demonstrators—citizens who echoed cherished American values in their rallies and came from all walks of life—confounded U.S. policy makers. Washington teetered between sympathy with the peaceful protesters and its deep commitments to Mubarak and the strategic partnership American officials had forged with him.

As the Arab Spring extended into summer and fall, the situation became even more confusing for American officials and made it increasingly difficult for them to devise a consistent policy. They looked on, offering little more than a few words of admonishment, as U.S. allies such as Bahrain's King Hamad ibn Isa al-Khalifa mercilessly attacked peaceful street protestors—and prevented medical personnel from treating them. To quell the protests, the beleaguered king even called in troops from neighboring countries, principally Saudi Arabia, whose regime established itself as the bulwark for the crumbling autocratic regimes in the region, at least the Sunni-dominated ones.

Simultaneously, the United States quickly initiated NATO military intervention against its long-time foe Muammar Qaddafi, who had held onto power in Libya for forty-two years. NATO forces mercilessly pounded Qaddafi's, aiding the rebels fighting him and eventually ensuring his demise. But if Washington acted resolutely against Qaddafi, it did little more than slap the wrist of another adversary, Bashar al-Asad, whose own eleven-year rule in Syria followed on the thirty-year presidency of his father. Like Bahrain's king, both of these leaders, who had consistently tried to thwart U.S. policies in the Middle East, unleashed their security forces to maul their own citizens.

The Obama administration was caught in an untenable situation. It sought to preserve the key elements that had underpinned American foreign policy in the Middle East for practically every president since World War II. These included close working ties with the likes of Mubarak and President Ali Abdullah Saleh of Yemen, in power for more than thirty years, who also battered his own peacefully protesting population but eventually was ousted. Those principles of American policy included, too, an odd reliance on ostensible enemies, like Qaddafi and al-Asad, to hold together diverse social forces in their countries that might otherwise be at one another's throats and to stave off Islamic militant groups such as al-Qaeda.

At the same time, the Obama team had to face a Middle East that had entered yet another one of its once-every-thirty-years transformations. Suddenly, the old principles of American policy were proving ever more anachronistic. Policy makers balanced precariously between their commitments to aging, flailing dictators and to core American values such as democracy and the right to peaceful protest. Those values had been stated forcefully in Obama's very first foreign-policy address abroad, his Cairo speech, on June 4, 2009, just four months into his presidency.

The effort to preserve U.S. influence in this key region was further complicated by the steep slide in America's reputation in the Middle East that had occurred during George W. Bush's years as president. From the outset, Obama had sought to reverse that downswing by appealing directly to the people of the region—the Cairo speech being the most prominent example—even as his administration continued to cooperate closely with the leaders repressing those very people.

At this writing, the new regional dynamics—the coalitions, fault lines, dominant conflicts, state-society relations, and central regional powers that will emerge from the current transformation—are far from clear. At least four new patterns may be emerging:

1. Disparate sectarian, kinship-based, tribal, and regional forces that had coexisted uneasily under strong-arm dictators may descend into fragmented patterns of violence, especially where state institutions to mediate conflict fail to develop
2. Where such state institutions do manage to develop and take root, societies, broadly conceived, will have a much greater voice in directing their states, but that voice may be divided between sparring democratic secular and political Islamic forces, each of which also may face internal tensions and conflicts
3. Iran's influence in the region, including the regional bloc that it assembled in the 1980s, 1990s, and 2000s, may diminish in importance and even crumble; Iran itself may no longer be the singular fulcrum for regional dynamics that it had been; and Shiites (and Alawis and Alevis) throughout the region (led by Iran) will find a strong backlash against the resurgence they experienced following the Iranian Revolution
4. Turkey has already moved from a neutral facilitator in the region to a stakeholder in the unfolding dynamics, attempting to gain influence with emerging Islamic regimes and teaming with Saudi Arabia to combat Shiite-dominated polities, especially Syria
5. Israel may also find itself with diminished regional influence as its conflict with the Palestinians festers and its former cooperation with Turkey and Egypt declines
6. U.S. power to shape events in the region may be substantially diminished as well, leaving a region without clear global or regional powers that can take the lead in shaping the region

Strategic Partnerships

For the United States, as American leaders attempt to maintain the foothold in the region first established in the 1940s, the latest Mideast transformation may be momentous. Will the techniques and tactics that Washington used in the latter half of the twentieth century and those it employed in the first decade of the twenty-first be relevant or effective any longer? What *were* the tools that American administrations used during the two-thirds of a century leading up to the Green Movement in Iran and the Arab Spring? The answers to those questions lie in the global approach that Washington took as it forged its new world role after the Second World War.

By the latter stages of World War II, the United States had become the colossus among world powers. The country's extraordinary military and economic dominance notwithstanding, FDR and his successors for the rest of the twentieth century rejected go-it-alone methods to protect what they saw as U.S. interests and to project the country's strength. Instead, every American president after Roosevelt, with the important exception of George W. Bush, aimed to exercise global power by seeking out *strategic partnerships* with key local powers, a policy Roosevelt had inaugurated during his rendezvous with Saudi Arabia's Ibn Saud at the Great Bitter Lake.

Washington sought out regional powers to work with and through, which helped limit America's own expenditure of resources in various parts of the world. Using the NATO alliance and America's special partnership with Great Britain as models, post–World War II U.S. presidents aimed to build regional coalitions and strengthen local powers around the world. They intended to share power to some degree so that carefully chosen allies could assume some of the security burden in local arenas. The hope was to enable the United States to play a global role without being stretched too thin financially or militarily.

Strategic partners, American presidents believed, could do for the United States what the country could not or would not do regionally. This would help secure American national interests, as each administration defined them, even while limiting U.S. presence abroad. The road to such ties, though, was rocky. President after president discovered that such partners were hard to come by outside Europe—from Latin America to Africa to South Asia, American administrations looked in vain for those regions' "Great Britains." Instead of deeply rooted partnerships with leaders who broadly represented their populations, as they had in the British case, U.S. leaders ended up with ties to autocratic state heads, like Mubarak, who often had tenuous if not repressive relationships to their own people. These leaders were, ironically, "strongmen" who headed extraordinarily "weak" states (Migdal 1988).

In their search for strategic partners, U.S. administrations fared better during some periods than others. The 1970s were the high point, when the United States was able to construct and maintain several key partnerships, including with Egypt, Iran, Israel, and Turkey. But overall, the presence of the United States in the Middle East has been a troubled one. The 1950s and 1960s, for example, produced endless difficulties, as several elaborate plans for partnerships with regional powers and for regional military alliances—Egypt and the Baghdad Pact, respectively, were the most notable examples—utterly collapsed.

More recently, the first decade of the twenty-first century was, perhaps, the bleakest period for the United States in the region: America was subjected to the devastating September 11 attack, which had been undertaken by a group of Middle Easterners. It suffered through the failure to seal the deal between Palestinians and Israelis at Camp David in 2000; the brutal, years-long violence that followed the Camp David debacle; the costly, drawn-out American war in Iraq; the failure of sanctions to stem Iran's nuclear program; the rising power of nonstate groups—Hezbollah, Hamas, and al-Qaeda—whose anti-Americanism seemed endemic and played on the growing anti-Americanism among Mideast publics; the deadly attack, most likely by al-Qaeda, on the U.S. Navy destroyer USS *Cole* in the port of Aden, Yemen, in 2000; and more.

It was also a decade in which, at first, American officials in the George W. Bush administration foreswore altogether the long-accepted idea of finding a strategic partner (see chapter 10). Even after Barack Obama reversed course, his administration discovered that finding a path toward viable strategic partnerships was proving to be frustrating. Obama's aims and practices ran headlong into the newly unleashed sentiments of the region's peoples during the Arab Spring.

Some of the reasons for America's foreign-policy difficulties in the area have been generic, that is, as likely to be relevant in Africa as in the Middle East: the fragility of many regimes and states outside Western Europe, their new and shaky relationships with their own societies, and the absence of established patterns of regional interaction for what were mostly new states. But such generic factors ignore the critical, distinctive factors—the unique institutional characteristics, as Peter Katzenstein (2005, 234) termed them—of each region.

In the Middle East, I argue, the efforts of various administrations foundered on factors specific to the area. Attempts by American policy makers to impose cookie-cutter solutions, like the NATO and Great Britain models, on the unique configurations and patterns of the Mideast regional system led to recurring frustrations. The obstacles to success in using the standard models for policy making included the rapid flux of the area, particularly the major transformation of Mideast regional dynamics after 1979, which Washington was slow to understand; the choice of potential partners, especially in the Arab world, that failed to live up to expectations; and the Palestine-Israel conflict.

On the last factor, presidents from Dwight D. Eisenhower on eyed Israel, with its strong state, powerful military, democratic institutions, and pro-American stance, as potentially Washington's most potent strategic partner. But the unending conflict between Arabs and Jews in Israel/Palestine meant that drawing close to Israel threatened to alienate critical Arab states, including the most populous and wealthy ones. For decades, administrations were divided over whether Israel was a strategic asset or liability, leaning sometimes to one side and sometimes to the other. I inquire in the concluding chapter whether the transformations in the Middle East now provide an opportunity for Washington to cut through this Gordian knot.

Today, the United States faces a region in upheaval. Popular forces have now challenged—and occasionally toppled—fragile, sclerotic regimes marked by tenuous, sometimes hostile relations with their own societies. In this tumultuous environment, no panacea exists for the United States to transcend all its past difficulties and establish a stable, untroubled Mideast presence. The kind of firm strategic partnerships that the United States found in Europe—with Great Britain and, later, Germany—is simply not possible in the Middle East.

Still, in the darkest days of the dark decade of the 2000s, a plan was floated by the Saudi king: the Arab Peace Initiative, which possibly could cut through some of the grave difficulties that American presidents repeatedly encountered in the region. Surprisingly, though, the United States did little to promote the plan at the time. In the final chapter, I will argue that this plan, now shelved for a decade, still can provide the basis for a productive role for the United States in the current tempest of the

Middle East. If not a panacea, it still holds out a formula for partnerships that would enable America to meet the grave challenges it faces today in this difficult region.

Chapter 2 will set the stage for the story of America's attempts to navigate the Middle East as it has undergone its three major transformations in regional dynamics since World War II. It begins by analyzing the framework for America's place in the world developed by Roosevelt and Truman, a framework that had a lasting effect on U.S. global foreign policy. It will then look at how and why the Middle East specifically became such a central concern—even obsession—for American foreign-policy makers. What sorts of national interests did president after president see in the Middle East, impelling them toward sustained involvement in the region no matter how painful that participation turned out to be?

Chapters 3 and 4 will then begin the story of America's checkered history of seeking partners in the Middle East during and after the Cold War. Chapter 3 will explore the tortuous road that American presidential administrations traveled as they tried to establish a place for the United States in the Middle East during the first couple of decades of the Cold War. The attempt to achieve a permanent role in the area came just as the region was experiencing the extraordinary transformation that included the achievement of Israeli independence and the Free Officers coup, which opened the door for Arab nationalism to sweep through the area. Trying to establish military alliances and forge strategic partnerships with the likes of the shah of Iran proved far trickier than American officials had imagined.

Chapter 4 will pay special attention to the ongoing struggles inside presidential administrations that took place over the question of whether Israel could serve as a possible strategic asset or simply would be a liability and to how relations with Israel affected overall U.S. strategic prospects in the region. An unlikely war, the Black September War of 1970, answered that question for a time and opened a new period of partnerships in the region for the United States.

The partnerships that the United States forged in the 1970s, however, quickly came under tremendous strain, and by 1990 they were mostly in tatters. Chapters 5 and 6 explore two wars, the 1973 Arab-Israeli War and the 1990–1991 Gulf War. Those wars demonstrate the difficulty the United States had in attaining secure strategic partnerships, particularly with Israel.

American prospects were deeply affected not only by relations with Israel but also by other factors related to the remarkable transformation in the region's dynamics that began in 1979, the topic of chapters 7 through 9. Chapters 10 and 11 will explore the grave difficulties that U.S. policy makers experienced during the decade after 9/11, embodied primarily in the Iraq War. The trauma of 9/11 mixed with the new ways of thinking about America's place in the world that had begun to develop after the collapse of the Soviet Union, and together these shaped policy toward the Middle East during the Bush and Obama presidencies (chapters 10 and 11). Finally, the last part of the book will look back and look forward. Chapter 12 will bring together the changes in Middle East regional dynamics and American policies as an everyday player, concluding with the disastrous decade of the 2000s. Then, the final chapter will analyze the dilemmas generated by the Green Movement in Iran and, especially, the Arab Spring and discuss the possibilities for the United States in this turbulent region in coming years.

2 America's Place in the Middle East

America's Global Strategy

It was in the early years after the Second World War that Washington opted for its distinctive strategy on how to play out its role as the preeminent global power, how to mark its presence beyond its own shores as the now-dominant power in the world. U.S. leaders chose, quite self-consciously, the mechanisms for establishing America's place internationally. Important echoes of the way Great Britain had played that global role in the eighteenth and nineteenth centuries could be heard, particularly the emphasis on maritime power and free trade. But the Roosevelt and Truman administrations did steer a different course through the turbulent waters of the mid-twentieth century, rejecting many of the methods by which earlier world powers, including Britain, had gained control far beyond their own borders.

Serious thinking about establishing a durable world order came even at the height of fighting during World War II. Here is how the journalist Forrest Davis, clearly speaking for the president, wrote about "Roosevelt's World Blueprint," the title of his famous article that appeared in the *Saturday Evening Post* in April 1943:

For the third time since Napoleon, the nations have a chance to remake the structure of the western world. This time the east is also involved. The President, devoting what may well be the most constructive thinking of his career to the job, quite naturally hopes to see the mistakes of 1815 and 1919 avoided. He deeply feels that mankind should not be subjected to a second disaster of the magnitude of Versailles in one generation. (Davis 1943, 21)

Much of Roosevelt's blueprint eventually succumbed to the tensions and challenges of the early postwar era, particularly the start of the Cold War. Still, substantial parts of the Roosevelt design came to be inscribed into America's long-term global strategy. How did FDR see America's place in the world? First, his administration planned for the United States to be present and active practically everywhere across the globe—Europe, Africa, Latin America, the Middle East, all across Asia. No nook or cranny was to be left out. With the United States producing half of the world's manufactured goods in the mid-1940s and its industrialists looking for new markets—and with a military that emerged largely intact from the war—the United States was in a position to be a truly global power.

Second, the Roosevelt team aimed to exercise America's vast power through a web of mostly new, acronymed international organizations in which all the world's states would participate. The United Nations (UN), the International Trade Organization (ITO), the International Monetary Fund (IMF), and others would be the vehicles for the United States to build an order, with rational and knowable rules, that would serve both America and the world. This visionary blueprint held risks for the United States and for other states as well. All had to sacrifice some of their precious sovereign powers. The United States, while still holding the equivalent of the role of chairman of the board and a 51 percent share in the new world order, would agree to have its wings clipped by other states, which would hold the other 49 percent share (Cumings 1981, 102).

As the dominant world power in the eighteenth and nineteenth centuries, Great Britain had shared power abroad, too. But its sharing was largely a local affair, the collaboration between British colonial officials on the ground and native potentates. The United States, in contrast, would actually share control with other *states*, through the new international institutions, although it was evident that it would be the first among equals. Harold E. Stassen, Roosevelt's delegate to the United Nations Conference in San Francisco, emphasized "that we do not subscribe to the extreme view of nationalistic sovereignty; that we realize that neither this nation nor any other nation can be a law unto itself . . . and that we are willing to delegate a limited portion of our national sovereignty to our United Nations organization" (*Time* 1945).

Third, Roosevelt imagined an inner circle of the world's states, a club of the most powerful countries, whose members would work cooperatively to insure the proper functioning of the new international institutions and act in partnership against troublemakers. This club mimicked the Concert of Europe, which had been created in 1815 in the wake of the catastrophic Napoleonic Wars. In Roosevelt's mind, the United States would be the police chief, and the other large powers, police captains. Together, they would take central responsibility for supervising and monitoring the international organizations and maintaining order in their global "precincts." The other powers would be America's major wartime allies—Great Britain, the Soviet Union, and China. With the United States, they would make up Roosevelt's Four Policemen. The essence of Roosevelt's idea was adopted in December 1945 at a conference of the major powers' foreign ministers—the meeting that produced the so-called Moscow Agreement. At that meeting, there was talk of a league of great powers.

The idea of the Four Policemen was seen by the journalist and public intellectual Walter Lippmann (1943) as the key to establishing an enduring postwar order: "The underlying principle, the controlling conception, of the whole agreement is that the four great powers are the four principal policemen of the post-war world." The notion of the Four Policemen was embodied in the UN Security Council's permanent members (with the addition of France).

And fourth, Roosevelt eschewed the sort of territorial control, both of land masses and the high seas, that previous world powers had achieved. In Davis's (1943, 109) words in the 1943 *Saturday Evening Post* article, "The President disagrees with those who foresee the United states forever embroiled in foreign quarrels and required to keep large military forces abroad." Colonies and imperial territories would no longer be the means to maintain the control and presence of the world's chief power in the far corners of the globe.

That said, the United States did not forego territorial control altogether. Even as Roosevelt and his aides planned the postwar order, Washington had every intention, for example, of taking the Philippines back from the

Japanese and of reinstituting American control there. Still, to Roosevelt's mind, securing and maintaining empire posed all sorts of costs, both economic and moral, especially for a world power that was itself a former set of colonies. America's great economic advantage at the end of the war—its plants were intact and highly efficient, its manufactured goods almost uniformly superior to those of others—and its tremendous naval power enabled it to dominate markets without requiring the extensive land grabs that earlier imperial powers had needed.

While Roosevelt's idea of eschewing vast territorial empires had practical as well as moral advantages, it did end up complicating America's projection of global power in subsequent years. American policy makers simply did not have the storehouse of knowledge about local cultures around the world and connections to locally powerful figures that the British had gained. Years of governing colonies and collaborating with strongmen had given a great number of British colonial officers (and those of other colonial powers) a sometimes skewed but still close look at far-flung societies. A much more limited cadre of U.S. officials enjoyed that sort of intimate contact with societies that the United States was trying to shape and influence.

Without the connections and knowledge that came out of ruling vast foreign territories, American policy makers had much less social capital with which to build strong and enduring ties abroad. The distance of U.S. policy makers from other societies led too often to the illusion that collaborating with autocratic leaders meant they were actually joining with the broader societies. Most U.S. strategic relationships turned out to be regime to regime (or U.S. state to foreign regime) and lacked the society-to-society dimensions that the model relationship with the British did. They were instead tactical marriages of convenience with regime leaders that did not penetrate deeply into other societies.

Once tensions with the Soviet Union became insurmountable, in 1947–1948, and after the Chinese communists took control in 1949, Truman officials gave up on or modified Roosevelt's vision. They settled on something less than the universality of Roosevelt's ambitions and accepted U.S. exclusion from exercising power in Eastern Europe, the sprawling Soviet Union, and then China after the defeat of the Kuomintang. Still, Truman and his successors continued to stake claims for American influence just about everywhere else in the world.

Roosevelt's successors also dropped the notion of a small number of policemen, but they did not scrap the principle that American power would, in some large measure, be expressed through some of the new institutions, such as the IMF, that Roosevelt had conceived. Other institutions were scotched, like the ITO, although a descendant appeared decades later in the guise of the World Trade Organization (WTO). Still other international organizations fell victim to the Cold War, such as the effectiveness of the Security Council.

Truman and succeeding presidents stuck, in principle, with the idea of not creating a territorial empire like that of the British, although the United States did end up occupying and controlling some significant expanses of territory at various times after World War II—the Philippines, Okinawa, and Iraq, among others. Their main tack in creating a physical American presence in the far reaches of the world as the Cold War intensified, however, was a string of military bases spread around the globe. Dwarfing all previous world powers, the United States has maintained hundreds of such bases in all parts of the world: there are probably more than seven hundred, along with hundreds of other smaller military installations, although firm numbers are hard to come by. These bases became the physical presence and forward thrust of American might around the globe. To Chalmers Johnson, America's military and economic presence meant the creation of its own sort of empire, one "based on the projection of military power to every corner of the world and on the use of American capital and markets to force global economic integration on our terms, at whatever costs to others" (Lippmann 1943; Johnson 2004, 7).

Once the Soviet sphere of influence was established in Eastern Europe and universality was off the table, starting around 1947, Truman officials made another fateful choice about how America's world presence would be manifested. Although the United States would be a major player almost everywhere, one region would be given pride of place. Truman officials chose Western Europe as the area where it would center its foreign policy. Other regions might have been chosen, particularly Latin America. As far back as FDR's first inaugural address, in 1933, his administration had signaled a shift to the Good Neighbor Policy in Latin America. That policy largely brought a change in tone in U.S. relations with other countries in the Americas. But it was the Marshall Plan in 1947 and the creation of the North Atlantic Treaty Organization in 1949, focusing on Europe, that indicated where the United States would invest most of its hardcore international resources and attention. East Asia quickly slid into second place.

Western Europe was not only afforded pride of place in American foreign policy; it became in officials' minds the archetype for Washington in two ways. First, it signaled a move away from Roosevelt's notions of a single world stage to foreign policy being played out on a series of smaller, regional stages. It is difficult to define what a region is generically and even where particular regions begin and end. They are mental constructs more than hard geographical realities. Still, American foreign-policy makers consistently talked about regions as if there were clear distinctions among parts of the world and that each had its own unique dynamics. The Middle East was no exception in this regard.[1] Policies like the Marshall Plan and the formation of NATO thus became the basis for broader American action around the world, action geared toward the special conditions of and challenges in particular regions. Second, Western Europe was also a model for the way that the Truman administration organized American entry into the region. That process involved fashioning one or several strategic relationships with core regional powers and the formation of a broader regional military alliance.

Building on its close cooperation with Great Britain during World War II, from the signing of the Atlantic Charter and the lend-lease legislation (60 percent of whose funds went to Britain) in 1941, U.S. policy makers maintained America's special relationship with Britain after the war. Beyond the direct support that Britain could offer the United States in the region, it also served as America's trusted agent within NATO and other regional multilateral organizations. Additionally, once the dust settled after the dismemberment of Germany and, then, the unification of three of its four parts into the Federal Republic of Germany, foreign-policy officials also forged a strategic relationship with the new Germany. Indeed, for much of the Cold War, the United States exerted considerable power through its political and economic ties to and military presence in West Germany. And, in the early decades of the Cold War, U.S. officials also pushed hard for European unity in order to create an even larger bloc on which it could rely.

As the United States formulated policies for other parts of the world, it fell back on this European formula. It set out to build security alliances like NATO, that is, military-treaty organizations, such as the Southeast Asia Treaty Organization (SEATO) and the Central Treaty Organization (CENTO). These coalitions mobilized the members for mutual protection and cooperation, and they enshrined the equality of the members through an understanding of noninterference in one another's domestic affairs. These alliances were all constructed with the Soviet Union in mind. In Europe, however, NATO, along with aid through the Marshall Plan, had far-reaching ramifications beyond the Cold War. Armies returned to their barracks in most cases and stayed out of their countries' politics (Greece and Turkey were exceptions at several limited key points); the growth of civil society was promoted; and internecine regional warfare ended.

What worked well in Europe, though, did not necessarily translate well to other areas. One key factor was whether the region could produce "core states that support U.S. power and purpose" (Katzenstein 2005, 13). Great Britain and then West Germany (and later the European Community) gave the United States tremendous leverage in Western Europe. In East Asia, Japan played that role, and, increasingly, Korea did as well.

But in Africa, South Asia, the Americas, Southeast Asia, and the Middle East, the search for strategic partners was less successful. Formal and informal alliances did not necessarily send the military back to the barracks, foster the flowering of civil society, or put an end to regional hostilities. The difficulties that the United States faced in transposing its Western Europe/Great Britain model to the rest of the world lie at the heart of America's experience as a global power since the middle of the twentieth century.

The Middle East at the Center of Global Affairs

In no area of the world were America's struggles in establishing a workable foreign policy more telling or more important than in the Middle East. This region was no backwater or distant corner that could be safely ignored. Just the opposite: since World War II, the region has been at the epicenter of international relations and American involvement abroad. As one writer put it, "The Middle East has become a metaphor for the world" (Schalit 2009, 20).

The Middle East's centrality for the United States as the world's leading power should be of no surprise. Its location, at the juncture of three continents, has made the region loom large in the eyes of world powers from the days of Alexander the Great and the Roman Empire on. The first two decades of the twentieth century added two additional factors that brought the attention of the then leading world power, Great Britain—the discovery of oil and the creation of the Soviet Union.

From the time of the Bolshevik Revolution in 1917, the Soviet Union played a major role in Britain's thinking about its strategic interests in the Middle East, just as it would for the United States a generation later. At the end of World War I and during the interwar years, British foreign and colonial officers fretted about the revolutionary aims of the USSR. They worried about the possibility of its expansion southward by fomenting communist takeovers in the remnants of the Ottoman Empire. The British worried that both the overland and sea routes to India, the colony around which their global strategy revolved, could be jeopardized through Soviet successes, as could access to the rich Middle East oilfields then coming on line. The first major oil fields in the Middle East began to be exploited during the first decade of the twentieth century, and the British, in an all-out race with other powers, sought as many special concessions for drilling as possible.

Even before the Bolshevik Revolution and the subsequent Soviet withdrawal from World War I, the British and French began to plan for a new post-Ottoman Middle East, dividing it into spheres of influence in the secret 1916 Sykes-Picot Agreement (Klieman 1970, 1990). Unrest in parts of the Middle East in the rocky aftermath of the war further provoked British concerns about the fate of the region, especially in light of what they interpreted as revolutionary Soviet goals there. These worries led them to seek local allies anywhere they could find them. British officials and non-officials made all sorts of promises, many of them contradictory, to cement local Middle East alliances—to Zionists, various minority groups, Arabs, and the French.

In their pacts, promises, and drawing of new borders, the British—along with the French—sketched the layout of the new Middle East. They drew the contours of what would eventually become independent states, and, in Egypt and the territories they ruled through League of Nations mandates, they deeply influenced the local distribution of power, favoring some social forces over others and pitting some groups against others. The radically changing distribution of power in the region, not least because of these British alliances, inevitably produced gloating winners and disgruntled losers among local officials, political leaders, clan and village heads, tribal chiefs, and others.

Remarkable parallels to these sorts of British security concerns and policies after World War I were evident, as well, in the aftermath of the Second World War. But now it was the United States demonstrating anxiety about the bear from the north and making all kinds of alliances. U.S.

officials expressed grave concerns about Soviet penetration into an area whose oil resources and geographic centrality were crucial to the revival of the world economy in the aftermath of the Great Depression and the war. For both the British after World War I and the United States after World War II, the challenge of somehow blocking southward penetration of the Soviets did not necessarily offer a clear blueprint for how to proceed in the Middle East—which policies to adopt, which allies to choose, where to concentrate resources and efforts.

The complexity and diversity of the myriad social groups on the ground in the region—tribal, religious, ethnic, clan based, and more—presented the global powers with a dizzying array of policy choices. Inside the British and, later, U.S. governments, different factions offered a variety of approaches—from hard line to accommodative, from military intervention to political engagement—for checking the rising tide of Soviet influence. The former territories of the Ottoman Empire were brimming with social and political groups, often in deep struggle with one another, making the forging of coalitions with local parties confusing and uncertain.

And, once the new states of the Middle East began to crystallize and take shape, the differences among them opened the possibility that any regional groupings that the British and, then, the United States might forge could create openings for closer Soviet ties to the regional opponents of the British and U.S. allies. In short, diplomacy was fraught with uncertainty and danger. Clear strategic aims did not lead either to clear tactics or a clear-cut set of policies. As opposed to the grand statements of government leaders and the neat theories of academic realists and neorealists, pursuing a coherent strategy turned out to be messy business.

For the United States as for Great Britain, the Middle East has exerted a magnetic pull. Not only were its location at the crossroads of Africa, Asia, and Europe and its huge stores of petroleum important, but strong domestic constituencies concerned with it have weighed in heavily on American policy debates. It simply could not be ignored in the way that, say, Africa has been relatively neglected in U.S. policy for long stretches of time.

To say that the Middle East has been at the center of global affairs and of America's role in the world since World War II is not to minimize the importance of other regions. During the Cold War, after all, there were epic, drawn-out showdowns between the superpowers in Central Europe and in East Asia, during which the Middle East took a decidedly back seat. The Berlin crises of 1948–1949 and 1961, the civil war in China leading to the communist victory in 1947, and the Korean War were all moments of truth for the superpowers.

A sign of the value of these other regions to Washington was the number of troops stationed in them. During the Cold War, 300,000 to 400,000 American military personnel were on duty in Europe. In northeastern Asia, the number after the Korean War remained well above 100,000 and, for some time, was in excess of 200,000, with as many as 60,000 in South Korea and a high of 19,000 in Taiwan. The Middle East, on the other hand, held fewer than 25,000 American armed forces at the height of the Cold War (with the exception of one volatile year, 1958, when it spiked to almost 40,000). By the end of the 1970s, considerably fewer than 10,000 American troops were stationed in the area, and many of these were in Turkey, pointed toward the USSR and not the rest of the Middle East.

But even with the undisputed importance of both Central Europe and Asia during the Cold War, those areas did not provide the same sort of ongoing foreign policy conundrums that the Middle East did. Northeastern Asia and Europe settled into definitive patterns in terms of superpower interaction. Each was characterized by massive stalemates—a faceoff of conventional and nonconventional forces and weapons—in which neither side could make much headway. There were flare-ups, to be sure, with various probes by each side—and several spine-tingling crises. And there were shifts in policy, such as détente or arms-control negotiations. But these crises and shifts were not serendipitous; they grew out of the immovable faceoff in the two regions. The sides learned that they were engaged in a little-changing deadlock in Central Europe and northeastern Asia, in which one's friends and foes were clear and in which neither side could budge the other. Any bright new policy idea was likely to have only a marginal effect on the situation on the ground.

The Middle East, in contrast, held no such stable stalemates. Allies and enemies shifted dizzyingly. Expectations were constantly upended. The largest, most powerful country in the region, Egypt, for example, started out the Cold War allying with the West, jumped to the Soviet side after the transformation marked by the Free Officers coup in 1952, and then moved back again toward the United States after the subsequent regional transformation that started in 1979. All this jockeying occurred over the course of three decades and all while Egypt, ironically, played a leading role in the Non-Aligned Movement, its successive superpower ties notwithstanding. Officials in both the United States and the Soviet

Union saw the Middle East as an unsettled area where they could make tangible gains in the Cold War and, at the same time, as a region so volatile that it could quickly become the focus of a superpower showdown.

The Middle East Looms Large in American Eyes

What made the Middle East so valuable to the two superpowers? For the Soviet Union, the Middle East was its southern gateway to the Mediterranean, Africa, and Asia. The warm-water sea route from the Black Sea through the Bosporus and Dardanelles provided a critical lifeline. It is no wonder that today the Russians continue to try to stake out a significant role in the region. For the Soviets, the new self-proclaimed socialist regimes that developed in the core Arab countries in the 1950s offered fertile ground for establishing a foothold beyond the USSR's own backyard of Eastern Europe. The Soviets had eyed the Middle East as a prize since the Bolshevik Revolution in 1917 and, in the post–World War II environment, felt that the opportunities now existed to expand their power beyond their sphere of influence in Eastern Europe.

The United States, too, defined the Middle East as crucial to securing U.S. national interests. From Roosevelt and Truman to George W. Bush and Barack Obama, American presidents have considered the goings-on in the Middle East as key for the United States. Oil, of course, is one prime reason for that claim. Government officials expressed concern over the control of oil reserves before and after World War II, and, in recent decades, if not speaking of "control," they worried about "access" to reserves. Robert Vitalis (2007, 2009) has raised serious questions about whether such control or access for Washington ever did—or could—come out of a strong American presence in the Middle East. Nonetheless, the saliency of oil led to a strong belief—or a mirage, as Vitalis calls it— by American policy makers that exercising the country's muscle in the region was a guarantee of sufficient oil flow.

What lay behind the construction of such a belief—myth or not—by policy makers is not hard to fathom. Oil is the most traded commodity in the world today. Coming out of World War II, U.S. officials were deeply concerned about supplies of oil in any future wars, especially prolonged conventional wars. Even though there were often gluts of oil, concern about future production grew. As time went on after World War II, U.S. petroleum output became increasingly inadequate to meet the country's unquenchable thirst for oil. In 1950, less than 10 percent of American oil needs were met with imports; today, that figure is around 60 percent: out of the 20 million or so barrels that America consumes daily, 12 million are imported.

Coupled with growing dependency on imports is the cold reality that most of that oil is in the Middle East. Out of an estimated 1.2 billion barrels of world petroleum reserves, around 60 percent lie in the Middle East. By far, the biggest estimated reserves are in Saudi Arabia, which itself is in some ways an American invention (Vitalis 2007). Numbers three and four on the list of countries with the most estimated reserves are Iran and Iraq; together they have a bit less than Saudi Arabia's total. Half of the top sixteen countries in the world in estimated petroleum reserves are in the Middle East and North Africa. Even if those figures for reserves are themselves questionable—another mirage—U.S. policy makers have taken them seriously. America itself, which now consumes about a fifth of the world's oil production, holds less than 2 percent of global reserves. The preponderance of the Middle East in oil has amplified the region's importance in the minds of government officials.

Oil helps explain the U.S. preoccupation with the region, but it is far from the whole story of America's ongoing presence in the Middle East. Indeed, at times, oil seemed to recede markedly in the considerations of various U.S. administrations.[2] The area also holds many of the world's busiest shipping lanes. Fewer than a dozen vulnerable waterways around the world, known as chokepoints, carry a huge proportion of shipping and are crucial to the global economy. Four of these chokepoints are in the Middle East: the Suez Canal, connecting Europe to Asia; the Strait of Hormuz, from the Persian Gulf into the Indian Ocean; Bab el-Mandab, from the Red Sea also to the Indian Ocean; and the Bosporus and Dardanelles, or Turkish straits, from the Black Sea to the Mediterranean. One might also add the Strait of Sicily, between Italy and Tunisia, which effectively divides the Mediterranean into two seas.

Of course, much of the concern with these shipping routes revolves around oil, too. The Strait of Hormuz alone carries 40 percent of the oil shipped globally. For the United States, which has about 95 percent of its oil imports arrive by sea, free access through these chokepoints was paramount in the thinking of generations of American officials. But these seaways carry a large share of all sorts of other shipped commodities, too. They are vulnerable to state blockades, pirates, tanker spills, and more. Two of the three trade routes from Europe to Asia—through the

Suez Canal and by way of the sea-land route from the Mediterranean, then overland to the Persian Gulf—cut through the Middle East (the third route is around the Horn of Africa). Policy makers understood in the decade or so after World War II that direct control over these water passages was not viable, just as direct control over oil reserves by the U.S. government or even U.S.-based companies was a chimera in the age of global nationalism. American influence over shipping would have to come through other means, and strong relations with states whose coastlines were along these waterways seemed like a safe bet to Washington officials.

Besides the chokepoints, the region's strategic location placed the Middle East at the center of U.S. concerns in other ways, as well. At the crossroads of Asia, Africa, and Europe, events in the area have spilled readily over into Africa, the Balkans, Afghanistan and Pakistan, the Caucasus, and Central Asia, all highly volatile areas themselves. I will discuss in chapter 10 how important this spillover effect was to the George W. Bush administration's refashioning of American strategic policy in the region. It is not only Mideast tensions that has spread to neighboring areas; instability in these regions has fed back to events in the Middle East as well. Afghanistan since the Soviet invasion in 1978 is a prime example of a bordering area generating conflicts and social forces that have added to the already bubbling pot of Middle East volatility.

Beyond the region's strategic resources and location, which helped fuel the belief among policy makers that a strong U.S. presence in the region would secure American interests, other Americans have also found reasons to put the Middle East high on their list of areas of concern. As far back as the nineteenth century, religion drew American Christian pilgrims, travelers (including Mark Twain), and archaeologists (who were seeking physical evidence for Christian Bible teachings). After Palestine was carved out of the Ottoman Empire in the wake of World War I, the competing and overlapping concerns of Christians and Jews (and, more recently, Muslims) in the United States worked their way into public discourse and policy. And the religious importance of the region to Americans does not seem to have diminished at all over time.

Once Israel was created as a state in 1948, American Jews increasingly came to identify with it. The 1967 war deepened American Jewish connections to Israel. In the lead up to the war, Israel's existence seemed to many Jews to hang by a thread, which increased their anxiety. After Israel's overwhelming victory, many American Jews seemed to undergo a psychic change in the process of the transition from anxiety to triumph, identifying strongly with the Jewish state. Powerful American Jewish organizations, both religious and secular ones, weighed in on issues affecting Israel and worked to keep the Middle East at the top of the U.S. foreign-policy agenda. AIPAC, the American Israel Public Affairs Committee, became one of the most powerful lobbies in Washington. It labeled itself America's pro-Israel lobby, working at both the grassroots and national levels on America's policies in the Middle East. Until the last few years, the major Jewish communal and religious institutions and AIPAC spoke largely in a singular voice. Now, American Jewish organizations have fragmented, adding multiple voices to the policy debates, but all still clamor to have the Middle East as central to U.S policy. Christians, too—especially evangelical Christians—have elevated the issue of Israel to unprecedented heights in the last couple of decades.

All in all, the welfare of Israel has become one of the highest-priority issues in the United States, not just for specific constituencies but in terms of overall public sentiment and the views of key public officials, especially in Congress. It is important to stress here that affection for Israel, which has waxed and waned in the United States but has been generally extremely high, and the power of AIPAC have been important factors in U.S.-Israel relations and America's overall role in the Middle East. But they are insufficient, as I will show in coming chapters, to explain the existence or absence of a *strategic* partnership between the two countries.

That is, contrary to the argument put forth by the political scientists John Mearsheimer and Stephen Walt (2006a, 2006b, 2007), the power of the Israel lobby and affection for Israel among policy makers and the public *cannot* explain the course of U.S. policy in the Middle East (more on this in the final chapter). What was critical in determining and pursuing U.S. interests was when *and* if U.S. policy makers saw Israel as a partner that could further American interests in the region and undertake missions and tasks for the United States that it could not do itself. Affection for Israel and the power of the Israel lobby are pieces in the much larger puzzle of American foreign policy in the region.

Other constituencies have also added to the pressure to consider the Middle East first in sorting out American strategic interests. Even in the early decades of the twentieth century, a variety of groups voiced strong views on what the United States should be doing in the Middle East. A few, such as oil-company representatives and missionaries, went beyond speaking up to creating their own facts on the ground in the Middle East. They established a presence there and undertook their own "policies." Their actions could and did drag public policy into issues and arenas that government officials might have preferred to avoid. These private groups could frequently act relatively independently of public policy making, further affecting America's position and presence in the region.

In recent decades, the Middle East has etched itself even more sharply into daily life in America (McAlister 2001). There has been expanding involvement in public policy making of domestic groups concerned with everything from Israel to America's loss of energy independence. Additionally, the number of individuals and groups creating their own facts on the ground in the region has grown exponentially—from American Jews settling on the West Bank, to American Arabs disbursing remittances among family members, to the financier Warren Buffett and innumerable other investors sinking their capital into Middle East business ventures.

Just as for the countries of the Middle East (or any other countries, for that matter), U.S. foreign policy has been the product of more than a handful of officials sitting around a table figuring out what America's national interests are and effecting policy to further those interests. Foreign policy stems in great part from the complexity of state-society relations in the United States—the strength that officials can (or cannot) draw from the state's relationship to its own citizens, the mobilization of specific groups in society over certain foreign-policy issues, and more. Policy is the byproduct, too, of internecine conflicts within the state: between Congress and the executive and within the bureaucracy. And foreign policy proceeds as well from the competing alliances of factions of the state with different social forces.

To complicate matters even more, state-society and intrastate relations are not static factors in the construction of foreign policy. Who sits at the table and whose voice has resonance change over time. In the United States, in the immediate aftermath of the Second World War, a small group of what were called "Wise Men" made foreign policy, determining what they considered the best strategic path for the country (more on them in chapter 4). They were certainly not immune to domestic considerations, but their autonomy was remarkable by today's standards. Ethnic, religious, business, and other groups could certainly voice their views at the ballot box and in other settings and thus influence the Wise Men to some measure, but most did not have the ability to mobilize around issues and affect debates the way they do today. The Vietnam War was a watershed for the United States in terms of the impact of social forces on foreign-policy making.

Similarly, the bureaucracy was much simpler back then; today, many more government officials are involved in international affairs and are part of a much more complex organizational structure. Here, the primary milestone was the National Security Act of 1947, which created the Department of Defense, the National Security Council, and the Central Intelligence Agency. Later, key documents issued by the National Security Council, such as NSC-68, hugely expanded the security and foreign-policy purviews of the American state. And all those new bureaus and agencies did not necessarily mesh together. Different bureaus and agencies have had very different stances on specific issues. Foreign-policy making, in short, has moved from a relatively insulated arena with a limited number of actors to a tumultuous realm with countless players inside and outside the government.

That there are multiple voices constructing foreign policy means that there is no singular set of national interests expressed in American (or any other country's) foreign policy. Policy and interests are the outcome of an often raucous process in which competing coalitions and conflicting voices mix in sometimes unexpected ways. Mearsheimer and Walt's (2006a, 2006b, 2007) claim that one group, the Israel lobby, has diverted the United States from its *true* national interests rests on the naïve assumption that such an objective, singular set of *true* interests actually exists.

My concern in the chapters that follow, however, is not the state-society relations *in the United States* that have shaped America's behavior in the world. That is a topic for another book. Rather than the origins of foreign policy, my focus is on America in the world, or, in this case, the Middle East. In the following pages, I characterize the United States, as it has navigated the complexity of both interstate *and* local state-society relations, as a critical and sometimes befuddled player in this crucial region. For simplicity's sake, I follow the actions of the key senior figures involved in foreign-policy making inside various U.S. administrations.[3] I am cognizant of the importance of others in the process, such as Congress, officials who execute policy in the field, and relevant social groups and governmental organizations, but here I do not say much about them. The policy makers themselves present themselves as if they are above the fray, as if they are not simply one more set of actors in a multiactor process but the singular rational interpreters of an objective set of national interests. That, of course, is mythmaking. It is important to keep in mind, even if it is not the subject of this book, that their actions and beliefs have been deeply influenced by their relationship to American society and to other forces in the state.

The Cold War Context

The centrality of the Middle East for U.S. policy makers, their definition of the American national interests that lie in the region, and their attempts to etch a place for the United States in the Mideast landscape all emerged in the context of the Cold War. American officials from the Truman administration through those of Ronald Reagan and George H. W. Bush understood the area almost exclusively through the lens of the superpower competition between the United States and the Soviet Union.

One of the most surprising elements of my research for this book was how relatively little top-level officials knew or cared about the intricacies of foreign countries and regional dynamics. It was the Cold War context that interested them. Even before he became president, Reagan stressed the Cold War frame in which American administrations grasped the goings-on in the Middle East: "Stripped of rhetoric, the paramount American interest in the Middle East is to prevent the region from falling under the domination of the Soviet Union." He went on to tie the Cold War dimension to oil, warning, "Any American government which allowed oil supplies to its allies to be placed in question almost certainly invites the neutralization of Western Europe and Japan, the encirclement of China, and—eventually—its own isolation" (Reagan 1979).

While Reagan's rhetoric was strong, he did not differ substantially from the presidents who preceded him. Just two years after the end of the Second World War, in which the Soviets and Americans were allied, key policy makers in the Truman administration were already painting a dark portrait of Soviet intentions. They represented the world as divided between the United States and its allies, pushing for democracy and global market access, on one side, and the Soviet Union and its "satellites," with their revolutionary, totalitarian goals, on the other. Soviet policy makers soon drew a mirror portrait of their own. This concept of U.S.-Soviet bipolarity as the key structure of the world—as opposed to, say, north-south differences, other possible understandings of the key organizational elements of the world, or regional dynamics as relatively autonomous—endured as the dominant image of how the world was put together for more than four decades after World War II.

More than the balance of power of the nineteenth century and, certainly, of the unipolar world after 1989, the understanding of Cold War bipolarity generated a remarkably simple—indeed, simplistic—set of strategic goals among the superpowers' foreign-policy makers. Each pole aimed, first and foremost, to thwart the other. Beyond that, policy makers sought to create global conditions that could further their own side's power, knowing full well that any such gains would be seen as losses by the other side. Each international action and event was thus sucked into the vortex of the Cold War, thereby reinforcing the image of bipolarity as *the* way to understand how the world works.

Nowhere was this simple formula more obvious than in the volatile Middle East. In the United States, where most political and policy divisions were often aired publicly, in the case of foreign policy little argument could be found about strategic goals during the Cold War. To be sure, there were murmurs of dissent by revisionist historians, Roosevelt-style globalists, and advocates of "rollback," among others. But their opposition, while making occasional, small inroads into the making of foreign policy, was largely overwhelmed by the broad consensus among policy makers and a good portion of the public over strategic goals. The domestic Red Scare in the 1950s and its carryover into subsequent decades fueled the restricted and limited way that top-level officials understood the world and the Middle East.

The minimal dissent over goals, though, did not translate into any sort of agreement about means. Among the foreign-policy establishment, important differences about how to proceed, how to achieve agreed-upon goals, marked almost any issue on the agenda. And among the broader public, dissension was the order of the day, as well. From the antinuclear protests of the 1950s to the movement advocating "no first-use" of nuclear weapons in the 1980s, deep divisions appeared in the American public over how to maximize the country's interests. These divisions were progressively exacerbated as foreign policy drew more active interest and involvement by a host of social groups.

Establishing a coherent foreign policy for the Middle East, a region that was so important internationally and that mobilized such strong emotions and political participation domestically, was not going to be an easy business. While almost all policy makers simply shoved the region into the Cold War box as a way to identify American interests in the area, dissension reigned over how the United States should pursue those interests. The central question for the region became with whom to ally. Chapter 3 begins the analysis of how American officials set out to establish a place for the United States in the Middle East, all the while maintaining their outlook framed by bipolarity. It starts with the foundering efforts in the first decades of the Cold War to forge strategic relationships in the region; chapter 4 then explores how an unlikely war changed U.S. fortunes in the area and led to an enduring strategic partnership.

PART II

The Cold War and Its Aftermath

3 Failed Partnerships and Fragile Partners

Even before the guns of World War II fell silent, the United States moved to become a highly involved player in the Middle East. Preoccupied with wartime petroleum supplies, mindful of fading British (and French) power in the area, and concerned over growing Soviet strength, U.S. policy makers turned their attention increasingly to the Middle East and were drawn quickly into the region's complex and changing dynamics. Later, even when presidents such as Richard M. Nixon tried to slide the area down their list of priorities, it always somehow insinuated itself back to the top of their agenda. Over time, the region became a daily fact of life in the United States, not only for presidents and policy makers but for the general public as well—soldiers, their families, investors, Israel lovers and haters, and just plain citizens.

With all the attention that foreign-policy specialists paid to the Middle East, though, they did not necessarily have an easy time deciphering it or deciding exactly where American interests lay there. And even when U.S. concerns did seem clear to them, policy makers found it difficult to mesh those interests with the complex dynamics of the area. The region's multiple lines of cleavage and layers of conflict—oil-rich and oil-poor states, Arabs and Jews, Arabs and other non-Arabs, rulers and ruled, monarchies and republics, states and ethnic minorities, secular and Islamic forces, Sunnis and Shiites, Christians and Muslims—have made the Middle East into an impossible Rubik's Cube. Add to all those struggles inside the region the domestic divisions and strongly held views in the United States itself on Mideast issues, and elegant and coherent policy making seemed nearly unattainable. In the end, it was very difficult for American officials to figure out which states to befriend and which to oppose, whether to cajole or coerce, how U.S. national interests should be understood, and where they lay.

This chapter explores Washington's attempts to forge a place for itself and a line of action in the region after World War II. Those efforts came in the context of the growing rivalry with the Soviet Union, the frame used by every administration for practically all international policy making for nearly half a century. Under President Harry S. Truman, U.S. policy makers set out an ambitious strategy to contain and confront the Soviet Union in nearly every nook and cranny of the world, at least where the Soviets did not already hold sway. Truman's successor, Dwight D. Eisenhower, quickly realized that such a strategy was, on the face of it, unsustainable and threatened to bankrupt the United States.

The answer that his and subsequent administrations hit upon was to secure local strategic partners and build military alliances that could contain communism. But these solutions generated difficult problems for U.S. foreign-policy makers when they were applied outside Europe. During the first two decades of the Cold War, American officials looked on as the Soviet Union secured an increasingly strong foothold in the Middle East, especially in the dynamic new Arab nationalist republics of the region—Egypt, Syria, and Iraq. The Eisenhower administration tried to counter Soviet encroachment and successes in a number of ways, including close collaboration with Iran and a military alliance grounded in the Middle East. But the partnership with Iran, which was born under shady circumstances, never yielded the hoped-for results, and multiple efforts to establish a military-treaty organization like NATO turned out to be equally frustrating.

Discovering an International Strategy in the Cold War

The year 1947 turned out to be pivotal for American foreign-policy officials. It was then that the Cold War began, and it defined the parameters for international relations for most of the rest of the twentieth century. As in other regions, the ongoing rivalry with the Soviet Union became the lens through which American officials saw and interpreted almost any event of interest in the area. The Cold War also increasingly trimmed the sails of policy makers both in the United States and the Soviet Union. As the two superpowers faced each other, backed by their massive armies in Central Europe and, later, their frightening nuclear arsenals, policy makers were dissuaded from adopting overly risky or adventurous plans. And when they did, as in the Cuban Missile Crisis in 1962, the world tottered on the brink of destruction, further sobering them once the crisis ended.

The result was an evolving strategy for both superpowers that might be called a "chastened doctrine." A chastened doctrine is one with built-in hedges. While hedges were not foolproof, as evidenced by the periodic global crises that punctuated the Cold War period, they did provide some important safeguards for the superpowers as they tried to win advantages in various parts of the globe. Hedges allowed for escape hatches from particular policies, they built ambiguity or multiple scenarios into plans of action, and they used allies or clients both to deflect responsibility and share burdens. For much of the Cold War, the hedges employed by American policy makers included shoring up local allies and attempting to offload regional functions onto them. The term "client states" that came to be applied to these local allies reflected the asymmetric nature of the relationship. The United States was clearly the senior partner. The tactic of building up such states became a central component of American foreign policy in almost every region of the world.

In the late 1940s, the Truman administration set the direction for future foreign policy. It developed the ideas of creating security alliances, like NATO, and helping selected states, like Great Britain, refortify themselves. But the idea of using those alliances and partnerships as hedges, in which the United States gave up a modicum of control to local agents, came more gradually. For the Truman administration, security-treaty organizations and strategic partnerships were less about ceding burdens and responsibilities to other states, although there was some of that, than they were about circling the wagons against Soviet encroachment.

The growing conflict with the USSR led Truman to deemphasize Roosevelt's ideas of shared governance through international institutions, as in the plan for the Four Policemen. Instead, his administration adopted a chest-thumping foreign policy in which the United States assumed an almost unfettered role of global leadership. Its doctrine was laid out in

1950 in one of the most important documents of the Cold War, NSC-68, a National Security Council study advocating the active, leading role of the United States globally to fight against the spread of communism. If Roosevelt had imagined a 51 percent share in world leadership for the United States, Truman aimed for something more like 85 percent (Cumings 1981, 130).

The move away from Truman's strategy of overwhelming dominance by the United States and toward the adoption of a chastened doctrine with built-in hedges to policies and, inevitably, some loss of control came slowly. The impetus was, first, the frightening head-to-head confrontations of the superpowers, which began as early as the Truman era, with the Berlin Crisis in 1948. But the chastened doctrine took full root as the Korean War dragged on, with the concern as much about economic disaster as it was about the fear of mutual annihilation.

The Korean War sapped American resources. Immediately after his election in 1952, Dwight D. Eisenhower became deeply concerned about "overstretch," of expending so many resources internationally as to imperil the U.S. economy. His New Look policy, which cut military spending, undergirded the idea that the United States would need strategic partners to share the burdens of foreign policy, particularly in beating back communism. The New Look, in effect, reined in some of the unfettered ambitions expressed in NSC-68.

By the last stages of the Korean War, Washington officials had cemented this key line of policy making, which would remain in place, more or less, until the end of the Cold War: beefing up selected states so that they could reduce America's global burden. Strengthening friendly regimes, they hoped, would decrease their chances of being overturned by pro-Soviet forces and bolster them for assuming important regional tasks or simply serving as credible regional deterrents. They could also act as shills, deflecting responsibility from the United States and allowing American deniability of its local meddling. The form stayed the same as in the Truman era—NATO-like alliances and special relationships with key states—but now Washington was much more willing to use that format as a way to offload responsibility and costs to its partners.

The downside of this policy thrust was that in various areas—not least the Middle East—containing the Soviet Union by buttressing friendly governments or even wheedling pro-Soviet states into the American orbit primarily involved allying with all sorts of regimes, no matter what the quality of their relationships with their own societies. States with deeply problematic ties to their own population found it hard to institutionalize, and they remained chronically weak. Moreover, with Washington adopting a high-minded tone in foreign policy, extolling American virtues of democracy and openness, partnerships with regimes that practiced just the opposite, or U.S. officials' engaging in nefarious acts to bring friendly governments to power, made America's lofty purposes seem like a sham. In short, the pull of competing forces in the Middle East and other regions—autocrats willing to throw their hat into the U.S. ring and social forces seeking American support for broader participation in their own governance—was as pertinent to Truman and Eisenhower at the outset of the Cold War as it was to Obama during the Arab Spring decades after the end of the Cold War.

Seeking a Place in the Middle East in the Cold War: Fragile Partners

It was that first year of the Cold War, 1947, in which policy makers began the journey of fashioning the way the United States would insert itself into the Middle East, specifically. The Truman White House set down the road of creating a security alliance in the region and identifying key states to fortify. But divisions arose immediately over which states those might be. Internal debates emerged in the context of two issues that occupied Washington that year, and both of which would continue to vex foreign-policy officials until the present day. The first issue was that the degree of fragility and weakness of states in the region raised the question if *any* of them could be reliable partners. The second, which I will return to in the next chapter, was the Jewish-Arab conflict in Palestine, which was coming to a head and was demanding that some hard decisions be made by Washington.

Alarmed in 1947 over the creation of a Soviet sphere of influence in Eastern Europe, the Truman administration feared that governments in the Middle East and in Western Europe, too, were susceptible to falling to communism or, at least, under Soviet sway. Truman aides fretted over the strength of communist parties in Europe, especially in France and Italy, as well as the Iranian communist party, the Tudeh. In what they called the Near East, they worried less about such political parties working within democratic systems than about communist insurgencies, particularly in Greece and Turkey. Claiming that the Soviets were behind the instability in Western Europe and the Middle East—a claim of dubious validity—they quickly slapped together policies to prevent further Soviet gains in those parts of the world. A 1947 National Security Council memorandum set out the importance of the area, the perceived threat, and the imperative for the United States:

> The security of the Eastern Mediterranean and of the Middle East is vital to the security of the United States. . . . The security of the whole Eastern Mediterranean and of the Middle East would be jeopardized if the Soviet Union should succeed in its efforts to obtain control of any one of the following countries: Italy, Greece, Turkey, or Iran. In view of the foregoing, it should be the policy of the United States, in accordance with the principles and spirit of the Charter of the United Nations to support the security of the Eastern Mediterranean. (U.S. Department of State 1947, 545)

The 1947 European Recovery Program, better known as the Marshall Plan, received most of the publicity in trying to stem the tide of communism. But even before Secretary of State George C. Marshall had sketched his plan for rehabilitating Western Europe, he had helped draft the Truman Doctrine, the first of many postwar presidential doctrines, most of which were aimed at the Middle East. The Truman Doctrine was a tough-minded policy designed to aid Greece and Turkey in the eastern Mediterranean in fighting off what the administration took to be Soviet-inspired communist insurgencies.

U.S. support came in the wake of Britain's decision to end its own aid to these governments. Severely battered by World War II and stretched to the breaking point, Britain could no longer be the power in the Middle East it had been in prewar days. The passing of the torch from the British to the United States in the Middle East marked the start of the Cold War and the opening salvo of U.S. efforts to contain Soviet influence, much as Britain had aimed to prevent Soviet penetration into the Middle East a generation earlier.[1] The Truman Doctrine was subsequently complemented in 1950 by the aggressive doctrine set out in NSC-68. The Cold War had officially come to the Middle East.

The legend of the Marshall Plan's effectiveness has become a central part of America's and Western Europe's historical narratives about themselves. In the Middle East, though, no such cheery story emerged. While Greece and Turkey staved off the purported Soviet-fed communist threats, U.S. officials found it much more difficult to build an effective regionwide set of policies aimed at containing Soviet influence than they had in Western Europe. No iron curtains were possible in the Middle East. Indeed, the Soviets made huge gains in the region during the two decades after the beginning of the Cold War. American officials simply were not able to identify willing and able partners in the area to stave off the Soviets. Washington pinned its hopes on a variety of doomed security blueprints and dubious potential partners, including Saudi Arabia, Turkey, Iran, Iraq, and Egypt. A review of all these cases of dashed American hopes is beyond what I can do here, but a look at two sets of events in the 1950s—the 1953 coup in Iran and the attempts for most of the decade to create a regional security pact—demonstrates how difficult it was for American policy makers to find solid ground in the region.

Partnering with Iran

The overthrow in 1953 of Iranian Prime Minister Mohammad Mossadeq became one of the more infamous episodes of the entire Cold War. U.S. officials long denied their involvement in the coup d'état. But a secret CIA history documenting the agency's hand in deposing the premier and exposing American disingenuousness was leaked in the late 1960s, and the full text was published by the New York Times on its website in 2000 (Wilber 1969). The strikingly explicit account was written the year after the plot was executed. It affirmed what observers had long suspected: U.S. intelligence had aided disgruntled Iranian factions, including the military brass that deposed the democratically elected government. In 2000, almost half a century after the coup, Secretary of State Madeleine Albright acknowledged the American role and the justified resentment of many Iranians toward the United States.

The outcome of the coup was the strengthening of the hand of Iran's monarch, Mohammad Reza Shah Pahlavi. While the CIA account may have overstated the U.S. role (Azimi 2004, Gasiorowski 2004)—the Iranians themselves, whose role historically has been underappreciated, were the initiators of the coup—the coincidence of American interests with those of Mossadeq's opponents, along with fumbling and factions among Mossadeq supporters, enabled the fall of the prime minister and the attendant rise of the shah's power.

Mossadeq, an outspoken nationalist, had earned the ire of the British Foreign Office (it had labeled him a demagogue and a windbag) at a time when the British were still hanging onto a day-to-day presence in the Middle East. Until their humiliation in the Suez War of 1956, the British continued to believe that they could maintain at least a foothold in the area, even in the face of their much-reduced international power and the rise of anti-imperialist, nationalist sentiment, especially in the Arab world. What angered the British Foreign Office in Iran, specifically, was a series of provocative reforms that Mossadeq promoted, first as a member of parliament (Majlis) and then in his two brief stints as prime minister in the early 1950s. None of the reforms in Iran was more important to the British than that related to oil.

The British had occupied Iran during World War II, precisely to insure control over the country's petroleum during the fighting, enabling a steady flow to their beleaguered ally, the Soviet Union. After the war, the British remained in charge through the Anglo-Iranian Oil Company, half-owned by the British government. They bristled at the very notion of local control of the oil. Mossadeq's plans to nationalize the company and having the Iranian state take charge of the country's oil reserves infuriated the British. The parliament chose Mossadeq as prime minister and then, following his lead, passed legislation nationalizing the oil. The British watched helplessly as the Iranians assumed control of the company's refineries, in 1951.

This was more than just an economic move. Mossadeq presented the takeover as the end of foreign control of Iran and of the Iranians. Despite the national fervor that the takeover generated among the Iranian people (and direct national control of natural resources was an idea that would spread like wildfire in the postcolonial world of the 1950s and 1960s), the shah, then still in his early thirties and limited in his powers, sided with the British, not Mossadeq, in the dispute. His reasons for close ties to Great Britain had little to do with the British hope to retain control of the oilfields. Uncertain of his hold on power, the shah was unnerved by *other* reforms then percolating in the Majlis. Most worrisome to him were efforts to undercut royal power further, especially over the question of who would control the military, the prime minister and his cabinet or the shah himself.

British policy makers were intent on reversing what they saw as an alarming set of events (as they were a bit later, in 1956, in their disastrous effort to undo Egypt's nationalization of the Suez Canal). But their attempts amounted to nothing. They tried bringing Mossadeq and the Iranian government to account in the World Court for stealing British property. They slapped an embargo on Iran. They froze Iran's sterling assets, banned exports to the country, and enforced a blockade that prevented tankers from loading Iranian oil. They also joined with the United States in creating the so-called Seven Sisters, the major British and American oil companies that formed what was labeled the "Consortium for Iran."

The Seven Sisters dominated all facets of the oil business for a short while, but the tide was rising against them and the Western powers standing behind them. Mossadeq's Iran was not alone in attempting to gain control over the mineral resources under its soil from Western powers and their multinational companies. Its nationalization laws were an early volley in a worldwide battle by Third World mineral producers. Over the course of the next two decades, control over mineral resources became a central plank in the Third World's demands, in what later came to be known as the New International Economic Order (NIEO). Iran turned out to be one of the few NIEO successes. Control over the wellheads— but not necessarily over processing and transport—fell steadily out of the hands of the Western powers and the Seven Sisters. Indeed, the shift to direct control of oil reserves by the producing countries tended to make many of the conceptions of some American foreign-policy makers anachronistic by the 1960s and 1970s, although a number still held on to the pipedream of continuing Western control over oil reserves.

All the British fulminating and sanctions did nothing restore the previous situation. Mossadeq closed down the British embassy and sent its personnel packing. Still intent on undoing the Iranian nationalization, the British approached American intelligence about the possibility of deposing the duly elected Mossadeq. At the time, Eisenhower's aides seemed to be as concerned with possible Soviet gains in Iran as with the question of who owned the oil. In fact, under Truman, who had been much more supportive of Mossadeq than Eisenhower later would be, the Americans had inched away from Britain's strident call for retention of control over Iran's oil. At one point, Truman had even vetoed a British-proposed military action against the Iranians.

Once Eisenhower took office, though, Washington's tone changed. As usual, American officials interpreted local events in terms of the U.S.-Soviet rivalry. Indeed, C. M. Woodhouse, a senior agent with Britain's Secret Intelligence Service, was key in framing Iranian events for the new American administration: "I was convinced from the first that any effort to forestall a Soviet coup in Iran would require a joint Anglo-American effort. The Americans would be more likely to work with us if they saw the problem as one of containing Communism rather than restoring the position of the AIOC [Anglo-Iranian Oil Company]" (Woodhouse 1982, 110). Woodhouse was an old-school imperialist who had little patience with those "who experienced," in the words of the historian Fakreddin Azimi, "the conspicuous power and arrogance of the British empire" (Azimi 2004, 100), such as it was in the early 1950s. Woodhouse wrote in his memoir that "the Iranians lived in a world of fantasy and imagination. An attractive symptom of it was that most of their statues in public places were of poets—Firdausi, Hafiz, Sa'adi—rather than kings and generals" (Woodhouse 1982, 114). His condescension notwithstanding, Woodhouse feared the role of Iran's active communist party, the Tudeh, which lined up behind Mossadeq. He conveyed his concerns to Eisenhower aides, who were similarly worried about Iran's possible tilt toward the USSR (Woodhouse 1982, 117).

There was evidence that the Soviets had supported separatist movements inside Iran after the war. Some Washington officials spoke ominously in the McCarthy-saturated political environment of the time about Iran becoming a second China. The domestic hysteria helped inflate the threat the Tudeh presented; in fact, it was a party with limited appeal (mostly in the urban areas) and riven by factionalism (Behrooz 2004). Nonetheless, the introduction to the CIA's secret history demonstrates how seriously U.S. officials took the threat of a communist takeover to be: "It was estimated that Iran was in real danger of falling behind the Iron Curtain; if that happened it would mean a victory for the Soviets in the Cold War and a major setback for the West in the Middle East. No remedial action other than the covert action plan set forth below could be found to improve the existing state of affairs" (Wilber 1969, xiii).

The Eisenhower administration, through CIA Director Allen W. Dulles, eventually acceded to the British entreaties for supporting a coup, hoping to replace Mossadeq's "government with one which would govern Iran according to constructive policies" (Wilber 1969, iii–iv). The aim was to enlist the shah, whose father had been pushed aside by the British in the 1940s, to join the anti-Mossadeq plot brewing among the prime minister's Iranian opponents. For U.S. officials, the shah promised to be both a leader whom they could manipulate as well as a long-term strategic partner to help protect the Middle East from Soviet advances. But the shah dithered as one powerful American figure after another tried to convince him to sign off on the coup—including General H. Norman Schwarzkopf, the father of the military leader of the First Gulf War in 1990–1991, who would make his own strong mark on the region, and Kermit Roosevelt, the CIA officer who oversaw the American role in the plot and the grandson of President Theodore Roosevelt.

The shah's irresoluteness should have tipped off the Americans that even once Mossadeq was deposed, the Iranian monarch would prove to be a pusillanimous partner. And that was the case. Various administrations armed the shah's military to the teeth and leaned heavily on the Iranians to assume a leadership role in the Persian Gulf region, where they hoped that Iran could deter Soviet mischief making aimed at fragile Arab monarchies and, indeed, play an active role in the entire Middle East.

Here was the strategic partner, presidents from Eisenhower and Nixon believed, that could serve as a major pro-American agent, deterring Soviet encroachment and generally reducing the American burden of leadership in the region. The shah certainly felt indebted to the United States, as evidenced in his line to Kermit Roosevelt, quoted by Gasiorowski (1987, 278): "I owe my throne to God, my people, my army—and to you." Gasiorowski wryly added, "Although each of these forces may have played a role in the coup, this statement would have been more accurate if the Shah had reversed their order of importance." I cannot speak to God's role in securing the shah's throne, but the people played little of a role in the coup and remained distant from the regime in subsequent years.

The shah never wavered in his pro-American stance and was praised to the skies by the likes of Nixon and his national security advisor and, later, secretary of state Henry Kissinger. Nonetheless, Iran did not turn out to be the partner for whom Eisenhower and his successors had hoped. The shah never did manage to institutionalize his rule deeply in Iranian society. Nor did he show much interest in playing a leadership role in the region. In fact, other than a rather passive role in U.S.-inspired security arrangements, to be discussed below, and a nefarious pact with Saddam Hussein to squelch Kurdish aspirations in Iraq in the mid-1970s, the shah's Iran largely turned its back on the Middle East. When crises struck that touched on America's role in the area, as in 1956, 1958, 1967, and 1973, Iran played a negligible role. In fact, it was in the heyday of the shah's rule and his partnership with the United States that the Soviets made their big gains in the region.

The shah and the various presidents with whom he interacted, from Truman to Jimmy Carter, spoke repeatedly of the abiding Iranian-American friendship. The problem was that this partnership, a partnership with a weak, despotic regime destined to crumble in the most important revolution in modern Middle East history, gave the United States only limited leverage in the region as a whole. The situation from 1953 through the shah's ouster in 1979 was a precursor of later American administrations' difficulties with the likes of Hosni Mubarak: the ties during the dictator's tenure did not deliver nearly as much as U.S. officials hoped for, in large part because of the weakness of regimes that lacked popular participation and support. When popular uprisings finally unseated the dictators, the United States was viewed as having served as a key prop to the ousted repressive regime.

In the case of Iran, Mossadeq's overthrow, as Gasiorowski (1987, 261) comments, was a landmark, just not the sort of landmark Washington wanted:

> In retrospect, the United States sponsored coup d'état in Iran of August 19, 1953, has emerged as a critical event in postwar world history. The government of Prime Minister Mohammad Mossadeq which was ousted in the coup was the last popular, democratically oriented government to hold office in Iran. The regime replacing it was a dictatorship that suppressed all forms of popular political activity, producing tension that contributed greatly to the 1978–1979 Iranian revolution. . . . The 1953 coup also marked the first peacetime use of covert action by the United States to overthrow a foreign government. As such, it was an important precedent for events like the 1954 coup in Guatemala and the 1973 overthrow of Salvador Allende in Chile, and made the United States a key target of the Iranian Revolution.

Seeking a Security Pact

If the attempt to secure Iran as an American strategic partner brought mixed results at best, another effort to build such collaborations in the immediate postwar period had even less success. In this case, the United States sought to anchor its presence in the Middle East and offload responsibilities to local agents through the creation of a security pact similar to NATO. While the British had pushed such an idea for the Middle East in one form or another from 1947 on, it was not until 1950, the year the Korean War broke out and NSC-68 was adopted, that Washington showed any substantial interest in the proposal. Over the course of the 1950s, such a military alliance, with the goal of hemming in the Soviet Union on its southern border, took a variety of guises.

Policy makers generated a riot of acronyms but to little avail. MEC (Middle East Command), MEDO (Middle East Defense Organization), BP (Baghdad Pact), and CENTO (Central Treaty Organization) all were short-lived multilateral security plans or agreements meant to repel the Soviets through shared British-American–Middle Eastern military cooperation. The British and Americans, though, had somewhat different goals for any security alliance: "For the British, the MEC and MEDO were primarily devices for preserving their leading role in the Middle East, while sharing some of its burdens; the United States, in contrast, was interested in a broader political approach to the Middle East. Washington was also insistent that it could assume no substantial defence burdens in the region" (Yeşilbursa 2005, 8).

Washington's warming to the idea of a Middle East security pact came during the last stages of the Truman administration. The head of the Policy Planning Staff, Paul Nitze, reacting to growing instability in Egypt at the beginning of 1952 and to waning British power, suggested the creation of a military-treaty organization for the region. His notion was a coalition, MEDO, with Arab states, especially Egypt, as the key participants. Both Truman and his secretary of state, Dean Acheson, bought into the concept, but nothing came of the idea with only months left in the life of the administration.

It was during the Eisenhower years that a concerted effort was made to fashion a Mideast military alliance. The New Look policy and the directive putting it into effect, NSC-162/2, constituted a retrenchment from Truman's seemingly limitless ambitions earlier in the Cold War, which had been articulated in NSC-68. The cutbacks undergirded the idea that the United States would need strategic partners to share the burdens of foreign policy, particularly in beating back or at least containing communism. After only four months in power, Eisenhower had his secretary of state, John Foster Dulles (the brother of Allen, the CIA director so central in the Mossadeq affair), undertake a grand tour of the Middle East. Covering eleven countries in twenty days, it was the first trip by an American secretary of state to the area. One implicit question that Dulles needed to answer was whether Nitze's earlier ideas for a Middle East Defense Organization were still viable.

Dulles returned home from the Middle East with a concrete set of ideas. He felt that Arab states were more concerned with Israel than with communism and, as I shall note below, that any tilt toward Israel by the United States would gravely hurt the latter's image among the region's Arabs. More to the point of the moment, he concluded that Arab nationalism was on the rise and that it was lending instability to the Arab world. His analysis of Arab nationalism was nuanced and not altogether negative. He certainly recognized the deep appeal it generated. As his trip faded in memory, though, Dulles adopted an increasingly negative view of Arab nationalism, in the end concluding that it was practically indistinguishable from communism as an anti-American force.

But in the immediate aftermath of his trip, Dulles's reasoning was that the turmoil in Egypt and other Arab countries stemming from Arab nationalist sentiments made the old regimes unreliable as partners; he did at the time hold out hope that future nationalist regimes could possibly team up with the United States. Nitze's earlier conception of a security agreement grounded in Egypt's participation would not work at the moment. Instead, Dulles argued, the United States must look to a "Northern Tier" of states, mostly (but not exclusively) in the Middle East, to seal the area from Soviet influence. If events settled down in Egypt, which Dulles initially hoped they would after the 1952 Free Officers Revolution (Dulles met with the figurehead leader of the revolution, Muhammad Naguib), it could join a Northern Tier alliance later (Hahn 2003, 94).

The Northern Tier conception caught on among American policy makers and took a number of forms over the next half-dozen years. Its pillars would be Turkey, in the Middle East, and Pakistan, bridging the Middle East and South Asia. Both countries were already committed to U.S.-led containment organizations through NATO and SEATO. In fact, Dulles saw the new Northern Tier arrangement as a vital link between the European and Asian alliances, tightening the noose around the Soviet Union. The various iterations of such a Northern Tier coalition largely in the Middle East resulted finally in 1955 in the Turkish-Iraqi Pact of Mutual Cooperation. It in quick order added Britain, Pakistan, and its fifth member, Iran, to become the much-heralded Baghdad Pact.

By then, American-Egyptian relations had soured, and the new nationalist regime in Cairo became an outspoken opponent of the new security pact. Washington was deeply implicated in all facets of the treaty organization. But after considerable internal debate, the United States did not become an actual member. Its final decision not to join—although its representatives served on some key committees in the organization—doomed the Baghdad Pact. As a spokesman for Iran, Iraq, Pakistan, and Turkey put it to Dulles, without the United States, "we are four zeros and those only add up to zero" (Podeh 2003, 112).

Eisenhower aides had concluded that with or without U.S. participation, the idea of a strategic partnership would not carry much weight. *Without* American membership, as a supposedly indigenous undertaking, the organization added up, in the words of the spokesman, to a zero plus a rapidly fading Great Britain. *With* American participation, the United States would have totally overshadowed its weak comembers. The fragility of the organization was highlighted when the tottering Iraqi monarchy succumbed in 1958 to the gathering storm of Arab nationalism, less than three years after the pact was cobbled together. When the new Iraqi nationalist regime withdrew formally from the organization, the coalition's name was changed to CENTO, and it limped along until the 1979 Iranian Revolution, when it died a quiet death.

For the Eisenhower administration, the failure of the Baghdad Pact was a serious blow. Not only did the security alliance fail to provide a link between NATO and SEATO; it also became an insignificant relic even before the Iraqi Revolution, never mind in its guise as CENTO. As their members held inconsequential meetings under the benign gaze of the United States, the Soviets in the 1950s and 1960s cemented ties with the three states that most influenced regional dynamics—Egypt, Iraq, and Syria. Washington seemed to be flailing as it floated a number of (sometimes contradictory) plans to reverse Soviet gains or at least prevent further Soviet successes in the region. The Eisenhower Doctrine of 1958 appeared to eschew the earlier idea of finding viable strategic partners; it instead reverted to America's going it alone. It authorized deploying American troops in countries seeking help against "overt armed aggression from any nation controlled by international communism."

In 1958, in NSC directive 5820/1, the administration reversed what had become its total rejection of Arab nationalism. Now American officials sought to accommodate it and the idea of Arab unity as a way of weaning nationalist regimes away from the Soviets. But this tack failed as well. Washington seemed to have little concrete knowledge and understanding of the Middle East and was stymied in its attempts to impose a set of ideas that had worked in Western Europe but had little relevance in the Mideast region. It would not be the last administration that would suc-cumb to "the flaws of applying a globalist analytical methodology to the Middle East—in lieu of a serious appreciation of the regional dynamics in the area" (Lesch 2003, 133). Podeh (2003) summed up the woeful attempt by the United States to establish itself in the Middle East in the early part of the Cold War:

> The greatest mistake of the United States was its failure to compre-hend Arab psychology in the postcolonial era and the depth of Arab rivalries. The belief that Nasser could be enticed to join a Western-led pact if only the price was right or that it would be possible to "build" King Sa'ud as an alternative Arab leader to Nasser attested to the shortsightedness of U.S. thinking.

In short, the two decades following 1947 did not go well in the Mid-dle East for American policy makers. U.S. efforts at building a barri-cade against Soviet influence through the creation of local alliances and partnerships faltered. In those years, the Soviet Union made major gains in the area. Rapid and destabilizing changes in the region played into So-viet hands. As France and Britain, which had taken quasi colonies in the area after World War I (officially, League of Nations Mandates), lost their imperial foothold, the postcolonial Arab states that emerged in their wake faced major instability. Coup after coup in Syria and major revolutions in Egypt (1952) and Iraq (1958) demonstrated the difficulty for the United States of aligning itself with dictatorships that had little connection to their own rapidly changing societies. If there was a lesson to be learned about the shaky foundations of alliances with dictators and regimes that had few institutional ties to their own populations, Washington failed to learn it. Preoccupied with the global structure of power, administration after administration was indifferent to the state-society relations and re-gional dynamics that were the underpinnings of power.

Postwar U.S. policy makers witnessed the emergence of new nation-alist regimes in Egypt, Iraq, and Syria, which replaced the old Western-dominated territories and governments. One by one these three major Arab states lined up behind the Soviets, and each took on a strong anti-Western bias. Arab nationalism, with its overtones of anti-imperialism, anti-Americanism, and socialism, had provided an opening for Soviet influence in the 1950s. The Soviets backed the nationalist regimes and supported their program of pan-Arabism, including its most important tenet, Arab political unity through the creation of a single Arab state. American hopes of finding strategic partners among the most populous Arab states in the heart of the Middle East and of creating a NATO-like security pact were in tatters by the end of the 1950s.

The Middle East became the key region where the USSR could and did make real headway in extending its influence beyond its immediate eastern and western borders. Indeed, the Middle East catapulted the Soviets into becoming a truly global superpower in the latter half of the 1950s, enjoying vast influence beyond what they claimed to be their natural sphere. They were sitting high in a region that held undeniable importance to the United States.

In retrospect, the Middle East was the area where Soviet world influence peaked—and where it most piqued the United States. In 1970, President Nixon, who tended to see almost every regional event in terms of the superpower rivalry, noted, "If there is one thing that can be said, over the past ten years the American position in the Mediterranean has been rapidly deteriorating and has deteriorated there more than any place in the world" (Nixon 1970). The historian Michael Oren, who became the Israeli ambassador to the United States in 2009, described how dour the American position was during the first two years of Nixon's presidency: "In Libya, the dashing and often delusional Colonel Muammar Qadhafi (or Qaddafi) had ousted King Idris, closed the Wheelus air base, and warmly allied himself with the Kremlin. Soviet arms streamed into Algeria and Sudan, and thousands of Red Army advisers deployed in Egypt, South Yemen, Syria, and Iraq. . . . [And there was] escalating lawlessness in Jordan" (Oren 2007, 529). Even after the tide began to turn in Washington's favor, Kissinger (1979, 1263) pointed to the continued ascendancy of the Soviets in the Middle East during the last year of Nixon's first term:

> The real issue in 1972 was that the required balance within an area essential for the security, and even more the prosperity, of all industrial democracies appeared in grave jeopardy. More than 15,000 Soviet troops were still in Egypt, with which we had as yet no diplomatic relations and which was tied to the Soviet Union by a Friendship Treaty signed a year earlier. . . . On April 9, the Soviet Union had concluded a similar Friendship Treaty with Iraq, followed by massive deliveries of the most advanced modern weapons. Syria had long since been a major recipient of Soviet arms—and had

invaded moderate Jordan twenty months earlier. Britain at the end of 1971 had just completed the historic withdrawal of its forces and military protection from the Persian Gulf at the precise moment when radical Iraq was being put into a position by Soviet arms to assert traditional hegemonic aims. Our friends—Saudi Arabia, Jordan, the Emirates—were being encircled.

Whatever strategic partnerships and military alliances the United States had attempted to put in place during the 1950s and 1960s had not panned out. Washington experienced grave difficulties in the quarter-century after World War II in finding its way in the Middle East. Its strategy of imposing formulas based on the models it derived from its successes in NATO and its strategic tie to Great Britain without due concern for specific Mideast dynamics had not yielded it much.

4 Finding a Place in the Middle East

A New Partnership Develops out of Black September

After a quarter of a century of frustration, American policy makers finally began making some progress in achieving their goals in the Middle East. The 1970s certainly were not smooth sailing—the oil boycott of 1973 and the Iranian Revolution of 1979, to take two critical events, were painful body blows. Still, in terms of their own goals of containing and even pushing back the Soviet Union and establishing stable strategic partnerships, U.S. officials finally began to enjoy some favorable outcomes. This chapter turns to a key turning point for American's presence in the Middle East, the events surrounding the Black September War in 1970. That civil war in Jordan, it turns out, led to a new, if unanticipated, strategic relationship for the United States that lasted until the end of the Cold War. For two decades, it lent a modicum of clarity to how U.S. policy makers would navigate this critical region—a clarity that eclipsed the floundering that American officials experienced in the 1950s and 1960s and that would subsequently be lost in the post–Cold War era.

In that same quarter-century after World War II that the United States was learning just how fragile and weak the states in the Middle East were, another issue, the future of Palestine, created further dilemmas on how to find a reliable strategic partner in the Middle East. Like the British after World War I, the Roosevelt and Truman administrations discovered that the issue of Palestine-Israel, Jews and Arabs, had pushed itself to the top of their agendas. And, like the British, U.S. presidents in the post–World War II environment found that Palestine was a minefield that lay before them in trying to construct a consistent strategy in the Middle East.

Problems in Palestine had begun to devil the British almost as soon as World War I ended. Domestic violence erupted in the territory even before the League of Nations Mandate, which legitimated British occupation and rule there, was ratified. And violence broke out periodically throughout the entire period of British rule, right up to Britain's ignoble exit in May 1948.

In 1917, the British government had issued the Balfour Declaration, which declared "sympathy with Jewish Zionist aspirations," in the words of Foreign Secretary Arthur James Balfour in a letter to the British Jewish leader Baron Rothschild. The declaration supported "the establishment in Palestine of a national home for the Jewish people." But, already in 1914 and 1915, the British had made contradictory promises in a set of letters called the McMahon-Hussein Correspondence to the Sharif Hussein of Mecca, if he would lead an Arab revolt against the Ottomans during World War I. Those assurances included the statement that "Great Britain is prepared to recognize and uphold the independence of the Arabs in all the regions lying within the frontiers proposed by the Sharif of Mecca."

By 1920, the first violence involving Jews and Arabs in Palestine broke out, violence that has continued on and off, mostly on, until this very day, almost a century later. Increasingly befuddled by local events in Palestine, the British vacillated between strong support of the Zionist project and of the emerging Palestinian Arab national movement, which began to take root in the 1920s. Different elements of the British state, both in London and in Palestine itself, sympathized with one side or the other, making the coalescence of a coherent overall strategic policy by the British chimerical. Those internal conflicts were a harbinger of the internecine battles that would be fought inside the American government a generation later.

Just as for the British, the importance of the Palestine issue for the United States stretched beyond the parochial struggle of Arabs and Jews in a small strip of desolate land on the eastern shore of the Mediterranean Sea. The problem lay at the heart of America's broader strategic hopes as postwar presidents charted a course for the United States to be an everyday player in the Mideast regional system. Even before Israel became independent, American relations with the future Jewish state came to be defined by both sides of the debate, those favoring close ties with Israel and those wanting to distance the United States from it, as one of enduring importance for national security.

An all-important vote in the United Nations on the partition of Palestine into Jewish and Arab states was looming in November 1947. On the heels of the adoption of the Truman Doctrine, U.S. officials began to consider whether the creation of a Jewish state would help or harm U.S. efforts to contain communism, the principal American concern. The initial thinking among officials in the State Department and the Defense Department was that such a state would only complicate matters for the United States and make the fending off of the expansion of Soviet influence even more difficult. Although the United States voted for the partition plan, UN General Assembly Resolution 181, on November 29, 1947, some American officials continued maneuvering until almost the day of Israel's independence, May 15, 1948, to try to forestall the creation of the Jewish state.

Inside the Truman administration in 1948, two powerful personalities faced off over the question of whether Middle East alliances should be pursued largely with the new Arab governments of the region or should include Israel, even at the inevitable cost of weakening U.S.-Arab ties. On one side stood Clark Clifford, who would become a giant in postwar affairs, advising presidents over nearly half a century. He began as a naval aide to Truman and moved on to become his White House Counsel from 1946 through 1950. Clifford's highest office was as President Lyndon Johnson's secretary of defense, but he probably exerted the most influence during the Truman years. He sat almost daily with the president in head-to-head sessions as Truman's confidante to review domestic and foreign issues. He also played a major role in presidential politics, particularly in engineering Truman's unexpected, narrow victory over Governor Thomas E. Dewey of New York in the 1948 presidential race.

Opposing Clifford on the Palestine issue was Secretary of State Marshall, the author of the Marshall Plan and Truman Doctrine. By 1947, he was already one of the storied figures in American history. His military career took him to the rank of general, and he served as chief of staff before his retirement from the army. After the war, he became Truman's secretary of state in 1947 and, later, his secretary of defense.

The backdrop of the Clifford-Marshall confrontation in May 1948 lay in Britain's impending, final, ignominious withdrawal from Palestine. Prior to the end of World War I, the British, as mentioned, had already twice promised Palestine, first to the Arabs as part of a large national state and then to the Jews as their national home. These promises, in-cidentally, were on top of yet another British promise, embodied in the Sykes-Picot agreement with France in 1916, which envisioned neither an independent Arab nor Jewish state but a Middle East divided between the two European powers.

In any case, in 1939, the British made yet another promise, in a famous White Paper, this time to the local Palestinian Arab national movement, for an independent state for Palestinian Arabs. By 1947, beaten down by World War II and as confused as ever about how to proceed in Palestine, the British threw the intractable issue of what was to become of the coun-try to the United Nations. Although some British officials harbored hopes that the United Nations would call Britain back to play some sort of major role, possibly in administering a UN trusteeship, in fact the entry of the United Nations into the mix marked the beginning of the end for the Brit-ish as a major power in Palestine and, more generally, in the Middle East.

In its famous (and, to some, infamous) vote of November 29, 1947, the UN General Assembly voted to partition Palestine into two states, one Arab and one Jewish, and to establish Jerusalem as an international city to be administered by the United Nations itself. Within two days of the UN vote on General Assembly Resolution 181, renewed fighting broke out between Jews and Arabs. That civil war continued through the entire painstaking five and a half months of British withdrawal, which was com-pleted on May 14, 1948.

As the fighting raged on, the United Nations reconsidered the schema created by Resolution 181, deliberating over a number of plans that would have put off the creation of the two states, including a UN trusteeship and the appointment of a mediator. But as the final British retreat neared, the U.S. government received word that Zionist leaders would soon declare an independent Jewish state in the parts of Palestine that they controlled, which, if effective, would have derailed any other possible plans for the country.

Whether to lead the way in recognizing the new Jewish state that was about to be declared (no one in the administration knew then that it would be called Israel) or to withhold recognition and possibly thwart the cre-ation of the state: that was the question that led to the Clifford-Marshall faceoff in Truman's office (Benson 1997). Recognition of the Jewish state was a question that Clifford, in his recollections as told to Ambassador Richard Holbrooke, labeled as "an issue of fundamental and enduring national security importance." He also characterized it as a matter that, "if not resolved, threatened to split and wreck the Administration" (Holbrooke 2008).

The stakes were high inside the U.S. foreign-policy apparatus, and the two sides in the confrontation were by no means symmetrical. A quarter of a century Clifford's senior, Marshall had accumulated vast experience in foreign affairs both as a soldier and a statesman. He was, in Clifford's own words, "a legendary war hero whom President Truman revered. . . . The President regarded his Secretary of State, General of the Army George C. Marshall, as 'the greatest living American.'" At the time, Clifford had almost no grounding in international affairs. He was, as Marshall was quick to point out, a domestic-policy and political advisor who had little if no standing on foreign-policy issues. Moreover, Marshall's position reflected the views of the great majority of the foreign-policy establishment, including the State Department bureaucracy, which he headed. Marshall's position, according to Clifford,

> was shared by almost every member of the brilliant and now-legendary group of men, later referred to as "the Wise Men," who were then in the process of creating a postwar foreign policy that would endure for more than forty years. The opposition included the respected Undersecretary of State, Robert Lovett; his predecessor, Dean Acheson; the number-three man in the State Department, Charles Bohlen; the brilliant chief of the Policy Planning Staff, George F. Kennan; the dynamic and driven Secretary of Defense, James V. Forrestal; and a man with whom I would disagree again twenty years later when we served together in the Cabinet, Dean Rusk, then the Director of the Office of United Nations Affairs.

On May 12, 1948, forty-eight hours before the end of British rule in Palestine, in a tense meeting in Truman's office, Marshall argued strongly that the United States should not recognize the imminent new Jewish state and aim instead for some sort of trusteeship and ceasefire. His reasons were not hard to fathom. Recognition of the new state would cause irreparable harm to U.S. relations with the Arabs in the region, who outnumbered the Jews by an order of fifty to one. Their overwhelming numbers alone led policy makers to the conclusion that they would prevail in the ongoing fighting, especially after the Arab states joined the conflict, which was widely anticipated once the British finally completed their withdrawal.

Secretary of Defense Forrestal and others were outspoken, too, about the importance of oil in their thinking. And they did not leave the Soviet Union out of their considerations. Lovett argued, in fact, that British and American intelligence reports indicated that the Soviets were sending Jews and communist agents into Palestine from the Black Sea area, thereby putting the recognition issue into the context of the recently declared Truman Doctrine. In brief, U.S. interests in the Middle East, especially in light of the developing Cold War with the Soviet Union, Marshall and the others argued, demanded a pro-Arab policy stance, which meant not recognizing the Jewish state.

Beyond their stated arguments, the group of Wise Men were confronting a turn in the making of foreign policy in the United States, one that threatened their own ability to dictate U.S. actions abroad. The Wise Men were almost all patrician figures from notable Protestant families, holding degrees from the most prestigious universities. They came from a narrow but influential slice of American life, seeing themselves as the guardians of the American way and, certainly, of the U.S. place in the world. Marshall himself, for example, was from an old and respected Virginia family that also included the legendary chief justice John Marshall. Lovett was a product of a select prep school, a member of the exclusive Skull and Bones Society at Yale, and a postgraduate at Harvard. His father was head of the Union Pacific Railroad. Like Lovett, Acheson went to Yale, where he was a member of the Scroll and Key Society, and Harvard, where he received his law degree. His parents both came from prominent American families. Coming from more modest backgrounds, Kennan and Forrestal still made their way to Princeton University, which they used as a launching pad for their storied careers.

In a way, foreign policy was this group's sandbox. At times these Wise Men demonstrated impatience not only with Kansas-born Clifford, who was not an Ivy League graduate nor a scion of a famous family, but also of small-town Truman himself. Indeed, in the lead up to the meeting in the president's office, Truman had felt the contempt of the group, charging that the State Department had gone behind his back and countermanded a promise that he had made.

Now, in 1948, this powerful group was experiencing serious challenges to its previously unquestioned dominance in the foreign-policy arena, and not only inside the administration. The Palestine question was the first of a series of postwar international issues that brought new social forces in America into the discussion. Underlying much of Marshall's and others' anger in the room that day was the challenge to their exclusive control over foreign policy. While American Jews were by no means unanimous in their support of Zionism, many of them did support the creation of a Jewish state, and they were highly mobilized in expressing their views. As the debate over a new Jewish state took place, Jewish voices could not be ignored. Their influence in the room, even without their physical presence, was keenly felt by Marshall and the others. And it was not at all appreciated.

Clifford offered a strong rebuttal to Marshall, making six arguments to the president. Among them was the notion that the idea of a trusteeship, supported by Marshall and the others present, presupposed a single Palestine where Jews and Arabs could live side by side peaceably, which Clifford felt was wholly unrealistic. Interestingly, this argument still resonates today in the debate over a two-state or one-state solution to the Israeli-Palestinian conflict. Another of his points stressed the need to preempt the Soviet Union in recognizing the new Jewish state first. A couple of his arguments were moral in nature, but the most telling was his final assertion, which was a strategic one, in which Clifford for the first time expressed the view that a Jewish state could and would enhance the interests and security of the United States:

> In an area as unstable as the Middle East, where there is not now and never has been any tradition of democratic government, it is important for the long-range security of our country, and indeed the world, that a nation committed to the democratic system be established there, one on which we can rely. The new Jewish state can be such a place. We should strengthen it in its infancy by prompt recognition.

The argument that occurred in the president's office on May 12 was deep and bitter. Marshall recorded his own take on the debate immediately afterward, reflecting his biting anger over what had occurred:

> I remarked to the President that, speaking objectively, I could not help but think that suggestions made by Mr. Clifford were wrong. I thought that to adopt these suggestions would have precisely the opposite effect from that intended by Mr. Clifford. The transparent dodge to win a few votes would not in fact achieve this purpose. The great dignity of the office of the President would be seriously

diminished. The counsel offered by Mr. Clifford was based on domestic political considerations, while the problem which confronted us was international. I said bluntly that if the President were to follow Mr. Clifford's advice and if in the elections I were to vote, I would vote against the President.

Clifford indignantly denied Marshall's charges that his position stemmed from the need "to win a few votes." But their differences over *how* to further U.S. strategic interests in the Middle East, such as repelling the Soviet Union and guaranteeing access to oil, interests that were not at all in dispute in the room, continued to resonate in the halls of government for decades afterward. Would U.S. interests be better secured through close ties to the Arabs or to Israel? While Clifford ultimately triumphed in the immediate issue at hand—and the United States did indeed lead the way in the diplomatic recognition of Israel—it was the position of the Wise Men that soon became ascendant in U.S. policy in the Middle East, namely, that the interests and security of the United States, especially in the tumultuous waters of the Cold War, were best served through a pro-Arab policy.

With the rise of the revolutionary Arab nationalist regimes, starting with the Free Officers Revolution in Egypt in 1952, policy makers feared that Clifford's approach would give the Soviet Union openings to the awakening Arab core in the Middle East. Throughout the Suez Crisis, the aborted attempts at a NATO-style military alliance in the region (METO, CENTO, and the Baghdad Pact), and the 1960s and beyond, most of the relevant State Department officers and many others held to Marshall's position that the long-term strategic interests of the United States lay in the Arab Middle East. Strong ties to Israel could subvert the country's ability to achieve its strategic aims.

Clifford's contrary stance, that the long-range security of the United States lay in a strong, democratic Jewish state, a stance that had ultimately won the day with Truman, remained in the mix as well. But it was a decidedly minority position among policy makers for the two decades after that heated May 12, 1948, meeting. After Secretary of State Dulles's Mideast tour in 1953, for example, he pointedly commented, "The United States should seek to allay the deep resentment against it that has resulted from the creation of Israel" (*New York Times* 1953). Indeed, the question of whether Israel is a strategic asset or liability has remained open until the present time. As I will show in this and the following chapters, changing world and regional conditions greatly influenced how that question was answered at different moments in time.

Part of the reason that Clifford's pro-Israel position maintained some traction, even if it was not dominant during the 1950s and 1960s, was the inability of the United States at that time to establish enduring relations with the key Arab states and to secure strong strategic partners in the region. As noted above, the Soviet Union managed to make major inroads in the Middle East. It provided military and economic support, signed friendship treaties, educated Arab leaders at its universities, stood behind the nationalist regimes at the United Nations and in other international bodies, and more.

This support enabled the Soviet Union to forge alliances with the revolutionary Arab nationalist regimes, notably the core Middle East countries of Syria and Iraq (both run by factions of the nationalist Ba'ath Party) as well as Egypt, the biggest prize of all. Egypt was the largest country in the region and was a powerhouse regionally and throughout the nonaligned world. The United States was left largely with the smaller monarchies among the Arab states, such as Jordan and Saudi Arabia, which time seemed to have passed by, even if, in the case of Saudi Arabia and the Gulf states, they controlled vast oil reserves.

The recurring frustrations that Eisenhower faced, especially during his second administration, in trying to secure strategic partners among the core Arab states or through the Northern Tier led to some rethinking of basic American assumptions. To be sure, caution continued to reign among Eisenhower aides about cozying up too closely to Israel, for fear of undermining America's role in the Arab world. As I mentioned, hope of weaning the Arab nationalist regimes away from the Soviets revived in the later Eisenhower years, and the United States also did not want to alienate its remaining Arab allies, such as Saudi Arabia.

Nonetheless, there was a slowly dawning realization among some American officials that Israel's formidable military power in the Middle East could possibly be useful in furthering American interests. As still-surviving U.S.-supported Arab states—Lebanon and Jordan—tottered in the late 1950s, some Eisenhower aides increasingly grew to appreciate how even the specter of Israeli military intervention could blunt both Soviet and Arab nationalist agitation against those regimes. Although the Eisenhower administration had pitted itself against Israel in the 1956 Suez crisis, American officials nonetheless marveled at the way the Israeli military machine had powered quickly across the Sinai Desert to the Suez Canal in that war. The newfound confidence of Egypt and Arab nationalism after the failure of the Suez War to reverse Egypt's nationalization of the canal, as well as the series of blows to American Arab allies in the region after Suez, had administration officials looking at Israel in a new light. The political scientist Zeev Maoz noted how Israel's military standing changed following the Suez War, despite that Israel was forced to cede its wartime gains in territory. In addition,

> Israeli-French ties deepened. Israel was assured of a relatively free flow of modern weapons. The French agreed to provide Israel with a nuclear reactor, which developed into the Israeli military nuclear capability in the late 1960s. The French also agreed to develop ballistic missiles for Israel. The balance of power that emerged out of the Sinai War was clearly and significantly in Israel's favor.
>
> (Maoz 1988, 77)

The international-relations specialist Abraham Ben-Zvi found that "President Eisenhower became increasingly predisposed, during his second term in the White House, to reassess his original vision of Israel as a strategic liability and a major impediment to Washington's regional plans" (Ben-Zvi 2007, 3–4).

The key to the attraction of the arguments among Eisenhower aides that Israel was a country to be embraced and depended upon lay in their concern not so much for Israel as for Jordan in the wake of the Iraqi revolution and Arab nationalist hostility to the United States (Ben-Zvi 2007, 3–4). America's friend King Hussein seemed to be hanging on by his fingernails, and Israel's growing military reputation and proximity made it an appealing counterweight to the pressures on the young king. It needs to be added that strong actors in the State Department, CIA, and elsewhere continued to reject any thought that Israel could further American interests in the Middle East, but they were now being challenged by others arguing precisely that. For the moment, however, those seeing Israel as a strategic liability prevailed.

That view continued to dominate in the 1960s. As late as 1965 and 1966, Washington's wariness about establishing closer ties to Israel remained, as seen in "the Johnson administration's determination not to sign a defense treaty with Israel" (Levey 2004, 258). Secretary of State Dean Rusk continued to be "a powerful opponent of closer U.S. Israeli relations," just as he had been during that tense meeting in Truman's office almost two decades earlier, "and he warned Johnson of the delete-rious effect that arms to Israel would have upon relations with the Arab states" (Levey 2004, 260).

Johnson reluctantly did end up signing a major arms agreement with Israel, despite Rusk's objections, largely to offset a deal with Jordan. But the president made it very clear that he did not intend the sale to Israel to signal the formation of a strategic relationship; it was a one-time deal only, he insisted. Interestingly, Johnson's declaration fell on deaf ears in Israel, where leaders saw the arms deal as the budding of a long-term strategic relationship.[1] And, as it turned out, they read the situation better than did Johnson.

No matter what Israeli officials believed, until the June 1967 War, at least, most U.S. foreign-policy aides in Washington "thought that Ameri-can support for Israel would inevitably drive the Arabs into the arms of Moscow. . . . A hard-headed calculus of interest placed limits on . . . sup-port. Up until the mid-1960s, almost no American military aid went to Israel, and even economic aid was modest" (Quandt 2004, 61).

Like Israel's military prowess in the Suez War of 1956, the overwhelm-ing Israeli victory in the 1967 War turned heads in the U.S. foreign-policy establishment. Israel began to be seen in a new light—a regional power that could possibly team with the United States to help achieve Wash-ington's regional goals, especially in deterring Soviet client states from acting aggressively against America's remaining Arab allies. Addition-ally, the 1967 War mobilized the American Jewish community as a much more unified and vociferous voice in foreign-policy issues involving Is-rael. But it was not until 1970 that Clifford's assertion that Israel was a strategic plus for the United States, one outweighing the costs that the United States would pay in its relations with Arab countries by drawing closer to Israel, actually became the position of an American adminis-tration. It was a small war in which neither the United States nor Israel fought, the war called Black September by the Palestinians, that in the end swung foreign policy to the Clifford position.

Prelude to Black September: The Hijackings

The 1967 War turned the Middle East upside down. To start, at the end of the six days of fighting, Israel occupied the Egyptian-controlled Sinai Desert and Gaza Strip, the Syrian Golan Heights, and the Jordanian-governed West Bank. Israel now ruled over all of the for-mer Palestine Mandate and more. Besides directly governing the large majority of Palestinian Arabs for the first time, Israel also sat on land that had been ruled by two key Arab nationalist regimes, Syria and Egypt. Second, the UN Security Council adopted Resolution 242, providing the first comprehensive framework for solving the Arab-Israeli conflict, prin-cipally involving the exchange of occupied territories for recognition and peace.[2]

Third, Arab nationalism was shattered: Egypt and Syria, two principal carriers of its banner, had been utterly humiliated in the war. In fact, Arab nationalism—the ideology and movement calling for the unifica-tion of the Arab world into a single state—would never return to its lofty pre-1967 status in the Arab world. Fourth, Jordan was severed in two. Its glorious time as the ruler of the two banks of the Jordan ended, probably forever. Fifth, Soviet prestige and influence in the region suffered a major blow, one from which it never recovered. Indeed, I believe that three criti-cal events in the 1960s marked the beginning of the end for the USSR as a superpower with global pretensions: the revelation of the Sino-Soviet split in Asia, the Cuban Missile Crisis in Latin America, and the 1967 War in the Middle East.

Besides all these international changes effected by the war, Palestinian resistance against Israel also shifted dramatically. During the pre-1967 period, opposition by the Palestinians to Israel had been a three-legged stool: nettlesome, if often uncoordinated, fedayeen (or guerrilla freedom fighters) raids into Israel, which usually inflicted limited damage; out-spoken support by Palestinians for Arab nationalism as the force that would soon liberate Palestine from Israeli control; and, from 1964 on, the new Palestine Liberation Organization, whose bark was far greater than its bite.

After the 1967 War, fedayeen raids continued, but now in a much more coordinated fashion, while Arab nationalism evaporated as a seri-ous carrier of the Palestinian cause. The biggest change in Palestinian resistance, though, came in the transformation of the Palestine Libera-tion Organization. The PLO had been created in 1964 by a convention of hundreds of Palestinian leaders in Jerusalem, on the heels of an enabling decision by the Arab League. But from its inception it had been largely under the thumb of Egypt's nationalist leader, President Gamal Abdul Nasser. While its chairman, Ahmad Shukeiry, was shrill in his doomsday threats against Israel, the organization accomplished very little in its early years. But under the new leadership of Yasser Arafat, who with his Fatah faction of fighters gained control of the organization in 1969, the PLO emerged as a much more independent force. It was an umbrella bringing together a number of factions engaging in acts of sabotage against Israel, including the dominant Fatah and a number of smaller factions, such as the Popular Front for the Liberation of Palestine. Armed struggle became the PLO's signature call, aiming for the liberation of all of former British Palestine, which now included Israel and the territories it had conquered in the war.

Arafat's initial attempt at undermining Israel came in the summer of 1967, immediately after the war, when he set out to establish Fatah in the occupied West Bank and, in Maoist fashion, foment the struggle from within. When the Israeli military made short shrift of those plans, Fatah and other factions established their headquarters in Arab states—in the case of Fatah and a number of others, in Jordan—carrying out cross-border raids into Israel. Jordan was an excellent candidate for Arafat's establishing a home base where there would be little interference in PLO affairs by the government. The Kingdom of Jordan had the longest border with Israel, which was very difficult to monitor. The monarchy there, under King Hussein, had faced a series of crises as the young king attempted to secure control in the 1950s, and, at one point, he had to call on British intervention. And the 1967 War, which had seen Arab nationalist regimes pull the reluctant king into the tempest, had rocked it badly. In fact, Jordan had suffered the greatest losses of any of the combatants.

From the time that Fatah moved its forces to Jordan, it directly and indirectly challenged the Jordanian state's control over its own territory, and other PLO factions also joined the fray against the monarchy. For a brief moment, Jordanian forces and Fatah fighters had seemed to stand shoulder to shoulder. In the Battle of Karameh in 1968, most notably, Jordanian soldiers and Fatah guerrillas had fought together against an Israeli incursion undertaken in reprisal for Fatah's blowing up of an Israeli school bus. The fighting led to serious Israeli casualties, and the battle became a major landmark for Fatah as it established itself as the premier Palestinian resistance force. Indeed, Karameh paved the way for Fatah to take control of the PLO.

Following the battle, though, Fatah tended to discount the Jordanian army's role in the battle. Its forces, along with fighters from a number of other Palestinian resistance organizations that were popping up, began ignoring Jordanian law and establishing their own rule in parts of the country. They set up checkpoints, commandeered cars and other supplies, and collected taxes from the population. "They established their own police force, tribunals, prisons, as well as education, welfare and health services (schools, dispensaries and hospitals)" (Nevo 2008, 21). It is a matter of dispute whether Arafat directed this activity against the regime, protected others who perpetrated it, simply tolerated it, or failed to control it.

Whatever the case, the growing autonomy of Fatah and the PLO as a whole, once Arafat became the organization's chairman, was a dire threat to an already wounded Jordanian regime. Some fedayeen spoke openly of taking over the country, which had been the eastern part of British Palestine until the British separated it in 1922 from the territory west of the Jordan River, creating Transjordan for the Hashemite family, under the rule of King Hussein's grandfather Abdullah. The PLO fighters saw the possibility of a current takeover of Jordan as a first step to liberating all of Palestine. A worried King Hussein found Jordanian sovereignty slipping away.

Throughout 1969 and 1970, violence between Jordan and PLO groups escalated. In one incident in February 1970, as many as three hundred people were killed, and similar skirmishes continued through the spring. In June 1970, two weeks of running battles between the Jordan Arab Army (the successor to Jordan's Arab Legion) and guerrillas went on until an Arab mediation team intervened to bring a halt to the fighting. That month saw an attempt on the king's life. Later in June, the Jordanian government signed an agreement with Arafat in which it ceded much of its authority, giving the guerrillas practically unfettered freedom of movement in Jordan. The deal clearly demonstrated the upper hand of the PLO groups.

But despite all the concessions, that agreement brought almost no respite for the beleaguered Jordanian regime. Fighting continued between Jordanian forces and PLO fighters on and off throughout the summer, and guerrillas were calling for a general strike and large-scale civil disobedience in the country. In Zarqa, in the north of the country, they controlled one of Jordan's key oil refineries. Toward summer's end, King Hussein escaped another assassination attempt, one of many over the years. In fact, President Nixon (1970, 251) dryly commented in an off-the-record speech, "Jordan, a country where you wonder why anybody would ever insure the king. I am sure nobody does." Indeed, from the heady time of the Battle of Karameh and its immediate aftermath, it seemed that the guerrillas had been more interested in toppling King Hussein than in confronting Israel. Remaining in character, Nixon administration Middle East hands understood the events through a Cold War lens. They looked on worriedly as U.S-supported Jordan came under increasing pressure from the Soviet-supported PLO.

It was not Fatah but another PLO faction that brought the crisis between the regime and guerrillas to a head. The Popular Front for the Liberation of Palestine (PFLP), under the leadership of George Habash, had already engaged in a number of dazzling international raids in 1969 and 1970, including the hijacking of an Israeli El Al plane and attacks on El Al, Swiss Air, and TWA airliners. They had struck Israeli embassies, bombed a Jerusalem supermarket, and fired on an Israeli bus. Now, in early September 1970, they undertook one of the most spectacular acts of piracy in history, hijacking four planes flying international routes—three flown by Pan Am, Swiss Air, and TWA, on September 6, and a BOAC flight on September 9 (an additional hijacking, of an El Al Israeli passenger liner, was attempted on September 6 but failed). Three of the four were flown to Zarqa, in Jordan, and then blown up there on September 12, after the passengers had been evacuated. The firestorm was recorded by British TV and broadcast around the world. The fourth hijacked jet, the Pan Am airliner, was blown up in Cairo.

For King Hussein, the explosions in the desert were the culmination of all the events threatening his authority over the last couple of years. They were a sign to the entire world of Jordan's weakness and a public humiliation of the king. The hijackings in that fateful September by the PFLP forced the king's hand. Fedayeen declared part of Jordan, Irbid, as a liberated zone, and they spoke openly of a final battle against the monarchy.

Operating under newly declared martial law, King Hussein reorganized his government and the top military leadership. While he created a military cabinet, he also brought back a tough-minded civilian and former prime minister, Wasfi al-Tal, to help lead a war against Arafat, the hijackers, and the PLO. On September 16, only days after the airliners had been blown up, the Jordanian army was poised to move against the PLO. One report has them actually delaying until September 17, after King Hussein's sister-in-law, "Princess Firyal, paid a visit to the family fortune-teller in London, after which she warned Hussein that the 16th was an unfavourable date for the Hashemites" (Ashton 2006, 104).

Bad omens or not, over the next few days, the king's forces inflicted heavy blows on the PLO army, the PLA. The PLA, now under the direct command of Yasser Arafat, suffered bad losses particularly around the Jordanian capital, Amman. Losses were less severe in other parts of the country, but the upper hand had now shifted to the Jordanians. By the end of September, the Jordanian army had largely defeated the Palestinian forces. Another attempt at an Arab League–inspired separation of forces brought Arafat and his forces some respite, but over the next ten months fighting flared on and off, punctuated by the occasional short-lived agreement between the combatants.

The end of the fighting saw a total rout of the PLO forces and the expulsion of the PLO groups from Jordan. Thousands of Palestinians died in the months of fighting, especially in the first week of battles, leading to the naming of the war by the Palestinians as Black September. A year after that fateful September, Wasfi al-Tal was shot down on the streets of Cairo. One unverified report told of how one of the assassins "kneeled over the dying Tal and licked the blood flowing from his wounds and then declared to the horrified onlookers, 'We are Black September!'" (Tyler 2009, 110; Dobson 1974, 110). The report may well be apocryphal, but its very dissemination speaks to the hatred the Palestinian guerrillas held for the king and his aides. From that time on, the term "Black September" became the moniker for the notorious terrorist group most infamous for its kidnapping and murder of eleven Israeli athletes at the Munich Olympics in 1972.

The Internationalization of Black September

It was those few days in the middle of September 1970 that were critical—for Jordan, the PLO, and the overall configuration of the Middle East in the global power struggle of the Cold War. Immediately after the hijackings, even before King Hussein launched the war against the Palestinian forces, President Nixon pushed for the bombing of the PFLP positions in Jordan, but that did not occur. Both Kissinger and Secretary of Defense Melvin Laird tried to rein Nixon in. Kissinger reminded Nixon of contingency planning undertaken that summer, which had the Israelis as the lead player. More immediately, Laird used a refrain from the Vietnam War, telling Nixon that cloud cover prevented the United States from bombing the hijackers. Clouds in Jordan in summertime? Not likely. Laird's ruse was probably a way to buy time to defuse the president's anger over the hijackings, and it worked: Nixon did not raise the issue of American bombing again.

But the United States did make all sorts of threatening war noises following the hijackings, including publicly shifting military aircraft to Turkey, putting the 82nd Airborne Division on alert, and moving the Sixth Fleet from port. The British, in an act opposed by the United States, negotiated for the release of those hostages who had not already been freed by the hijackers—women and children had been let go earlier, while mostly Jewish men, fifty-four in all, continued to be held. The deal was for the remaining hostages in exchange for PFLP members who were prisoners. Among these prisoners was the infamous Leila Khaled, the poster girl for the PFLP, who had been captured in the foiled attempt to hijack the El Al plane on September 6.

U.S. officials were not the only ones watching the events with concern. Jordan's neighbors also looked on warily. The Arab nationalist regimes in Syria and Iraq made ominous sounds about protecting the PLO from harm. Iraq already had a sizeable contingent of troops in Jordan, and Syria's were available to strike. When King Hussein did move against the PLO, both countries openly threatened the Jordanians.

The stakes were high for both the United States and the Soviet Union. The PLO and its backers in Syria and Iraq were all solidly in the Soviet camp; Jordan was a staunch U.S. ally. Nixon and Kissinger, as expected, immediately put the crisis into the Cold War context, largely ignoring the intricacies of intra-Arab politics. Indeed, Kissinger believed that the Soviet reticence to act directly by putting pressure on its clients to release all the hostages quickly cost the Kremlin dearly. "Soviet prestige would have been demonstrated and reinforced," he wrote. "But by getting too greedy—by not helping to rein in their clients—the Soviets gave us the opportunity to restore the equilibrium before the balance of forces had been fundamentally changed" (Kissinger 1979, 609).

The administration was convinced that the outcome of the Jordanian-PLO fighting, as well as the posturing by Syria and Iraq, could be very consequential for the two superpowers as they jockeyed for dominance in the Middle East. The United States was bogged down at the time in Vietnam and had invaded Cambodia only months before. The invasion had provoked significant domestic dissent, leading to the shooting of four Kent State University students by the Ohio National Guard at a campus protest—an event that deeply traumatized the American people.

Indeed, despite all the movement of C-130 cargo planes and aircraft carriers to the Middle East, not to mention Nixon's bellicose public language that he was prepared to intervene in the crisis, the United States was basically unwilling to become involved militarily on behalf of Jordan. There were simply too many other fires both international and domestic to put out. To be sure, the Americans engaged in a number of feints and sleights of hand that hinted at possible military intervention. But even though Kissinger gave the impression of a resolute United States causing fear among the hijackers and nationalist Arabs (or "radical Arab states," as he liked to call them), the United States appeared largely powerless given its commitments in Southeast Asia and turmoil at home (Kissinger 1979, 609–612).

Still, the Nixon administration did see the possible toppling of King Hussein as a potential American foreign-policy disaster. Beyond that, U.S. policy makers worried that the internecine conflict in Jordan could blow up, leading to a larger regional war including Israel and the nationalist Arab regimes, and such a regional war held the potential to balloon into a U.S.-USSR confrontation, as well. As Quandt (2005, 79) put it, "Egypt and the Soviet Union could . . . be drawn in, which might lead to a U.S.-Soviet confrontation, the fear that all along had haunted Nixon and Kissinger. . . . Even if the Soviet Union was not directly involved, the symbolism of a fedayeen victory would work to Moscow's advantage." Another commentator echoed Nixon's deep concerns that the crisis could escalate into a U.S.-Soviet clash: "Hovering above the Jordanian Crisis throughout was the looming prospect of superpower confrontation, which fit rather neatly into Nixon's tendency to downgrade the significance of local or regional developments and instead view events in terms of superpower rivalry" (Siniver 2008, 116).

The administration was more concerned about an Iraqi intervention than a Syrian one, but actually the opposite occurred. The Iraqis backed off from their earlier threat by withdrawing their 12,000 troops from Zarqa on September 17, a day after the king had unleashed his army against PLO forces. But worst-case scenarios seemed to be realized the next day. Armored forces from Syria made good on the earlier Syrian threats; on September 18 they crossed into Jordan and engaged the Jordanian army. The Syrians publicly labeled the forces as a Syrian-based division of the Palestine Liberation Army. The PLA did lead the way, but it was clear that the bulk of the armored convoy was Syrian, not Palestinian.

The invading forces quickly took control of the town of Irbid and broke communications among Jordanian units. Three days after the invasion, on September 21, King Hussein sent a desperate telegram to Washington through the American embassy in Amman.

> Situation deteriorating dangerously following Syrian massive invasion. Northern forces disjointed. Irbid occupied. This having disastrous effect on tired troops in the capital and surroundings. After continuous action and shortage supplies Military Governor and Commander in Chief advise I request immediate physical intervention both air and land as per the authorization of government to safeguard sovereignty, territorial integrity and independence of Jordan. Immediate air strikes on invading forces from any quarter plus air cover are imperative. Wish earliest word on length of time it may require your forces to land when requested which might be very soon. (U.S. Department of State, Office of the Historian 1970)

Although the king's alarmist description was overblown, it did send shockwaves through the Nixon administration. Two years into his presidency, Nixon had begun to move Middle East policy from the State Department, where open concern had been expressed about the United States favoring Israel too heavily, to the White House. A National Security Council working group led by Kissinger had already determined earlier in the summer that the United States was not positioned to intervene in case of just such a threat as occurred in Jordan in September and that Israel was better placed to respond militarily (Quandt 2004, 77). Also, from the moment that the crisis began, the United States leaned heavily on Israeli intelligence; American intelligence sources in the area were weak (Rabin 1996, 188).

Of course, a possible Israeli incursion was fraught with all sorts of political difficulties, particularly since Jordan and Israel had fought a cataclysmic war only three years earlier. Jordan still had deep suspicions that Israel would use the present crisis to grab yet more Jordanian land. Additionally, the Middle East, beyond the crisis in Jordan, seemed at the moment to be a tinderbox. Israel and Egypt had signed a tenuous ceasefire ending their War of Attrition just a month before the hijackings. Israeli Prime Minister Golda Meir and Ambassador to the U.S. Yitzhak Rabin were even at this moment still engaged in difficult talks with the United

States regarding that ceasefire and peace initiatives associated with the truce (Rabin 1996). Secretary of State William Rogers's department, which tended to be more attuned to the multiple intricacies of the Middle East than the White House team, had been nudged aside in the crisis in favor of Kissinger's leadership. Kissinger's style dovetailed with Nixon's in downgrading these local aspects in favor of the Cold War framework. Nixon reported Kissinger as saying, "It looks like the Soviets are pushing the Syrians and the Syrians are pushing the Palestinians. The Palestinians don't need much pushing" (Nixon 1978, 483).

When the actual Syrian attack occurred, Kissinger reiterated the limitations that the United States faced. Possible U.S. military intervention, he wrote, would mean that "we would be stretched to near the breaking point in two widely separated theaters and naked in the face of any new contingency." Still, Kissinger saw the urgency of the situation, as always, in the context of the Cold War. "I had no doubt that this challenge had to be met," he recollected. "If we failed to act the Middle East crisis would deepen as radicals and their Soviet sponsors seized the initiative. If we succeeded, the Arab moderates would receive a new lease on life" (Kissinger 1979).

Kissinger and Secretary of State Rogers received progressively dire reports from Jordan on the Syrian incursion and the collapse of the Jordanian forces. Their determination, which they conveyed to Nixon, was that only direct Israeli intervention could stem the Syrian successes. Nixon gave a "go" to military Israeli action, first agreeing to an Israeli air strike against the Syrian forces and, after receiving word from Israel that such an airstrike alone would not suffice, to a possible ground action. The U.S. administration was now putting its own strategic fate in the hands of the Israelis.

Kissinger quickly became the point man in the efforts to save what the White House saw as its rapidly sinking ally, Jordan, and its own position in the Middle East. Kissinger began a series of consultations with Ambassador Yitzhak Rabin, the former chief of staff who had orchestrated Israel's stunning victories in the 1967 War and a future Israeli prime minister. Just before the crisis, relations between the United States and Israel had been strained over the ceasefire to end the War of Attrition between Israel and Egypt. The tension over the truce and violations of it came in the context of a longer-term wariness on both sides about the U.S.-Israel relationship. All that said, it was clear to both Kissinger and

Rabin that the White House now was leaning heavily on Israel to prevent the fall of an American ally and the triumph of Soviet allies in the region. Kissinger first relayed the Jordanian plea for help to Israel and, when Rabin demanded it, indicated that the United States would publicly support Israeli intervention. Here is Rabin's (1996) recollection:

> "I'm surprised to hear the United States passing on messages of this kind like some sort of mailman," I told Kissinger. . . .
> "Do you advise Israel to do it?" I pressed.
> "Yes," he said, "subject to your considerations."

Even before Israel's military moves in the crisis, it was providing key intelligence as to what was actually happening in the Jordanian-Syrian fighting. Israeli intelligence reported that there were as many as 250 to three hundred Syrian tanks in the region of Irbid. While this figure was probably exaggerated, the report confirmed White House fears about the scale of the Syrian attack. Israel then massed armored forces on its side of the border, north of the West Bank. This area directly faced Irbid and was very close to the Syrian border. Only a day after Washington's receipt of the king's urgent telegram, on September 22, Israeli forces were already in place, prepared to attack. Israel's flanking of the Syrian forces emboldened the king to order the Jordanian Royal Air Force to attack the Syrian tanks, and the Jordanian forces did remarkably well. Amazingly, for reasons that still have never been fully laid out, the Syrian air force, under the command of the country's defense minister and soon-to-be president Hafez al-Asad, failed to provide air cover for the Syrian armor. Indeed, Asad's decision not to involve his air force may have been a deliberate maneuver to pave the way for his takeover of the Syrian government later that fall.

All sorts of contingencies were laid out in those couple of days following King Hussein's call for help, with messages speeding back and forth between Israel and the United States, largely through the key interlocutors Rabin and Kissinger. Israel's preference was to stage an attack on the Syrians in Jordan, sending a couple hundred tanks toward Irbid, buttressed by air strikes. The Israelis agreed to leave Jordan once its goals were accomplished. But the king balked at what would be perceived as his obvious reliance on Israel. Instead, he pushed for the Israeli incursion to be in Syria itself. Fearing a Soviet response to such an attack, Israel sought and received some guarantees from the United States for a worst-case scenario of Soviet moves against it.

All these plans and messages, though, were unnecessary. Four factors seemed to induce the Syrian armor to turn tail and retreat to Syria on September 23–24, without Israel firing a single bullet; in fact, all that Israel actually did militarily was to use its air force to buzz the Syrian forces. First and probably foremost, Israel's massing of its own forces on the border appeared to lead the Syrians to the conclusion that this internecine war in Jordan was not worth the possibility of a new war with Israel. Second, the Jordanians put up a better fight against the Syrians—both on the ground and in air strikes—than King Hussein's panicked telegram would have indicated. In fact, Rabin himself saw Jordanian resistance as the key factor (Rubinovitz 2010, 700–701). The Jordanian air strikes, in particular, led to significant Syrian losses. Indeed, Jordan's strong showing led the historian Nigel Ashton (2006, 94) to scoff at the charge that the king was a "puppet in search of a puppeteer." But Ashton probably overestimated Hussein's autonomy. In any case, the king expressed his appreciation of Israeli help in the crisis (Zak 1996, 44), which seemed to indicate that he realized it was not his Jordanian forces alone that turned the tide.

Third, President Nixon gave interviews that hinted at direct U.S. intervention, although that never really seemed to be on the table. Nevertheless, the illusion of American strength and determination played a role in the crisis. Finally, the absence of air support from the Syrian air force put the Syrian armor at grave risk. Hafez al-Asad appears to have been playing a high-stakes game with his principal rival for power in Syria, Salah Jadid, who had sent in the Syrian tanks in the first place. Indeed, Asad, who later denied this allegation, did use the Black September War as a springboard to the Syrian presidency in the coup d'état he pulled off almost immediately after the ill-founded Jordanian intervention.

With the Syrians gone, Jordan was able to achieve a total victory in the war. Palestinians, both PLO members and many innocent others, suffered heavy casualties. Estimates range from 2,500 to 25,000 killed (the figure was probably toward the lower end). Neighboring Arab countries did not countenance the Jordanian onslaught against the PLO, but they could do little to stop it other than shun the Jordanian regime. President Nasser of Egypt, probably the most influential man in the entire Middle East, attempted to broker an agreement between Jordan and the PLO on

September 27. He succeeded in having the king and Arafat agree to an end to the hostilities and to have the PLO operate outside Jordan's cities, largely on Israel's border. The next day Nasser died of a heart attack, and the agreement, as others before and after it, fell apart. By July 1971, the PLO was totally routed by the Arab Legion and banished from Jordan. Arafat slipped out of Jordan dressed as a woman, bringing to mind the escape of Haj Amin al-Husseini, the Palestinian leader of an earlier era, when he was being hunted by the British. The PLO's new headquarters were now in Lebanon, which was to lead to yet another interesting chapter in the history of the modern Middle East.

The United States Finds a Strategic Partner

At the end of the twentieth century, Samuel L. Lewis, the former American ambassador to Israel, listed a number of factors contributing to what were already then the long, close U.S.-Israeli ties. The final factor in his list was the so-called strategic relationship between the two states. "It first emerged," he wrote, "in the Nixon Administration during the 'Black September' 1970 crisis over the Palestine Liberation Organization (PLO)/Syrian challenge to King Hussein of Jordan" (Lewis 1999, 365). The strategic relationship that Lewis wrote about, while harking back to Clark Clifford's arguments in 1948 and to the rethinking of America's place in the Middle East in the second Eisenhower administration, was forged during that critical week in September 1970. Helping the United States "represented a very important opportunity for Israel to show it was a reliable asset in the Middle East. Israel had no intention of losing this opportunity, even though there was concern about the wisdom of saving Hussein's regime" (Rubinovitz 2010).

For the White House, seeing Israel as an asset came after a long period during which the dominant view was precisely the opposite—that Israel was a strategic liability. As William Quandt, who served on the National Security Council during the Carter administration put it, before Black September the long-held view was that "Israel was more of an embarrassment for U.S. policy than a strategic asset. Even if Israel was an impressive military power [after 1967], that power could be used only to defend Israel, not to advance American interests elsewhere in the region" (Quandt 2005, 84).

FIGURE 4.1   President Nixon, Henry Kissinger, and Prime Minister Golda Meir of Israel, meeting in the Oval Office, March 1, 1973.
Source: Courtesy of Richard Nixon Presidential Library and Museum.

In the aftermath of the Black September War, however, that perspective of Israel as an embarrassment faded. The White House was well aware that Israel had made an overburdened and overstretched United States look strong and resolute. "Nixon wished for the United States to appear strong militarily and in command politically," wrote Adam Garfinkle (1985, 137). "Since the truth was quite the reverse, the image of the crisis that the president and Kissinger managed to construct was, in its own way, a diplomatic marvel." American foreign-policy officials—at least those based in the White House—saw Israel as providing the United States with the invaluable strategic assistance that made that diplomatic marvel possible. Rabin (1996, 189) wrote:

> These events had a far-reaching impact on U.S. relations. Israel's willingness to cooperate closely with the United States in protecting American interests in the region altered her image in the eyes of many officials in Washington. We were considered a partner— not equal to the United States, but nevertheless a valuable ally in a vital region during times of crisis.

On September 25, Kissinger phoned me and asked me, on behalf of the president, to convey a message to our prime minister: "The president will never forget Israel's role in preventing the deterioration in Jordan and in blocking the attempt to overturn the regime there. He said that the United States is fortunate in having an ally like Israel in the Middle East. These events will be taken into account in all future developments." This was probably the most far-reaching statement ever made by a president of the United States on the mutuality of the alliance between the two countries. I had never heard anything like it and still look back on that pronouncement with nostalgia.

Without using its own forces at all and with limited use of other resources, Washington was able to have considerable sway in the region, using Israel's power as a deterrent force. Indeed, after Black September and Nasser's death at the end of the crisis, his replacement, Anwar Sadat, reassessed the positions of the Soviet Union and the United States in the Middle East. His conclusion was unequivocal in the wake of Soviet ineffectiveness in the 1967 War and then again in Black September: Soviet power, including its ability to assist Egypt in reclaiming the Sinai Desert from Israel, was in decline. The United States, with its strong ties to Israel, held the critical cards.

The new regard for the United States as the power that mattered in the Middle East drew in good part from the Rabin-Kissinger collaboration in September 1970. Kissinger alluded to the opening that the 1970 collaboration with Israel presented to the United States in the region, writing in his memoirs of how the events "opened the road for the diplomacy of the years that followed" (Kissinger 1979, 601). The new U.S. relationship with Israel as time went on was not without its tensions. Even in the immediate aftermath of the Syrian invasion, administration officials, including Nixon himself, were worried about Israel's taking the partnership as a carte blanche. They wanted Israel to know that it would be the United States that would initiate action within the parameters of the partnership (*Minutes of a National Security Council Meeting* 2008). As will be seen in chapter 5, even more severe tensions would arise a few years later, in the aftermath of the 1973 War involving Israel, Egypt, and Syria, both in the administrations of Nixon and his successor, Gerald Ford.

But all those tensions did not erase the afterglow of Black September. Appreciation of Israel as a strategic partner had replaced embarrassment, and this lasted for the next two decades; indeed, in some ways the strategic partnership grew. In the 1980s, intelligence sharing, joint assessments of Israel's security needs to maintain a qualitative military edge in the region, and military-staff cooperation became staples of the Israel-U.S. relationship. The underpinning of all those activities, though, would quickly evaporate in 1990, as will be discussed in chapter 6. The environment that had promoted Israel to America's leading strategic partner in the region changed dramatically. That sudden change came with the termination of the Cold War and manifested itself more fully after Iraq's invasion of Kuwait in 1990. While Israelis were shocked by the U.S. turnaround in 1990, a change in the calculus of American policy makers could already be discerned in the years before that, as the next chapter will show.

5 The Strategic Partnership Faces Strains

The Yom Kippur War and the Changing Calculus of

U.S. Foreign Policy

By Washington's original yardstick of what success in the Cold War entailed—namely, U.S. gains at the expense of the Soviet Union—the two decades after the Black September War constituted the most successful period in the Middle East. The United States enjoyed strong relationships with the area's three major non-Arab powers—Turkey, Israel, and Iran—at least until the shah was overthrown in 1979. And even after the Iranian Revolution, the new regime at least did not defect to the Soviet side. In the Arab world, the Soviets were in retreat, especially with the expulsion of their advisors from Egypt prior to the Israeli-Arab 1973 War and, after the war, Egypt's switch to the American camp. That change initiated a long period of close collaboration between Washington officials and the regime headed by Anwar Sadat and then Hosni Mubarak. That collaboration greased the wheels of an Egyptian-Israeli peace and enabled U.S. policy makers to constitute their long-sought-after partnership, a triad of Egypt, Israel, and the United States, which could serve as a deterrent to anything Washington officials would consider to be Soviet adventurism.

Outside the framework of the Cold War, though, events in the Middle East should have been more worrisome to American policy makers.

Iran's revolution in 1979 not only ousted a close U.S. ally; it also ushered in a rabidly anti-American regime with a program of exporting its model of an Islamic-based state. Additionally, in the year after that revolution, 1980, a brutal coup in Turkey both put democracy on hold there (in the short term) and had the unintended effect of opening the door to political and economic participation of new religious and social forces (in the long term). These groups would eventually question some of the fundamental tenets of Turkey's foreign policy, including its slavishness to American security concerns.

Events in the Arab world should have been even more alarming to American administrations. Leaders who came to power in the 1970s and 1980s simply would not go away, and as time went on, their populations became more and more alienated from them. The regimes themselves increasingly became very narrowly based. In addition, the entire Middle East regional system was undergoing a major transformation, one that would in time refashion the ideology and the distribution of power in the region, creating grave new challenges for the United States.

American administrations for the two decades after 1970, however, paid little heed to these warning signs. Instead, they relished the unexpected opportunities that came out of the events beginning with the four hijackings in September 1970. Officials in Nixon's White House basked in the success associated with the triumph of King Hussein and his regime over the PLO and Syrians. They and their successors took advantage of that victory to marginalize the Soviet Union in the Middle East. Their success on that score and in forging partnerships with key Mideast states veiled the troubles brewing beneath the surface.

Like other aspects of U.S. policy that seemed to be doing well, the key strategic tie with Israel that was established during the Black September crisis in 1970 looked to be on solid ground. But here too appearances hid lurking difficulties. The U.S.-Israel relationship actually came under growing pressure and changed qualitatively during the two decades after Black September. To be sure, the continuing, even deepening, relationship should not be discounted, even in the face of building strain, as the Cold War slowly defused and then finally ended. But there were clouds on the horizon foretelling the demise of the U.S.-Israel strategic relationship at the very moment that the Soviet Union disintegrated.

The continuation of the strategic marriage in the couple of decades after 1970 could be seen in the substantially increased U.S. military and nonmilitary aid to Israel, especially after the peace with Egypt. High-level military technology was also transferred to Israel. On occasion, the technology flow went the other way, as well, with Israel providing the United States with new military technological capabilities, although the relationship was highly asymmetric, with the United States as the top dog. The two established a two-way transfer of intelligence on a regular basis, and Israel continued to serve as a military bulwark against any possible mischief making in Jordan. Israel swapped military and intelligence information in the decade after Black September with another American ally, the shah's Iran, as well, which also aided U.S. policy makers.

The fall of the shah in 1979 seemed only to enhance Israel's strategic value to Washington. Ronald Reagan commented on Israel in an op-ed piece a year before his election, demonstrating how the Cold War continued to dominate thinking about the Middle East, even during a period when Soviet fortunes in the region were flagging badly:

> The fall of Iran has increased Israel's value as perhaps the only remaining strategic asset in the region on which the United States can truly rely; other pro-Western states in the region, especially Saudi Arabia and the smaller Gulf kingdoms, are weak and vulnerable. . . . [Israel's] intelligence services provide critical guidance to ongoing regional development, the technical know-how of her specialists could be used to service American equipment in a crisis, and her facilities and airfields could provide a secure point of access if required at a moment of emergency. Further, Soviet planners must constantly take into account the effective dominance of the Israeli forces and especially its air force, over critical zones of access and transit in the region. In a moment of crisis the knowledge that this air force can create a zone of danger and uncertainty to the U.S.S.R. must greatly restrict Soviet options and thereby facilitate the task of American planners. . . . Only by full appreciation of the critical role of the State of Israel plays in our strategic calculus can we build the foundation for thwarting Moscow's designs on territories and resources vital to our security and our national wellbeing.
>
> (Reagan 1979)

Candidate Reagan's unequivocal Cold War language was already somewhat anachronistic in 1979. The relationship with the Soviet Union was by then in the throes of change, and so too, as a result, was the strategic relationship with Israel, which came under growing stress. Israel's utility for the United States lay in great part in the advantages it could deliver in the context of a zero-sum rivalry with the Soviets. The 1970s had already brought some superpower rapprochement through détente, nuclear-arms negotiations, and trade talks.

International phenomena that could not be shoved into the Cold War frame, most notably the Iranian Revolution and, later, the 1980–1988 Iran-Iraq War, were popping up. In the aftermath of 1962's frightening Cuban Missile Crisis, the two superpowers had become increasingly aware that their rivalry was not simply a zero-sum game in which a gain by one automatically translated into a loss by the other—and in which every world event was defined by their rivalry. It took years for the superpowers to assimilate that lesson fully and adhere to a "chastened" doctrine, but over time they became leery of pushing too hard to gain regional advantages, for fear of igniting yet another nuclear showdown. The slow transformation of the U.S.-Soviet rivalry into generally a positive-sum game, in which both sides "won" in certain circumstances, signaled trouble for America's strategic relationship with Israel.

This chapter explores how the waning intensity of the Cold War in the 1970s and 1980s and, then, the end of bipolarity altogether in 1990 made U.S. policy makers' chosen international strategy of creating partnerships with a regional strategic partner even more difficult to achieve and maintain. It begins by exploring the gathering clouds in America's strategic relations with Israel during the last two decades of the Cold War. Shortly after the Black September War, another Mideast war revealed some of those underlying tensions. The October 1973 War was a crucible for U.S.-Israeli ties, as American officials brought their changing relations with the Soviet Union (and Egypt) into the calculus of their interaction with Israel. While the U.S.-Israeli strategic relationship survived the 1973 War, it did so only in the context of a much more complex set of international and regional interactions.

As U.S. officials moved away from a single-minded set of policies grounded in a zero-sum relationship with the Soviets, they found that bloody conflicts such as the 1973 War and, later, the Iran-Iraq War offered both new opportunities and numerous pitfalls. They also discovered that the new environment could muddle relations with existing strategic allies. As we will see in chapter 6, the new opportunities and pitfalls became strikingly evident once the Cold War ended. In the Gulf War of 1990–1991, the first major post–Cold War global crisis, which took place just as the Soviet Union was being dismembered, the U.S.-Israel strategic relationship did not survive; it unraveled. Israeli leaders were shocked to find suddenly that the White House considered Israel not a strategic asset but a liability.

The Double Edge of the American-Israeli Strategic Relationship

Even in the very midst of the Black September crisis, nearly a decade before Reagan's op-ed article, some in the Nixon administration voiced caution about using the strategic relationship with Israel to procure Cold War gains in the Middle East. Such victories, they warned, might be antithetical to achieving other goals regarding the Soviets, especially if, as Garfinkle (1985) put it, the United States and Soviet Union were moving from confrontation to "pragmatic accommodation." He pointed to the following questions that the White House grappled with regarding the Soviet-American relationship and how they played out in the Black September crisis:

> Is the pursuit of U.S. interests in the Middle East best served by pragmatic accommodation with the Soviet Union in the region or by the maximum feasible exclusion of Soviet influence? Depending on the answer, to what extent is the close U.S. relationship with Israel a strategic asset or liability? At that time [of the Black September War], the happy ending to the crisis from the American point of view vindicated those within the Nixon administration who argued for the exclusion of the Soviets from the area, in part by denying their clients any benefit from Soviet military aid, and those who saw closer U.S.-Israeli ties as a major asset in this endeavor.

The question of whether to seek advantages over the Soviets or pragmatic accommodation with them was a real one, and it recurred throughout the rest of the Cold War. It impinged strongly on Washington's Mideast policies, including its strategic relationship with Israel. Increasingly, that relationship became a double-edged sword. At the same time that it held all the possibilities that Reagan had enumerated for gaining advantage over the Soviets in the region and thwarting their ambitions, it also ran the danger of sabotaging the new global accommodative relationship with the USSR and even leading to a global crisis.

To be sure, the temptations to make gains in the Middle East at the Soviets' expense were great, and the possibilities in the 1970s were never better. The poor showing of the Soviet Union's allies and the ineffective actions of the Soviets themselves, first in the 1967 War and then in the Black September War, eroded Soviet prestige and leverage in the area. Even as he pursued détente with the USSR, National Security Advisor and, later, Secretary of State Kissinger believed the time was also ripe for the United States to pick some fruit from the Soviet tree, to lure key Soviet allies, with Egypt at the top of the list, from the Soviet sphere of influence.

The risks of Washington's winning advantages at the expense of the Soviets, however, were high. Gambling that Soviet influence could be excluded from the region or at least marginalized ran the danger of upsetting the shared understandings developing between the superpowers in other arenas. It could lead even to a global crisis on par with the Cuban Missile crisis. Israel's utility as a strategic partner lay on the side of the equation in which the United States sought gains in a zero-sum relationship with the USSR; if the United States instead aimed for compromises and deals with the Soviets, the tie to Israel was far less valuable and possibly even counterproductive.

The special relationship with Israel was a mixed blessing for the United States in another way, as well. Soon after the Black September War and the death of Nasser, Egypt's new president, Anwar Sadat, came to believe that the newly forged U.S.-Israeli strategic relationship was not entirely negative for his country; it could also be exploited by Egypt. Sadat distanced Egypt from the Soviets starting in 1972, a process that gained steam after the October 1973 War. He concluded that the highly intertwined Israeli-American relationship gave the White House unusual leverage over Israel. That U.S. clout, Sadat hoped, could be used to Egypt's advantage. The risks of undoing the improved ties with the Soviets aside, Nixon White House aides salivated over the prospect of winning over as major a Soviet ally as Egypt to the American side.

Kissinger and other Nixon aides understood in the first couple of years of the 1970s that attracting the Egyptians would mean some tension with Israel. Indeed, if the administration was to mediate effectively between the two enemies, it would be pushing Israel into positions with which the Israeli leadership was not at all comfortable. On one side, then, the strong strategic tie to Israel could be used by the Nixon aides as a card to win over the Egyptians. On the other, the administration would have to distance itself from Israel to some degree—disentangle what it defined as U.S. interests from Israel's—if it were to succeed in attracting Egypt to the American camp.

The tension generated by the double-edged nature of the strategic ties with Israel was evident in how the United States navigated its delicate ties with both the USSR and Egypt after the Black September War. Despite Reagan's trumpeting of the unproblematic nature of the connection with Israel, during the period before he came to power and even during his two terms there was in fact both close cooperation and ongoing tension in the American-Israeli relationship. The strategic connection, which elevated Israel into an asset (Schoenbaum 1993, 182) survived and even deepened after 1970, but it also took a battering at various times. A closer look at the 1973 October War (variously called the Yom Kippur War and the Ramadan War) demonstrates the complexity and inner contradictions of the strategic relationship, as the United States sought to secure and expand its role in the region while at the same time developing an array of accommodative ties to the Soviets.

The October War of 1973: High-Stakes Games in the Middle East

The fighting began on October 6, 1973, in a coordinated attack by Egypt and Syria on Israel. Attempting to reverse Israel's gains in the 1967 War, Syria aimed a missile at Tel Aviv and drove its armored corps into the lightly defended Israeli-occupied Golan Heights. At the same time, Egyptian forces crossed the Suez Canal, which also held just a smattering of Israeli soldiers, and sent commandos deep into the occupied Sinai Desert. My wife, Marcy, and I were in Israel at the time, confounded as the usual calm and solemnity of Yom Kippur were shattered by the deafening clamor of an all-out military mobilization. Trucks revved their engines, and civilian men were running in every imaginable direction, trying to find their way to their reserve units. While trying to meet up with me (in this pre-cell-phone era), Marcy could not make sense of the recurrent calls for "ironing! ironing!" (*gee'hoots*) as she wheeled our baby's stroller through the streets. It turned out the shouts were announcing not ironing but a full-scale military "mobilization" (*gee'yoos*). She located me somehow, despite the confusion.

Shortly after we found each other, a shrill siren pierced the air, and kind strangers herded us and our infant into an apartment building's bomb shelter. We and the Israelis huddled around us remained clueless for what seemed like an interminable amount of time. Eventually, the radio, usually silent on Yom Kippur, crackled and then reported that Israel was under attack, and we were instructed to wait for the all-clear signal, which came a couple of hours later. We endured the rest of the war in blacked-out Tel Aviv, in and out of bomb shelters, listening to constant broadcasts of Israeli successes—lies, at first, and then reflecting the actual changing military balance in Israel's favor, starting around October 14. For the first week of the war, Israeli officials kept any bad news from the public—not only the military setbacks in the field but the rapidly diminishing supply of guns and bullets, as well.

Once Israel gained the upper hand, especially on the front with Egypt in the Sinai Desert, the United States and USSR began increasingly to be drawn into the maelstrom. After maddening holdups that confounded Israeli leaders, the United States began a major airlift to replenish Israeli military supplies. The delay was an attempt by key U.S. officials to demonstrate to Israel the asymmetric nature of the partnership and to demonstrate U.S. leverage, which would come in handy once the fighting stopped.

The Soviet Union not only resupplied the Egyptians, but as Egypt's and Syria's forces lost momentum and then started to reel, it also began to take a more active diplomatic role. In the midst of this stepped-up superpower activity, the rapprochement between them, which had progressed so far in the early 1970s, threatened to disintegrate. Only a year before the October War, the United States and the USSR had agreed upon the first limitations on nuclear arms, the so-called SALT I agreements. Now, in the latter days of the three-week October War, misunderstandings between the superpowers threatened to undo their advances and lead to direct confrontation, even a nuclear showdown.

The stakes were high. As one historian of the conflict described the situation of the United States and the USSR as the war went on, "They could not stand aloof because the success or failure of their clients reflected directly on their status as superpowers" (Rabinovich 2004, 319). For both, events in the Middle East were seen through the prism of their own competition, and that rivalry threatened to overshadow anything happening in the Golan Heights and Sinai Desert. One study of the war put it this way: "For Kissinger, the Arab-Israeli conflict was basically a problem in Soviet-American relations" (Maghroori and Gorman 1981,

29). In the end, the superpowers avoided going to the brink; self-restraint and superpower cooperative diplomacy carried the day, even at the expense of their relations with their allies Israel and Egypt.

During the last week of the war, America's ally Israel stood to build on a daring military action that had been led by General Ariel Sharon. Sharon directed a small Israeli force that slithered through the crease between two Egyptian armies, crossed the Suez Canal, and established a beachhead on its western bank, creating a corridor between the two Egyptian armies. It then fortified and expanded its presence across the canal, moving twenty thousand troops and heavy weapons through the corridor. It soon threatened to encircle completely and cut off all the supply lines of one of those armies, Egypt's Third Army, leaving it without any escape route. The assessment by many analysts in both Moscow and Washington was that if the Israelis succeeded, they could march almost unhindered on to Cairo and depose the Egyptian regime.

That scenario unnerved officials in the Soviet Union and even in the United States. Soviet leaders feared yet another blow to their prestige if their client fell. Washington, having witnessed the cooling of Egyptian-Soviet relations the year before the war, hoped to win the Sadat regime over to the American camp or at least to see the United States as the only viable interlocutor in gaining Israeli concessions. In the words of Janice Gross Stein (2003, 213), Nixon and Kissinger "shared the Soviet objective of preventing an Egyptian defeat because it would seriously compromise their central objective of creating a postwar political monopoly." Additionally, doomsday scenarios began to be aired. Cairo's collapse could precipitate Soviet intervention to save the Egyptians, and that in turn could lead America to act to protect Israel. Both Soviet and American officials worried about these scenarios and the possibility of a direct superpower confrontation.

The noose that Israel was tightening around Egypt's Third Army prompted a dizzying four days of diplomacy and even nuclear saber rattling. It began on October 22 with UN Security Council Resolution 338, negotiated between the two superpowers, calling for a ceasefire.[1] It did not end until the fighting itself finally came to a close on October 26. Agreement on securing a halt to the fighting was itself a turnaround. In the first couple of weeks of the war, first the Soviet Union and then the United States had not shown much interest in effecting a Security Council–mandated ceasefire. The Soviets viewed the early successes of the Arab armies with satisfaction. And during the first two weeks of the war, White House officials did not hold as dark a view as Israeli officials did about Israeli prospects.

The American aides played a complex game, which demonstrated their ambivalence about their ties to Israel. Zeev Maoz (2006, 159–160) put it this way:

> Kissinger realized that, paradoxically, the Yom Kippur War offered a unique opportunity for jump-starting a peace process in the region. Sadat, in Kissinger's view, launched the war in order to invite the United States to mediate between itself and Israel. However, if the war ended in a clear one-sided victory, the defeated party would have revenge—rather than diplomacy—on its mind, while the victor would want to reap the full diplomatic fruits of the military victory. Thus, the war had to end in a stalemate if both sides were to make the necessary concessions it would take in order for mediation to be effective. . . . Kissinger managed to fend off a number of Israeli ideas that would have undermined the new goals of the United States.

The ceasefire calculus changed radically once Israel had crossed to the west bank of the canal and threatened the very existence of the entire Third Army. It was then that the Soviets reacted. They pushed hard for an armistice, even summoning Secretary of State Kissinger to Moscow for what they called "urgent consultations." The very fact that face-to-face consultations aimed at joint action took place indicated how far the two superpowers had moved toward pragmatic accommodations with each other.

As he hurriedly flew to Moscow, Kissinger's motives were complex. He had not hesitated for a moment to go to Moscow for joint consultations. Still, he continued to be interested in displacing the USSR as Egypt's favorite superpower. In that sense, he felt that Soviet insistence on a truce could be beneficial to the United States. Sadat would see U.S. support for the ceasefire as having helped save Egypt's Third Army and, arguably, his entire regime.

Kissinger also unequivocally saw Israel as the principal U.S. ally. After the initial delays, the United States had engineered a massive airlift of military materiel to Israel during the war. Kissinger would not have been at all unhappy if Israel gained further advantage in the war, using American-supplied weapons. He hinted to Israeli officials that the United States would tolerate brief additional fighting by Israelis during the grey period in which the ceasefire was to take effect so that Israel could secure the encirclement of the Third Army (but not, Kissinger stressed, its destruction). His encouragement to the Israelis came despite America's apparent cooperation with the Soviets to secure an *immediate* truce. During Kissinger's forty-hour trip to Moscow, the two sides had worked feverishly to hammer out the details of the ceasefire. Before flying off to Tel Aviv from Moscow, Kissinger assured the Soviets that he would secure the Israeli acceptance of the truce.

The combat, as Kissinger's wink to the Israelis portended, did not stop, as the Soviet leaders had hoped. Acting on Kissinger's go-ahead for a limited amount of fighting before the ceasefire took hold, the Israelis continued pressing their advantage. Soviet alarm grew quickly. Worried about a potential deathblow to the Egyptian regime if the Third Army were totally surrounded, Kremlin leaders excoriated the Israelis and proposed, following the prompts of Sadat, joint intervention by the superpowers. Playing with Roosevelt's image, the Soviets proposed the equivalent of the Two Policemen to enforce the ceasefire.

Ominously, a letter by Soviet General Secretary Leonid Brezhnev threatened "taking appropriate steps unilaterally" if the two powers could not act together. The threat was a red flag to the Nixon team. In response to Moscow's tough words, the United States raised its nuclear-alert levels to DEFCON (Defense Condition) 3, the highest state of peacetime alert. The superpowers seemed on the road to an eyeball-to-eyeball nuclear confrontation. The U.S. administration now interpreted the war as a Soviet test of its resolve, and the issue of reining in Israel quickly diminished in importance (Stein 2003).

Only a bit more than a decade removed from the Cuban Missile Crisis, officials of both superpowers recoiled from what they had gotten themselves into. Fearing the repercussions of a nuclear showdown, the two sides looked for ways to deescalate the crisis. Soviet Premier Alexei Kosygin reflected the mindset of officials on both sides: "It is not reasonable to become engaged in a war with the United States because of Egypt and Syria" (Rabinovich 2004, 484). And, he might have added, it would have been unreasonable to threaten the gains the two sides had made in "pragmatic accommodation," as evidenced by Kissinger's trip to Moscow only days earlier. The Soviet Union implicitly withdrew its threat of unilateral intervention, and the United States sent a conciliatory letter to the Soviets. They began to talk of "mutual trust" and the need for a diplomatic solution. The substance and tone of the many exchanges between officials from the two countries in the last week of October reflected the return by both to a risk-averse strategy.

In the end, both sides acted to head off a full-scale superpower showdown; they were determined not to let local events in the Middle East drag them into a global crisis. The Nixon administration hedged its support for Israel by leaning heavily on it to allow medical supplies, food, and water to reach the now fully encircled Third Army. Kissinger was adamant with the Israelis that they not undertake to destroy the trapped Egyptian forces.

Israel's view of the situation was quite different from that of the Nixon administration, especially once the administration moved from gaining advantages at the expense of the Soviets to working with them to deescalate the crisis. Rather than defuse or end the crisis, "the Israeli leaders used every resource at their disposal to secure the military victory" (Stein 2003). But with the United States and the Soviets aligned against them, the Israelis could not extend their victory by strangling or destroying the Third Army; they could do little but honor the ceasefire and wait for American diplomacy to dictate the next steps to them.

After the truce was finally secured and observed, a dramatic new chapter in Middle East history began. With the superpower confrontation behind him, Kissinger was able to continue his attempts to gain advantages in the Middle East at the expense of the Soviets. Using shuttle diplomacy, he employed his leverage with Israel (as well as Egypt's precarious situation) to initiate the first direct negotiations between the two Mideast enemies, brokered by the United States. These started with simple separation-of-forces agreements and eventually moved onto substantive political issues.

The initial agreement to move all Israeli troops to the east of the Suez Canal and Egyptian troops to the west of the canal was a dramatic harbinger that the Middle East system was about to change in dramatic ways. The complex combination of American policy makers' assurances of Israel's importance to the United States, their subtle distancing of themselves from Israel as they embraced Sadat, and the pressure they exerted on Israel moved the two mortal enemies, Egypt and Israel, toward their own pragmatic accommodation. By moving out of the black-and-white mold of the Cold War, Kissinger succeeded in securing an agreement between the two regional powers at a moment when the two had suffered grievous losses. I stood at the Suez Canal the day the forces of the two regional powers began withdrawing across it. Not familiar with the Sinai Desert, I asked a soldier about the beautiful ripples of sand for as far as the eye could see. He looked at the ripples and then at me and said, "Those are not ripples; those are bodies covered with sand."

Kissinger's success in moving the parties toward their first agreement had the effect, according to Dowty (1984, 301–302), "of making the U.S. role central and excluding the Soviets (in the words of one aide, Kissinger took personal delight in seeing the Soviets on the outside). . . . U.S. prestige benefited enormously from the disengagement [of forces]." These American-brokered military-level talks produced a historic separation of forces and opened the door to further political negotiations in the 1970s, which finally led to the heralded Israeli-Egyptian peace treaty.

But the journey toward that historic agreement was an not easy one for Israeli policy makers. Perhaps the most difficult moment came when the Israeli leaders Prime Minister Yitzhak Rabin and Defense Minister Shimon Peres rebuffed Kissinger's proposal in 1975, during the presidency of Gerald Ford. Israel's opposition prompted the administration to announce a "reassessment" of U.S. relations with Israel, with hints of possible sanctions against it, which deeply shook the Israeli leadership as well as the general population. Although the bilateral crisis had been resolved, signs of difficulty in the strategic relationship were clear.

Washington's Heyday in the Middle East

In the October War, the superpowers simultaneously recognized the volatility of the Middle East—both their opportunity for gains in a rapidly changing, unstable region and the high stakes that their moves entailed. In the fast-paced action of late October 1973, the United States managed to outmaneuver the Soviet Union. Washington used diplomacy to placate Soviet leaders and to deescalate the superpower crisis. But its ability both to assist *and* pressure Israel was not lost on Egypt. Before the fighting began, in July 1972, in a then unheralded event, Sadat had expelled some 17,000 Soviet advisers from his country. After the war, he edged away from the Soviet Union and into the American camp. For the United States, Egypt's shift was one of the biggest diplomatic victories of the Cold War.

Egypt's new pro-U.S. orientation ushered in the most stable few years of America's post–World War II presence in the Middle East. At no time during Washington's sixty-year effort to fashion a Mideast policy did American officials find truly smooth sailing. But if one period stands out for going the way that officials hoped, it would be the time from the Black September War in 1970 up until the Iranian Revolution in 1979.

After the Nixon administration managed to wean Egypt away from the Soviet Union and establish its own close relationship with the largest and most powerful Arab state, the White House was then able to guide the Egyptian-Israeli relationship for most of the 1970s. The culmination of American efforts came during President Jimmy Carter's hosting of the Camp David Summit in 1978. The accords reached at that extraordinary meeting paved the way for the Israeli-Egyptian peace treaty, perhaps the most important diplomatic achievement of the last half-century in the Middle East.

To be sure, Washington was not without its serious setbacks in the region during the 1970s, including the Arab oil-producers' boycott of 1973. Even during that crisis, though, the United States contrived to steer a huge portion of the petrodollars that accrued from the spike in oil prices to American banks. Equally important, partnerships existed in the 1970s with the four most powerful states in the area: Israel, Egypt, Iran, and Turkey. By the 1980s, however, one of those relationships was in tatters, and the others were under stress. The most dramatic turnabout occurred with Iran, of course. With the fall of the shah's regime in 1979, the most anti-American regime anywhere came to power. Egypt entered a downward spiral after Sadat's assassination at a ceremony commemorating what Egyptians still see as the major victory in the October 1973 War, eight years to the day after the beginning of that war. Starting in the 1980s, Egypt's strength was progressively emasculated (as will be discussed more extensively in chapter 7), and, with that, its utility to the United States as a partner diminished, although certainly not to zero. Turkey remained a key partner, but already changes were brewing there based on the 1980 military coup, which would slowly reshape Turkish-American relations.

Washington's strategic partnership with Israel remained, but as the October War demonstrated, the connection suffered from America's other global and regional goals: to deescalate tensions with the Soviet Union and to win the friendship of the most powerful Arab state, Egypt. The October War had shown the Israelis that their close relationship with the United States could work in two ways—they could benefit from American support (as the giant airlift had demonstrated), but they might have to bend under American pressure (as the order to leave the Third Army intact showed).

The critical airlift of weapons from the United States to Israel in the midst of the war, when Israeli supplies were quickly running out, saved the Israelis from disaster. No one in the Tel Aviv vicinity at the time can forget how the buildings of the city shook as a giant Lockheed C-5A Galaxy heavy-cargo transport plane loaded with munitions landed every few minutes. The airlift validated Nixon's reported words, "We will not let Israel go down the tubes" (Schoenbaum 1993). But even the airlift was not unambiguous support, as the delay in supplying the weapons indicated. The United States sought "to aid Israel without being conspicuous and without helping too much. Both Kissinger and [Secretary of Defense James] Schlesinger publicly acknowledged delay [in sending Israel the weapons] by choice as a way of effecting an early cease-fire" (Schoenbaum 1993).

FIGURE 5.1   Anwar Sadat, Jimmy Carter, and Menahem Begin at the Camp David Accords Signing Ceremony, September 17, 1978.
Source: Courtesy Jimmy Carter Presidential Library.

The U.S.-Israel strategic relationship went on to survive the rest of the Cold War and, in some ways, flourish. Israel, for example, was the partner for America's first-ever free-trade agreement. For Israel, the agreement was a godsend. At the time, it was in dire economic straits, and although the free-trade pact was not the only factor that helped pull the Israeli economy out of its tailspin in the mid-1980s, it did help at a critical moment.

Iran-Contra

Around the same time, the mid-1980s, the depth of the strategic relationship could be seen in another realm, as well. Israelis and Americans collaborated in an ironic venture to deliver missiles to the nemesis of both, revolutionary Iran, perhaps the most vocal anti-American and anti-Israeli state in the world. Moreover, the United States had slapped an arms embargo on Iran. The weapons shipments were part of the shady, nefarious Iran-Contra dealings. Key Israeli figures, along with a faction in the Reagan White House, naïvely hoped to effect some sort of softening in the attitudes of the Iranian rulers.

Reagan staffers who cooperated with the Israelis had another key motive in selling arms to Iran. They were hoping funds accrued in the Iran deal could be quietly transferred to aid the Contras, who were fighting to topple the leftist Sandinista government in power in Nicaragua. The essence of the deal involved the sale of weapons in Israel's hands to Iran. The United States would then resupply Israel, taking the cash that Israel had garnered from the transaction and diverting it to the Contras. Like the sale of arms to the embargoed Iranians, support for the Contras had to be under the table. In 1982, Congress had passed what was known as the Boland Amendment, denying American funding to the Contras. Israeli officials spurned any role in the Contra part of the equation (although Reagan aides did approach them to assist in arming the right-wing Nicaraguan rebels).

If Israel managed to sidestep the Contras controversy, Israeli figures did act as middlemen between the White House officials acting illegally and the Iranians, establishing a secret back channel to Tehran. Israeli officials and private businessmen used their old ties with Iranian politicians who had survived the revolutionary change in Iran to engineer an arms deal. That deal came in the context of perhaps the bloodiest of all

Mideast wars, the Iran-Iraq War, a World War I–style grinding affair that lasted from 1980 to 1988 and took roughly half a million lives.

For Israeli leaders, an aggressive Iraq (it was Iraq that initiated the war through an invasion of Iran), separated territorially from Israel only by the precarious Kingdom of Jordan, seemed to pose a far greater danger than Iran, which, despite its bombast, was in the throes of revolutionary chaos. And for Reagan officials, a victory by a Soviet client state, Iraq, was more ominous than one by even the hostage-taking Iranians, who held the Soviets in contempt. For both the Israeli and some (but by no means all) U.S. officials, at least at that point in time in the early phases of the conflict, Iran appeared to be the more vulnerable combatant and the lesser of the two evils fighting the bloody war.

The Israeli leaders thus found common cause with the Reagan team and maneuvered with them to prevent an all-out Iraqi victory in the early stages of the war by supplying TOW missiles to Iran. In the end, the funds never did reach the Contras. The deal devolved into trading the arms to Iran for its help in gaining the release of American and Israeli hostages taken during the Lebanese Civil War.

Even the cooperation with the Americans in supplying the Iranians with weapons, however, demonstrated to the Israelis the double-edged nature of the strategic relationship. Eventually members of the Reagan administration were exposed in 1986 for going behind the back of Congress and acting illegally in the arms-for-hostages trade and in attempting to use profits from the arms sale to aid the Contras. Reagan staffers caught in the crosshairs of the scandal, what came to be called the Iran-Contra affair, tried to pin the blame on Israel.

Although that blatant ploy in passing the buck failed, the U.S.-Israel strategic relationship continued to be fraught with tension. Reagan's unequivocal words in 1979 about Israel as a strategic asset did not prevent the strain in the relationship from continuing and sometimes growing during his presidency. This period was also one of restructuring (*perestroika*) and opening (*glasnost*) in the Soviet Union, which softened the Reagan administration's earlier hard-line Cold War positions. The new superpower accommodation—as evidenced in the Reykjavík Summit between Reagan and Secretary-General of the Communist Party Mikhail Gorbachev shortly after the Iran-Contra scandal broke, as well as the landmark 1987 nuclear treaty with the Soviets—further eroded Israel's value as a wedge for the United States against Soviet influence in the Middle East. Indeed, by the latter stages of the Iran-Iraq War, the Reagan administration considered the Soviet-Iraqi tie of such little consequence that it switched its allegiance, such as it was, to the now more vulnerable combatant, Iraq. Indeed, as I will note below, U.S. intelligence was critical in thwarting the Iranians as they drove toward what seemed like a probable victory in the last stages of the war. The strategic relationship between Israel and the United States survived the Cold War, but it was encountering strain even before the collapse of the USSR.

After the Cold War

Once the Berlin Wall came down, the international environment changed dramatically. The clear parameters and strategic goals associated with bipolarity, where two major world powers face off and largely define world politics, were gone. There was no longer a clear sense of the country's strategic interests or goals in the new post–Cold War world. New, highly mobilized constituencies were now arguing for a variety of conflicting goals and policies—a sharp departure from the Cold War years. U.S. policy makers faced a difficult environment in which to steward America's place in the world. Some critics of President Bill Clinton's foreign policy, for example, derided it "as 'social work' that is too easily swayed by ethnic lobbies, public opinion polls, and media buzz" (Walt 2000).

In fact, if one had to characterize American foreign policy during the terms of the first two post–Cold War presidents, George H. W. Bush and Clinton, it would be as a cacophonous, reactive, and ad hoc enterprise without clear guiding principles or goals. The world sped headlong into an unrecognizable future, with only one superpower left standing. Michael Howard (1988), a doyen of the study of twentieth-century international relations, described foreign policy under George H. W. Bush in these uncertain conditions (not unflatteringly, by the way): "All the United States could do, in Bush's words, was encourage, guide, and manage change. This required seat-of-the-pants planning, not a Wilsonian vision of a new world order."

While more critical in tone, the comments on Bill Clinton's foreign policy by Richard Haass (2000, 136), the head of the prestigious Council on Foreign Relations and holder of numerous foreign-policy posts, sounded the same theme: "The Clinton era was marked by a preference for symbolism over substance and short-term crisis management over long-term strategizing." In chapters 10 and 11, I will show how subsequent American foreign policy, in the twenty-first century under the second President Bush, George W. Bush, and then Barack Obama, took a dramatic turn away from the seat-of-the-pants policy making found in the elder Bush and Clinton administrations. But for the 1990s at least, Howard's phrase, "seat-of-the-pants," captures the making of foreign policy in the United States quite nicely.

In the dying embers of the Cold War, the new global environment tested the policy makers of the first Bush presidency almost immediately in—where else?—the Middle East. Iraq's invasion of Kuwait on August 2, 1990, when the Soviet Union was already on its deathbed, raised pressing questions of how the United States would respond now that the bipolar structure of global politics no longer held. The answers that the Americans gave to those questions surprised the Iraqis, stunned the Israelis, delighted the Syrians, and changed the U.S.-Israeli relationship dramatically.

6 The Strategic Relationship Unravels

The End of the Cold War and the Gulf War of 1990–1991

For almost all the parties involved, the Gulf War in 1990 proved to be a revelation: it turned many of their assumptions and expectations about the world and America's role in it upside down. For government leaders of Syria, a long-time Soviet client state, for example, the demise of the Soviet Union must have initially appeared to be an unmitigated disaster. Gone was the superpower that had given the Syrian state aid, trained and supplied its military, defended it in world forums, and stood behind it in regional conflicts. And for Israeli officials, the first reaction must have been pure joy: Israel's backer and strategic partner, the United States, had triumphed. Israeli leaders could only feel that they had bet on the right horse in the Cold War, and the Syrians, just the opposite. Yet in the months after Iraq's invasion of Kuwait, the United States was sweet-talking Syria, wooing it into the coalition being knitted together to oppose Iraqi President Saddam Hussein. And at the same time, U.S. policy makers were giving the cold shoulder to Israel, all but publicly renouncing the strategic relationship that had tied the two together since Black September.

In the following section, I look at the period before the actual invasion. For President Saddam Hussein and his foreign-policy entourage in Iraq, the old rules of the game for action in the Middle East seemed to have evaporated in the first half of 1990. The old constraints of the Cold War no longer held. The invasion of Kuwait can be understood in the context of the Iraqis' take on how the global structure now presented a very different set of possibilities to them. The following section then focuses on the postinvasion period, the long autumn of 1990, when all the Iraqi assumptions about American intentions proved wrong. To counter the Iraqis, the United States gathered a new set of strategic partners. Markedly missing from America's strategic entourage was the partner that had emerged as so critical in the Black September War, Israel. The following section then looks at how the strategic relationship between the United States and Israel was turned on its head, from one of mutual dependence to one in which Israel became an American strategic liability.

The Lead-up to Invasion

Unfortunately, we were not privy to the thinking of Saddam Hussein in the summer of 1990, the period leading up to Iraq's startling attack on neighboring Kuwait. But his actions and words lent themselves to an interpretation of his strategic considerations; he too perceived the global environment changing so dramatically in 1989 and 1990. Strong hints about the direction of his thinking emerged, in particular, from a remarkable and widely reported meeting that he had with the American ambassador to Iraq in the week before his forces invaded Kuwait. Their conversation was captured by British journalists and reproduced by media around the world.

After the debacle of the Reagan administration's early efforts to aid Iran in the Iran-Iraq War, Iraq's relationship with the United States began to improve, if incrementally. Stepping back from the abyss of the 1960s and 1970s, when Iraq, as the leading revolutionary Arab nationalist regime after Egypt, had landed firmly in the Soviet camp, during the mid-1980s the United States and Iraq reconciled some, but certainly not all, of their differences. The principal motivator for the improvement in relations ironically was that same Iran-Iraq War in which the United States, in the Iran-Contra Affair, participated in the provision of missiles to beleaguered Iran. But after that, the pendulum began to swing markedly.

In the three decades since the Islamic Revolution and the taking of U.S. hostages in Tehran, in 1979, probably no country has irked the United States more consistently than Iran. Support by the United States for revolutionary Iran in its war with Iraq, then, was out of character, especially in the wake of the bitter memory of American hostages having been held in the U.S. embassy in Tehran. The American tilt toward Iran came out of a variety of motives: continuing disgust with the nationalist leadership of Saddam Hussein in Iraq, the desire to use Iranian good offices to free American hostages taken in the Lebanese Civil War, the blind hope that the Iranian regime would change its stripes, and the desire to secure extralegal funds for the Nicaraguan Contras. Important Reagan aides had not only facilitated the supply of antitank missiles; they had also provided Iran with critical intelligence on Iraqi military deployments and plans. Part of their motivation came from the misguided view that the Soviets stood to gain through an Iranian defeat; they crammed even the Iran-Iraq War into their dominant model for seeing the world, the Cold War.

However, by the time that the Iran-Contra scandal broke in 1986, Washington had already shifted its limited backing to Iraq. After the brief flirtation with Iran during the early stages of the war and with the upper hand in the fighting shifting from Iraq to Iran, the Reagan White House set its sights on containing Iran. Indeed, key groups inside the CIA and White House had felt all along that Iran was the main enemy and had bristled at the transfer of intelligence to the Islamic Republic and at the cooperation with the Israelis in supplying missiles to the Iranians. Saddam Hussein's earlier expulsion of the Palestinian Abu Nidal Organization, a splinter group from Arafat's Fatah and the perpetrator of grizzly acts of international violence, had greased the wheels for a new tilt in U.S. policy. Saddam's turning on his erstwhile ally, Abu Nidal, paved the way for the United States to remove Iraq from the State Department list of state sponsors of terrorism and develop better relations.

Reagan officials moved to redirect U.S. support toward the now beleaguered Iraqis. In the words of George H. W. Bush's secretary of state, James A. Baker III, "The policy toward Iraq that President Bush had inherited from the Reagan administration was grounded in a determination to thwart the expansionist aspirations of the revolutionary government of Iran" (Baker 1995, 261). The United States reestablished diplomatic ties with Iraq (which had been severed since the June 1967 War), provided agricultural grain credits, shared vital military intelligence with the Iraqi army, and, using American warships, protected Baghdad's oil exports aboard reflagged neutral ships. American support for Iraq was tested by the Iraqi bombing of an American warship, the *Stark*, which killed thirty-seven American sailors, but the aid continued; the White House wrote off the attack as inadvertent.

In true Machiavellian fashion, Iraq benefited in its ties to the United States by simply being the enemy of America's enemy. American satellite photographs pinpointed critical Iranian installations, which the Iraqis used to direct their bombers, breaking the momentum the Iranians had gained in the latter stages of the war. When an Iranian mine downed an American ship, the United States hit the Iranians hard, sinking a number of warships. With losses mounting, Iran was forced to agree to an end to the war.

While relations between the United States and Iraq were by no means warm—and, in fact, mutual grievances were regularly sounded, as were warnings by Washington about Iraq using chemical or biological warfare against groups in Iraq—the extreme hostility between the two states had eased considerably by early 1990. Some harsh speeches starting in February 1990 by Saddam about the specter of American imperialism in the absence of Soviet opposition did cause concern in Washington, but relations were not nearly as bad as they had been a decade earlier. By April 1990, however, a clear downward spiral in U.S.-Iraq relations was underway. The United States suspended its agricultural credits to Iraq, and Saddam Hussein's anti-American rhetoric heated up.

The eight-plus-year brutal war with Iran had crippled Iraq in a number of ways, not least of all economically. It had run up debts of around $70 billion during the fighting. Even though it had huge oil reserves, the price of oil was at that time relatively low, limiting the foreign currency coming into its treasury. The possibility of incorporating oil-rich Kuwait into Iraq was a tempting and relatively easy solution for some of those accumulated problems.

There was no shortage of Iraqi grievances concerning Kuwait. Iraqi nationalist leaders had long complained about its oil-rich neighbor. For one, they saw the British separation of Kuwait from Iraq in 1913 as an illegitimate, colonial act—one that left Iraq nearly landlocked, with the prime Gulf coast going to Kuwait. The partition also robbed Iraq of a huge share of its oil reserves. Reclaiming Kuwait as Iraq's nineteenth province, in Saddam's words, would restore the essence of the preimperial order. Beyond that, Arab nationalist thought rejected altogether the legitimacy of separate petroleum-rich, lightly populated states such as Kuwait. Arab nationalists saw the oil as a general, national Arab resource. That sort of thinking made not only Kuwaiti state leaders nervous but increased anxiety about Iraq's intentions in other Gulf states and in Saudi Arabia. And when Iraq was not questioning Kuwait's legitimacy as a state, it carped about their shared border.

The immediate catalyst for Iraqi anger toward Kuwait in 1990, whether real or contrived, was the claim that Kuwait was slant drilling in the long-disputed, shared Rumaila oilfield, stealing nearly $2.5 billion worth of oil from Iraqi reserves. Tensions rose throughout the spring and summer: Saddam Hussein made dire threats against Kuwait, and Kuwaiti leaders delivered some ill-advised anti-Iraqi invective of their own. Iraqi leaders also issued veiled statements that Kuwait was part of an anti-Iraqi cabal that included unnamed foreign powers. The United States, clearly the prime unnamed power, suffered now from being the friend of Iraq's enemy (Kuwait), an ironic twist on its earlier closeness to Iraq, which was the enemy of America's enemy Iran. The Middle East is a dizzying place.

In the spring, Saddam turned the rhetoric against Israel up a notch, as well (Telhami 1994), presenting Iraq as the Arab world's nationalist bastion. It made similar claims regarding its central position as the pre-eminent Arab nationalist power in another context, too. Iraq was deeply in debt to both Saudi Arabia and Kuwait, as a result of loans it had taken during the Iran-Iraq War. It now wanted those debts canceled as well as additional billions in aid from those countries for the reconstruction of Iraq (Salinger 1995, 596). It reasoned that it had defended Arab national interests, particularly those of the weak Saudis and the Gulf states, in the fight against a revolutionary Islamic power, Iran, and that it should have been compensated for its action.

Saddam Hussein had well understood the dynamic of the Cold War, in which every regional act was interpreted in the context of the zero-sum calculation of the two superpowers. The bipolar understanding of the world by the superpowers had hamstrung his regional aspirations. Almost every possible move would be met with firm U.S. opposition, directly or through its regional clients, as the United States would interpret any Iraqi achievement as a Soviet gain, as well. The sole exception was when what had been a U.S.-supported Iran transformed, in 1979, into a state that suddenly was both vulnerable and anathema to the Americans. An Iraqi move against Iran could not be interpreted as either anti-American or leading to Soviet gains. Saddam Hussein did use that opening to attack Iran in 1980, touching off the Iran-Iraq War, which lasted close to nine years, but without much success. In fact, Iraq emerged from that war badly bruised, with upward of two hundred thousand Iraqis killed (the Iranians probably lost one-and-a-half to two times that number). Whatever the exact number of casualties, Iraq paid a high toll for Saddam's adventure. Additionally, during the war, Israel had destroyed Iraq's nascent nuclear facility in a daring bombing raid.

Other than the attack on Iran—a state anathema to both superpowers—the Iraqi regime had been hamstrung in attempting any other foreign adventures by the constraints posed by bipolarity and by the risk that a military action would be interpreted by the United States as a Soviet gain. Now, with the Cold War over, Saddam Hussein had to wonder if the barriers that the United States had thrown in front of his earlier ambitions would still be there. Indeed, could America's official neutrality in the Iran-Iraq War and its actual tilt toward Iraq in the latter years of the war not be a harbinger of America's new role in the post–Cold War Middle East? As to the point at hand, would the Bush administration see the United States as having a dog in a possible Iraq-Kuwaiti fight?

That question may have been answered for Saddam in the conversation alluded to earlier. At the high point of the Iraqi-Kuwaiti tensions, the U.S. ambassador to Iraq, April Glaspie, met with the Iraqi president just eight days before the Iraqi invasion of Kuwait. The transcript of the conversation has Saddam simultaneously lecturing the United States, reassuring it on the question of oil, and seeking to glean from Glaspie just how the United States would react to a possible Iraqi action against Kuwait.

After listening to Saddam's hectoring remarks for some time, Glaspie began, "I have a direct instruction from President Bush to improve our relations with Iraq." Her remarks were not a fluke; they echoed a statement that U.S. Assistant Secretary of State John Kelly had made to Saddam back in February. From there Glaspie turned to the movement of Iraqi troops to the Kuwaiti border, probing for the reasons for the massive deployment. Saddam Hussein's response was typically elliptical, alluding to a coming Iraqi attack if a last round of negotiations with the Kuwaitis failed.

At the end of the conversation he asked outright, "What is the United States' opinion on this?" The ambassador answered, "We have no opinion on the Arab-Arab conflicts, like your border disagreement with Kuwait." Glaspie was echoing a cable that had gone out to all embassies only a week before. She went on to say that Secretary of State James A. Baker III directed her to emphasize the instruction that the Kuwait issue is not associated with America. Glaspie's remarks probably reinforced Saddam Hussein's thinking that the end of the Cold War had opened a new door strategically. His larger foreign-policy ambitions must have seemed within reach.

The U.S. Assembles a Coalition

The Middle East pundit Shibley Telhami (1994) has argued that it was unlikely that the go-ahead for such a complex operation as the invasion of Kuwait hinged on a single conversation only a week before the action. Still, the tête-à-tête with the American ambassador must have mattered to Saddam Hussein as he moved toward a final decision. Once the invasion occurred, he would quickly discover precisely the opposite of what Glaspie had assured him: the Kuwait issue was indeed associated with America. The strong Bush response was the first among several key surprises for—and indications of miscalculations by—Saddam.

The next rude awakening for the Iraqi president was how this conflict, tucked away in the corner of the Middle East, mushroomed into an international crisis of major proportions, mobilizing global forces against him. The invasion and the war that ensued became "the first major postwar crisis not to have an overriding East-West dimension" (Halliday 1991, 223). It was not a negligible brush war, by any means. In fact, the conflict involved the biggest mobilization of forces since the Korean War. For the Middle East there was "no comparable crisis involving both regional and extra-regional forces since the First World War" (Halliday 1991).

A final shock for Saddam was the reaction of the Arab world to the lightning-quick invasion and conquest of Kuwait. Waving the banner of Arab nationalism, Saddam expected nationalist sentiments to generate a tsunami of support for his action in much of the Arab world. Some of that support was evident on the Arab street, especially among Palestinians. But for the most part, no mass backing materialized from the broad Arab public. Nor, critically, did support come from other Arab regimes, aside from some desultory encouragement on the part of Jordan, Libya, Yemen, and the PLO, hardly the major players in the Middle East.

The First Surprise: The U.S. Reaction

Just as rapid as the invasion itself was the chorus of criticism of Iraq's actions, which were led by the strong, negative response by the

Bush administration. Almost immediately, the Bush team moved on the diplomatic front, focusing on the United Nations, and then quickly began rattling sabers. There has been much speculation about the reasons behind the vociferous U.S. reaction. After all, Saddam's calculation—that the United States did not have the motive to intervene in this regional fight once the Cold War context was gone—was not without merit. Iraq had gone to some lengths in assuring the United States that it did not intend to withhold oil or work to raise oil prices.

Yet oil did quickly become a U.S. concern once the invasion started. Desert Shield, the U.S. operation to reverse the Iraqi occupation of Kuwait, was initiated with the first deployment of U.S. armed forces to Saudi Arabia on August 7, only days after the invasion. Protecting the regime that sat on the world's largest oil reserves and that supported the United States in issues of oil pricing was prominent in the thinking of Bush and his foreign-policy team. At one point early on, the United States claimed that the way Iraqi forces were deployed in Kuwait suggested that they had designs on Saudi Arabia. The reports of the threatening configuration of Iraqi troops caused great anxiety in Washington that Iraq would not stop with Kuwait, especially if the United States did not draw clear redlines. But in the days after the invasion, the Iraqi forces in fact did not deploy in a way that threatened Saudi Arabia.

Still, U.S. policy makers certainly had an eye on the oil issue and were well versed on the dispute within OPEC between Iraq and Saudi Arabia on whether to aim for high (the Iraqi preference) or low (the Saudi—and American—position) world oil prices. After the war, one unnamed U.S. official was famously quoted as saying, "We need the oil. It's nice to talk about standing up for freedom, but Kuwait and Saudi Arabia are not exactly democracies, and if their principal export were oranges, a mid-level State Department official would have issued a statement, and we would have closed Washington down for August" (Aarts and Renner 1991, 25).

Besides oil, U.S. officials paraded a number of other rationales for their actions before the American public and potential international partners. They spoke of the seriousness of Iraq's open breach of the UN Charter in its attack on Kuwait. Additionally, they cited Iraq's miserable record on human rights and the threat the regime posed to the Kuwaiti population. The most famous brouhaha over human rights came when it was reported—and then backed by President Bush—that Iraqi forces had taken babies from incubators in a hospital in Kuwait, allowing the infants to perish on the hospital floor. The charge turned out to be a fraud, but it gained wide publicity and even seemed to affect the debate in Congress (MacArthur 2004, 44).

Finally, U.S. officials emphasized the danger that Iraq posed in its possible use of chemical, biological, and nuclear weapons. This refrain would carry forward all the way to the second war against Iraq by the United States, in 2003, when the issue became a major political football. In 1990, weapons of mass destruction (WMD) by so-called rogue states or nonstate groups were first emerging as a significant preoccupation among policy makers, especially as the concerns about future unsecured Soviet nuclear weapons grew in the face of the decay of the erstwhile Soviet empire.

Fears over WMD in Iraq were not without foundation or precedent. The regime had employed chemical weapons against the enemy during the Iran-Iraq War—as well as against its own citizens, the rebellious Kurds in the north of the country. Iraq's nuclear reactor, Osirak, had already been a cause of consternation for other powers in the Middle East. The Iranians succeeded in damaging it in 1980, early in their war against Iraq. A year later, Israel struck the facility, largely disabling it. While it is not certain that the site was actually to be used for the manufacture of nuclear bombs, the Israeli attack did seem to prod the Iraqis into a more serious nuclear-weapons program. In the lead-up to the Gulf War, Iraq appeared to reactivate Osirak, but the site was finally destroyed in one of the many U.S. airstrikes in January 1991.

But in the end, none of rationales that U.S. spokespeople trotted out in August and September explains how vociferously the American government reacted to the invasion of Kuwait. For all the posturing about oil, there were few indications that U.S. leaders believed that oil supplies were threatened in the short or long run. And Bush's strong language against Iraq seemed to predate any explicit concerns with oil. Nor were the UN Charter, human rights, or WMD the actual motivations for the tough stance that U.S. leaders assumed. For all the sincerity with which Bush officials presented these rationales, the administration seemed not to have acted on the basis of any of these reasons. The rationales came fast and furiously in the days after August 2, but they appeared as ad hoc justifications for a decision that had preceded them. In this initial crisis of the postbipolar world, the reaction produced the rationales, not the opposite.

The very absence of a clear set of strategic goals, like those that had existed during the Cold War, was critical in the scale of U.S. actions once the invasion occurred. As Telhami (1994, 163) put it, the decision to use military force "preceded a clear vision of the specific objectives of the deployment, which evolved as the crisis went on. The question that remained was of size and shape." With the Cold War winding down, uncertainty reigned in Washington on questions of what exactly U.S. interests were and which real risks the country faced in the future. With Saddam's bold action, talk of peace dividends and a new era in which the atomic clock would no longer be permanently fixed at five minutes to midnight was rendered suddenly moot, at least for the moment. Now there was little on hand in Washington to fall back on in terms of doctrine once the attack occurred. In other words, it was not at all clear to American officials what exactly the Iraqi attack meant for the United States. With the end of the Cold War, it was not evident what the United States hoped to achieve or what its interests in the events in the Middle East really were.

Without a clear doctrine, no rationale jumped off the page as *the* reason to react so strongly to the invasion, although the very uncertainty of the global structure itself suggested that *some* reaction was needed. So, instead of deducing a clear imperative for action, seat-of-the-pants policy making dominated. Not necessarily cynically, the U.S. policy makers sought to find the rationale for their instinctual response to the uncertainty that surrounded them as the crisis unfolded. In the unpredictable—even frightening—environment of the end of Soviet influence in the Middle East, in a world in which the old rules for strategic action were no longer operative, the Iraqi invasion struck an ominous chord among policy makers. The Gulf War was the first of a series of post–Cold War U.S. military interventions and wars in the 1990s—Somalia in 1992, Haiti in 1994, Bosnia in 1994–1996, and more—that reversed the traditional relationship between strategic rationale and action. The 1990s were a decade without clear strategic imperatives, leading to military action that created its own self-fulfilling rationales.

The Second Surprise: A Regional Dogfight Becomes a Major Global Crisis

Saddam Hussein hoped that his indications to the United States on keeping oil flowing—at reasonable prices—would mollify Americans and others. Before the Kuwaiti crisis, he had spoken in global terms of the threat of imperialism. In a world where only one superpower was left standing, he felt that the Middle East, including Arab national autonomy, was in jeopardy. But immediately before the invasion he tried hard to disengage the regional ruckus with Kuwait from global politics. While the Iran-Iraq War of the 1980s had ended badly for him, the Iraqi president could draw a valuable lesson from it: when a local war—even one involving two major oil producers—did not threaten the world structure of power, global powers could look the other way or, at least, minimize their involvement. Focusing on issues such as borders, debt repayment, and slant drilling, Saddam hoped that the local conflict with Kuwait would remain local.

Again, he badly miscalculated. Starting with sharply worded UN resolutions and moving to the rapid deployment of U.S. military forces in Saudi Arabia, the United States began an international campaign, days after the invasion, to reverse the Iraqi action completely. Once the dust settled, the central plank in that campaign was to assemble an international coalition based on the multiple UN resolutions adopted after the invasion. American attention quickly turned to assembling a coalition of states to confront Iraq and to finding financing for the coming war. Secretary of State James Baker became the administration's interlocutor with leaders of possible coalition partners.

The idea of a coalition was rooted in the principle of American foreign-policy making that had dominated since Eisenhower's New Look doctrine: find partners to share the burden of America's global role. And that principle received added backing from the U.S. economic situation at the end of the Cold War. In 1990, the U.S. federal deficit seemed to be spiraling out of control, as was the country's trade deficit. Japan was supplanting the United States as the world's most dynamic economy. Gains in American labor productivity were painfully small. In piecing together the coalition, Baker aimed to provide troops to complement American forces, but, what was probably even more important, he focused on countries that could contribute badly needed cash for the looming war.

Establishing a coalition was no easy task, and not just because of the usual logistical problems in inducing so many parties to cooperate in a difficult and costly enterprise. On a more fundamental level, the end of bipolarity presented major challenges in establishing an action-oriented alliance. As one article put it a few years after the crisis, "Because the political fault lines of the cold war have disappeared, there are few accepted political criteria for sharing those security burdens that are perceived collectively" (Bennett, Lepgold, and Unger 1994, 39).

It was an open question in 1990 whether military alliances such as NATO, constructed precisely with the Cold War in mind, made sense in the new global environment. And, if not, American officials would have to create something *de novo* instead. For a large number of heterogeneous states, with their own individual interests and concerns, not to speak of their domestic political constraints, to join such a newly constructed alliance was not an easy decision. For officials from around the world, the more ominous the crisis, the easier it would be to make the decision to participate in the crisis. In other words, coalition making itself demanded a global crisis of major proportions.

The incentive was thus very high for the U.S. officials to make sure that others—potential allies—would see the Iraqi invasion in that light, as a threat to the global order and to the individual countries that benefited from the stability of that order. American interests thus directly contravened the Iraqi leaders' strategy of keeping the conflict local. The Americans employed a number of means to globalize the crisis. First, they used the United Nations as the organizing mechanism for the coalition. Resolution 660 quickly censured the Iraqis and called for a withdrawal from Kuwait. A further UN vote, Resolution 678, at the end of November, authorized the reversal of the Iraqi conquest through "all necessary means." These resolutions and others had the effect of transforming a regional crisis into a global one, bringing the world body to apply sanctions against Iraq and frame the invasion as one threatening the United Nations and the entire international community. Eventually, the war was waged under UN auspices, even though in almost every way imaginable the United States was clearly in charge.

Washington signaled the seriousness of the issue by implementing Operation Desert Shield. It not only deployed U.S. aircraft in Saudi Arabia but also quickly placed army and marine ground troops in the country. And American leaders kept the pressure up. On October 31, Bush doubled the number of U.S. troops in the region, making clear the enormity of the problem at hand. In the end, the number of U.S. forces in the Middle East was greater than for any conflict in half a century. Eventually, Operation Desert Shield became Desert Storm, the war against Iraq by the U.S.-led coalition; it employed nearly three-quarters of a million men and women from thirty-four countries.

The making of the coalition developed a momentum of its own. Secretary of State James Baker traveled around the globe seeking recruits for the coalition. As he added key players, the pressure on others to join grew. Baker's message was that Iraq's assault was an attack on the entire global community. The coalition included familiar allies, such as France, Greece, and the United Kingdom. But it also brought in unlikely participants, such as Bangladesh, Niger, and Singapore. Baker succeeded in gaining commitments from Germany and Japan for resources totaling over $16 billion, in addition to money he raised from Saudi Arabia and Gulf states. "At a time of economic uncertainty at home," Baker (1995, 288) later wrote, "it would be politically impossible to sustain domestic support for the operation unless we demonstrated that Uncle Sam wasn't footing the bill while others with pockets as deep as ours sat on the sidelines." These financial commitments came in what came to be called the Tin Cup Trip that he made around the world. As the United States added country after country to the coalition, perhaps most shocking of all, at least to long-time observers of Middle East affairs, was the success in recruiting the majority of Arab states: Bahrain, Egypt, the exiled Kuwaiti regime (of course), Morocco, Oman, Qatar, Saudi Arabia, and Syria.

The Third Surprise: Iraq Stands Alone

U.S. success in gaining Arab participation in the coalition was, indeed, surprising. The immediate reaction among the Arab states had struck the same key that had been heard repeatedly over the previous forty years: the conflict should be handled as an Arab family spat. Only a day after Iraq attacked, the Arab League passed a resolution sounding two themes—the need for the Arab states to handle the problem themselves and a sharp warning to outside powers to stay clear of the conflict. But their resolve on both points quickly dissolved.

From the outset, the United States worked to avoid framing the crisis as America against the Arab world (another key reason to make the crisis global, rather than allowing it to remain local or regional). The United States had made important gains in the Middle East since the darkest days of the Cold War, before 1970, and it was loathe to let its improved situation slip away in what might be perceived as a war against the Arabs. The United States thus put tremendous resources into recruiting Arab and other Muslim states into the coalition. Saudi Lieutenant General Prince Khalid bin Sultan bin Abdul Aziz al-Saud was appointed as a commander of the coalition forces. While the real power lay in the hands of the commander-in-chief of the Central Command, U.S. General Norman H. Schwarzkopf, the symbolism of an Arab as commander was significant. On a practical level, some of the Arab armies that became part of the fighting force agreed to report only to Arab commanders, justifying to themselves and their civilian populations their attacking a fellow Arab state. Diplomatically, the Arab League called for Iraq's withdrawal from Kuwait (with only Iraq, Libya, and the PLO dissenting), but no opposition was offered to a U.S.-led solution if the Arab League effort did not work, which it didn't.

The Bush administration sought to play on precisely the issue that Saddam Hussein had raised in his speeches on U.S. imperialism earlier in 1990. That is, American officials understood that, as the sole remaining superpower, the United States sparked fear, engendering a desire by most states not to cross it. As Hilal Khashan (2001, 159), a professor at the American University in Beirut put it later, "Nearly all Arab countries now cherish good relations with the United States."

More than that, the United States was counting on the fact that the most important Arab states—Egypt, Saudi Arabia, and even Syria—had individual interests that would lead them to oppose the Iraqi invasion. The United States saw the new era as one in which ideology—in this case, Arab nationalist ideology—would occupy a back seat; realpolitik would become the guiding principles of states. Here is how the noted Harvard Middle East scholar Nadav Safran (1990) reflected this sort of thinking in an article he wrote the month after the Iraqi invasion:

> It is not hard to see why the directly affected Arab governments lined up with the United States. They share a common perception of the implications of Iraq's invasion of Kuwait that is uncannily close to the basic American view. They all believe that if Hussein could get away with annexing Kuwait by force, he would not only command the formidable combined oil resources of his own country and Kuwait; he would also be able to cow the Saudis and the emirates into doing his bidding, and would thus control in effect more than half the world's oil reserves and oil trade. That would give him enormous financial means, great diplomatic leverage, and vast access to instruments of military power. He would then be in a position to seek to unify or dominate the Arab countries.

Saddam Hussein pinned his hopes for support in the Arab world on nationalist sentiments among Arabs in the street that could override officials' adopting an every-man-for-himself mentality. His bet was that Arab nationalism and its underlying attachment to the concept of Arab unity would trump the reservations of individual regimes about the invasion. But that was a serious miscalculation. His hoped-for street demonstrations barely materialized. With the exception of Palestinians in the occupied territories and in Jordan, popular support for Iraq and Saddam was muted. And, as noted, the Arab regimes lined up with the United States.

As I will discuss in both chapters 8 and 10, Arab nationalism simply no longer held the power that it had a generation earlier. Indeed, the Gulf War was to be a watershed for Arab states, moving them away from the collective-style foreign policy that Arab nationalist ideology demanded. While the Arab League and the idea of collective foreign policy did not disappear altogether, more conventional decision making increasingly prevailed, based on each state's individual interests, or at least the way the leaders defined those interests. International politics in the Middle East after the Gulf War looked to be grounded more in the standard theories of international-relations specialists than it had earlier.

In any case, after the 1967 War and, then, Egypt's peace treaty with Israel in 1979, Saddam had envisioned the passing of the torch from Egypt to Iraq as the new dominant carrier of Arab nationalism. Nationalist feelings, he may have reasoned, would have been especially aroused in 1990. Palestinian suffering, the central symbolic issue in Arab nationalism, was prominent at the moment in the daily press because of the harsh Israeli response to the ongoing Palestinian intifada, or uprising, and the absence of movement toward solving the Palestinian problem. As a result, anti-Israel feelings in Arab countries ran especially high. As a consequence, anti-American sentiment also spiked, because of U.S. support of what was seen as Israeli intransigence. Coupling his attack against Iraq with ominous threats against Israel, Saddam Hussein anticipated a wave of Arab support for Iraq as the standard bearer of Arab nationalism and Palestinian liberation. He badly misjudged, however, how severely the 1967 War had wounded pan-Arabism and how weak a force it was now, in 1990.

My own conversations with elites in a number of Arab countries in the early 1990s indicated that while the Palestinian issue remained important among individuals at the time, other social and political problems were crowding it out. Many expressed anxiety that the end of the

Cold War would marginalize Arab states in world affairs. Additionally, they viewed with grave concern the moves toward "Europe 1992," with its promise of greater economic integration. There was particular concern over the impending Maastricht Treaty, which eventually created the European Union in 1993. The fear of Arab elites was that economic integration in Europe would leave the Arab states excluded from the new European club and its robust economy. They worried that the structure of the new world economy, with the increasing domination of regional blocs such as the European Union and NAFTA (which was also being negotiated at the time and came into force at the beginning of 1994), was going to leave them on the outside looking in. In brief, the rapidly changing global environment pushed elites in Arab states away from marching to the drummer of Arab nationalism and toward the type of thinking that privileged individual state interests.

Some Arab states, such as Egypt, navigated this challenging new global environment on their own, distancing themselves from the dictates of Arab nationalism. A number sought to negotiate their own deals with the European community. Still others created international organizations of their own, outside the existing pan-Arab structures. Saudi Arabia, Kuwait, Bahrain, Qatar, Oman, and the United Arab Emirates created the Gulf Cooperation Council in the early 1980s and strengthened it as the decade wore on. In 1991, the North African states created a similar economic community, the Arab Maghreb Union. None of the Arab states found Iraq's call for loyalty to the old Arab nationalism compelling. For Saddam Hussein and his government, this move toward smaller economic customs unions as well as the inward-looking orientation among other Arab states meant that Iraq stood alone in the wake of its attack on Kuwait.

Israel and the Gulf War

Secretary of State Baker's pursuit of a broad coalition against Iraq knew almost no bounds. He recruited states from North America, South America, Western Europe, Eastern Europe, Africa, South Asia, Southeast Asia, as well as Australia and New Zealand. His most impressive achievements, though, were in the Middle East, where he gained the support of Turkey and most of the Arab states. He managed to have states such as Turkey and Syria, which held longstanding grievances against each other, stand shoulder to shoulder in opposition to Iraq. His approach involved personal diplomacy, cajoling, and veiled threats of possible reductions in aid if an invited state did not join. Thomas R. Pickering, the U.S. ambassador to the United Nations during the war, was reported to have quoted Baker after the UN vote authorizing the coalition's war against Iraq. After the Yeminis had voted against the resolution, Baker told their ambassador that "it was the most expensive vote they'd ever cast" (Lynch 2006, A19). And in fact, American aid to Yemen did dry up after that.

The sole exception to the inclusiveness the United States sought in its broad anti-Iraqi coalition was Israel. Once America's favored strategic partner in the Middle East, Israel now found itself on the outside. To ascertain how unsettling this was to Israeli leaders, it is worth quoting at length Israel's then top journalist on military affairs, Ze'ev Schiff (1991, 21–22), who wrote immediately after the war:

> Until the outbreak of war, Washington did everything possible to keep Jerusalem at arm's length so that no one could possibly entertain the slightest suspicion that Israel had any connection with the anti-Iraq coalition. President Bush and Secretary of State James A. Baker even avoided speaking to Israeli Prime Minister Yitzak Shamir on the phone. Israeli Defense Minister Moshe Arens almost forced himself on Defense Secretary Dick Cheney by going to the Pentagon uninvited, under the auspices of a Washington research institute.
>
> Jerusalem was less concerned by the meeting between President Bush and Syrian President Hafez al-Assad than by America's refusal to discuss, even secretly, the various military options available to Israel in the event that it were attacked by Iraq and had to respond immediately. The cooperation between the two countries' intelligence agencies was minimal at this stage, and there were no consultations on operational matters—to the point where doubts arose in Israel about the significance and seriousness of the strategic cooperation between the two countries.

This shunning of Israel by U.S. officials was a threefold shock for Israeli officials. First, while Israel's relationship with the United States had been marked by moments of tension and dissent over the previous two decades, it was one that rested on the bedrock of mutual need. For Israel, the support of the United States in terms of military and economic aid, weapon deliveries, and support in international bodies was critical. For the United States, Israel's military presence and strength, deterrent capabilities, and human intelligence all had helped secure America's place in the Middle East for the last two decades of the Cold War. Israeli leaders had basked in the strategic relationship with the United States in the 1970s and 1980s, even as occasional tensions had surfaced; the sudden distancing of Washington from Israel after the Iraqi invasion therefore hit Israelis hard.

A second factor augmenting Israel's surprise stemmed from its leaders' reading of the global events in the five years prior to the Iraqi invasion. Israeli officials and commentators had believed that all the changes in the Soviet bloc in the last half the 1980s could only bode well for Israel. The thinking was that the disintegration of the communist bloc would open a vastly expanded flow of highly skilled immigrants to Israel, which in fact did occur. Around one million immigrants came to Israel from the former Soviet Union in the 1990s, with over 10 percent of them having advanced technical skills. Israelis also believed that the Soviet disintegration would work against Israel's enemies, such as Syria, Iraq, and the PLO. The collapse of communism, then, could only enhance the position of Israel as the most reliable ally of the winner of the Cold War. Israeli leaders watched, for example, as the United States, in 1988–1989, put great pressure on a now highly vulnerable PLO to recognize Israel and for Arafat to "totally and absolutely renounce all forms of terrorism." All expectations in Israel were that the end of the Cold War would only enhance Israel's position as the key strategic ally for the United States in the region.

Finally, in the immediate aftermath of the Iraqi invasion in 1990, Israeli leaders imagined that they would be highly valuable to the United States as Washington moved to put military pressure on Iraq, possibly including a war. After all, as Israeli leaders tried to convey to the United States, they possessed anything and everything that U.S. forces might want in the region. They had the most sophisticated ports, the best hospitals and medical personnel, the most advanced logistics, and the most reliable intelligence. And most important, Israel had the best fighting forces in the region. What more could the United States want?

The shock was palpable, therefore, when the American leaders avoided their Israeli counterparts and spurned their offers of assistance in the war against Iraq. The moment of revelation came on September 29, 1990, less than two months after the Iraqi invasion, when a senior White House aide was quoted as saying, "Our message number one, two, and three to Israel is to keep out of this at all costs" (Hiro 1992, 209). Israel's Prime Minister Yitzhak Shamir countered with a cry in the dark, but to no avail: "They fail to understand that Israel is Washington's only reliable ally. The Arabs need the U.S. more than Bush needs the Arabs" (Hiro 1992).

Even after the initial rejection, Israeli leaders worked to prove Israel's strategic value to the United States. In early January, Shamir met with Jordan's King Hussein, who felt caught in a vise between Iraq and Israel, especially as Saddam Hussein's language promising the liberation of Palestine heated up. Hussein implored Shamir to see Jordan as a buffer state between Israel and Iraq and to give assurances it would not use Jordanian territory, including its airspace, for military purposes. The king's aim was to go to Iraq with Israel's promise, hoping to gain a similar commitment from Iraq. "From this encounter," writes Moshe Zak (1996, 39), "Shamir surmised that Jordanian involvement in the war threatened to bring the Hashemite Kingdom to its end, so that yet again, Israel's strategic perspective required it to defend Jordan's existence and its position as a buffer state between Israel and Iraq." But even Shamir's willingness to rescue the king once more did not move Bush officials to reconsider its shunning of Israel.

Saddam Hussein well understood the U.S. position on Israel. No matter what Prime Minister Shamir believed, if Israel participated in the coalition or in a possible war against Iraq, the U.S.-led alliance would quickly unravel. Arab states were quite clear that Israel's participation in the coalition would be a game breaker, leading to their exit from the alliance. Regimes in other Muslim countries might have easily followed suit. That message was why the U.S. aide quoted above emphasized the need to exclude Israel, and, at the same time, it was the reason that Saddam went to great lengths to do just the opposite: somehow draw Israel into the crisis. Provoking Israel could provide him with a much-needed wedge to undo the coalition. And that was the route he selected: he began his provocations in the period between the invasion and the beginning of the American bombing of Iraq on January 16, 1991, threatening to set fire to the oilfields in the region and to attack Israel.

Repeatedly, he claimed that Kuwait was step one of his design—and the liberation of Palestine, step two. Giving such prominence to the Palestinian issue was quite deliberate on Saddam's part. His hope was not only to goad Israel into direct involvement in the war. He also believed that by playing the Palestinian card he could arouse the Arab street in his favor. Popular pressure, he calculated, could induce the Arab regimes to abandon the coalition.

Once the bombing of Iraq began in January, Saddam moved from a war of words against Israel to a direct military attack on it as a means to draw it into the fighting—again, with the aim of undermining the U.S.-led coalition and Arab participation in it. Iraq fired thirty-nine missiles at Tel Aviv and Haifa. The fear in Israel was that the missiles would hold biological or chemical weapons, and Israel moved quickly to supply everyone in the country with gas masks. Israelis fitted safe, sealed rooms in their homes to which they retreated during the nineteen volleys of rockets that the Iraqi forces fired. There was damage, to be sure—3,300 apartments were damaged; a small number of people died, mostly from heart attacks; and the Israeli economy suffered badly, a loss of upward of $3 billion. But the chemical and biological weapons never came.

U.S. leaders addressed the attacks on Israel, attempting to blunt Saddam's strategy of inducing Israel to retaliate. American military commanders received orders to make the identification and destruction of rocket launch sites a high priority—detracting to some extent from other dimensions of the attack in Kuwait and Iraq by the coalition forces. Improved intelligence on when missiles were actually fired, which was conveyed immediately to Israel, gave Israelis a few precious extra minutes to find shelter before the rockets hit. The United States also supplied the Israelis with batteries of Patriot antimissile missiles, most of which ended up missing the incoming rockets.

But for all this assistance, the central thrust of American communications to the Israeli government was precisely the same as the one delivered by the White House aide back in September: messages one, two, and three were to keep out of the war and eschew any retaliation. Israel "was reduced to depending on the United States even in a sphere in which its forces might have found better operational solutions" (Schiff 1991, 23). Israeli leaders chafed under the restrictions the United States put on them. Military commanders in Israel felt that they could do a better job than the Americans in finding and destroying the missiles. They resented the lack of a ground operation by coalition forces to ferret out the missile sites. In the end, though, they became passive spectators in this critical war in their backyard—a war that was wreaking havoc on them.

Conclusion

The Gulf War of 1990–1991 was among a handful of massive military operations that came to characterize the post–Cold War period. And it was significant, too, as the first battle of that era. Saddam Hussein calculated that the old incentives that drew global powers into costly ventures in the Middle East no longer obtained. Local conflicts, he reasoned, could remain local without sucking outside powers into them, as had been the case with the bipolar structure of the Cold War. And theoretically, at least, his judgment was not so far fetched.

Events, however, did not proceed as he imagined they would. In this first major crisis after the collapse of the Soviet Union, American officials simply did not operate on the basis of a clear rationale as to where the country's interests lay in the emerging new world structure. In the new uncertain environment, the Bush administration lashed out at this first instance of one country swallowing another. The rationales for the strong U.S. reaction came later. The Americans surprised Iraq's government not only with the scale of their response but also with their determination to transform the crisis from a regional fight into an international brouhaha.

As the U.S. government pieced together its far-flung coalition, Saddam Hussein's hope was to undermine that alliance's unity, particularly Arab participation in it. But once again, he misjudged the lay of the land. Arab nationalism and solidarity, which he counted on, held little influence in 1990. The Palestinian issue, while generating heartfelt indignation in the Arab world—along with anti-American sentiments—had been watered down by the anxiety that the new world order created among Arab elites. Many calculated that this was not the moment to cross the sole remaining superpower, the United States.

For the Bush administration, the process of reacting to the invasion of Kuwait created a new strategic stance for the United States internationally and, particularly, in the Middle East. American policy makers had gone back and forth on the strategic value of Israel versus the Arab states from the Truman administration on. After 1970 and the Black September War, though, they found that they could have their cake and eat it too. A strong strategic relationship with Israel, a country that had proved itself so militarily powerful in the 1967 War, had enabled the United States to beat back the moves of Soviet clients against U.S. ally Jordan. That strategic relationship had also led to the reconsideration by Egypt, the strongest, largest Arab state and the outspoken leader of Arab nationalism, of its position in Cold War, abandoning the Soviet camp for a seat at the American table. From 1970–1990, Israel was not only the largest recipient of American aid; it was also a key strategic partner in achieving U.S. dominance in the Middle East.

The process of coalition making, as the United States readied for war against Iraq, led to a severe turnaround in its strategic policy. Israel suddenly became a strategic liability. U.S. officials viewed it as the monkey wrench that could wreck its carefully constructed global alliance. The Palestinian question loomed ever larger as having the potential to undo all the American handiwork in lining up Arab countries as diverse as monarchical Morocco and nationalist, republican Syria to participate in the American-led coalition.

In stark contrast to the heyday of the Israeli strategic relationship with the United States during the Black September War and afterward, Israel now found itself to be an embarrassment, asked to become invisible. Its active role in this first test of the post–Cold War world was reduced nearly to zero. "Although cooperation between Israel and the United States improved in terms of sharing intelligence," wrote Schiff (1991), "it remained severely limited in the operational sphere, even after Israel had come under attack by Iraqi missiles. From this standpoint Israel remained an outsider—though attention was paid to its advice on how to attack the missiles in western Iraq."

Israeli leaders and the public alike expressed extreme frustration that they had to sit on their hands as an enemy power attacked them. But U.S. officials had made it abundantly clear that no Israeli retaliation was permitted. In fact, the most damage to Israel was done to its pride and deterrent capabilities. The war was the first since Israel's War of Independence, more than four decades earlier, in which the enemy inflicted damage on Israel's home front. And it was the first in which the Israeli military sat on its hands as the country absorbed enemy blows.

Israel's change from strategic partner to strategic liability was not simply situational and temporary. In the years after the Gulf War, Israeli officials put forth any number of rationales for its strategic importance to the United States. They offered their prowess in intelligence as a basis for reestablishing the strategic relationship. And, from the time of the emergence of al-Qaeda, they suggested their importance as partners in what came to be called the worldwide war on terror. The moral sentiments that Clark Clifford had referred to in 1948 and President Kennedy had alluded to in his reference to a *special relationship* still kept Israeli-American ties very strong at most times. Indeed, the special relationship flourished in the sixteen years of the presidencies of Bill Clinton and George W. Bush. But the U.S.-Israeli relationship no longer rested on the solid foundation of a mutual *strategic partnership*. Israel depended on the United States, but the United States no longer depended on Israel.

U.S. officials felt that they had struck gold in the coalition that fought the war against Saddam Hussein in 1991. Their partnerships in the region had multiplied, including oil-rich and oil-poor states, Arab nationalist republics and traditional monarchies, old allies and new ones that had been in the Soviet camp. With the defeat of Saddam Hussein, American officials thought they were on the verge of a new era, one with a secure new role in the Middle East. For the first time, they now had permanent ground forces in the region. The future promised even more successes than those after Black September and the October 1973 War. Washington did not see the dark clouds on the horizon. U.S. officials paid little heed to the transformation of Mideast regional dynamics. The entire Middle East regional system was changing in the 1980s and 1990s—the subject of the next three chapters—and the American position became increasingly tenuous. Washington's indifference to that transformation would prove to hold grave consequences in the twenty-first century.

PART III

A Transformed Region

The Rise and Fall of the Arab Middle East

7   A Changing Lineup of Regional Powerhouses

The efforts of the United States to establish a role for itself in the Middle East after World War II hinged on finding one or more strategic partners and building a security alliance encompassing the region. The attempts to stitch together a military alliance, though, were little more than fiascos. And selecting partners that could assume some burdens and do for the United States what Washington was unable or unwilling to do itself turned out to be fraught with all sorts of difficulties.

For several brief periods, Washington believed that it had finally hit the jackpot in partnering in the region. The establishment of the Baghdad Pact in 1955 set Washington hearts racing, but the nationalist revolution in Iraq in 1958 made short shrift of those hopes. Later, in the 1970s, American administrations struck partnerships simultaneously with Israel, Egypt, and Iran, in addition to its longstanding ties to Turkey, and moved to marginalize the Soviet Union in the region. The shah's demise in 1979 was a major blow. And the slow erosion of power in Egypt after Sadat's assassination in 1981 and its isolation in the Arab world after the peace treaty with Israel also cut into its effectiveness as a partner. Indeed, only one leg of the stool, Israel, stood firmly in place in the last decade of the Cold War.

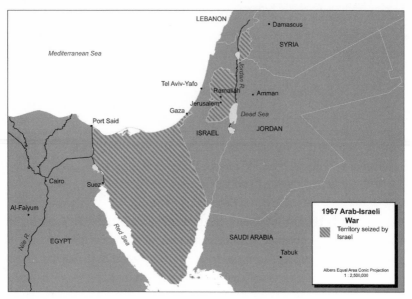

MAP 7.1

Another seemingly strong set of partnerships came at the end of the Cold War, when the Bush administration created its far-flung coalition in response to Iraq's 1990 invasion of Kuwait. Establishing the coalition did come with a cost: jettisoning Washington's twenty-year-old strategic partnership with Israel. Still, American aides believed that the coalition had succeeded in forging ties with Arab states (plus Turkey) that would be the long-term foundation for a U.S. presence in the region, bridging into the twenty-first century. That foundation, however, quickly crumbled.

Three Sparks That Ignited the Middle East

Pivotal events with deep repercussions undercut American efforts in finding steadfast regional partners. In the last third of the twentieth century, three cataclysmic moments with long-lasting effects were key in triggering fundamental changes in the Mideast regional system. Each directly affected America's role in the area. The 1967 Arab-Israeli War, the 1979 Iranian Revolution, and the end of the Cold War were catalysts for critical changes in the overall configuration of power in the Middle East and for America's prospects in the region. Starting in the mid-1960s, the dynamics of the area were transformed: the major regional powers, the fault lines of conflict, the substance of interstate relations, and the dominant ideologies changed dramatically from what they had been in the generation following World War II. By the end of the millennium, it was no longer your mother's Middle East.

The June 1967 War

Brief but explosive, the four-country clash that began on June 5, 1967, left deep scars, and they are clearly visible even nearly half a century later. Issues of occupied territories, the absence of permanent boundaries, the Palestinian political future and refugee problem, and never-ending instability have continued to haunt the area and the United States up to this very day. The June War initiated the downward slide of the Soviet Union in the Middle East—and globally—and opened the door for a new, more productive role for the United States in the region. The war's outcome spelled the near-death of Arab nationalism as well as the rapid decline of Arab core states as the primary Mideast powers. It turned Israel into a regional powerhouse. For better or for worse (mostly worse), its outcomes etched themselves profoundly into Israeli society and politics. And it deeply transformed the lives of Israel's new subjects in the occupied territories. The aftermath of the combat also created fertile ground for the emergence in the Middle East of a new dominant ideology, political Islam, and of powerful nonstate players, starting with the PLO under Yasser Arafat's leadership in 1968, both of which became major forces in reconfiguring the Middle East.

Teetering on its heels in the month leading up to the 1967 War, Israel emerged from the six days of combat as a major regional power, while its strongest opponents—Egypt and Syria—were gravely damaged not only militarily but more deeply in terms of their long-term influence in the area. Indeed, neither state ever fully recovered its share of regional power. Reacting to the remilitarization of the Sinai Peninsula (it had been demilitarized after the 1956 Suez War) and the blockade of the Straits of Tiran in May 1967, following a spring of growing tension, Israel initiated the fighting with a devastating airstrike on Egypt.

The attack was a bold move, aimed at the most powerful country in the Middle East, and it was devastating. The bombing destroyed the Egyptian air force as its planes sat on the tarmac. Israel immediately followed the airstrike by overrunning the armored and ground forces, first of Egypt in the Sinai Peninsula and then, quickly, Syria, in the Golan Heights, and

Jordan, in the West Bank. In less than a week, old borders dissolved, as did the balance of power in the region. Israel ended up occupying parts of all three of the countries that it fought in the war. It now ruled the heart of the eastern Mediterranean, from the Suez Canal all the way to the Jordan River, from Sharm el-Sheikh to Lebanon.

The nationalist Arab core of the region, especially Egypt and Syria, was badly battered. Egypt, the biggest and most important combatant, eventually did retrieve the bulk of its lost territory, the Sinai, in its peace treaty with Israel a dozen years after the war. But that came at the steep price of sacrificing its dominant leadership in the Arab world. All the other occupied lands—the Gaza Strip (formerly administered by Egypt, which practically severed its ties with Gaza at the time of the 1979 treaty), the West Bank, and the Golan Heights—have remained in limbo.

The Golan Heights was formally annexed by Israel but has remained the subject of intermittent negotiations and mediation efforts for return to Syria. Occupied Jerusalem was also formally annexed, and it, too, has remained on the table in on-again, off-again negotiations. The West Bank evolved, through the Oslo Peace Process in the 1990s, into a hodgepodge of contested zones of authority of Israel and the Palestine Authority. As a whole, the West Bank and Jerusalem have been fraught with tension between a ballooning population of hundreds of thousands of Israeli settlers and nearly two million Arab inhabitants. And unruly Gaza was administered by Israel until it abandoned Gaza in 2005, in its much heralded "disengagement." It has been ruled by Hamas since its brief, fratricidal war with Fatah in 2006–2007. Like the Golan Heights and the West Bank, the Gaza Strip has also been the subject of sporadic negotiations—sometimes between Israel and the Palestinians and, more often recently, as part of reconciliation talks between the Palestine Authority and Hamas.

Prior to the June 1967 War, Palestinians had pinned their hopes on the Arab states and the dream of Arab unity for the elimination of Israel and restitution of their homeland. A central plank of the Arab nationalist ideology was Palestinian redemption as part of the Arab nation's renaissance. The 1967 War changed all that. Palestinians used the debacle and the bitter disappointment of the war to build a new, independent strategy for *Palestinian*, rather than broader *Arab*, national redemption. That strategy centered on the PLO. But still today, Palestinians' status remains as indeterminate as ever. The upshot of that war has left open, festering sores in the occupied territories, the core Arab countries, and Israel itself. These sores continue to torment the Middle East.

The Iranian Revolution

The second major catalyst for the transformation of the Middle East was the high-voltage uprising against the shah of Iran, a dozen years after the 1967 Arab-Israeli War. Like that war, the Iranian Revolution had long-lasting repercussions that have continued to ripple through the entire area decades after the revolutionary moment. Overnight, it transmuted a close U.S. ally in the region into its most bitter enemy.

In the region itself, the revolution sparked the transformation of the political, religious, and cultural topography of the Middle East. It provoked the resurgence and unrest of Shiites throughout the region and, more broadly, of political Islam in the Middle East and beyond. The revolution's success initiated and demonstrated to other Muslims in the region the efficacy of an Islamic republic, of a refashioned Islam that could be a practical basis for twentieth- and twenty-first-century political rule. Additionally, Iran now, much more than under the shah, bored in on its relationships and role in the Middle East. The Islamic Republic was a *revolutionary* regime in the true sense of the word: it was bent on exporting its dramatically old-new conceptions of how state and society should be organized to anywhere that Muslims lived in great numbers, and especially to other Mideast countries. The revolution in Iran was, quite simply, the most important domestic upheaval in modern Middle East history.

Following more than a year of agitation in Iran, the regime of Shah Mohammad Reza Pahlavi, which had seemed invincible only a short time before, proved to be a house of cards and collapsed in January-February 1979. Multiple groups and interests—from merchants to mullahs—converged to topple the monarchy. But it was the Shiite religious forces, led spiritually by the exiled Ayatollah Ruhollah Khomeini, that dominated the opposition to the shah and controlled the revolution.

Trotskyite and other secular, revolutionary groups that had happily joined the religious forces in ousting the shah suffered brutal elimination and repression by the Islamic forces as soon as the new order was established. I, as someone who had been caught up in the romanticism of the revolution, remember sitting stunned as I heard one of my graduate students recount her own experience. She and her fiancé, both Trotskyites, had fought shoulder to shoulder with the Islamists to topple the shah. But soon after the Ayatollah assumed power, both were rounded up and stuck in prison. One day, my student was summoned by the guards. She watched in horror as her fiancé was executed, and then she, too, was hauled in front of the firing squad. For reasons unknown to her, the bullets went sailing over her head. A short time later, she was able to flee and eventually ended up at the University of Washington in Seattle, traumatized but still in one piece.

The fall of the shah was another monarchical domino falling in the Middle East—following those in Egypt (1952), Iraq (1958), and Libya (1969)—giving way to a people's republic. But this republic was different from the national republics that had preceded it. On April 1, 1979, the population overwhelmingly voted "yes" to create an *Islamic* republic, a new concept in Middle East history, indeed, in world annals. Khomeini then declared the establishment of the new republic, with a constitution underscoring the Islamic principles that would guide the new regime.

Within months, the revolution began to fan global and regional flames. In November, student supporters of the regime seized sixty-six hostages in the U.S. embassy in Tehran. Most were held for over a year, aggravating a deep, still-unresolved rift between the United States and Iran, one dating back to the CIA role in the overthrow of Mosaddeq. That same month, signs began to surface that the religious fervor of the Iranian Revolution was having a profound, agitating effect outside the country, as numbers of religious Islamic youth throughout the region took heart from the Iranian success story. Some, but by no means all, of these effects abroad were actively promoted by Iranian Revolutionary Guards and others in the regime. The Revolutionary Guards, or Army of the Guardians of the Islamic Revolution, were formed after the revolution as part of the Iranian army and came to take an active role in almost all facets of Iranian life, stamping them with a revolutionary, religious character. Their actions, though, did not stop at Iran's borders.

Perhaps the most spectacular event outside Iran that seemed to be inspired by the revolution occurred in monarchical Saudi Arabia, whose own brand of fervent Islam, Wahhabism, came to be pitted against the new revolutionary, republican impulses coming out of Iran. A group of Islamic militants declaring the appearance of the Mahdi, or Messiah, took over the Grand Mosque in Mecca, Islam's holiest city, in November 1979. Their seizure lasted for a couple of weeks, leading to hundreds of deaths of Saudi forces, Muslim pilgrims, and the militants themselves.

The action in the heart of Islam foreshadowed a bevy of attacks in other countries by dedicated Islamic militants, including the most spectacular, the assassination of President Sadat of Egypt in 1981. Repeatedly, fingers were pointed at Iran. And barely a year after the fall of the shah's regime, Iraq invaded Iran, in part because of what Saddam Hussein considered a revolutionary call to the Shiites of Iraq by Iranian militants and partly to take advantage of the disorder inside in Iran.

The End of the Cold War

The third triggering phenomenon for the changed regional system was the demise of the Soviet Union. The global competition with the Soviets, which had been such a decisive factor in international relations and which had made the Middle East into a Cold War playfield, simply went up in smoke. Although the United States had gradually gained the upper hand over the USSR in the region over the previous two decades, the final disintegration of the Soviet Union in 1991 eliminated what had been a major regional calculus since the late 1940s—the pitting of the superpowers and their respective client states against each other. While events in the region certainly held their own local meaning and resonance, both superpowers had consistently reframed those events in the context of their own global confrontation.

Now, the United States became the sole outside power with a hovering presence and an enduring influence on regimes and relations in the area. I use the word "imperial" to describe America's new role in the Middle East—a role unchallenged by other global powers and that was at once dominant and domineering. That new imperial role was hinted at already in 1990–1991, during the First Gulf War, and was confirmed in 2003 when the United States again invaded Iraq, ousted the old regime, and then set out to reshape the country—and the region—via an extended occupation. For the last two decades, the United States has been the Middle East's eight-hundred-pound gorilla.

The rapid global restructuring of the late 1980s—the crumbling of the Soviet empire, the end of the Cold War, the now unchallenged preeminence of the United States—was like a tsunami, transforming basic international and transnational relationships in every corner of the world. And the Middle East was no exception. In that volatile region, the changing international structure was felt as keenly as anywhere. Iraq, as discussed in chapter 6, was the first to test the waters of the post–Cold War world, gauging how far an ambitious, aggressive state could push the envelope of the new order. Saddam Hussein's ill-fated adventure in Kuwait in 1990 focused world attention on the Middle East and its internal problems just as global bipolarity was evaporating into thin air. It certainly entwined the United States into the region in unprecedented ways.

By the time the global picture changed in the late 1980s and early 1990s with the crumbling of the Soviet Union, the Middle East had already undergone major changes of its own. The region was highly unsettled, brimming with powerful forces that had barely existed a generation earlier. For foreign-policy makers in the United States, the last superpower left standing, with an already strong presence in the Middle East, this transformed region was very much an enigma. The combination of enigma and highly stepped-up involvement to become the imperial power in the area was not a good one.

Generally speaking, foreign-policy making in the United States after the Cold War was already complicated by the lack of clarity about what American interests actually were now that there was no Soviet Union with which to contend—the seat-of-the-pants syndrome. U.S. decision making for the Middle East was rendered even more rudderless by the failure of American officials to assimilate the changes that had overtaken the region. Only after 9/11, in both the Bush and Obama administrations, were there concerted efforts both to redefine and delineate American global interests and come to terms with the now transformed Middle East. To be sure, the responses of these two American administrations to global and regional events (the subject of chapters 10 and 11) were wildly different. Still, both were reacting to a Middle East that American officials now understood to have changed dramatically from the post–World War II era.

The June 1967 War, Iranian Revolution, and collapse of the Soviet Union served as catalysts, changing the central dynamics of the region. The central fault lines after these cataclysmic global and regional events were no longer the same. The global superpower standoff that had played out repeatedly in the Middle East gave way to a single imperial power, the United States, having major sway in the region and now establishing the permanent presence of its troops there. Israel's conflict with the Arab states, led by Egypt, now became a largely Palestinian-Israeli conflict. The cleavage that had divided monarchies from nationalist republics dissolved almost entirely as sworn enemies, like the regimes in Saudi Arabia and Egypt, now joined hands to act in the region. Iran and Turkey, which had mostly turned their backs on the doings in the area, became major players, and Iran dominated a bloc that stretched from sea to sea, the Gulf to the Mediterranean. Arab nationalism, which had both divided nationalist republics from others, particularly monarchies, and also set the nationalist republics upon one another, became increasingly irrelevant. Now political Islam was the touchstone, dividing states from one another and rending states and societies internally.

Forces that had held sway during the early decades of the Cold War crumbled and gave way to new sets of forces starting in the 1980s. These old and new forces, so critical in shaping the dynamics of the Middle East, are the topic of the remainder of this chapter and the next two. In this chapter, I analyze the key actors in the Mideast struggles and how they changed from the post–World War II period to the post–Cold War period. The Middle East was transformed by an entire changing of the guard in terms of the *leading states*, the preeminent regional powers, which have most prominently shaped the dynamics of the area. In chapter 8, I explore another change in key actors, as the monopoly of a certain kind of player, *state* actors—as the prominent players in the Middle East—cracked, creating new openings for the growing influence of *nonstate forces*.

In chapter 9, I continue the analysis of the disintegration of old forces and the succession of new, very different forces, exploring two key changes within Islam and how they also were tied to the transformation of Middle East dynamics. Chapter 9 will explore how the dominant ideology of the Middle East in the 1950s and 1960s, Arab nationalism, gave way to a new religious-political ideology rooted in Islam. And it will look at how, within the broad Islamic majority, Sunni dominance was challenged by a resurgent Shiism across a broad swath of the region. The chapter will then analyze how these changing sets of forces—the change in the roster of leading powers, the emergence of powerful nonstate actors, the move from Arab nationalism to political Islam as the primary ideology, and the rise of Shiism—have combined to produce a new configuration of power in the Middle East, one with deep implications for the United States.

The Changing of the Guard from the Arab Core to the Non-Arab Periphery

The twentieth century in the Middle East, especially the period after World War II, was the Arab century. During the last throes of the Ottoman Empire, various Arab leaders and elites had made a number of bids for the Arabs to wrest control from Istanbul and become the dominant players in the Middle East. The most notable was Muhammad Ali, the Ottoman-appointed wali of Egypt and Sudan during practically the entire first half of the nineteenth century, who radically reformed governance in Egypt and restructured its military. His reforms were so successful, in fact, that his well-oiled machine challenged the flaccid Ottomans for control of the entire Middle East, well beyond his home base of Egypt. Under the field leadership of his son Ibrahim Pasha, Muhammad Ali's army conquered the Levant, including what is today Lebanon, Palestine, and Syria. And he seemed on the verge of taking the Anatolian heart of the empire as well, threatening to topple the Ottoman dynasty. Only intervention by the European powers forced his retreat, preserving Ottoman rule in the region.

Later in the nineteenth century, the forerunners of modern Arab nationalism began to envision a post-Ottoman Middle East, one dominated by a unified Arab state. But those musings did not amount to much. More serious was the Arab Revolt of 1916–1918, in which Arab armed forces colluded with the British to oppose the Ottomans (who had made the fatal mistake of allying with the Germans in World War I). The Arab Revolt helped change the face of the Middle East, ending the Ottoman Empire's long run—nearly half a millennium—as ruler of the Arab Middle East.

This revolt has gained wide recognition in part because of the role of T. E. Lawrence, the colorful Lawrence of Arabia. Lawrence, a British army captain and adventurer, helped organize the Arab fighters, who were led by the sons of Hussein bin Ali, commonly known as Sharif Hussein. He was head of the Hashemite dynasty, which was at the center of a series of tribal alliances around the Hejaz, in the western portion of the Arabian peninsula, and held great prestige as a direct descendant of the Prophet Muhammad. It was the Ottomans who had appointed him Grand Sharif in Mecca, Islam's holiest city.

In 1916, Sharif Hussein joined forces with the British under the belief that once the Ottomans were defeated, Great Britain would support a unified Arab state ruled by the Hashemites and stretching from Persia to the Mediterranean. Sharif Hussein's sons, Faisal and Abdullah, did end up after the war as the titular heads of some of that territory, Iraq and Trans-Jordan, respectively. The British, however, hardly lived up to their promises and instead dominated the region themselves (along with their colonial compatriots, the French).

Only after World War II, more than a century after Muhammad Ali had first bid for regional power, did Arabs come truly to hold sway in the Middle East—and, even then, in much different terms from what Arab leaders had envisioned. Two revolutions—actually, glorified coups d'état—marked the transition to the new Arab-centered configuration of power in the region. The first and most important was the Free Officers Revolution of 1952 in Egypt. Led by Colonel Gamal Abdul Nasser, the revolution ousted Egypt's corrupt King Farouk and quickly turned to putting an end to direct and indirect British military control and political influence in Egypt. Nasser, though, did not limit his horizons to Egypt or even only the Middle East; he carried the banner of anticolonialism around the world and became a leading force in the newly emerging global Non-Aligned Movement. He was a charismatic figure who hatched the movement along with two other now legendary figures, India's Jawaharlal Nehru, the first prime minister of India, and Yugoslavia's Marshall Tito, the heroic antifascist leader of World War II.

For fifteen years after the revolution, Nasser deftly guided Egypt through a profound domestic transformation under a socialist banner (which actually looked a lot more like state-led capitalism) and projected it into a leading role in the Middle East and beyond. He managed to nationalize the Suez Canal and withstand the British-French-Israeli axis in the Suez War of 1956, which aimed to return control of the canal to the European powers. And he developed a close relationship with the Soviet Union, starting with the Aswan High Dam project, in which the Russians replaced the Americans as principal funders in 1955. The Soviets' aid opened the way for their expanded influence throughout the region. Those fifteen years were heady times for Egypt—at home, in the Mideast, and in the larger world. In 1972, a couple of years after Nasser's death, I happened to be the graduate tutor of Benazir Bhutto, the future prime minister of Pakistan, at the time that her father, Zulfikar Ali Bhutto, became Pakistan's president. I asked Benazir whether her father had been her political hero growing up. "Not at all," she replied. "Nasser was my hero."

Less remarkable than the Free Officers Revolution was the Iraqi 14th July Revolution, in 1958. Here, as in Egypt, the military coup d'état unseated the monarch, in this case King Faisal II. Faisal II was the great-grandson of Sharif Hussein and the grandson of Faisal, who had been the primary military leader of the Arab Revolt in 1916 and the first king of the newly formed Iraq (after a failed attempt to set up his kingship in Syria). The fall of Faisal II in 1958 further diminished the once-powerful Hashemite dynasty, leaving as a Hashemite head of state only King

Hussein of Jordan (another great-grandson of Sharif Hussein), and he too was tottering at the time.

The Hashemite dynasty had been the leading force in the Arab world during World War I and its immediate aftermath. But its loss of influence started soon after and continued through the ignoble fall of Faisal II in Iraq. The Hashemite decline actually had begun with none other than Hussein bin Ali, who had graduated (with British support) from Grand Sharif of Mecca to King of the Hejaz. Then, with the abolition of the Turkish caliphate, Sharif Hussein declared himself caliph of the world's Muslims and king of all the Arabs. Titles aside, his glory days were few. By 1924, he had been routed by the Saudis, who took control of most of the Arabian Peninsula, and forced into exile in Iraq, where he died in 1931. The toppling of the Hashemites in Iraq in 1958 signaled the triumph of a new breed of Arab leaders committed to the old dream of a dominant single Arab state: the republican nationalists, bent on Arab unity based on popular rule, in the mold of Nasser.

From the time of the Free Officers Revolution in Egypt in 1952, the monarchy in Iraq, led day to day by Prime Minister Nuri al-Said, had faced increasing pressure from homegrown antimonarchical Arab nationalists. These forces looked to both Egypt, under Nasser's control, and Syria, with its rising pan-Arab Ba'ath Party. The stress on the Iraqi regime only increased when Egypt and Syria merged to form the United Arab Republic early in 1958. That was a year of nationalist-inspired turmoil throughout the Arab Middle East, which rocked the old Arab regimes and paved the way for the young, vibrant Arab nationalists. Jordan and Lebanon stood on the brink of falling to the new nationalist forces, but it was in Iraq that the nationalists had their principal success. With the triumph of the military coup in Iraq, whose leaders professed unwavering support for pan-Arabism, the leading Arab countries seemed on the verge of achieving the nationalist dream of a single, united Arab state shaping the modern Middle East.

Arab nationalist regimes remained ascendant in the Middle East after 1958 but not in the form of a united Arab state, as they had hoped. By 1961, Syria had withdrawn from the United Arab Republic, which Nasser had dominated—a bitter pill for Nasser and other Arab nationalists throughout the region to swallow. The Arab nationalist regimes found themselves more at one another's throats than cooperating in the creation of a pan-Arab regime. The dynamics of the Middle East now revolved around the rivalries and intrigues among the three most important Arab nationalist regimes—Egypt, Iraq, and Syria; their domestic political intrigues, particularly in Syria and Iraq, both ruled by changing factions of the Ba'ath Party; and their place in the global politics of the Cold War, especially once Egypt switched from the Soviet to the U.S. camp after the 1973 Arab-Israeli War.

Patrick Seale (1986), a noted journalist covering the Middle East for decades, made the argument that the central dynamic of the Middle East during the post–World War II era reproduced a rivalry that dated back to antiquity. That competition was between those who controlled the two great river systems of the Middle East, the Nile and the Tigris-Euphrates. Over the millennia, he argued, the dominant dynamics in the region were the rivalry between the civilizations of Egypt and Mesopotamia. Seale saw the postwar era also to have been characterized by this ancient enmity, now between the two Arab nationalist regimes in Egypt and Iraq. What had tipped the balance of power in one direction or another through the ages was the disposition of Syria. When Syria was controlled by or allied with one of the two powers, that bloc tended to dominate. The twentieth century was no different, he maintains, and the dynamic of the Middle East revolved around the title of Seale's book, *The Struggle for Syria.* Syria was no cipher in the regional power dynamic, though. In the 1970s and 1980s, particularly under the leadership of Hafez al-Asad, it revived ideas of Greater Syria, bringing Lebanon firmly under its umbrella and aiming to do the same with the Jordanians and the PLO (Maoz 1988).

Other countries in the region were also candidates to be major players in shaping the security, politics, culture, ideology, and economics of the Middle East. Among the Arab states, Saudi Arabia was a prime prospect, largely because of its huge oil resources. To be sure, there were moments in which it played a strong regional role, as in the Yemeni Civil War in 1962 (where pro-Nasser nationalist forces were pitted against traditional powers, which the Saudis supported) and the emergence of OPEC, the oil-producers' cartel, in 1973. For the most part, though, Saudi Arabia's leaders tended to be inward looking and very cautious in their foreign policy. They shied away from imprinting their stamp on the larger region in terms of their religious Wahhabism or in any other way. Saudi Arabia's foreign policy tended to be mostly defensive and reactive. The country's dependence on the United States also mitigated its regional influence. Its greatest influence in the region over the years tended to be among the traditional Arab regimes in Yemen, the country with which it shared the Arabian Peninsula, and the Gulf, where it was the dominant power in the Gulf Cooperation Council, founded in 1981 largely to fend off revolutionary Iran.

The three non-Arab states of the Middle East also seemed to be logical choices as major powers, which could shape the region in multiple ways. Iran, Israel, and Turkey were all dynamic states with formidable militaries. But none emerged as a powerful regional actor to challenge the Arab core during the Cold War era. The regimes in Iran under the shah and republican Turkey, both strongly allied with the United States, took only limited interest in the Middle East and broader regional affairs. Under the shah, Iran was mostly inward looking and self-absorbed.

Through their White Revolution, Iranian leaders hoped to distance the country from the pack of economic underachievers in the Middle East. The leadership focused its attention not so much on the region but on the United States, especially after the CIA-promoted 1953 coup that propped up the young shah. While American presidents from Eisenhower to Carter prompted the Iranian leadership to assume a greater role in Middle East affairs and supplied the Iranian army with vast stores of arms to help them play that role, the Iranians never did become a major regional player during the shah's rule.

Only after the Iranian Revolution in 1979, which was committed to spreading Islamic rule, did Iran's new regime begin to take a much more active and sustained role in Middle East political, military, and religious affairs. But it took some time. While, as mentioned, some meddling in neighboring regimes was going on (Iranian Revolutionary Guards, for example, were said to be actively involved in aiding Shiite militias in the Lebanese Civil War in the early 1980s), in addition to the pure inspirational effect of the Islamic Revolution on those in neighboring countries, the Iran-Iraq War drained Iran's attention and resources for almost the entire decade of the 1980s.

Turkey, too, looked away from the Middle East in the decades after World War II. The creation of the republic in 1923 had involved a traumatic break with the near territories of the Ottoman Empire, including the Arab lands to the south. After the war, two other foreign factors preoccupied Turkish policy makers, and both drew their attention away from the Middle East. The first was the country's incorporation into NATO and its growing desire, as time went on, to be integrated into Europe, leading eventually to its application for full membership in the European Union. And the second was the longstanding rivalry with Greece, which was also tied to its invasion of Cyprus in 1974.

On top of that, after the harsh 1980 military coup in Turkey, the country's army focused largely on its extended war with the Kurdish resistance movement. The sometimes violent resistance to the Turkish state was led by the Kurdistan Workers' Party, popularly known as the PKK. As with Iran, Middle East issues did crop up for Turkey, such as its water disputes with Syria and Iraq and its resentment over Syria's role as a haven for PKK guerrillas (leading to the threat of a Turkish invasion). But these issues did not add up to a concerted effort on the part of the Turkish state to play an ongoing, influential role in regional affairs.

Israel's case was different from those of Iran and Turkey. It found itself, like it or not, deeply involved in regional affairs. That engagement, though, was practically entirely through an almost endless series of wars—in 1948–1949, 1956, 1967, 1970, 1973, 1978, and 1982. There is no doubt that Israel affected the region deeply through those wars, especially the 1967 War. The country's effect on the region, however, was largely limited to the negative influence of its wars, especially prior to 1970. In terms of economics, diplomacy, and culture, its influence was practically nil, at least until its treaty with Egypt in 1979, and limited even after that. The great historian Albert Hourani wrote in the foreword to Seale's book that in terms of the wider stage of regional politics in the years after World War II, "Israel, newly created and occupied with its own problems, played a part which may seem to a later generation to have been surprisingly passive" (Seale 1986, xii).

Israel by no means could be ignored in understanding the Middle East in the first decades after it achieved independence, but its one-dimensional role kept it from being a central agent in shaping the daily relations of the region. It was not that Israel's leaders were uninterested in the region; they strived to forge ties with Turkey and Iran, the other non-Arab powers, and with non-Arab and religious minorities in largely Muslim Arab countries, such as the Kurds in Iraq and Lebanese Christians. On the whole, however, it was only after the Black September War in 1970 that Israel showed signs of becoming a shaper of regional affairs. And it was only in the 1990s that Israel played a sustained part in the Middle East drama beyond the military sphere.

To sum up, for the key decades after World War II, the region truly was the *Arab* Middle East. The influential actors in molding the international relations of the area for most of the Cold War era—from ideology to economics to security—were the core nationalist Arab powers. These states were at the forefront of each of the four struggles that constituted the central dynamics of the region in the postwar era. The first was the Cold War, with the three Arab nationalist states all moving into the Soviet orbit. Their friendship treaties with the USSR created the high-water mark of Soviet influence in the region and, possibly, worldwide. Egypt's defection from the Soviet camp in 1973 signaled the end of the Soviet era in the area and the reassertion of American dominance, which only grew over time.

The second key feature of the region's dynamics was the Arab-Israeli conflict, which generated war after war, crisis after crisis. Each of the three Arab states engaged in at least one war with Israel, and Egypt and Syria, multiple wars. Those two states led the charge against the Jewish state, assuming the responsibility for the restoration of Palestinian rights. Third, these nationalist republics formed a winning coalition against the alternative forms of Arab rule, the monarchies and the Lebanese confessional system. And a final central dynamic in the region was the machinations among Egypt, Iraq, and Syria themselves, which were often highly complex, sometimes even bizarre. At one moment, these states issued statements about their intentions to unite, aiming to fulfill the dream of a single Arab state, and, in the next moment, they hurled invective at one another.

While the dream of a unified Arab state dominating the region faded after the demise in 1961 of the Syrian-Egyptian condominium, the nationalist regimes still exerted tremendous influence with other states and with the people on the street throughout the region. Understanding the culture, politics, economics, and security of the region after World War II, especially in the 1950s and 1960s but even forward into the following decades, meant focusing on the actions and relations of the three primary states—Egypt, Iraq, and Syria.

All that changed quickly, though. By the end of the last century and the first decade of the current one, a whole new cast of states had stepped into the central roles in regional affairs that the core Arab states had occupied earlier. Part of that change resulted from the steady erosion of the foundation of power in Egypt, Iraq, and Syria; part came from the now active interest of two of the largest and strongest countries, Iran and Turkey, in regional affairs; and part was attributable to the increasing integration of Israel into the region on a political, diplomatic level, beginning with the Madrid Peace Conference at the end of 1991.

Much of this sea change came through the relative slippage, both regionally and globally, of the key Arab republics, especially when compared to the non-Arab states, namely Iran, Israel, and Turkey. The poor performance of Arab countries across a variety of indicators was captured in a remarkable document, the *Arab Human Development Report*, written by Arab intellectuals and published first in 2002 by the United Nations Development Programme and the Arab Fund for Economic and Social Development. In subsequent years, the report's findings were updated, but the core message stayed the same.

The report did not mince words. The authors lamented, for example, that the Arab states had failed to catch the democratic wave washing over much of Asia, Africa, and Latin America in the latter stages of the twentieth century. "There is a substantial lag," the authors wrote, "between Arab countries and other regions in terms of participatory governance" (*Arab Human Development Report* 2002, 21). Egypt, Iraq, and Syria all remained stubbornly authoritarian, with regimes that stultified and repressed off-message voices and new ideas. The odd mixture in these regimes of a populist base and iron-fisted rule was caught in book titles such as *Republic of Fear* (Kanan 1989), on Saddam Hussein's Iraq, and *Ambiguities of Domination* (Weeden 1999), on Hafez al-Asad's Syria. In these states, the dissemination of information was carefully controlled, even in the new global Age of Information.

Rulers—in what were supposed to be popular republics—had virtually endless runs in power. Hosni Mubarak was president of Egypt for nearly thirty years and, in his final year or two, tried to manipulate politics so that his son could succeed him. Hafez al-Asad, after his ascent to supreme power following the Black September War, also lasted in Syria for three decades until his death in 2000; his son, Bashir, has been at the helm ever since. The infamous Saddam Hussein ruled for a mere twenty-four years before being ousted by the U.S. invasion in 2003.

Beyond the length of their reigns, these dictators oversaw states whose capabilities for governance were low. Bureaucracies stifled initiative. Opportunities for mobility were few. The harsh police states that these autocrats built resulted in institutional sclerosis both in the states themselves and in the larger societies, which they kept under tight and constant surveillance.

Institutional inflexibility had dire effects economically. The Arab Middle East fared poorly during the last two decades of the twentieth century: "After increasing at rapid rates between 1963 and 1980, GDP per capita stagnated over the following two decades. In fact, GDP per capita in the region as a whole was lower in the year 2000 than in 1980. . . . The growth performance of the Arab world after 1980 was disappointing across the board" (Sala-i-Martin and Artadi 2002, 22–24). In 1980, for example, Egypt, Syria, and Turkey all had incomes that ranged around $1,000–$2,000 per capita, with Egypt on the low end and Turkey, the high. By 2009, Egypt and Syria had grown modestly to $4,620 and $5,690 in current dollars, respectively. Compare those figures with Turkey's, whose per capita income grew to $13,730. (See figure 7.1 for a comparison of the income growth of the principal Arab and non-Arab states.) A good part of the blame for poor economic performance lies at the feet of the state. In Egypt, for example, it has been estimated that around 35 percent of business people's time has been spent dealing with problems related to government regulation (Sala-i-Martin and Artadi 2002, 30). In effect, the bureaucracy strangled the economy.

And each of the three core Arab republics had specific issues that diminished its once bright prospects as the twentieth century came to an end, ranging from Saddam's misguided foreign adventures in Iran and Kuwait to Egypt's break with the rest of the Arab world as a result of its 1979 treaty with Israel. In Iraq, Saddam eventually brought on his own demise and the relegation of Iraq to the status of "problem" rather than player. In the case of Syria, here is Rodman's (1991, 2) description of its government's misadventures: "Syria had been deflated by the cumulative effect of its economic weakness, its Lebanon quagmire, its humiliation by the Soviets (who rejected Syria's bid for strategic parity with Israel) and even the Palestinian uprising in the Israeli occupied territories, which punctured Asad's claims to be a major player in the Palestinian game." In the mid-2000s, it suffered a number of disastrous events, including the Israeli bombing of its putative nuclear site in 2007 and its role in

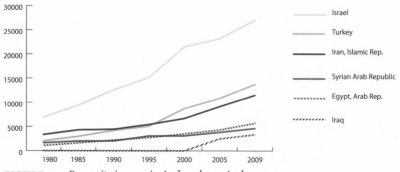

FIGURE 7.1 Per capita income in Arab and non-Arab powers.

the assassination of Rafiq Hariri, the former Lebanese prime minister, in 2005.

Even on the eve of the Arab Spring, Arab states could not be simply dismissed in terms of their effect on regional dynamics. Egypt remained the most important Arab country and exercised influence well beyond its borders. It is today larger in population than France or the United Kingdom and, by now, may well have surpassed Germany. While its future is still uncertain in the post-Mubarak era, it still has a daunting army, and it continues to play an active role in Arab affairs and in Israeli-Arab relations. Saudi Arabia, especially, in the 2000s assumed a more active part in regional affairs, notably on security issues. And its tremendous wealth makes it impossible to ignore. Syria, too, rebounded somewhat from the ill-fated events of the mid-2000s. In the latter part of the first decade of the twenty-first century, before popular protests unsettled the Asad regime, Syria managed to reassert its influence in Lebanon (especially through its alliance with Hezbollah) and reconcile with Turkey and, to some degree, Saudi Arabia.

Still, no Arab state today, with the possible exception of Egypt because of its sheer size, could be labeled one of the major regional leaders. In the years prior to the Arab Spring, the dictators of Egypt, Iraq, and Syria, through their fiascos abroad and their stifling policies at home, helped make their states much less formidable players in regional affairs than they had been earlier, although each certainly continued to exert some influence in the region. Egypt's descent, perhaps, has been the most remarkable, simply because it was the dominant regional power in the early postwar decades. Today, the Middle East analyst Samer Shehata says of Egypt that it is "decaying," and the newspaper article that quotes him speaks of "Egypt's flagging regional influence" (Stack 2009). Another expert, Emad Gad, of the Ahram Center for Political and Strategic Studies in Cairo, says that "Egypt's role is receding regionally, and its cards are limited" (Slackman 2009). In the midst of the turmoil that would undo Mubarak, the *New York Times* reporter Anthony Shadid (2011) wrote of a degraded "Egypt, once the dynamic, uncontested leader of the Arab world, whose foreign policy now often amounts to an appendix tacked onto American mediation in Israeli-Palestinian negotiations."

Syria's and Egypt's descent into second-tier regional powers occurred gradually; Iraq slipped, too, from the time of the Iran-Iraq War on and then fell off the cliff, of course, with the American invasion of the country in 2003. Saudi Arabia has stayed a second-level regional power through the years. Among all these Arab states, Egypt has remained the most influential but has still been considerably diminished.

At the same time that the Arab core countries stumbled, the non-Arab states on the territorial periphery of the region began to play a much bigger role in the Middle East, transforming the power game in the region. Most important, by far, has been Iran, which I will return to at the end of the chapter 9. Suffice it to say here that the revolutionary regime paid far closer attention to Middle East affairs and became much more involved in events in the "near abroad" than the shah's regime ever had. Lebanon, Palestine, Iraq, the Gulf states, and Israel all became targets of a new aggressive foreign policy in the region by the Islamic Republic, and overtures were made to Turkey, Syria, and the Shiite leadership of Iraq. By the beginning of the twenty-first century, Iran became the single most important Middle East country shaping the region, a fact that the administration of George W. Bush was slow to grasp.

Iran's deposing of Egypt as regional kingpin can be seen in an important measure of both governmental and economic capacity, electrical-power consumption. Despite the disruption of the revolution, the war with Iraq, and U.S.-led international sanctions, Iran pushed its electrical-power consumption from around 275 kilowatt hours per capita in 1971 to 2,325 in 2007. Compare those figures with Egypt's growth from around 200 (nearly three-quarters of Iran's kWh per person) to only 1,384 (only 60 percent of Iran's per capita kWh).

With the victory of an Islamic-oriented party in 1996 for the first time in modern Turkey's history, that country began a slow, if not always steady, process of moving its foreign-policy focus toward the Middle East. The Islamic-leaning Rafah (Welfare) Party, elected in 1996, did not last long, forced out by Turkey's secularist, nationalist military and, later, the Constitutional Court. But its successor, the Justice and Development Party, widely known as AKP, continued the move toward more sustained engagement in Turkey's "near abroad," including Central Asia and the Middle East. Prime Minister Recep Tayyip Erdoğan of the AKP and his foreign minister, Ahmet Davutoğlu, broke many of the old taboos deeply embedded in the Turkish Republic's foreign policy. Davutoğlu, in particular, was key in refocusing on Turkey's neighborhood.

The government moved Turkey toward establishing diplomatic ties with Armenia. That initiative came in the face of the historic enmity between Turks and Armenians stemming from the Armenian genocide in 1915, when the Ottoman government targeted its Armenian population. Government actions during World War I and in the war's immediate aftermath resulted in the death of over a million Armenians. The talks on ties were preceded by a memorable visit by the Turkish president to Armenia. In the same vein, Erdoğan helped normalize relations with Turkey's historic enemy Greece. Ties improved after Greece extended its hand to help Turkey after the latter's devastating earthquake in 1999. In the Middle East, Turkey repaired its long-tattered relations with Syria while keeping a wary eye on events in Iraq after the American invasion, especially in the Kurdish sector.

Erdoğan's first foreign visit was to Iran, with which he negotiated an energy deal. That visit and Turkey's refusal to serve as a staging ground for the United States when it attacked Iraq in 2003 signaled a move away from the United States as one of two central axes of Turkish foreign policy (along with seeking membership in the European Union). And, even on EU membership, Turkey made achieving that less central to its overall foreign policy. Davutoğlu, a leading intellectual, came to the position of foreign minister with the idea of rethinking Turkey's strategic positioning. He wrote about his vision in a widely circulated article (Davutoğlu 2008) and later reformulated Turkey's Red Book, an accounting of Turkey's strategic threats and opportunities.

As Turkey shifted toward a Middle East focus, its ties with Israel became increasingly problematic. In 2008, Turkey quietly began to serve as a go-between, attempting to bridge the deep Israeli-Syrian differences, but with little success. Once that effort came to an end, relations quickly began to unravel. The secular-leaning army continued its strong military relations with that country. But the army—and, indeed, the entire secular political establishment—was weakened considerably by Erdoğan. The government, at the same time, tilted away from Israel, strengthening ties with the Arab world. A very public shouting match in 2009 between Erdoğan and Israel's president, Shimon Peres, at a panel at the World Economic Forum in Davos following the Gaza War was followed during the next couple of years by harsh criticism of Israel for its treatment of the Palestinians. The straw that broke the camel's back came in 2010, when a nongovernment Turkish flotilla sought to breach Israel's blockade of Hamas-run Gaza. Israeli sailors boarded the ships and, in the struggle that followed, ended up killing nine people, most of them Turks. The incident led to a new nadir in Turkish-Israeli relations and, at the same time, affirmed Turkey's place in Middle East affairs, even ones far from its borders.

As relations with Israel soured, ties with the Arab world deepened. In 2009, Turkey requested of the Egyptians, who had been trying to mediate between Hamas and Fatah, that Turkey be allowed to assume that task, although that initiative did not go far. In 2010, Erdoğan was the guest of honor at the Arab Summit Conference in Sirte, Libya. As Maddy-Weitzman (2010b, 22) commented, "Erdoğan's presence provided a stark indication of Turkey's new assertiveness in the region."

Turkey's new Mideast role was quite different from that of Iran or Israel. Its actions were not like those of a traditional military power, although its military was strong. The Turkish government edged away from its swaggering, confrontational policies with Armenia, Greece, Iraq, and Syria and edged toward a different sort of presence. It started acting more as a diplomatic facilitator that could traverse historic rifts in the area, such as between the Arabs and Israel, the various Palestinian factions, and Iran and Arab countries. Its attempts to play a broker-like role, including between Iran and America, signaled the sort of new functions that the country was assuming in the Middle East.

Much of Israel's changed position in the Middle East has occurred below the radar. Previously, it had long worked, with mixed success, to cultivate ties with non-Arab populations and states in the region. Turkey and Iran, at least until the 1979 revolution, were its primary targets, but it also courted other groups, such as Kurds (especially in Iraq) and Lebanese Christians. It also held various secret negotiations with Arab leaders, such as the kings of Jordan and Morocco. On the whole, though, Israel's influence during the Cold War period tended to be one-dimensional, based on its military rather than its diplomacy, and fairly limited. The peace treaty with Egypt gave the country its first opening to develop a sustained diplomatic presence in the heart of the Middle East, but even the new relationship with Egypt was what the Israelis called a cold peace, limiting its diplomatic possibilities. The Palestinian issue, the most important symbolic issue in all Arab countries, weighed heavily on Israel's foreign-policy options—as it still does.

Nonetheless, the flurry of peace negotiations in the 1990s paved the way for a new Israeli role in the Middle East. The negotiations started with the U.S.-driven Madrid Conference in December 1991. The conference, laboriously put together by the administration of George H. W. Bush, especially Secretary of State James A. Baker, developed a loose framework for comprehensive Arab-Israeli engagement. It also was the umbrella for more focused bilateral talks (including with the Palestinians, who came

FIGURE 7.2   Clinton presiding over the handshake of Prime Minister Yitzhak Rabin of Israel and Palestinian Liberation Organization chairman Yasser Arafat during the Middle East Peace Agreement signing ceremony, September 13,1993.
Source: Courtesy William J. Clinton Presidential Library.

in through the fig leaf of participating in the Jordanian delegation). And it initiated multilateral negotiations on issues of areawide concern. The talks, which quickly moved from Madrid to Washington, led to Israel's peace treaty with Jordan, Israel's second such treaty with an Arab country. The secret Oslo negotiations in 1993 that produced a historic Declaration of Principles between Israel and the PLO—agreeing to mutual recognition, a framework for solving their differences once and for all, and an end to armed conflict—opened even more doors for Israel throughout the region, some of them, front doors, others, back doors.

Oslo ultimately failed, and it was followed by a brutally violent period between Israel and the Palestinians during the al-Aqsa intifada in the 2000s. The intifada set back Israel's attempt to establish itself as a day-to-day actor in the region. Days after the uprising began, Bahrain, Morocco, and Oman closed their diplomatic missions, which had been established in the wake of Oslo. Even more pointedly, the brutal wars in Lebanon and Gaza in 2006 and 2008–2009 once again edged Israel back toward pariah status. Bolivia and Venezuela, for example, suspended diplomatic relations with Israel after the Gaza War. The countless group-to-group interactions (the so-called Track II, or backdoor, negotiations) that had mushroomed in the 1990s between Palestinians and Israelis—involving everyone from rabbis and imams to lawyers and environmentalists—dried up almost entirely after the outbreak of the intifada.

But the inroads Israel made during the Oslo years were not completely wiped out, by any means. Backdoor relations with a number of Arab governments seemed to continue, although neither side would confirm those contacts. The peace treaties with Jordan and Egypt remained intact, and Israel had intensive diplomatic relations with both. The second factor leading to Israel's new role in the Middle East involved the common perception by Arab regimes and Israel that Iran posed a major threat to their collective existence. That shared conviction led to growing, if quiet, strategic, military, and diplomatic coordination between Israel and its Arab neighbors. Much more on this later.

The ascendant roles in the dynamics of regional affairs passed from the hands of the core Arab states to those of the non-Arab powers on the territorial periphery of the region—Iran, Israel, and Turkey. What had been a Middle East dominated by the clashes, cooperation, and coalitions of the three primary Arab states during the Cold War now saw new powers, fault lines, and blocs as central to the area. From 1990 or so on, the three non-Arab states prevailed as the leading actors, bringing the era of the Arab-dominated Middle East to an end. Over the course of less than half a century, the Middle East has experienced "the decline of the power of Arab states, individually and collectively, and the corresponding clout of their non-Arab neighbors in the region—Turkey, Iran, and Israel" (Maddy-Weitzman 2010a). Singling out the preeminent position of Iran, Maddy-Weitzman noted, "The divided Arab system of states now confronts in its midst a non-Arab state able to project considerable power along with emotional appeal to large segments of its frustrated and young public. In essence, Iran now carries the flag of anti-Western militancy, which had belonged to earlier generations of Arab nationalists." It was truly a changing of the guard.

8 New Boys on the Block

Nonstate Actors

The roster of heavy hitters in the Middle East looked radically different by the beginning of the twenty-first century from what it had been in the 1950s, 1960s, and 1970s. In place of the secular, nationalist Arab states, which had previously defined the regional dynamics, was a potpourri of non-Arab states—Iran, Turkey, and Israel—each of which incorporated religion into the state and public life in differing ways. These states now had the dominant hand in defining the lines of competition and conflict and in establishing the rules of the game for regional interaction. These states, however, were not the only major players. Besides the changing lineup of leading states, the region also saw new sorts of players, nonstate actors, emerging as additional forces shaping Middle East dynamics. These new boys on the block put in their bid for places in the lineup, as well. And they played a major role in transforming the region.

The Retreat of the State

The period of decolonization in Africa and Asia, from 1947 to around 1965, was the heyday of the idea that independent states, including the new postcolonial states, would be the supreme actors across the globe; gone, it was thought, was the era of sprawling empires, powerful tribes, religion-based polities, and autonomous rajs and warlords. The new states were almost without exception avowedly secular, nationalist regimes. Just as the number of such independent states in the world tripled over those couple of decades—truly effecting a revolution on the world map—so, too, did the conviction take root that these states, sooner rather than later, would be robust: they would fully control their territories, monitor their borders, and make effective rules governing the everyday lives of their citizens. Indeed, the idea that the category of "citizen" would be an individuals' primary source of social belonging across the globe, displacing kin, religious, ethnic, tribal, and other identities, held strong among state elites and intellectuals worldwide.

But the new postcolonial states rarely lived up to their billing. By the twenty-first century, intellectuals had gone from propounding the inevitability of state control to lamenting how many states seemed so distant from the imagined European standard. They were labeled "quasi" states, or "proto"-states, or "collapsed" states, or "fragile" states, or "outlaw" states, or (a popular label these days) "failed" states, or, even, "mad" states (Chomsky 2006; Jackson 1990; Rotberg 2003, 2004; Simpson 2004; Zartman 1995). While among Middle East cases only Lebanon and possibly Yemen could be thought of at various times in these extreme terms, overall the region was no exception to this postcolonial experience: many states in the region failed to meet early expectations and had great difficulty establishing uniform, coordinated rule (or rules) across the territory they claimed. As noted above, the core Arab states suffered from the extended reign of autocratic leaders who, while managing to hold onto power, oversaw states that were increasingly stagnant. The fiction of the 1950s and 1960s that Middle East states were capable of broad and deep control of their territories and societies began to fade by the 1970s and 1980s.

Many states were simply unable to penetrate their own countryside consistently, provide basic services and infrastructure to their citizens, regulate movement of goods and people across their borders, and offer a modicum of justice and security. People could not count on an effective civil administration of society or a working security and judicial system to guard their well-being. Nor could they fall back on the institutions that they had leaned on in past centuries—clans, tribes, village organizations, and others. Increased mobility, hyperurbanization, and integration into the global economy all shook these old institutions to their roots. Many withered away or found their ability to regulate and protect their members' lives severely curtailed.

Into this void stepped a variety of new or renewed nonstate organizations—some quite local and others stretching across state borders. In the last couple of decades of the twentieth century, nonstate actors became serious players inside Middle East countries and, more broadly, in the regional system, adding yet another new factor transforming the Middle East at century's end. Nonstate actors certainly did not displace states, but they took their place alongside them as players shaping the region. They thrived precisely because states had failed on two fronts. First, states repeatedly failed to do what their leaders said they would do—provide security, justice, basic services, and an opportunity for a better life. Either through pure inefficiency or outright criminality, most states in the Middle East served their populations badly. In short, states promised much more than they delivered.

Second, riding a wave of neoliberal reform—sometimes called the Washington Consensus—Middle East states, starting in the late 1970s, self-consciously shrank. That is, they promised their citizens less and less. Their leaders jettisoned functions and discontinued services to their publics that they had earlier embraced and even tried to monopolize. While the retreat of the state was intended to spur rapid economic growth through privatization and the flowering of capitalism, in fact, growth lagged badly. Many citizens were left in desperate straits as incomes stagnated and services dried up. It was in this environment that countless nonstate organizations were born.

These actors came in many different shapes and stripes. Longstanding organizations thought to have been relegated to the dustbin of history, such as clans and tribes, reorganized themselves to deal with the challenges of twentieth-century life. They assumed (or reassumed) functions still publicly claimed by the state or ones now disowned by the state, ranging from settling disputes to providing security (Baylouny 2008, 2; Khoury and Kostiner 1990). They served as labor exchanges, welfare organizations, and aggregators of votes.

Additionally, new nonprofits, or nongovernmental organizations (NGOs), both homegrown and international, proliferated. They sometimes stepped in for the state in performing certain roles, such as offering health care or education; others became strong cause advocates, lamenting the state's failure to do what it was expected to do and pushing it to get the job done. Many NGOs focused on human rights, women's issues, development, health, social welfare, and democracy. Reorganized or new religious groups and organizations also played increasingly central roles in many countries in the provision of services, administration of justice, advocacy, and more.

Besides these sorts of largely peaceful organizations, violent nonstate actors—including militias, terrorist groups, gangs, and even some clans and tribes—multiplied and grew in importance as well. They challenged the fundamental marker that is supposed to distinguish states from other sorts of social organizations: their monopoly over the means of violence. Anne Marie Baylouny (2008, 1), in perhaps overly alarmist language, wrote about these violent players in the Middle East.

> The Middle East appears rife with violent non-state actors operating outside domestic law and international norms. Through state incapacity, economic reforms or war, increasing areas are untouched by state services or law. Territories are becoming effectively stateless even in the geographic heart of the state itself. States considered strong (Tunisia) or rich (Saudi Arabia) are similarly affected. . . . New actors and institutions fulfill roles previously considered the preserve of the state. Gangs, militias, thugs, local men of influence, and religious political parties are the main contenders for authority. . . . They establish authority through services to the community and legitimate it in religious, identity, or violent terms.

Nonstate actors helped transform the Middle East, and they had growing indirect and direct effects on the dynamics of the region. Indirectly, they affected states themselves, sometimes positively (such as by providing services, relieving pressure on an overburdened or incompetent state apparatus) but more frequently negatively. On the negative side, nonstate actors challenged state authority, helped undermine state coherence through alliances with fragments of the state, made state borders into sieves, competed with the state for citizen loyalty, crafted important alliances with foreign states and social forces, and more. Some even precipitated civil wars. Even small nonstate actors—a warlord's entourage, an NGO—cumulatively managed to drain the blood from states through a thousand pricks.

Nonstate Actors Affecting Regional Dynamics

In terms of directly shaping the regional power dynamics of the region, a handful of violent nonstate actors, almost all of them listed as terrorist organizations by the United States, emerged as key players, helping transform the Middle East. The most notable have been the PKK (Kurdistan Workers Party), al-Qaeda, the Muslim Brotherhood, the PLO, Hezbollah, and Hamas. All of them, besides the PKK, which has been an ethnic movement, have been deeply entwined at least in one of two major issues spanning the region, and sometimes both: the Israeli-Palestinian conflict and the growing political role of Islam. All of the nonstate organizations mentioned have played important roles in their countries of origin and have had a share of cross-border influence, as well; several have broadly influenced the regional dynamics of the Middle East after the Cold War.

The PKK: Lots of Bark in Regional Affairs but Little Bite

In its struggle for Kurdish rights and autonomy, the PKK has ranged beyond Turkey, especially into Syria and the Kurdish part of Iraq, but also into Europe, where for some time it had a formidable presence. For nearly a generation starting in 1984, it waged a violent struggle against the Turkish state. Led by the formidable Abdullah Öcalan, who was captured in Kenya in 1999 and is now in a Turkish prison, the PKK has had a deep effect on Turkish social and political life. Over the years, the struggle resulted in the death of about forty thousand combatants and civilians in Turkey, but its influence on regional dynamics was and continues to be limited.

Perhaps the PKK's central effect regionally was initially to exacerbate already testy relations between Turkey and its immediate neighbors Syria and Iraq. In its early years, during the 1980s, the head of the PKK, Öcalan, set up headquarters in Syria, and PKK raiding parties took refuge in Syria's hills. Once the Syrian regime acceded to Turkish pressure to stop providing a sanctuary to PKK leaders and fighters, though, Turkish-Syrian relations improved dramatically. Only the brutal attacks by the Asad regime against its own citizens during the Arab Spring of 2011 reversed what had been increasingly close ties.

The PKK also soured Turkish-Iraqi relations, as PKK units set up bases in the Kurdish hills of Iraq, as well. Especially with the establishment of the semiautonomous Kurdish Regional Government after the U.S. invasion and the demise of Saddam Hussein in 2003, tensions grew as PKK units took shelter under the wings of fellow Kurds in Iraq. Besides their distress over the protection afforded to PKK guerrillas, the Turkish government and military cast a wary eye over the entire Kurdish enterprise in post-Saddam Iraq. They feared that Iraqi Kurdish autonomy could provoke increased mobilization and violence on the part of Turkey's own Kurds.

As the Iraqi Kurdish experiment took hold, though, it did not seem to motivate Turkish Kurds to greater violence in Turkey or in cross-border actions. What did occur was the move by Turkish Kurds to seek in-country cultural and ethnic autonomy, while recognizing and legitimating the integrity of the Turkish state—not very different from what the Iraqi Kurds had already achieved. The road to that goal has not always been smooth. From prison, Öcalan did call for an end to violence, accepting negotiations with the Turkish state. And the Turkish state, in turn, opened the door for increased (though still limited) Kurdish autonomy. Periods of calm, however, have been punctuated by acts of violence when accommodation broke down.

On a regional level, the PKK's influence dropped markedly, particularly after Öcalan's arrest. While still fraught with tension, Turkey's ties with its neighbors have improved markedly. And when tensions have flared, they could be attributed to a number of factors, but less and less to the actions of the PKK, which has faded as a regional actor. Still, the potential for an influence on regional affairs remains. An Iranian offshoot of the PKK, the PJAK (Free Life Party of Kurdistan), has been engaged in a series of violent acts against the Iranian state in recent years. While these acts have not amounted to a serious threat to Iran, the Kurdish issue, especially Kurdish unity, and the PKK's central role in the Kurdish question, remain a largely untreated sore across four states—Turkey, Syria, Iraq, and Iran.

Al-Qaeda: Reshaping America's Place in the World

As a result of its devastating attacks on American soil in September 2001, al-Qaeda became the best-known nonstate actor around the world. Founded in the late 1980s by the Saudi magnate Osama bin

Laden, the organization was an outgrowth of the resistance of mujahedeen, or Muslim guerrillas fighting in the name of God, to the 1979 Soviet invasion of Afghanistan. The mujahedeen's struggle was occasionally aided by the United States, which once again defined the immediate
events—in this case, the bloody war the mujahedeen waged against Soviet occupation—exclusively in the zero-sum calculus of the Cold War.

Anti-Soviet resistance in Afghanistan lasted for almost the entire decade of the 1980s, leading in the end to the ignominious withdrawal of
Soviet forces in 1989. The Soviet invasion and the drawn-out guerrilla
war against it gave birth to a host of new religiously based ideas, organizations, and violent capabilities, all nurtured in the remote mountains of
Afghanistan at the very moment that the Iranian Revolution was reshaping the role of Islam in the modern world ideologically and practically. I
will explore further in chapter 9 how the reconfiguration of Islam contributed mightily to the transformation of the Middle East over the last
three decades.

Once the Soviets finally withdrew from Afghanistan in 1989, the end
of the Cold War quickly helped define the new organization of al-Qaeda.
Like Saddam Hussein, al-Qaeda's leaders were alarmed at the unipolar
structure of the world, particularly the now uncontested role of the United
States in the Middle East. The Gulf War of 1990–1991 confirmed their
concerns—the emergence of the United States as an imperial power with
a permanent military presence in the Middle East. Even more galling was
the collaboration of ostensibly Muslim regimes, such as Saudi Arabia, in
bringing non-Muslim military forces to the region.

Having come from around the world to fight in Afghanistan, the mostly
young mujahedeen had seen the Soviets as infidels attempting to impose
their will by force on the Muslim world. Along with the Taliban, which
took control of Afghanistan in 1996, during the post-Soviet trauma, al-
Qaeda became the most important offspring of the struggle against the
Soviets. Now, in the post-Soviet era, some of the same mujahedeen, wiser
and more experienced, took up the banner against America's imperial
presence on Muslim soil. They directed their wrath at the United States,
Israel, and the collaborating Muslim regimes in the region. Although an
alliance with the new revolutionary regime in Iran might have seemed
logical, al-Qaeda leaders saw the Iranian brand of Shiite Islam as little
more than idolatry and thus put the Iranians onto its long list of enemies.

The United States, like the Soviets earlier, was seen by al-Qaeda operatives as composed of infidels, largely Christian, and in cahoots with Jews

and Zionists. America's intention was to impose its will on Muslims, and this belief motivated bin Laden to expand al-Qaeda beyond its base in Afghanistan, encouraging the establishment of active cells in a number of Muslim African and Arab countries, including Iraq and Yemen. The organization's notoriety derived from the international splash caused by its grand acts of terrorism outside its central base in Afghanistan. The successful and unsuccessful acts of sabotage for which it claimed responsibility or to which it was linked by others range from the attack in 2000 on the USS *Cole* in the Yemeni port of Aden, killing seventeen American sailors, to the 2010 attempt of a Nigerian to blow up a plane with 288 passengers on board.

The most spectacular attack, of course, occurred on September 11, 2001, when al-Qaeda hijackers, commandeering four commercial jets, destroyed the Twin Towers of the World Trade Center in New York and badly damaged the Pentagon. More Americans were killed on American soil that day—almost three thousand—than by any other act of international war. That single event ushered in a new era in international relations and triggered a profound transformation of the Mideast region. The United States reacted to the attacks by initiating three wars, all of them in or on the periphery of the Middle East.

The first, the War on Terror, was also called the Global War on Terror and, by the Obama administration, the Overseas Contingency Operation. Whatever its name, it became an open-ended, worldwide set of operations principally directed at eliminating al-Qaeda. It was initiated by President George W. Bush within a week of 9/11. The Bush administration and, later, the Obama administration fought the war in part by strengthening their ties with Arab dictators. U.S. military and intelligence personnel worked hand in glove with these autocrats' regimes to combat local al-Qaeda cells and, as the war dragged on, gained permission from them to use America's weapon of choice, pilotless drones, to kill al-Qaeda figures.

These operations over time had a crippling effect on al-Qaeda, severely limiting its ability to undertake grandiose acts of terror globally, although not entirely stopping some fairly autonomous cells from operating in a number of Mideast countries and elsewhere. Success for such cells seemed to be greatest where state organizations were most limited: Somalia and Yemen. The greatest success the United States had in the War on Terror was the killing of bin Laden in Pakistan, on May, 2, 2011, nearly a full decade after the 9/11 attacks. Although, as I will discuss in chapter 10, the roots of the transformed role of the United States predated

9/11, al-Qaeda's audacious actions certainly sparked America's initiation of the War on Terror.

On the heels of that war, the Bush administration also began a second war, in Afghanistan, less than a month after 9/11, on October 7, 2001. That conflict turned out to be America's longest-lasting war. Its purposes changed through time, as each goal displaced the one before it: dislodging the ruling Taliban, as well as bin Laden and al-Qaeda, which were being given shelter by the Taliban; building the Afghani state, once the Taliban was routed within weeks of the war's start, into an efficient democracy responsive to its own population; and, finally, fortifying the military capability of the state sufficiently to withstand a resurgent Taliban.

In 2003, the United States undertook its third war in nineteen months, invading Iraq and putting an end to Ba'ath dominance and the regime of Saddam Hussein. Like the War on Terror and the war in Afghanistan, the Iraq War dragged on for the rest of the decade and beyond. While the Bush administration enumerated multiple rationales for the war in Iraq, including the charge that Saddam harbored weapons of mass destruction, one of its important arguments was the ties of Saddam to al-Qaeda. As it turns out, like the claims about Iraq possessing nuclear weapons and other weapons of mass destruction, the connections of Iraq to al-Qaeda remained unsubstantiated and likely never existed. Still, al-Qaeda's influence in transforming regional dynamics stemmed not only from its isolated spectacular acts of terror but extended to the myths that it *and* the Bush administration created about it.

Perhaps no actor has had as large an influence on Mideast regional affairs as al-Qaeda. But its influence was unlike that of the other major nonstate actors, whose strength derived from their painstaking work on the ground in building constituencies and mobilizing followers as the foundation for the violence that they used. Al-Qaeda's, in contrast, came largely through its singular success on that one day, September 11, 2001. For the most part, it was unable to build significant constituencies in the region before or after 9/11 nor a sustained presence on the ground to achieve its goals of ending American influence in the region and upending American-supported regimes.

On the whole, al-Qaeda's influence on Mideast dynamics after 9/11 through its organization and acts of violence did not amount to much. The Obama administration expressed fears during the Arab Spring that the fall and weakening of leaders, such as Mubarak in Egypt and Saleh in Yemen, would open doors for al-Qaeda influence, but little evidence to date has proven those fears to be grounded in the organization's actual capabilities. Its continuing effect on regional affairs has been in the power of the myths surrounding it to sustain America's wars in the area.

The Muslim Brotherhood: An Uncertain Actor in the New Middle East

The Muslim Brotherhood, or Ikhwan, is the oldest of the major nonstate actors in the Middle East, dating back to 1928. Through its slogan "Islam is the solution," it has fought to reshape, through Islam, both state and society in a variety of Arab countries. Its long-range aim was to create pious Muslims, establish Islamic states, and then unite those states through the reconstitution of the caliphate. The Ikhwan's home base has been Egypt, where it had profound effects throughout the twentieth century, and it finally achieved power following the ousting of Mubarak, in the twenty-first century. But it has also been a major opposition force, if not *the* major opposition force, in other countries as well, spawning branches and offshoots throughout the Middle East.

After Egypt's Free Officers Revolution in 1952, which brought Nasser and his successors Sadat and Mubarak to power, the Brotherhood used a variety of means to gain strength. It preached, provided social services, engaged in acts of violence, and participated in democratic politics. In the 1950s, the Ikhwan turned toward violence as a key tool in the face of the repression and violence that Nasser's regime used against it. In the latter part of Mubarak's rule, it eschewed such violence (earning the wrath of al-Qaeda for abandoning jihad, or holy war against infidels). And it added parliamentary participation by its members to its arsenal in order to challenge Egypt's secular state.

Throughout the republican period, the Brotherhood managed to hold itself together, often to expand its base in Egypt and beyond, despite the most trying conditions. Its leadership was rounded up, jailed for long periods, and killed. Some leaders broke with the organization because of its decision to use violence to achieve its goals. In the 1980s, after nearly three decades of repression, the organization and the state both backed off, to a degree. The Brotherhood largely gave up on violence in Egypt, and the Mubarak regime, while not allowing it to organize as a political party, did enable Brotherhood candidates to run for office. In the 2005 parliamentary elections, its members won eighty-eight seats, causing deep anxiety in the Mubarak government.

Intent not to let that happen again, security forces arrested over 1,200 Brotherhood members, including five parliamentary candidates, in the run-up to the 2010 parliamentary elections. Charges against the detainees included belonging to an illegal organization, distributing publications that undermined public security, and constituting a religious party (based on their motto, "Islam is the solution"). The government rigged the elections so that not a single Brotherhood member won a seat. The Mubarak's regime extreme actions against the Brotherhood in 2010, especially the total exclusion of its candidates in the elections, further eroded the legitimacy of the regime and helped pave the way for the protests in January and February 2011, which ousted the president, and the tremendous success of the Brotherhood in the country's first free elections.

The entry of the Muslim Brotherhood into the powerful demonstrations in Tahrir Square during the protests that engulfed Egypt in January and February 2011 was actually hesitant and halting. Its established leaders, who had overcome internal opposition to effect a major change away from antiregime violence, held back as the popular protests grew. Eventually, they allowed younger members of the Ikhwan, who had argued vehemently against sitting on the sidelines, to participate and, ultimately, help lead the movement. That role helped position it to triumph in the subsequent parliamentary elections and to have one of its own, Mohammed Morsi, win the first free presidential election.

Not only has the Brotherhood had profound effects in Egypt; it has also had a significant influence on some other parts of the Middle East, such as in Jordan, through offshoots that it has spawned. Throughout the region, the Ikhwan both benefited from the retreat of states and fed that process. It benefited by stepping into the voids that the state left—providing medical, educational, and other services as well as offering a coherent ideology and sense of identity. And the Brotherhood fed the weakening of the state—opening the door to other nonstate actors—by undermining the state's claims over a monopoly of violence and as the ultimate source of law. For years, it almost singlehandedly sustained an Islamic alternative to the reigning idea of a secular Arab nationalist state, paving the way for likes of the mujahedeen in Afghanistan and the Iranian revolutionaries.

With the fall of Mubarak in Egypt and its assumption of power, the Brotherhood faces a new, uncertain future. As a participant in the demonstrations associated with the Arab Spring and in democratic elections in the region, it has spawned both popular support and fear on the part of secular, national forces. The tightrope it walked as the ruling party in Egypt was evident in its new constitution in 2012, the fierce opposition by secular forces and Copts, and, ultimately, the military coup that deposed Morsi and his party in 2013.

Moreover, it has confronted a diverse set of forces within the Islamic religious world, which have questioned the Ikhwan on any number of issues, including its willingness to defer the establishment of the caliphate, or even Islamic states, to the distant future; its rejection of violence and of jihad, at least in terms of violent struggle; its purported religious moderation; its openness to non-Muslim groups; and its willingness to defer the establishment of Islamic law as the law of the land in Egypt. I already mentioned how al-Qaeda disdainfully saw the Muslim Brotherhood as giving up on the important principle of jihad. Other jihadist groups in Egypt and elsewhere (below, for example, I will show a similar phenomenon at play for Hamas, an offshoot of the Ikhwan) have leveled similar criticism.

From another direction has come disparagement from Salafists. That name is derived from the Arabic phrase for "righteous ancestors," referring to the virtuous model presented by the first three generations of Islamic leaders after the Prophet Muhammad. Salafists have been advocates of what they claim to be the forms of practice and belief that date back to the Prophet and these early generations of Islam. They have accused the Muslim Brotherhood of accommodation to forces antithetical to the true Islam. Their success as the second most popular bloc in the first Egyptian parliamentary elections established them as a formidable counterforce to the Brotherhood.

Even within this vise of opposing forces, the Brotherhood still remains the preeminent Islamic organization among Sunni Muslims in the region. It holds the ability to wield great power in shaping the future of the Middle East, especially after its electoral success in Egypt, but it is not yet clear in which directions it will push events.

The PLO: Paving the Road for Nonstate Actors in the Middle East

The Palestine Liberation Organization, a "front" incorporating ten smaller factions, is the second oldest among the region's major nonstate actors, after the Muslim Brotherhood. Like the Brotherhood, it formed and flowered before the period in which nonstate actors proliferated in the Middle East. Its activities traversed the Arab Middle East, across a variety of countries. As an early entrant to the field of such actors and as one that insinuated itself into multiple Middle East countries, the PLO became a trendsetter, staking out how it was possible for future groups to survive and even thrive in a world of states. But it also has been an outlier, because it, along with the PKK, are the only ones of the major nonstate actors that are secular; the others all have ridden the wave of Islamic renewal, which will be discussed in chapter 9.

The PLO was created in 1964, but its emergence as a fairly autonomous organization followed the bitter defeat of the Arabs in the 1967 War. Ironically, Israel's triumph created the space for this militant, flamboyant organization to flourish. It had notable successes in the 1970s, 1980s, and 1990s and had a hand in shaping regional dynamics; it is worth noting, too, that it also had some spectacular failures, most notably its expulsions from Jordan in 1970 and Lebanon in 1982.

The PLO's triumphs did not translate into coming even remotely close to achieving its original core goal of liberating Palestine from Israeli control. Instead, its lesser successes came in three other realms. First, under the leadership of Yasser Arafat, it managed to gain important regional and international recognition, both from individual countries and international organizations. Perhaps the most famous and infamous moment came when Arafat, now recovered from his humiliation of Black September and subsequent expulsion from Jordan, addressed the General Assembly of the United Nations in 1974. Standing below the crossed olive branches of the UN seal, he lifted his arms triumphantly to thunderous applause, revealing a holstered pistol on his waist (other accounts claim all Arafat had in his holster was a pair of sunglasses). That year, the PLO achieved official observer status at the United Nations.

Second, Arafat, mostly successfully, navigated the perilous waters of Arab politics. He fought off the attempts by powerful states, including Egypt, Iraq, and (especially) Syria, to dominate the organization at one time or another. Keeping the organization autonomous when it had no permanent territorial base was no easy feat. Beyond that, it transformed a central fault line in the Middle East from the Arab-Israeli conflict to the *Palestinian*-Israeli conflict.

Third, the PLO, after bitter internal disputes within the dominant Fatah faction and between Fatah and other smaller groups, modified its core goal. By the end of the 1980s, it settled in principle for a hoped-for state in the Israel-occupied Gaza Strip and the West Bank rather than the liberation of all of what had been British Palestine. In 1988, it actually declared the State of Palestine in those occupied territories, although that declaration did not have any actual effect on the ground. But the decision, which implicitly accepted Israel's sovereignty in the territory it ruled prior to the 1967 War, led eventually to the Oslo Accords, in 1993. That agreement paved the way for the triumphant return of the organization to Palestine and the establishment of the Palestine Authority (PA), all of which have had effects throughout the region.

While the PLO did not actually bring Israeli occupation to an end or achieve a Palestinian state in a practical sense, it did manage to govern Palestinians through the PA. Those successes in the twentieth century, however, were precarious. Starting in 2000, the PLO engaged in its own near self-immolation. It encouraged and organized the al-Aqsa intifada, a major uprising against Israeli occupation, which ended up decimating the PA's fragile infrastructure. And through internal fighting, blatant corruption, and its weak response to the challenge posed by Hamas, it came perilously close in the 2000s to losing its previously unquestioned status, validated by both the Arab League Rabat Conference and the United Nations, as the "sole legitimate representative of the Palestinian people."

But in its heyday the PLO enjoyed some remarkable achievements. It succeeded in putting the Palestinian plight at the top of the regional agenda and keeping it there. Eventually, it was able to overcome Israel's refusal to recognize or negotiate with it. While it did not actually manage to create a Palestinian state, the PLO gained widespread international recognition, including in Israel, for the *idea* of such a state. Through its international recognition, its ability to remain autonomous, and its success in becoming a governing power, the PLO demonstrated that violent nonstate actors could go far in shaping the dynamics of the Middle East.

While their situations were different in many respects, both Hezbollah and Hamas followed the PLO's lead in moving from being largely violent organizations to ones engaged in domestic politics, governance, and international negotiations, even as they still maintained and flouted their fighting character. And they have equaled or possibly surpassed the PLO in terms of popular appeal in the region. As Alastair Crooke writes, "Hezbollah and Hamas have seized the imagination of Muslims everywhere" (Tamimi 2007, ix).

Hezbollah: A Rising Star Among Nonstate Actors

The creation of Hezbollah, which means the "party of God," as a formidable violent nonstate actor came out of the deep abyss of Lebanon's fifteen-year civil war starting in 1975. As the central Lebanese state all but disappeared (its effective rule limited to a few hundred square meters in Beirut) and the Lebanese Armed Forces collapsed, multiple sectarian militias became the central actors in the country. The Shiites of Lebanon were among the poorest, fastest growing, and most oppressed groups in the country, and Hezbollah emerged after Israel's invasion of Lebanon in 1982 to represent them in the bitter conflict pitting the country's religious sects against one another and to resist Israel. Its animus was principally for the right-wing Christian Lebanese Phalangists and for Israel, but early on it made clear that it wanted to transform Lebanon entirely into an Islamic regime modeled on Iran. It signed onto Ayatollah Khomeini's idea of much broader Islamic political rule.

In the 1980s, Hezbollah made its mark through violence. It organized its Shiite recruits into an effective militia. It contended with the more established Amal organization for political supremacy among the Shiites. And it clashed with the Israeli-supported South Lebanon Army in the southern part of the country, where Shiites were concentrated. Additionally, although it usually did not take credit for them, Hezbollah used suicide attacks and kidnappings as key weapons during the civil war, including against the United States.

Once the Taif Agreement of 1990 brought an end to Lebanese civil strife, Hezbollah assumed a more complex profile. It certainly did not forsake violence. On the contrary, with Syrian backing, it was the single militia in Lebanon to snub the Taif Agreement's stipulation to disarm and disband all militias. It held onto its firepower and continued stocking up on more and better weapons. By 1997, Hezbollah forces were engaged in ongoing actions against Israel, which continued to occupy a strip of southern Lebanon. Those deadly attacks demoralized Israelis and eventually induced Israel to abandon Lebanon altogether in 2000. Only a postage-size strip of land, called Shebaa Farms, remained in Israel's hands, claimed for Lebanon by Hezbollah.

At the same time, Hezbollah assumed a much more social-political character. It expanded its cultural and social activities: vastly enlarging its social service network; creating a television station, al-Manar, which now operates in a number of countries around the world; and even entering the field of film production. While never turning its back on religion—on the contrary, power in the organization has continued to be vested almost exclusively in local religious leaders, who generally look to Iran's supreme religious leaders for guidance—the movement became deeply involved in Shiites' everyday problems, ranging from educating their children to finding adequate health care.

On the political level, with the blessing of Shiite Supreme Leader Ali Khamenei of Iran, who had succeeded Ayatollah Khomeini, Hezbollah entered Lebanon's electoral fray as a political party. Tactically, at least, it dropped its goal of turning Lebanon into an Iran-style Islamic republic while still maintaining that Lebanon's antiquated confessional agreements had to be abandoned. Over time, under the leadership of Sheikh Hassan Nasrallah, it became the single most powerful political organization in the country. Domestically, it established a coalition with other sectarian parties—the so-called March 8 Alliance. From 2008, it directly participated in the Lebanese government, holding nearly a third of the cabinet positions. And in 2011, much to the distress of the United States, it became the leading party in the government.

Even as Hezbollah assumed a parliamentary role, it did not shy away from the use of violence in Lebanon. Hezbollah operatives were implicated in the assassination of Lebanese Prime Minister Rafiq Hariri in 2005. For a time after the February assassination, it appeared as if that violence might backfire. The so-called Cedar Revolution seemed to reign in Hezbollah, forcing Syrian troops to be withdrawn from Lebanon. Hezbollah appeared to lose a powerful ally. Later, the Special Tribunal for Lebanon, an international court set up in 2009 to prosecute, under Lebanese law, those responsible for the assassination, presented four secret arrest warrants to Lebanese officials in 2011. Those names quickly became public, with the tribunal pointing its finger at four top Hezbollah leaders as responsible for the murder. Nasrallah quickly denied the allegations and denounced the legitimacy of the tribunal. But Hezbollah rebounded from the short-lived Cedar Revolution. In 2008, it again resorted to violence, enabling it to cement a powerful position inside volatile Lebanese politics. It went so far as to seize control of parts of Beirut in deadly fighting in May of that year, which it referred to as its Glorious Day.

But by the 1990s and especially in the 2000s, Hezbollah was more than simply a domestic powerhouse in Lebanon; it was also a notable international actor deeply affecting the Middle East as a whole. It found that it could lean heavily on Syria, even if Syrian troops were no longer in Lebanon, and it continued to line up with Iran, as well. In 2006, Argentine prosecutors charged Hezbollah with acting on behalf of Iran in bombing a Jewish Center in Argentina in 1994. Similarly, in April 2009, the Egyptian government arrested what it identified as a Hezbollah cell operating inside Egypt.

Its most notable international achievement, though, came in the brutal war it fought with Israel in 2006. In that war, both Hezbollah and Lebanon as a whole suffered massive damage, but the organization's strategy of hurling rockets into Israel also deeply disrupted Israeli society, even if it did not cause many casualties or physical damage. Many Israelis, for all the destruction their army rained on Lebanon and the limited damage they themselves experienced, saw the war as a defeat for their country. Hezbollah's mere survival against the formidable Israeli military machine and its ability to keep firing rockets at Israel even in the face of massive bombing and a large ground invasion drove home its claim of a "divine victory." The 2006 war made Hezbollah and Nasrallah the darlings of much of the Arab world. It retained that status until the bloody Syrian civil war that began in the Arab Spring in 2011. Hezbollah's active support of the Asad regime drew criticism across the Arab world.

All in all, Hezbollah has ranged far from its home in southern Lebanon. It has managed to become one of the most important forces over the last two decades in the new Middle East.

Hamas

Like Hezbollah, Hamas (an acronym for the Islamic Resistance Movement) exploded onto the Middle East scene in the late 1980s as a largely violent, religious nonstate actor and then gradually transformed itself into a multilayered social-political organization. It followed Hezbollah, too, in never abandoning its violent core; it continued to maintain a strong fighting component through its military command even as it branched into social services and electoral politics. And, like Hezbollah, it has become a major Mideast actor, principally in homegrown Palestinian and Israeli-Palestinian affairs but also on the broader tableau of the region.

Hamas's genesis was in Israeli prisons, where many young Palestinian resisters languished in the early 1980s, using their time to establish personal bonds that went beyond traditional kinship groups and plotting the end of Israeli occupation and the demise of Israel altogether. The formal organization was formed in 1987 in Gaza by Sheikh Ahmed Yassin as an offshoot of Egypt's Muslim Brotherhood. It was designed explicitly to engage in active resistance during the first Palestinian intifada, a stone-throwing uprising against Israeli occupation that began in December 1987 and went on for at least four years (Abu-Amr 1993, 5). Hamas adopted the position that, rather than waiting for the creation of an Islamic republic that would eventually free Palestine of Jewish control, the act itself of liberating Palestine would pave the way for an Islamic republic and a full-fledged Muslim way of life (Zuhur 2008, 46).

The rise of Hamas to the ranks of significant regional actors stemmed from its actions on two fronts, one in the fight against Israel and the other in intra-Palestinian affairs. Its primary goal has been the destruction of Israel and the liberation of Palestine, and it has promoted the idea of a popular uprising of Palestinians in the occupied territories as well as its own armed resistance as the means to that end. It issued its own pamphlets addressed to the population in the intifada and planned its own actions, but for the most part Hamas worked side by side with the local secular leadership and the PLO during the 1987–1991 uprising (Mishal and Sela 2006). During its gestation in the 1980s, it benefited from a light hand by Israel, as Israeli officials regarded the development of an internal opposition to the PLO positively.

But when the PLO accepted Israel's existence in the 1993 Oslo Accords—and, even before, when it indicated it would accept Israel and create a Palestinian state only in the West Bank and Gaza Strip—Hamas registered strong opposition, establishing itself as the primary counterweight to the PLO. In Israeli officials' eyes, Hamas leapfrogged the PLO as Israel's biggest nonstate threat, especially after Hamas began its campaign of suicide bombings in Israel after the signing of the Oslo Agreement. Hamas's position was that all of Palestine was a Muslim trust and that not a millimeter of it could be ceded to a non-Muslim entity. Israel's very existence was prima facie illegitimate and unacceptable.

With Hamas often outperforming the PLO in the intifada in the 1980s and in the provision of social services to the Palestinian population, what Mishal and Sela (1994, 2006) call its "winning card," it created the basis for powerful opposition to Arafat and the PLO after the signing of the Oslo Accords in 1993 (Kristianasen 1999, Knudsen 2005). Hamas labeled the accords a sellout and successfully used a variety of means, including multiple deadly suicide bombings, which it designated as "martyrdom operations," to sabotage them. At the same time, its leaders, particularly those based in the Gaza Strip, rhetorically attenuated their positions sufficiently—including floating the concept of a long-term ceasefire with Israel as early as 1994—so as to avoid all-out conflict with the PLO and to gain international recognition.

As time went on, even with Israel's killing of much of its top leadership, including Sheikh Yassin, the Hamas strategy of resistance gained in popularity as a "national agenda." In stark contrast, the PLO's strategy of negotiating with Israel, particularly during the long, difficult years of talks and implementation following the signing of the Oslo Accords, did not seem to yield the Palestinians many tangible gains (Hroub 2004). Israel's steady onslaught against Hamas leaders and operatives induced a portion of the leadership to set up shop first in Jordan and, once that country began to move toward a peace treaty with Israel, in Syria. Hamas's chief, Khaled Meshal, the most notable of these external leaders, used his platform in Syria to help establish Hamas as a rival to the PLO and spokesperson for the Palestinian resistance not only in Palestine but on the larger regional and even international stage.

Hamas, in brief, employed a triple strategy, which gradually moved it into the front ranks of Middle East nonstate actors. First, it continued using violent means, especially suicide bombings and, later, mobile rockets to strike at Israel. Second, the organization skillfully set itself apart from the PLO and PA through its "national agenda" of resistance and successful social services. During the mid-2000s, it was broadly perceived by Palestinians in Gaza—and in the West Bank, to a degree—as the honest provider, compared to the corrupt PLO. And third, it stayed within the framework of broader Palestinian institutions, competing against PLO lists and others in student and trade-union elections.

It flirted with the idea of participating in the 1996 PA legislative elections as well, but in the end it decided to endorse rather than directly field candidates. Hamas leaders hoped that this sort of democratic participation would help ease the international boycott against the organization and gain it international recognition and legitimacy (Tamimi 2007, 215). It finally took the plunge and participated directly in municipal elections in 2004–2005 and, then, later in 2006, in the all-important PA legislative elections. Those general elections turned out to be a watershed: it received 44 percent of the votes (against 41 percent for Fatah, the primary PLO faction). Hamas won a large majority of seats in the parliament.

Throughout 2005, as those elections drew near, tensions flared between Fatah and Hamas. Mahmoud Abbas, the successor to Arafat (who had died in 2004) as the Palestine Authority president and chairman of the PLO, even postponed the elections. And the conflict only worsened once the elections finally took place and Hamas emerged victorious. Lame-duck Fatah legislators granted Abbas vast new powers in anticipation of the Hamas majority in the parliament, and the president used his position to deny the Hamas-run government control of key institutions, setting up his own kind of parallel government, snubbing the Hamas electoral victory. Israel and Abbas's allies in the United States and Europe imposed economic sanctions on the Hamas-led government, seeking to strangle it.

Suddenly, Hamas was at the center of a whirlwind of international and regional events. Russia and Turkey invited Hamas leaders for talks, legitimating their standing. Jordan, after a tentative step toward rapprochement with Hamas, accused it of planning violent attacks inside Jordan, precipitating a full-fledged crisis between them. Egypt and Saudi Arabia tried to act as mediators between the Fatah and Hamas factions. Abbas's call for new elections was the breaking point. After a Saudi-brokered agreement failed (for which Hamas earned deep Saudi enmity), a fierce civil war between Fatah and Hamas erupted in the streets of Gaza in June 2007, with more than one hundred people killed.

By routing Fatah forces from Gaza, Hamas became a nonstate actor in charge of actual governing institutions, the rump institutions in Gaza of the Palestine Authority (Gunning 2008). These institutions were much more autonomous than those in the West Bank, where Abbas and the PLO kept control, because the Israelis unilaterally had disengaged from Gaza in 2005. For the last few years, Hamas has had two distinct faces: a nonstate actor and the government of Gaza. These roles have not always meshed well and have been a mixed blessing for Hamas. Its role as the governing body for Gaza helped establish the group as a force that no one in the Middle East could ignore and gained it increasing but still severely limited international legitimacy. But it also led to the crushing attack against it by Israel in the 2008–2009 Gaza War, which held it responsible for a barrage of missiles fired on Sderot and other Israeli towns from Gaza. The Israeli rationale was much the same in 2012, when it bombarded Gaza. An Egyptian-brokered ceasefire headed off an Israeli land invasion on this occasion. Unlike Hezbollah, Hamas broke with the Asad regime during the bloody Syrian civil war and, as a result, inched away from Iran and toward the new Muslim Brotherhood regime in Egypt (which, ironically, did not accept Hamas's embrace as warmly as Hamas leaders had hoped).

In the years to come, Hamas will remain a central cog in Middle Eastern affairs. Its success among Palestinians has rested on the social services it has provided and on its alternative national agenda at a time when there has been loss of faith in a negotiated settlement with Israel. As a nonstate actor, it articulated its central premises about the future, which, if effected, will touch not only Palestinians but Israelis, others in the Middle East, and the United States, as well. Those premises included

> a commitment to territorial maximalism with an eye toward the establishment of an Islamic state throughout all of Mandatory Palestine—and on the wreckages of the state of Israel. This vision replaces the political realism that accepts the framework of a two-state solution: Israel alongside a Palestinian state. . . . [Its] perception of the Palestinian-Israeli conflict [is] as a predetermined clash of destinies, instead of a conflict over boundaries.
>
> (Mishal and Sela 2006)

But as it has been drawn into elections, the institutions of the Palestine Authority, and, then, actually governing Gaza, Hamas has demonstrated a pragmatic side, at least rhetorically. Khaled Meshal and other leaders have indicated at various moments that while the organization is not ready to recognize Israel, it may be prepared to accept the coexistence of a Palestinian and Israeli state. In 2007, for example, he declared at a news conference, "There will remain a state called Israel. . . . The problem is not that there is an entity called Israel. The problem is that the Palestinian state is non-existent. . . . As a Palestinian today I speak of a Palestinian and Arab demand for a state on 1967 borders. It is true that in reality there will be an entity or state called Israel on the rest of Palestinian land" (Macguire and Owels 2007). At other times, though, as in the aftermath of the 2012 Israel-Hamas clash, when Meshal visited the Gaza Strip for the first time, he sounded an uncompromising line, demanding and predicting Israel's demise.

Hamas's place in the dynamics of the region are assured, but powerful forces pull it in opposing directions: toward accommodation with Israel and acceptance of the secular PA institutions, on one side, and toward wiping out Israel and establishing an Islamic republic, on the other. Some

Arabs have castigated Hamas for establishing Taliban-like rule in Gaza and have appealed to it to move from an extremist stance (Alhomayed 2009). In the same vein, Arab states, the American government, Europeans, and others have pulled the organization toward accommodation with Israel. Egypt, Turkey, and Saudi Arabia have all leaned on Hamas to reconcile with Fatah and accept the secular PA institutional framework.

At the same time, hardcore political Islamic activists have put pressure on Hamas to live up to its original premises, just as the Muslim Brotherhood has come under such criticism in Egypt. In 2009, for example, a group calling itself Jund Ansar Allah (Soldier of God) announced the establishment of the Islamic Emirate of Palestine, which would enforce Islamic law throughout Palestine. It accused Hamas of actually being a secular organization that falsely claimed an Islamic agenda, much as the Turkish AKP has done. Hamas responded violently, killing the leader of the group and his followers, but the incident demonstrated the tightrope that Hamas has to walk and the pressure it faces if it veers toward acceptance of secular institutions for Palestinians or from the ultimate goal of destroying Israel.

Conclusion

Changing and diverging state-society relations in the Middle East paved the way for the transformation of the central dynamics of the region. The top dogs, the fault lines of conflict, the explosive issues in the region, and the nature of the players all changed dramatically during the last quarter of the twentieth century. Chapter 7 analyzed the flip-flop of the region's leading powers—the sinking of the Arab core states and the rise of the three non-Arab states.

The stagnation of Arab politics in the Middle East not only helped lead to the turnaround in which non-Arab states rose to the top; it also prompted the emergence of powerful, violent nonstate actors. Hezbollah, Hamas, and al-Qaeda—the most disruptive of these nonstate players in recent years—have been labeled as terrorist organizations in the West, and there is no doubt that brutal violence specifically directed at civilians has been an important part of their repertoire. But in the cases of Hezbollah and Hamas, that designation belies the many other facets of these organizations that have thrust them into the central dynamics of the region. Neither has exerted the influence that the most powerful Mideast states have, but they both have been important elements in the transformation of the area. As the political scientist Barak Mendelsohn (2009, 2) has shown, globally the challenge posed by nonstate actors goes beyond violence or "the targeting of specific states for specific grievances to a rejection of the foundations of the Westphalian state-based order." On a regional level as well, the nonstate actors challenged the primacy of the Mideast state system in defining areawide dynamics.

U.S. foreign-policy officials dealing with the Middle East were drawn willy-nilly into the fallout of the 1967 War, the Iranian Revolution, and the demise of the Soviet Union. But they tended to be somewhat myopic in viewing these events, focusing on the immediate issues of occupation, hostages, and the like. Far less attention was paid to how these events became catalysts for the steady drip of change that ultimately transformed the Middle East regional system. Those incremental changes led to a new set of leading powers and to a new set of nonstate players who would shape the region in the early twenty-first century.

9   A Changing Islam and the Rise of the Islamic Republic of Iran

The factors analyzed in the last two chapters, the changing of the guard from the Arab to the non-Arab states and the empowerment of nonstate actors, were two crucial ingredients in changing the face of the Middle East. This chapter continues the analysis of the emergence of a newly transformed Middle East after the Cold War, exploring factors rooted less in institutions, like states and nonstate actors, and more in ideology and faith.

At the heart of these shifts has been a transformed Islam. While Islam historically has not ever undergone the sort of volcanic reformation that Christianity has, it nonetheless experienced deep changes in its history, particularly over the last two centuries. The engagement with modernity, including the ideas and forces of the Enlightenment, capitalism, and European colonialism and imperialism, has had lasting and far-reaching effects on Muslims personally and on Islam as a way of life and religion. Iza Hussin (forthcoming) has documented, for example, how the core of the religion, Islamic law, underwent major refashioning during the colonial period.

Islam has been transformed over the last two centuries. The system practiced as "Islamic law" in every state with Muslim majorities or

significant minorities changed from an uncodified and locally administered set of legal institutions and laws with wide-ranging jurisdiction to a codified, state-centered system with jurisdiction over
family law. For Muslims, this change was monumental, relegating
Islamic law to the private sphere and redefining the relationship
between Islam and state authority.

Islam did not stop evolving after the colonial and immediate postcolonial periods. Over the last generation, two changes within Islam became
important parts of the brew that transformed the dynamics of the Middle
East. First, a wave of renewed Sunni Islamic religiosity, often with a particular twist, swept through the region like a tsunami. A new brand of
Salafism marked a call for a "return" of Islam to original tenets and practices and for a purification through the abandonment of wayward, Western ways. Salafists have been literalists in terms of interpreting ancient
texts. Many have focused on the transformation of the individual and
have eschewed violence or even politics altogether. But, alongside this pious, nonpolitical Salafism has grown an overtly political and sometimes
violent brand of Islam.

This adaptation of Islam, what we can call political Islam, sought major political change. Those advocating political Islam have, like the nonpolitical Salafists, also pushed for spiritual purification, but their aim
has also been to win political authority. The key has been the assertion
that Islam can be the basis for political rule today. Political Islam has
called for the establishment of a new hybrid—Islamic republics. These
principles of Salafists and political Islam became the most powerful motivating ideas in the Middle East (and beyond) in the latter decades of the
twentieth century, displacing Arab nationalism as the primary ideology
that mobilized Arab publics.

A second change in Islam came in redefining the fault line between
the religion's two principal sects, Sunnis and Shiites. In many places
where the two sects had comingled, that line had long been marked by
Sunni dominance. But since the early 1980s, the long subservient Shiites,
spurred by the success of the Iranian Revolution, have become increasingly assertive across the region.

This chapter explores these two changes and how they contributed to
transforming the dynamics of the area. It then turns to how the institutional ingredients discussed in chapters 7 and 8, the new regional powers
and the growing importance of nonstate actors, mixed with the ideas and

beliefs discussed in this chapter, the rise of political Islam and the Shiites, to create an entirely new power configuration. If in the old dynamics
of the Middle East it was Egypt that sat at the center of the power configuration, as the principal focus on almost every front, in the new regional
configuration it is Iran that is poised in the eye of the storm.

The Heyday of Arab Nationalism

The postwar era was unequivocally the age of Arab nationalism
in the Middle East. Non-nationalist regimes, such as the monarchies,
emirates, and Lebanon's multiconfessional arrangement, were on the
defensive throughout the 1950s and 1960s and beyond. The pressure on
them was both on the international and domestic levels. In the region,
the old regimes came under tremendous political and military challenges
from neighboring popular-style nationalist regimes. And at home they
faced an increasingly mobilized public, especially involving young educated Arabs who were deeply dedicated to the tenets of pan-Arabism. Indeed, Arab nationalism was the single most powerful force in the Arab
world, one capable of mobilizing huge numbers of people throughout
the region. In the nationalists' thinking, all Arabic-speaking people were
organically connected and formed the basis for the nationalists' core goal,
Arab political unity (Dawisha 2003, 2).

The idea of creating a single modern Arab state began to take root during the latter part of the nineteenth century. Early Arab nationalists of the
Ottoman period generally had aimed, at least initially, for an expansion
of Arab autonomy within the empire, rather than demanding outright
independence. They were clearly influenced by the power of nationalist
sentiments and ferment in Europe and the growth of purposive nationalist movements, especially in Eastern Europe, challenging the Austro-
Hungarian, Ottoman, and Russian empires.

But the true watershed for the Arab nationalists was World War I. That
cataclysmic conflagration and Woodrow Wilson's promotion, after the
war, of self-determination as a central organizing principle of world politics were major turning points. A number of factors converged to make
the idea of a unitary Arab state in the Middle East conceivable. First, all
those empires in which nationalism had incubated during the late nineteenth and early twentieth century finally crumbled, splintering into what
were supposed to be multiple national states. What was most important

to the Arabs, of course, was the disintegration of the Ottoman Empire. Turkish dominance of the Arab lands suddenly came to an abrupt end.

A second factor spurring the imagination of nationalist Arabs was Britain's signing onto the notion of Arab self-rule, even before the fall of the Ottomans. The Arab Revolt against the Ottoman Empire, starting in 1916, was the quid pro quo for British backing of a unified Arab state. British letters—the famous McMahon Correspondence—all but assured the creation of a state in Arab lands in the event that the British prevailed in World War I, which they, of course, did.

Third, the initial successes of Zionism created a beachhead in the Arab heartland, particularly through the 1917 Balfour Declaration, affirming Britain's support for the construction of a Jewish national home in Palestine (in contradiction to its promises to the Arabs). The early gains of Zionism alarmed Arab elites, further mobilizing them to insure their own control of Arab-majority areas.

Fourth, colonialism and anticolonialism became central motifs in the region after World War I and thus inserted the Middle East into a budding worldwide maelstrom. And with European occupation and colonial control came anticolonial, nationalist ferment. The League of Nations created so-called Mandates in Iraq (the Mandate of Mesopotamia, as it was called), Palestine, Trans-Jordan (lopped off from Palestine), and Syria and Lebanon following the Ottoman demise. This barely disguised colonialism meant that the Arab areas were denied sovereignty, no matter what the British had promised during the war.

Arab territories were now, in effect, British and French colonies. And while the mandates assured inhabitants that their existence as independent nations could be *provisionally* recognized, the League of Nations, under the direction of the imperialist powers—including, of course, Britain—deemed these countries as still incapable of standing on their own. Britain's promises to the Arabs and the Jews notwithstanding, the promise that it actually fulfilled was one made to the French, and it contradicted its official assurances to the Arabs and Jews. The Sykes-Picot Agreement was a British secret deal with the French in 1916 to divide the Arab Middle East between them once the Ottoman Empire collapsed.

Britain and France became the new colonial powers, even if those colonies were dubbed mandates, with direct rule over the Arab heartland. The mandatory powers did later grant formal sovereignty to the Arabs, as in Iraq in 1932, but de facto the Europeans remained the preeminent powers in the former mandates. In Egypt, too, where no mandate existed,

Britain retained a strong hand in ruling the country during the inter-war years, even if it no longer officially remained an occupying power. The strong British presence was the target of Egypt's popular uprising in 1919, and it was an important factor in the strongly nationalist Free Officers Revolution in 1952.

Not surprisingly, all these sorts of European arrangements and du-plicity—mandates, ownership of the Suez Canal, informal occupation, contradictory agreements—led to increased frustration by Arabs and growing strife between the imperial powers and the local population. Murmurings among educated Arabs, particularly, began almost as soon as World War I and the 1919 Paris Peace Conference, or Versailles (which was a great disappointment to Arabs), was over. Arab nationalism, while still inchoate, began to gain momentum, eventually turning into the rallying call across the expanse of the Arab Middle East. In 1925 in Syria, the French encountered "the largest, longest, and most destructive of the Arab Middle Eastern revolts" (Provence 2005, 12). This anticolonial uprising, which included workers and peasants as much as intellectuals, foreshadowed post–World War II Arab nationalism in its ability to bridge regions, classes, and sects in Syria. It was the first and longest-lasting anticolonial insurgency in the Middle East.

Similarly, Great Britain faced powerful resistance in Iraq. The British had expected their hand-selected leader in Iraq, Faisal, the military head of the Arab Revolt in 1916, to be pliant. In actuality, he created a hotbed of nationalist thinking in the country. The key figure was Faisal's minister of education, Sati al-Husri, who became the foremost theorist of Arab nationalist thought, fleshing out the bare-bones Arab nationalist ideas circulating in the 1920s (Dawisha 2003, 48–74). Later, British domination was challenged in the bitter Anglo-Iraqi War, in May 1941, when the British finally ended up reoccupying the country in order to maintain their influence.

In short, the interwar years reshaped nationalist ideology and nationalist stirrings globally, as these movements became part and parcel of anticolonial, anti-imperial agitation. And in this the Middle East was no different from any other decolonizing region; it too was feeding off the sentiments pulsating throughout Africa and Asia. Arab nationalism became a true, complex ideology, with a sophisticated set of ideas tying it together. Just as important, it began to spread from a small group of intellectuals to the broad Arabic-speaking population, motivating them to take action against Western control and influence. Additionally, all these fires of anticolonial and anti-imperial agitation were fanned by the hopes generated by Wilson's doctrine of self-determination and by British promises to the Arabs during World War I, as well as by the fear engendered by the Zionist project.

After World War II, the expansion of Arab nationalism's reach accelerated rapidly. The now well-honed ideas produced a brand of nationalism in the region that reached well beyond select elites—who had often been minority Christians (such as Michel Aflaq, a founder of the nationalist Ba'ath Party, which eventually came to rule both Syria and Iraq). Arab nationalism became the stuff of the Arab street, as well, boasting adherents from across the social spectrum, lower classes and upper classes, Muslims and Christians. More than any other set of ideas, it could mobilize and unite Arab publics throughout the Middle East, from Morocco to Yemen.

Two events helped cement Arab nationalism as the ruling idea in the region after the war. First was the 1948–1949 Arab-Israeli War surrounding the creation of the state of Israel. The humiliating defeat of the combined Arab armies in that war precipitated agitation against the corrupt regimes whose armies had stumbled so badly in battle, leading eventually to the demise of a number of governments. Out of that war came the region's most important change, Nasser's regime in Egypt. It was the pitiful performance of the Egyptian state in that war that had galvanized the Free Officers, who undertook the coup led by Nasser. The first Arab-Israeli War also produced the issue that stirred the Arab street and united Arabs across the region, al-Naqba, the catastrophic displacement that befell the Arabs of Palestine (Kimmerling 2004). From 1948 until today, the Palestinian plight became the single issue that could unite Arabs of every stripe. The feelings that al-Naqba engendered have been truly heartfelt, from the western tip of North Africa all the way to the Persian Gulf. In the minds of Arabs everywhere, the demise of Palestinian political institutions and society demanded that a unified, powerful Arab state, the product of Arab nationalism, would step in as the solution for restoring Palestinian rights.

The second event leading to the deep and broad adoption of Arab nationalism was Nasser's nationalization of the Suez Canal in 1956. This brazen act, in defiance of the European powers that had dominated the region in the interwar years and that still exerted considerable influence more than a decade after World War II, electrified the broad Arab public. Nasser's ability to survive the subsequent Suez War in 1956 and withstand the British-French-Israeli attempt to return the canal to European control made his bold action of seizing the canal the high-water mark of Arab nationalism. Indeed, the British failure in 1956 in taking on Nasser and the subsequent wave of Arab nationalist-inspired unrest in British-supported regimes over the next two years spelled the end of Britain's forty-year "moment" in the Middle East, to use Hourani's word (quoted in the foreword of Seale 1986; Dawisha 2003, 173). A scholar of Arab nationalism characterized this period of nationalist success: "The old world was crumbling: traditional values and customs were questioned, old patterns of authority were coming increasingly under attack, and Nasirist Arab nationalism was leading the assault everywhere in the Arab world, even in its remotest areas and most traditional parts" (Dawisha 2003, 173).

If anything could be singled out as the marker characterizing the Middle East in the postwar era, it was Arab nationalism and its drive for a pan-Arab state. It led Palestinians to place their hope of upending Israel in the hands of the Arab nationalist regimes; it rocked the streets of Baghdad, Beirut, and Amman in 1958; it established the power of the Ba'ath Party in both Syria and Iraq; and it contributed to the civil wars in Yemen and Lebanon. In 1958, just two years after the nationalization of the canal and the humiliation of the British and French, Arab nationalists seemed on the cusp of fulfilling their dream of a single Arab state. Nasser's Egypt joined with Syria to erase the imperialist-created boundaries, creating a unified Arab nationalist state, the United Arab Republic (UAR).

For the United States, Arab nationalism posed immense challenges. Its hopes of fortifying the Middle East against Soviet influence through the creation of a NATO-like military alliance foundered on tensions between America's monarchical allies and the new nationalist regimes. And while the nationalist regimes joined the Non-Aligned Movement, in practice they inched closer to the USSR and openly attacked U.S. imperialism. Until the 1970s, the United States was left with a ragtag team of allies in the region, including the vulnerable monarchies and universally despised Israel. It was the Soviets that found in Arab nationalism a new lever for influence in the area.

But as the twentieth century wore on, Arab nationalism lost steam. The UAR remained intact for only three years and was dissolved in 1961, with fingers pointing in every direction. Over the next few years, there were starts and stops toward a new unified Arab state involving Egypt, Iraq, and Syria, but these efforts, too, devolved into bickering and inaction. More than any other factor, though, the 1967 Arab-Israeli War rocked Arab nationalism badly, both as an ideology motivating the Arab public and an ascendant political movement. Over the rest of the century, its influence in high politics and in the hearts of common people throughout the region steadily waned. Nasser died three years after the 1967 War, robbing the movement of its most charismatic leader. Under his successor, Anwar Sadat, Egypt began to put Egyptian interests ahead of general Arab interests. The nationalist Ba'athist regimes in Syria and Iraq became bitter enemies. Increasingly after 1967, Arab unity seemed to most an unattainable goal. Palestinians despaired that Arab nationalism could ever recover their rights, and they proceeded to take matters into their own hands, rather than wait for Arab political unity.

The Move to Islamic Militancy

Arab nationalism has been a modernist movement from the time that it was first conceived in the nineteenth century. Even as it associated with the larger anticolonial and anti-imperial streams in the Third World after World War II, it never lost its fundamental modernist dimensions. Its thinkers railed not against the universalist impulses of the Enlightenment but the particularistic expressions of those principles by imperialist Europeans asserting their own innate superiority. Arab nationalists embraced rationalism, human equality, and secularism.

The downward slide of Arab nationalism after 1967 opened the door for the domination of the region by a different ideology, political Islam, which rejected many of those same Enlightenment tenets. Political Islam was a set of ideas grounded in faith and religious practice, rather than rationalism; in hierarchies expressing differences between believers and others and between the sexes, rather than blanket human equality; and in the centrality of the authority of religion in both explaining how the world works and in state governance, rather than secularism.

The appeal of political Islam across countries and social classes has been remarkable, especially in the wake of an age that was declaring the death of God and religion. Its proponents did draw on many modern principles and practices in various facets of everyday life—from organization to technology. But much of its appeal lay in its rejection not only of European domination and arrogance but also of fundamental Western ideas and practices about individual and social life.

Those ideas and practices seemed to have accomplished little in improving the lot of most Muslims in the Middle East. Political Islam spoke to the deep sense of disappointment palpable through much of the Middle East and in different social classes about what the postcolonial period had wrought. And much of the blame for that disappointment was placed at the feet of modernist ideas, leading to a rejection of Western ways as well as disillusionment with Arab nationalism.

Political Islam's appeal has rested on a solid foundation of already existing Islamic faith and practice across the Middle East and beyond. Nationalists in the 1950s and 1960s had proclaimed the triumph of secularism. But most of the population, while often responding to the appeal and mobilizing power of Arab political unity, had still remained deeply steeped in Islamic practice and faith. What was different in the 1980s and after was the ability of the new adherents of political Islam to construct broad, successful movements asserting that a purified Islam rid of polluting Western ideas could be the basis for the political and social organization of Muslims *and* their states in the contemporary world.

And if anything demonstrated the actual potential of such an audacious idea, it was the creation of the Iranian Islamic Republic. The success of political Islam in overtaking Arab nationalism as the dominant motivator and mobilizer in the region started, ironically enough, in a non-Arab setting, Iran. Even more paradoxically, it began outside the dominant Sunni sect, among minority Shiites, who for centuries had been looked down upon by many Sunnis. If the 1967 War demonstrated to people across the region the ineffectiveness of the Arab nationalist solution, the Iranian Revolution did the opposite: it showed that political Islam could actually be realized and that Islam could be the basis of a contemporary, effective state. Ayatollahs in Iran took an age-old ethos, as Roy Mottahedeh (2009, 7) put it, and subjected it to an internal intellectual revolution, making it the basis for contemporary Islamic political rule. This act was the foundation for a new optimism, even among non-Shiites: that Islam could provide the political agenda for the future of Muslims.

For Ayatollah Khomeini, the Iranian Revolution was but the first step in establishing what he was confident would be an Islamic world order. Like the great modern revolutions that preceded it—the French, Russian, and Chinese—the Iranian Revolution, in the Ayatollah's theology, had to direct the energies of the revolutionaries outward, beyond the boundaries of the country, as well as inward—changing the larger world as well as themselves. Indeed, early on, one scholar labeled the Khomeini-led efforts an ideological crusade (Ramazani 1986, 2), and in many ways it became just that. Much of Khomeini's theological understanding of the eventual creation of an Islamic world order was grounded in the specifics of Shiite thinking:

> To the *faqih* [the preeminent figure who brings an understanding of Islamic law] belongs temporal as well as spiritual authority, which he should exercise in the absence of the Twelfth Imam [the critical historical and mythical figure distinguishing Shia from Sunni thought], who will appear (*zuhur*) ultimately as the *Mahdi* (Messiah) or the *Sahib-e Zaman* (master of the age) to establish just and equitable rule.   (Ramazani 1986, 20)

Sunnis rejected this entire theological underpinning. But the Sunni activists who promoted political Islam in the Arab world took heart from the Iranian Revolution's implementation of the central idea: establishing "temporal as well as spiritual authority." They took courage from the success of the Iranian Islamic Republic as a practical expression of Islam's ability to serve as the basis for contemporary political rule, even if Iran's brand of Islam was not theirs. The declaration of an Islamic state in Pakistan, also in 1979, and the incorporation of Islam into the foundation of the state in Malaysia in 1980 also gave heart to those espousing political Islam (Nasr 2001). In short, the practicalities of actually setting up an Islamic state, rather than the specific theological or ideological doctrines driving that process, is what whet the appetites of Sunni political activists in the Arab world.

While Iran showed that success was possible, the idea itself of using Islamic law as a basis for social and political renewal in the Arab world predated Ayatollah Khomeini and the Iranian Revolution. Pan-Islamic thinkers had taken on the dilemma of the weak, subjugated position of Arabs as early as the nineteenth century, alongside the early pan-Arab thinkers.

On one level, the rise of political Islam in the 1970s and 1980s etched itself in the hearts of many Muslims across the Middle East and beyond. It both prompted and drew succor from the renewed religiosity that has been evident in people's homes and in the public sphere. From headscarves to Friday prayers on the sidewalks of cities and towns, the deepening hold of Islam on people's daily practice and self-presentation has been evident almost everywhere. On a second level, the new ideology became a catalyst for new—and renewed—political movements and organizations. It was the basis for the new nonstate actors, discussed in the previous chapter, which have had such a profound effect on Middle East regional dynamics.

The first makings of a contemporary mass Islamic political movement came in 1928, when Hassan al-Banna established the Muslim Brotherhood in Egypt—not surprisingly only a few short years after the demise of the caliphate. The caliphs had been religious *and* civil-political leaders, the successors to the Prophet Muhammad. The sultans, or leaders, of the Ottoman Empire had held the position of caliph until the empire's demise. At that time, in 1924, the first leader of the Turkish Republic, Mustafa Kemal, or Atatürk, prompted the new Turkish Grand National Assembly to abolish the position of caliph altogether. The disappearance of the caliphate resonated among Muslims worldwide but especially among those in the Middle East.

In the wake of Atatürk's and the assembly's brazen act, al-Banna set out to engineer an Islamic-based spiritual *and* political renewal in Egypt and beyond. While they did not achieve power in Egypt until the recent Arab Spring—and never rose to power anywhere else—the Muslim Brothers managed to remain the most powerful of the Sunni Islamic movements. Their popularity remained high before their ascension to power in Egypt after the Arab Spring, despite almost unremitting suppression by the Egyptian government and other regimes. Much of their appeal has been to the poor, though the Ikhwan has also demonstrated a powerful attraction to students, professionals, and others who have also been disappointed with secularism's achievements, even with their advanced education.

Numerous other political Islamic organizations have popped up throughout the Middle East over the last couple of decades, many directly inspired or aided by the Muslim Brotherhood. These Islamic groups have professed many variants of political Islam, ranging from the highly violent, such as al-Qaeda, to those using nonviolent means, such as the Gülen movement (Kuru 2003). Many but not all have established a network of social services, including health clinics, kindergartens, schools, and other institutions, reinforcing their religious message with practices rooted in service to the people.

In Turkey, Islamic-oriented political parties have achieved political power and accepted the secular institutions of the state. Elsewhere, state regimes have hounded political Islamic organizations and their leaders

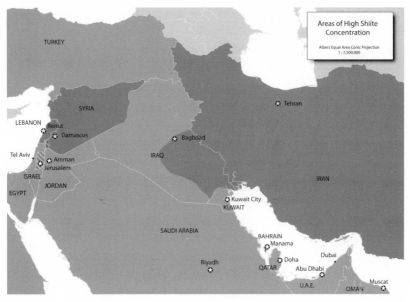

Areas of High Shiite Concentration

Albers Equal Area Conic Projection
1 : 7,500,000

MAP 9.1

(as in Tunisia), gone to war with them (as in Algeria), and co-opted them (as in Egypt, which also suppressed them off and on). Indeed, cooptation led to the incorporation of Islamic ideas and practices into ostensibly secular states, further strengthening the position of political Islamic thought. The ideological appeal of political Islam has struck fear into the hearts of Arab state leaders, and they have either sought to bring its proponents into the fold, lash out against them, or (as in Mubarak's Egypt) both. Political Islam became the most powerful set of ideas among Muslims from all walks of life across the Middle East in the last decades of the twentieth century, displacing Arab nationalism as the frontrunner. It became a major factor in transforming the region.

Resurgent Shiism

As the twentieth century drew to a close, the Middle East looked very different from the way it had appeared in the couple of decades after World War II. With the end of the Cold War, the Soviet presence vanished. The leading regional powers, the core Arab states, had faded. Arab nationalism, the ideology that had inspired millions of people to newfound hope and action, had lost its luster. A new brand of Islam—political Islam, with its many faces—gained traction, both through the Iranian Revolution and the new nonstate actors, which flexed their muscles throughout the region. And within Islam a tectonic shift occurred. That shift was in the Sunni-Shiite balance.

Shiites had long constituted the smaller, weaker sect in Islam, claiming just over 10 percent of the world's Muslim population. They have been concentrated primarily in the Middle East, especially in Iran, which is 90 percent Shiite; Iraq, about 60 percent; some of the Gulf states (Bahrain leads with about three-quarters Shiites; Kuwait, 30 percent); and Lebanon, where the lack of a census makes it difficult to know for sure, but by now Shiites are certainly at least a plurality of the population. While there are concentrations of Shiites outside the region, such as in India, the Middle East is the primary area where their communities can be found.

The split with the much larger Sunni sect dates back to the early generations of Islam in the seventh century. Shiites (literally, followers of Ali) rejected the main line of succession from the Prophet Mohammed, claiming instead the primacy of Ali, the son-in-law of the Prophet, and his descendants. The principal (but not only) Shiite account is that one of those descendants, the so-called twelfth imam, who became revered as an extraordinary, mythical figure, disappeared. Without him or a successor, Shiites lacked a central authority. Most (but, again, not all) Shiite believers—those called Twelvers—have held that the twelfth imam would one day return as the redeemer, or Mahdi.

Sunnis, in contrast, recognized the caliphate as the supreme central authority within Islam. The abolition of the caliphate in 1924 came to be considered a major tragedy for Islam by many contemporary political Sunnis. Besides these differences between Shiites and Sunnis on the issue of lines of succession and authority in Islam, important theological differences and contrasting modes of practice emerged.

Through the centuries, Sunnis have looked askance at Shiites' theology and religious practices. At best, Shiites were tolerated by Sunnis as somewhat misguided Muslims but Muslims nonetheless. One could even find intermarriage between them in some places. At worst, though, Shiites were viewed as nonbelieving, idol-worshipping apostates and actively persecuted. Examples abound of Sunni-Shiite coexistence, but one can also find numerous instances of discord and violent discrimination. What was generally true beyond differences in theology and practice in mixed communities, though, was that Sunnis tended to dominate economically, politically, and socially. Shiites, more often than not, were at the bottom of the social ladder, looking up at the more prosperous, powerful Sunnis. This pattern of stratification has held into contemporary times in many mixed areas, including Lebanon, Iraq, and Bahrain.

With the 1979 revolution in Iran, an overwhelmingly Shiite country, a new dynamic was put in motion, upsetting yet another longstanding regional pattern—Sunni dominance over Shiites. The success of the revolution earned admiration in large segments of the Muslim world, even among Sunnis who remained disdainful of Shiite theology. Shiite resurgence, however, did not end with the Iranian uprising in 1979. On the heels of the Iranian success came the creation of Hezbollah three years later, representing the Shiites of Lebanon and taking them to a new position of influence in that country—from perhaps the politically weakest large sect in the country to, in some respects, the strongest.

Iraqi Shiites, who had suffered brutal repression under Saddam Hussein, especially after their unsuccessful uprising in the wake of the 1990–1991 Gulf War, found themselves after the American invasion in 2003 suddenly in a new position of power. In Iraq's new power-sharing arrangement among Shiites, Sunnis, and Kurds, the Shiites were given the upper hand in key institutions, including the all-important position of prime minister.

In Bahrain, Shiites undertook a failed coup in 1981 on the heels of the Iranian Revolution, with the aim of creating an Iran-like Islamic republic. Shiites rose up there (again, unsuccessfully) in the 1990s. And the popular demonstrations in Bahrain during the Arab Spring in 2011 were spearheaded by Shiites, against the Sunni monarchy.

In Saudi Arabia, where Shiites make up somewhere between 15 and 20 percent of the population (and probably a third of the population in the Eastern Province), the small Shiite minority, sitting on crucial oil reserves, became more outspoken and electorally active after the Iranian Revolution. In 2009, they began engaging in antigovernment demonstrations and other actions. They were reacting to a long history of discrimination. Joshua Teitelbaum (2010) writes of their situation in Saudi Arabia:

In 1927, the Wahhabi ulama published a fatwa calling upon the Shiites to "convert" to Islam. Some Shiite notables complied, while others left the country. The publication and distribution of religious texts was forbidden, the Shiite call to prayer was outlawed, and centers of religious studies were dismantled. Specific Shiite customs such as grave visitation (*ziyarat al-qubur*) were forbidden, as were the Ashura commemorations. The Shiites have been vilified in textbooks, and generally have been made to feel like outcasts. Economically as well as socially, the Shiites have rarely been treated or led to believe that they are part of a common Saudi experience.

Almost everywhere in the Middle East where concentrations of Shiites exist, whether as the minority or majority, they became more assertive about their rights and status. At times, increased activism led to new coalitions and cooperation with other sects or ethnic groups, as in the Arab Spring protests in Bahrain, where Sunnis were welcomed into the demonstrations. In other instances, new tensions sprouted with Sunnis and others, as in Saudi Arabia in the last few years.

Beyond the realm of domestic politics, Shiite groups reached out across borders to other Shiites, from Iran to Iraq to Lebanon—and beyond. They traversed state borders through pilgrimages, donations, institution building, and politics. They engaged and offered aid to one another. Throughout the Middle East, the new assertiveness and political participation of Shiites was an important ingredient in the region's new brew. Perhaps the provocative title of the reporter Deborah Amos's (2010) book about the human tragedy stemming from the Iraq War, *Eclipse of the Sunnis*, overstates the case, but there certainly was a shift in power in the direction of the Shiites. Along with the rise of political Islam among Muslims of all stripes, the move in power toward the Shiites changed Islam itself and contributed to the overall transformation of the dynamics of the Middle East from 1979 to the outbreak of the Arab Spring. It was only in the wake of the Arab Spring—with the rise to power of the Sunni Muslim Brotherhood and the cracks in the Iranian bloc through the turmoil in Syria—that there seemed to be a reassertion of Sunni power and a Shiite retreat.

Egypt's Fading Star in the Middle East

How did all the elements of change discussed in this chapter and chapters 7 and 8—the surge of the Shiites, the growth of political Islam, the emergence of nonstate actors, and the change in the roster of the region's leading states—come together to create a new Middle East?

The weaving of these strands starts in the region's nucleus. In the 1950s and 1960s, Egypt was in the eye of the Middle East storm. Its imprint was unmistakable in all four of the change elements: Egypt was the leading Arab state and the preeminent power among the *core of Arab states* in the region. It demonstrated the *primacy of states* generally—particularly post-colonial states—as the central, nearly exclusive significant players in the area, dominating any nonstate pretenders to power, such as the fledgling PLO or Muslim Brotherhood. The country was the flag bearer of the most important motivating and mobilizing set of ideas in the region, *Arab nationalism*. And Egypt embodied the clear upper hand of *Sunni power* in the region. Sunnis' privileged status was more implicit than explicit, since Sunni ascendancy was largely an unquestioned premise at the time. Egypt's centrality put it at the forefront of every one of the struggles that shaped Mideast dynamics in those decades:

- Between the Soviet Union and the United States
- Between the monarchical *anciens régimes* and the popular national-ist republics
- Between Israel and the Arab states
- Among the troika of Arab nationalist regimes, which included Syria and Iraq, besides Egypt itself

By the end of the Cold War, however, the entire Middle East looked strikingly different. Egypt's star began to fade after the 1967 War, and by 1990 it was far from being the central regional player. Its domestic institutions had been diminished over time, and its regional status had suffered badly, particularly after the signing of the peace treaty with Israel in 1979. Additionally, Arab nationalism now barely made a blip on the radar screen. State organizations had lost their monopoly as the exclusive key players in the region, as a number of key nonstate actors joined the fray. And Sunnis no longer took their dominance within Islam as a given.

The old flashpoints had changed, too. The Cold War was over. Monarchical and republican Arab states were more likely to be working hand in hand than facing off against one another. The Arab-Israeli conflict still carried on (and on and on) but manifested itself now mostly (although certainly not exclusively) as the *Palestinian*-Israeli conflict; Egypt and Jordan had signed peace treaties with Israel, and other Arab regimes had ongoing contacts, including some security cooperation, with the Israelis.

And the old struggle involving the nationalist regimes of Egypt, Iraq, and Syria simply petered out.

Searching for a New Nucleus in Mideast Dynamics

Just as in the earlier Cold War era, understanding the radically changed contemporary Middle East begins with the global forces penetrating the area. During the Cold War, the U.S.-USSR rivalry had cast a long shadow over all of the relations in the region. Each superpower jockeyed for local strategic relationships in order to better position itself with respect to the other superpower. Once the Soviet Union collapsed, superpower competition, of course, was no longer a factor in the area.

Instead, since then, it has been the United States, largely unopposed by any other global powers, whose economic, political, and military presence and actions have been so deeply etched in the region. That influence has been exerted in multiple arenas in the Middle East through actively fighting wars, applying sanctions, offering mediation, proffering aid of various sorts, and much more. Conservatives (admiringly) and liberals (critically) both termed the United States' role as an imperial one (Vidal 2004, Newhouse 2003, Kurtz 2003), and, certainly, if imperial means a single dominating and domineering country, then the United States has fit the bill. The next two chapters explore how the very different presidential administrations of George W. Bush and Barack Obama understood the transformed Middle East and played this imperial role.

As in the Cold War, though, global forces during the last two decades have constituted only part of the Middle East's story. Like the global forces stemming from the period of U.S.-USSR competition, America's imperial influence since then has complemented, interacted with, and contended with the forces operating in the region. Middle East dynamics are sometimes opportunities but, more often, are limiting factors on American imperial control.

For U.S. officials, recognizing and understanding the Middle East's central dynamics, especially in a region that was so fundamentally transformed, were major challenges. It was not immediately clear to U.S. policy makers what the changes in the region actually were, what they added up to, or how to construct sensible, effective policies in response to them. Indeed, for two decades following the end of the Soviet presence in the Middle East, Washington struggled mightily with the challenge of figuring out exactly what the region had become, what its interests in the region now were, and how best to achieve its goals.

From 1990 on, the United States tried to identify where the new nucleus of Mideast dynamics have resided. Was there a country, like Egypt in the postwar period, that was the fulcrum for the dynamics of the region? Its first inclination, especially during the Reagan era, was to continue to see Egypt as precisely that country. American presidents since Eisenhower had recognized Egypt's primacy. Eisenhower's secretary of state, Dulles, had early on recognized the importance of Egypt, although he had framed that in largely negative terms. During the Nixon period, and continuing through the Ford and Carter administrations, Egypt continued to be seen as the nucleus of the region but now in a positive light.

Even in the 1980s, the Reagan years, when Egyptian leadership had been repudiated by the other Arab states and Egyptian institutions had begun their downward spiral, American officials persisted in seeing Egypt as the central regional actor. Indeed, Reagan built on the tie between Egypt and Israel that had been forged with the help of the Carter administration. Reagan took the strategic relationship with Israel seriously and saw Israel's new peace with Egypt as a building block for U.S. policy in the region. At the beginning of his presidency, Ronald Reagan invited Egyptian President Anwar Sadat to the United States, treated him royally, and lavished public praise on him.

But this was no longer the Egypt of the Nasser era, no longer the central fulcrum of Middle East dynamics. Perhaps the continued importance that American officials attached to U.S.-Egyptian relations stemmed from the fact that the United States had invested so heavily in Egypt after its peacemaking with Israel in the late 1970s. They hoped that Egypt could continue to play the leading role in the Middle East now that it sided with the United States and had made peace with Israel. That hope did not die easily and continued into the presidency of George H. W. Bush. But by the middle of the senior Bush's presidency, Egypt's stagnation was unmistakable, bringing into question how central it truly was to the dynamics of the region. As the largest country in the region, Egypt continued to play an important role in the Middle East—and does until this day—but it clearly was no longer the hub to which all spokes were attached.

Another candidate for U.S. officials to see as the fulcrum for regional dynamics might have been Turkey. U.S. presidents from Truman on all took U.S.-Turkish relations seriously. But in the 1970s and 1980s, concern existed in Washington about Turkey's stability. The 1970s were a difficult period for the Turkish regime, the descendants of Atatürk. Tensions with Greece, especially over the rule of Cyprus, led to the invasion of Cyprus in 1974, which was followed by considerable international criticism of Turkey. Domestically, the 1970s were a time of social upheaval and domestic violence, which was brought to a halt by a heavy-handed military coup in 1980. By 1984, some semblance of normalcy had returned to Turkish civil society and politics, but that year also saw the beginning of the long, violent campaign waged by Kurdish militants in the PKK. In the years that followed, Turkey both waged a brutal war against the PKK and turned its eyes increasingly to Europe, where its leaders hoped the country would be accepted as a full-fledged member of the emerging European Union.

For American officials, Turkey continued to play a central role in Middle East affairs, as in the 1990–1991 Gulf War, but few regarded it as the lever through which the United States could exert its influence in the region. In the 2000s, when Turkey was no longer ruled by Atatürk's heirs but by a new Islamic-leaning government, it did turn its primary foreign-policy attention to the Middle East. But by then the intimacy of U.S.-Turkish relations had dissipated. Turkish officials were less interested in serving as the U.S. stalking horse in the region and more intent on staking out an independent Turkish position as a regional facilitator.

Iran was yet another prospect for American officials to regard as the central node of Middle East affairs. In the aftermath of the enmity generated by the Iranian hostage crisis, of course, considering Iran as the center would have meant seeing it as a negative force and designing policies to throttle it (much as U.S. officials had seen Egypt negatively for most of the 1950s and 1960s). Still, even after the revolution and the enmity engendered by the hostage crisis, the Reagan administration did attempt to overcome the mutual bitterness and woo Iran through arms sales. As discussed in chapter 6, this was the period of the Iran-Iraq War, and Reagan's staff clearly tilted toward Iran in the early part of that conflict. Cold War thinking remained central to the Reagan administration, and Saddam Hussein's Iraq was, after all, a Soviet ally. But that effort to forge a positive link between the United States and Iran ended in the fiasco of the Iran-Contra Affair. Iran and the United States made no progress at all in repairing their tattered relations, and the second Reagan administration drifted into supporting Iraq over Iran.

Whether seen negatively or positively, in the late 1980s, 1990s, and into the early 2000s Iran gained only limited traction among U.S. officials as a candidate to be considered the leading power around which policy should be constructed. Certainly, there was talk in Washington of the Iranian threat, there were entreaties by Saudi Arabia and Egypt to take the Iran threat seriously, and there was even the shift in actual policy to support the hated Saddam Hussein in the latter stages of the Iran-Iraq War precisely because of the anxiety that revolutionary Iran engendered among U.S. officials. At the beginning of the Clinton presidency, there was even the proclamation of a new strategy, "dual containment." It drew on the Cold War notion of containment and identified both Iran and Iraq as key threats in the Middle East. But, like most attempts at grand strategy in the immediate post–Cold War period, it did not amount to much. There was an uptick of American troops in the region from earlier periods (excepting the period of the Gulf War), and there were sanctions levied on Iran. The policy, though, pitted the United States against two mortal enemies, which did not seem to make much sense.

In a period marked by "seat-of-the-pants" foreign policy, in the wake of the Cold War, U.S. officials tended to extinguish fires, rather than develop grand strategies like dual containment. Relatively little time and energy were expended on figuring out changing regional dynamics and on constructing overarching policies for the region revolving around a central threat. Perhaps, too, the relative neglect of Iran as the fulcrum for Mideast regional dynamics came from the consideration that Iran's power was bound to be limited, since it was neither Arab nor Sunni in a region whose majority was *both* Arab and Sunni; its anomalous position might have made it seem somewhat peripheral to the central dynamics of the area.

More likely, though, is that Iran receded in importance in the eyes of U.S. officials as they became increasingly fixated on *Iraq* as the key regional player, particularly with the invasion of Kuwait in 1990 and the no-fly zone imposed on Saddam Hussein's region after the Gulf War. By the late 1990s, neoconservatives were already drawing most attention to Iraq through their demands for regime change there. The preoccupation with Iraq came to full bloom in the administration of George W. Bush, as I will discuss in the next chapter.

But Iraq, for all of Saddam's bluster and adventurousness, was more identified with the dynamics of the old Middle East that had lost their luster—fading Arab power, a humbled Arab nationalism, beleaguered state-centered actors, and no longer unquestioned Sunni dominance—than with the new factors shaping the region. No one could deny the importance of Iraq, of course: it had invaded two neighbors (Iran and

Kuwait), rained missiles on another (Israel), and fought two wars against the United States and its allies, all in the course of a single generation. But the signs of its decline were evident long before its elimination as a regional power after the 2003 American invasion, even if U.S. policy makers had not recognized them.

The fixation with Iraq came to be built into the elaborate analytic underpinnings that drove American policy in the Middle East for most of the first decade of the twenty-first century—with disastrous consequences for both the United States and the Middle East. That is the topic of the next chapter. Here, I want to emphasize how perhaps the effect of becoming gun-shy of engagement with Iran after the Iran-Contra Affair and certainly the obsession with Iraq led U.S. analysts to miss the changing dynamics of the region. The fulcrum of the transformed Middle East in the post–Cold War period was no longer Egypt, and it was not Iraq; by the twenty-first century, it had indeed become Iran.

Iran's Rising Star in the Middle East

Iran emerged as the preeminent regional power after the Cold War. Its rise was tied to the new change factors analyzed in this chapter and the last: the changing of the guard to *non-Arab powers*, as the Arab states became increasingly hollowed out and the non-Arab powers redirected their attention to Mideast affairs; the rise of *political Islam* as the driving ideology just as Arab nationalism faltered; the growing role of *nonstate actors*, the most important of which, as will be discussed momentarily, allied with Iran; and, of course, the new prominence of *Shiites* in the Middle East configuration.

Riding the wave of all these change factors, Iran has taken center stage as a leading player in every one of the struggles that have come to define the region in the last two decades. Iran

- has led the clarion call against America's imperial position;
- has taken the lead in a bloc of states and nonstate actors that multiple Arab regimes and Israel have seen as existentially threatening;
- has been a driving force in the pressure that political Islam has put on secular (and some religious) regimes;
- and has injected itself into the Palestinian-Israeli conflict directly, through its leaders' questioning of Israel's right to exist and deny-

ing that the Holocaust actually occurred, which is so central to the Israeli narrative, and, indirectly, through its alliance with Hamas and Hezbollah.

In short, it is now Iran, not Egypt, that is in the eye of the Middle East storm and that is a primary force along every major fault line in the area.

An Iranian-Led Bloc

The key to understanding the dynamics in the transformed Middle East was not the highly reported war in Iraq, nor the Palestinian-Israeli conflict, but the issue of the emergence of an Iran-led bloc whose presence spanned the northern tier of the Middle East. This coalition of states and nonstates stretched from the Gulf all the way to the Mediterranean Sea. The territorial reach of this bloc was itself daunting. In addition to Iran, other members included Syria, Hezbollah, and Hamas. The Shiite-dominated Iraqi government, as well as key Shiite Iraqi militias, constituted tentative or potential components, as well. Indeed, close collaboration developed between Tehran and Iraq's regime leaders in the years following the 2003 American invasion. A variety of key Iraqi Shiite political leaders consulted closely with Iranian leaders after the March 2010 Iraqi national elections. The regular visits by Iraqi Shiite officials to Tehran have been "a stark indication of Iraq's geopolitical tilt eastward since Saddam's overthrow, towards Iran and away from the Arab system" (Maddy-Weitzman 2010b, 22).

Westward from Iran to Iraq, both of which touch the Persian Gulf, through the heartland of Syria, all the way to Hezbollah and Hamas perched on the eastern Mediterranean coast, this informal bloc stretched contiguously along the northern rim of the Middle East. The change factors that the last three chapters explored—the decline of Arab nationalist states, the surge of Shiism, and the emergence of political Islam and nonstate actors—were all important elements binding this bloc together, and this bloc was led by the non-Arab Islamic Republic of Iran. Additionally, Iran made headway in relations with East African countries, enhancing its naval presence along another regional waterway, the Red Sea. Iran, quite simply, emerged as the central element in the new Mideast regional system.

Shiism certainly has been a key component of the glue that helped form and maintain this coalition. But for all the fears that various Sunnis and non-Muslim outsiders expressed about a threatening homogeneous Shiite bloc, the actual connection between Iran and its various partners rested on Shiism as only one of several components. Even then, this religious connection was varied and complex. The most straightforward Shiite connection has been between Iran and Hezbollah. From its inception, Hezbollah has outwardly accepted the religious and political authority of the Iranian Islamic Republic and its clerical leaders. And while there are other geopolitical considerations linking Hezbollah and the Iranian regime, the bond between the two has rested on the foundation of shared Shiite beliefs, with the highest-ranking Iranian clerics having the last say.

Syria, in contrast to Hezbollah, had a much more complex connection to Iran. Shiism did play a role in forming a link between the countries, but in a fairly ambiguous and largely secondary manner. Syria is three-quarters Sunni, and Shiites constitute only a minute fraction of the population, making the Shiite bond seem initially irrelevant. The wild card in Syria, however, is the Alawites. They make up about 15 percent of the total population and come from a fairly remote region of the country. After Hafez al-Asad's rise to power in 1970, Syria's political and military leadership came from the Alawite sect. These leaders, who dominated Syrian political life, are like most other Alawites in recent times: they have been nationalistic and mostly secular, downplaying the importance of religion. Until the uprising in 2011, the al-Asad family's iron-fisted rule mostly kept a firm lid on sectarian tensions, making any Syrian Shiite tie to Iran seem improbable.

But beneath the secular veneer, Shiism has indeed played a role in Syria itself and in the connection to Iran. After Hafez al-Asad seized power following the Black September War in 1970, a strong claim was made in 1973 that the Alawites are actually Shiites, Twelver Shiites to be precise. This was controversial, since Alawites, while probably originally actually an offshoot of the Twelvers, have been thought of in a number of Middle East countries as not Muslims at all but as members of an heretical offshoot sect, even among Shiites who themselves have faced such accusations. An important Shiite imam born in Syria and serving on the Shiite Supreme Council of Lebanon, however, made the claim, through a key fatwa, or responsum, that Twelvers and Alawites are actually one and the same. In fact, it may well have been Hafez al-Asad who solicited the fatwa, seeking to establish the bona fides of Alawites as real Muslims as he consolidated his rule in an overwhelmingly Muslim country, even as he sought to impose a new secular nationalism on the population.

To be sure, the recent Syrian-Iranian alliance rested much more on a foundation of hard-nosed, shared interests than on religious affinity. Still, the fatwa asserting that the Alawites were actually legitimate Shiites helped cement the Syrian coalition with Iran and Syria's role as a conduit between Iran and Hezbollah. Additionally, the success of Hezbollah in Lebanon, especially in the 2006 war against Israel, and proselytizing by Iranians led to increasing Shiite successes in Syria. These successes included internal Syrian Muslim conversions to Shiism, something punishable as apostasy in some other Sunni-majority countries. Additionally, Iranians provided private funds for the restoration of Shiite tombs and shrines in Syria and built at least one Shiite religious school near Damascus, named after Iran's supreme leader, Ali Khamenei (Tabler 2007). Growing numbers of Shiite pilgrims from Iran, Iraq, and Syria itself flocked to a shrine in Syria, the grave of Zeinab, who was the daughter of the revered Ali and the granddaughter of the Prophet. All in all, Shiism fortified the link between Syria and Iran, although it did not constitute the most important connection between the two countries.

As with Syria, the Iraqi Shiites' connection with Iran has been complex and multilayered—not the more straightforward affinity marking the Iran-Hezbollah connection. Although the demise of Saddam Hussein was a huge plus for practically all Iraqi Shiites, they have been deeply divided since the American invasion in 2003. Key Shiite groups lined up with the United States; others doggedly fought against American occupation. Iranian leaders have been coy about any aid that they offered to Iraqi Shiite militias opposing the United States, but at various points in its war in Iraq American officials publicly charged Iran with meddling in Iraqi affairs by providing military support to Shiite fighting forces. They pointed to weapons with Iranian "signatures" on them that were used to attack American forces.

As the war dragged on, though, the Iranians went beyond military aid to opposition militias. They made overtures to the Shiites in the U.S.-supported government, as well. Among Shiites participating in the new Iraqi state, different factions, often pitted against one another, developed. Increasingly, Iranian officials served as peace brokers between opposing Shiite factions inside Iraq, moving away from their previous role as one-sided backers of rebels fighting against the American occupation. Such factionalism among Iraqi Shiites was highlighted in the 2010 elections and in the long aftermath of that election, in which the Iraqis first tried to form a government and then found that government foundering because of the enduring rifts. Iranian officials quietly threw their support behind some factions, shunned others, and acted as go-betweens in some cases. While Iranian officials certainly did not succeed in establishing Iraqi Shiites as a fixed part of their bloc, they made serious inroads into American influence with Iraqi Shiites, cooperating with them on a number of fronts.

A key figure in the developing Iranian-Iraqi ties was Nuri Kamel al-Maliki, who became prime minster of Iraq in 2006 and emerged as prime minister again in 2010, even after the hotly contested elections left him in second place. Al-Maliki had fled from Saddam Hussein's Iraq (where he had been sentenced to death for his resistance to the regime) before the Iran-Iraq War and spent most of the 1980s in Iran and the 1990s and beyond in Syria. In Syria, he cooperated with both the Iranian leadership and Hezbollah in his efforts to topple Saddam Hussein. When he rose to Iraq's top office in 2006, American officials believed al-Maliki was not as beholden to Iran as some other Iraq Shiite leaders, although they were still well aware of his previous Iranian ties. Still, tensions between the United States and al-Maliki flared on several occasions over the issue of his reaching out to Iran, including a visit he paid to Tehran in 2008. For his part, al-Maliki stated that he did not see good relations with Iran and with the United States as contradictory, a response that did not sit well with American officials prosecuting the war in Iraq while simultaneously confronting Iran in the Middle East.

Iran forged other connections to Shiites in Iraq, too. For example, it shared sponsorship of Arabic-language Internet sites and satellite TV stations with Iraqi Shiite militias. With those militias, Iranians broadcast Shiite religious programming into Syria. Iran also offered funds for Iraqi postwar reconstruction. Its exports to Iraq mushroomed. And Iranian tourists—close to a half million yearly—flocked to Shiite shrines in Iraq, bringing badly needed tourist business. All in all, Iran worked hard not to isolate its influence in Iraq to the anti-American Shiite militias, instead broadening its relations with multiple Iraqi Shiite groups and leaders, including those in power. If Iraq did not become an undisputed member of the Iran-led bloc, especially as the shaky government survived largely thanks to the American presence, it moved to repair the long-frayed Iran-Iraq relations.

The major exception to the Shiite connection in the Iran-led bloc was Hamas, an avowedly Sunni organization stemming from an overwhelmingly Sunni Palestinian population. Shiism was tossed around in Palestinian internecine struggles, mostly negatively. Fatah, for example, accused Hamas of being Shiite agents (Hamas, in turn, has countered that Fatah has been a lackey of Israel). Hamas, which was an offshoot of the Muslim Brotherhood, followed elements in the Brotherhood prior to its rise to power in Egypt in playing down Sunni-Shiite differences, especially in recent years. In fact, the Brotherhood even mediated sectarian disputes and largely avoided the sort of anti-Shiite rhetoric used by some Sunni groups in the Middle East. Not all Muslim Brothers in those years saw eye to eye on Shiism; one member, for example, wrote a paper asserting that Shiism was a fifth religious school of Islam, alongside the four Sunni schools, a claim that others in the Brotherhood strongly rejected. Still, prior to the Arab Spring the Ikhwan moved to dampen Sunni-Shiite differences and itself moved toward closer ties with Iran (Mahjar-Barducci 2009). Only after the Arab Spring could one see the division grow, as Hamas broke with Asad's Syria and thereby distanced itself from Iran, and the Muslim Brotherhood joined a Sunni bloc that pitted itself against the old regime in Syria.

For its part, Iran consistently presented itself as the voice of true Islam, which supersedes sectarian divides between Sunnis and Shiites, and appealed broadly to Sunnis. Its religious and political leaders addressed themselves to Sunni Muslims and saw no problem in allying with an avowedly Sunni group like Hamas. Hamas and the Muslim Brotherhood served as two important bridges for Iranian influence among the Middle East's Sunni majority. The critical link among Iran, Hamas, and the Muslim Brotherhood was their mutual dedication, regardless of sect, to militant political Islam, including the creation of Islamic republics.

As a nonstate actor, Hamas was clear from the time of its founding in 1987 about its Islamic militancy and its aim to create an Islamic republic. Once it began to participate in the democratic, secular political institutions of the Palestine Authority, and after it eventually wrested control of the Gaza Strip from Fatah, its position became much less black and white, much as Hezbollah's had once it became a political party in the multireligious environment of Lebanon. Hamas continued to claim that it respected the secular, pluralistic framework within which it operated, but, as time went on, its rule in Gaza increasingly emphasized the Islamic element. It adopted a "Yes for Virtue" campaign in the Gaza Strip, insisted on Islamic dress for schoolgirls, banned women from riding on the backs of motorbikes, insisted that female lawyers wear headscarves in court, and broke up mixed couples on Gaza's beach; more generally, it enforced a public space governed by Islamic law and norms. All these Hamas moves reflected Iran's position on appropriate "civil" behavior and helped cement the Iran-Hamas tie. That same sort of Islamic link—professing the ideals of Islamic temporal rule, enforcing Islamic norms in the public square, aiming for the creation of Islamic republics, and pushing the global mission of political Islam—reinforced Iran's ties with Shiite Hezbollah and some of the Iraqi Shiite militias, as well.

For Hamas, of course, the issue of Israel has been preeminent. And, here, Iran's unrelenting opposition to Israel was crucial in bringing Hamas into its fold, even without the Shiite connection. Ayatollah Khamenei, for example, referred to Israel as a cancerous tumor that has to be excised from the region. Iran's growing strategic prominence, especially as it enhanced its nuclear capabilities, coupled with such language sent shockwaves through Israel. The pronouncements questioning whether the Holocaust actually took place by Iranian President Mahmoud Ahmadinejad only heightened Israeli alarm. From Hamas's point of view, Iran's bellicose rhetoric on Israel and the Holocaust, in addition to its growing power, were important assets in the fight against Israel and in its opposition to the Fatah-led PLO, which accepted Israel as a legitimate state. Such support was in addition to any possible direct military aid by the Iranians to Hamas (which has been widely speculated about but not verified).

While Iran-Hamas ties rested on shared views of political Islam, the Iranian connection to the secular regime in Syria and some of the secular-leaning Shiite groups in Iraq was only muddied by Iran's militant stance promoting political Islam. Still, that Islam-based ideology was the most important to the Iranian leadership of all the ingredients bonding the disparate parts of its bloc. At the same time, with all the heterogeneous members of the coalition—states and nonstate actors, Shiites and Sunnis, secular and Islamic—Iran appealed to shared sentiments and strategic interests, from anti-Americanism to opposition to Israel, as means to strengthen ties inside the bloc. Much more than simply a "Shiite Crescent," the term coined by King Abdullah of Jordan and widely adopted by others, Iran fashioned a multifaceted alliance weaving a variety of actors with disparate motives for participating. The success of the coalition stemmed not from any single quality, such as Shiism or Islamic militancy, but in the combination of factors that proved so important in the post–Cold War Middle East. Only in the wake of the Arab Spring was the solidarity of that bloc diminished.

With its allies in hand, Iran sought to expand its power and influence. It worked to spread its religious message from the Arab Gulf states all the way to Morocco. In 2009, President Ahmadinejad hosted a summit meeting with President Hamid Karzai of Afghanistan and President Asif Ali Zardari of Pakistan, both staunch American allies. The *New York Times* called the summit "the latest sign of Iran's emergence as the regional power" (Perlez and Shah 2008). What brought the three together was their shared opposition to the Taliban, which has been waging armed insurgencies in both Afghanistan and Pakistan. The Taliban had purged Shiites in Afghanistan when it ruled the country prior to the American invasion and also fanned Sunni-Shiite conflict in Pakistan, drawing the ire of the Iranians. The amicable Pakistan-Afghanistan-Iran summit troubled American officials, who made every effort to isolate the Iranians, particularly because of Iran's recalcitrance on the nuclear issue. Indeed, U.S. leaders have been convinced that Iran is well on the way to producing a nuclear arsenal and missiles to carry the nuclear warheads. But the summit, along with the earlier visit of Iraqi Prime Minister al-Maliki, demonstrated Iran's prowess in using its leverage in neighboring South Asia, as well as the Middle East, even with countries considered to be strong allies of the United States.

On the Other Side of the Iranian-Led Bloc

Multiple conflicts have continued to haunt the Middle East in the twenty-first century. The United States invaded Iraq, fought a prolonged war there, and, even after it officially withdrew from combat, continued to have a looming physical presence in the country. Israel fought brutal wars with Palestinians in the al-Aqsa intifada, starting in 2000; Hezbollah, in 2006; and Hamas, in 2008–2009 and 2012. Turkey and the PKK waged a vicious, low-level war that started during the Cold War and has carried, off and on, into the 2000s. The wars in Afghanistan and Pakistan, on the periphery of the region, have leaked into the Middle East. The Arab Spring brought vicious civil wars in Libya and Syria and less intense conflicts in Bahrain and Yemen. As much as practically any area of the world, the Middle East has been a tinderbox, threatening not only those in the region but global peace, as well. With Israel already armed with nuclear weapons; Iran, seemingly on the verge; and Pakistan and India, in neighboring South Asia, loaded to the teeth with armed warheads, the Middle East holds the potential for sparking a global disaster.

Underlying many of the tensions in the area has been an ill-defined political conflict that so far has not generated direct fighting. On one side of the divide in that conflict has been the Iran-led bloc, including Hezbollah, Syria, some Iraqi Shiite groups, and Hamas until it edged out of the bloc during the Syrian civil war. What has existed on the other side of the divide, though, has been amorphous. To be sure, fear of and opposition to the Iran-led coalition have been widespread in the Middle East and beyond. Different states have had varying concerns about the bloc, but no unified opposition has yet to emerge. For example, Morocco, territorially far removed from the coalition members, has feared the Shiite component of the Iran-led bloc. Early in 2009, Morocco broke diplomatic relations with Iran, accusing its embassy of "intolerable interference in the internal affairs of the kingdom." The Moroccan Foreign Ministry specifically cited Iranian actions that threatened the religious unity of Morocco. The ministry's statement followed charges in the Moroccan press that the Iranians were actively proselytizing Shiism among Morocco's Sunni population.

In a similar vein, an ongoing uprising of Houthi Shiites in the northwestern corner of Yemen led to deteriorating relations between Sana'a and Tehran, as well as exacerbating tensions between Saudi Arabia and Iran. Starting in 2004, Yemeni officials complained of Iranian arms and other resources flowing to the rebels. In 2009, the Yemeni government claimed that it had seized an Iranian ship bearing weapons for the Shiite rebellion, which has grown in recent years. And the Iranians, in turn, expressed concern about the fate of Shiites in Yemen. Saudi forces also clashed with the Houthi forces, and Saudi officials watched what they took to be Iranian troublemaking in the Arabian Peninsula with a wary eye.

Officials in Saudi Arabia, the Gulf states, and Egypt under Mubarak similarly spoke in harsh terms about what they saw as Iranian adventurism and interference in their domestic affairs. The issue was not only Shiism per se but also the perceived threat of political Islam, generally, regardless of sectarian differences. The small Gulf states linked through the United Arab Emirates (UAE) have felt particularly vulnerable, with Iran breathing down their necks. Iran made significant headway in one of them, the city-state of Dubai, which became an economic powerhouse, a Middle Eastern Singapore. Dubai became a trading center for Iranians, with many businesspeople moving there permanently or temporarily. It also became a key site from which Iran imported gasoline. The other states quietly bristled at the growing role of Iran in Dubai, and when

Dubai's financial crisis hit in 2009, it is not surprising that other UAE members in a position to bail passed (only Abu Dhabi offered only limited help).

Saudi Arabia, an Islamic regime itself, has had strained relations with Iran since the Islamic Revolution. Fearing Iranian incitement of Saudi Islamic militants, who have opposed what they have seen as a corrupt regime that has abandoned the true tenets of Islam, Saudi officials have gone so far as to fingerprint Iranian pilgrims to Mecca and have pointed to Iran as being behind violent clashes in the holy city. Iran has worked to dampen the conflict in recent years, and President Ahmadinejad visited Riyadh in 2007 on a mission of reconciliation.

But the fear of Saudi officials lingers. They have watched anxiously as Iran has built up its naval presence in the Gulf of Aden. They have viewed the post–U.S. invasion Iraqi government as being solidly in the Iranian camp. Even after the attempted reconciliation between Iran and Saudi Arabia, the Saudis bombed the Shiite rebels in Yemen, in a countermove to Iranian aid to those rebels, and the Saudis continue to keep a wary eye on any possible connection between their own Shiite minority and Iran.

The Saudi actions continue a longstanding policy of opposing Iranian influence in the Arabian Peninsula. Saudi Arabia and five other Arab states—Bahrain, Kuwait, Oman, Qatar, and the United Arab Emirates—had created the Gulf Cooperation Council (GCC) in 1981, only two years after the Iranian Revolution, precisely with the Iranian threat in mind. Indeed, Saddam Hussein presented the Iran-Iraq War as a defense of the Arab states in the Arab Peninsula and the Gulf against a militant Islamic regime. In 2008 and 2009, a number of Arab states resumed official relations with Iraq (and forgave some Iraqi debts) in part to lure Iraq away from Iran and back into the Arab fold. Three decades after the creation of the GCC, the anxieties inside the Arab regimes about Iranian intentions and of Islamic militants who might be inspired by Iran have not abated. Only Qatar has spoken up against the GCC's and Sunni Arabs' unremitting opposition to Iran. In the turmoil of the Arab Spring in 2011, the GCC invited Jordan and Morocco (the other traditional monarchies in the region) to join. The issue of Iran figured into the consideration to expand. Reporting on a conversation with a former commander in the UAE, a correspondent of the London-based Arabic daily Asharq al-Awsat wrote, "By far the more pressing aspect of this expansion is the political one. The controversial stands of neighboring Iran are a source of concern for the GCC countries" (quoted in Middle East Policy Council 2011).

Alarm about Iran's intentions and the threats it poses has gone beyond the issue of Islam, however, and it often revolves around simple power relations. Arab leaders have had deep concerns about Iran's meddling in their domestic affairs, its nuclear program, its growing naval power, and more. Egyptian officials in the Mubarak period uncovered a Hezbollah cell, allegedly planning violent acts, operating in the country and immediately pointed fingers at Iran. Egyptian Foreign Minister Ahmed Abul Gheit saw Hezbollah as little more than a stalking horse for Iran: "Iran, and Iran's followers [a not-so-veiled reference to Hezbollah], want Egypt to become a maid of honor for the crowned Iranian queen when she enters the Middle East" (*Middle East Online* 2009). Abul Gheit's sarcasm grew out of thirty years of hostile relations, dating back to Sadat's giving refuge to the shah after the revolution. Egyptian officials harbored multiple apprehensions about Iran: its nuclear aspirations, its conventional military power, the allies it has collected, its Islamic ideology, and its connection to Egyptian Islamic militants, especially the Muslim Brothers.

The columnist Tariq Alhomayed expressed this generalized fear of the Iran-led bloc's power explicitly in an editorial in *Asharq al-Awsat*: "The dispute is not about the Shia doctrine or the Shia in the Arab world; it is about the spread of Iranian influence in the Arab countries and Iran's continuous attempts to export its revolution to these countries under the banner of so-called political Shiafication. This is the crux of the matter" (Mahjar-Barducci 2009).

In the post–Arab Spring period, the new Egyptian regime immediately disowned Mubarak's Iran policy. Officials noted that the new Egypt held no animosity toward Iran. For the first time since the Iranian Revolution, the two countries resumed diplomatic relations and exchanged ambassadors. Egypt's new president, Mohammed Morsi, even traveled to Iran for the meeting of the Non-Aligned Movement. But the path to improved relations was strewn with potential minefields. Iran and the new Egypt supported opposite sides of the Syrian civil war. Egypt seemed to be moving closer to a Sunni bloc that was actively assisting the rebels against the Iran-supported Asad regime in Syria. For Egypt, as for Turkey, the Syrian civil war seemed to signify not only a battle against a repressive regime but a fight by Sunnis to escape Shiite (in this case, Alawite) domination.

Anxieties about Iran have been expressed repeatedly in other Arab states as well, including Saudi Arabia and the Gulf states. And it has not been the Arab Muslim states of the region only whose leaders have seen Iran and its bloc as the key challenges to their own prospects and to

Mideast dynamics more generally. Israel's deep alarm about the Iranian threat has also been tied to political Islam, in this case, to Iran's allies, the nonstate actors with which Israel has fought its last two wars, Hezbollah and Hamas. But, as with the Arab states, Israel's foreboding over what it sees as the Iranian peril has focused on issues of power, especially the likelihood of an Iranian nuclear capability, along with Iran's unrelenting anti-Israel propaganda. By no means, though, have Israel and the Arab states that have expressed similar anxieties about Iran and its allies united in into the semblance of a counterbloc. On the contrary, the states on the other side of the bloc have remained fundamentally divided. It was this division that may have prompted the Saudis to propose the Arab Peace Initiative in 2002. I will discuss that possibility more in chapter 13.

The Middle East today remains as much of a tinderbox as it was during the dark years of the Cold War. Back then, conflicts in the region twice, in 1967 and 1973, led to nuclear saber rattling by the superpowers, whose hands were in almost every conflict and struggle in the area. Today, the superpower rivalry has disappeared, and the conflicts related to global bipolarity have mostly dissipated. The region has been changed into something entirely different: there are new forces, cleavages, and conflicts.

The end of the Cold War and the transformation of the Middle East, however, have not diminished American involvement in the area. On the contrary, its looming presence grew after the demise of the Soviet Union. At first, the focus of U.S. officials was principally on Iraq and the Palestinian-Israeli conflict. As time went on, the focus of Washington was also very much on Iran, its bloc stretching across the northern rim of the region, and the threats—real or imagined—it posed to U.S. allies—from Saudi Arabia and the GCC to Egypt to Israel.

The triad of issues—Iraq, Iran, and Palestine-Israel—intersected repeatedly in the first decade of the twenty-first century, and all seemed to tie imperial America into knots. In that decade, the United States saw itself drowning in a long, costly war in Iraq; failing repeatedly to make headway on the Palestine-Israel conflict; and taking a series of ineffective steps to curb Iran's influence and thwart its purported nuclear-weapons program. Through it all, America's popular standing in the region fell precipitously, which not only limited Washington's range of action but also put Washington's Mideast strongmen collaborators in growing peril. George W. Bush, as I will explore in the next chapter, attempted to go beyond putting out fires one by one and, instead, to bring a coherence to American foreign policy in the Middle East, one that might link the various challenges that the United States faced. But that effort failed miserably.

Barack Obama drew back from Bush's bold, even adventurous, integrated set of policies. The Obama administration tried to fashion an alternative path, as I will discuss in chapter 11. It tackled separately the ongoing war in Iraq, the stubborn Palestine-Israel conflict, the threats posed by Iran, and the War on Terror. While it achieved limited success in Iraq and little more than frustration on Israel-Palestine and Iran, several key events occurred, largely independently of anything that the United States was doing in the region, that provided new opportunities for Washington in the second decade of the twenty-first century. One of these events was the 2009 elections in Iran and their violent aftermath. The charges of electoral fraud that rang through Iran and the brutal repression of those trying to reverse the rigged election bloodied Iran and weakened it in the region. A second set of events was the tumult of the Arab Spring in 2011. For all the glee of Iranian leaders at the fall of Tunisia's Ben-Ali and Egypt's Mubarak, the regionwide protests actually further weakened Iran, at least indirectly. The demonstrations hinted at the limits of Iranian power and affirmed key values associated with the United States. They also shook Syria, Iran's key ally. I will turn to these events and their creation of new openings for the United States in chapter 13.

PART IV

The United States and the New Middle East in the Twenty-First Century

10 The Bush Administration and the Arc of Instability

George W. Bush's election to the presidency in 2000 marked the most radical change in U.S. foreign policy in at least half a century and probably one of the sharpest turns in all of American history. The new administration transformed both the underlying principles and conduct of foreign policy. Part of the change was almost inevitable. The end of the Cold War had closed the door on a chapter of U.S. international history and opened a new one, demanding a fundamental reconsideration of America's place in the world. And within the first year of the Bush presidency, the attacks of 9/11 demanded yet another rethinking of U.S. foreign policy.

In the Middle East, the change in the direction of American policy making was no less dramatic than elsewhere. In fact, the new administration's policies were more ominous for the Mideast region than for practically any other area of the world. The new policies eschewed the predilection of Cold War presidents to share the burden of world leadership with key strategic partners and through military alliances. And even more than its immediate predecessors, the presidency of George W. Bush missed the totality of the transformation that had overtaken the Middle East, making the United States all the more vulnerable to the new currents in the region.

After the end of the Cold War, it took some time—in fact, nearly the entire period of the administrations of George H. W. Bush and Bill Clinton—to map out the new lay of the land. As I noted in chapters 5 and 6, U.S. foreign policy in the 1990s tended to be seat of the pants rather than driven by a coherent vision; it was more ad hoc than it was based on an overarching assessment of the threats and opportunities for the United States in the post–Cold War world. Policy makers still did not have a firm grasp on how, or even if, the various parts of the world fit together conceptually in some comprehensive schema. With the inauguration of the new Bush administration in 2001, nearly a dozen years had passed since the fall of the Berlin Wall. Those years provided ample opportunity to fit the pieces together. Policy makers and policy thinkers could now develop a cogent understanding of the world and America's place in it. And even though after his election George W. Bush saw his mandate, such as it was, in terms of domestic reform, the attacks on the World Trade Center and Pentagon on September 11, 2001, shifted his administration's focus to the world outside and demanded an immediate course of action.

However, more factors than just the passing of time and the urgency created by 9/11 helped account for the profound change in the way America conducted its international affairs during the Bush presidency. The years leading up to his election witnessed a veritable hothouse of new ideas among conservatives on how to think about the world and what America's role in it should be. The roots of the radical change in the tenor of foreign-policy making in the United States during Bush's first term stemmed from those new ideas—how they portrayed the world and how the United States should behave in it.

This chapter asserts that the set of ideas that were developed in the 1990s by key conservative thinkers and out-of-work Republican policy makers drove American foreign policy in the 2000s; they provided a basis for developing a course of action after 9/11. Those ideas put the Middle East generally and Iraq in particular at the center of American foreign policy. It was here, the thinking went, that the biggest threats to U.S. security were centered, and it was in this region that American global leadership could play a transformative role in creating a safer world. In the Middle East and numerous other regions where violence, dictatorships, and terrorism now reigned, the United States could unleash freedom and democracy.

Those ideas, I will show, were built on untenable assumptions and a fundamental misreading of the Middle East. They missed the important transformation that the region had undergone over the last decades of the twentieth century. They led the United States into a protracted war and a foreign policy that failed to confront directly the biggest challenges that the country faced. Much of the failure stemmed from the assumption that the world could be understood systemically. That is, if one were to grasp the underlying principles of how the world as a whole now worked, one could then fashion and adopt effective policies. Similar to much thinking during the Cold War, at least in this one respect, the conservative theorists downplayed the importance of appreciating the distinctiveness and knowing the ins and outs of particular spots around the globe. As a result, for the Middle East, they missed the foundational changes that were occurring at the end of the twentieth century—those discussed in the last three chapters—and this had disastrous results.

After the election of Bill Clinton, Republicans who had previously been fully occupied in positions of power now found themselves with the opportunity to contemplate how international affairs had changed. They could mull over why they were now sitting on the sidelines. For the Republican Party, which had been in office, remarkably, for twenty out of the previous twenty-four years, the Clinton presidency was an unwelcome and unfamiliar change. Still, it afforded its theorists the forced leisure to step back and think broadly and deeply about what the Republican party stood for in a now reconfigured world. Even when these sorts of opportunities do present themselves, former policy makers, sitting in cushy think tanks or schools of international affairs, do not always use these opportunities wisely. They fail to confront the fundamental questions of how the world has changed and why they were not returned to power by the voters. In fact, I would venture to say that most often they do not grapple with these questions at all. But to their credit, a number of key Republican former officials and aides did exactly that, rethinking the fundamentals of their approach to U.S. foreign policy.

The next section distills the world vision that these thinkers developed and their shaping of that vision into a foreign-policy agenda. In the subsequent section, I look at how George W. Bush, who had expressed open skepticism about the kinds of ideas developed by these thinkers, eventually adopted those concepts himself and built them into the cornerstone of his presidency. The following two sections delve into America's official statement of its world agenda after 9/11, "The National Security Strategy of the United States of America," and the conceptual thread that pulled it together, what I call the "arc of instability." The chapter then turns to the theory of change adopted by the Bush administration, what some have called the "reverse domino theory," and how the Middle East held pride of place in that theory for how the United States would achieve its strategic goals globally. Those ideas became the foundation for America's war in Iraq. Finally, I analyze the faulty assumptions that underlay the Bush administration's conceptions of global change and the Middle East and how those led the country into a quagmire in the region.

A New View of the World

The people who developed the ideas that would later become the basis for American foreign policy in the Bush years came to be known as neoconservatives, or neocons. But the neoconservatism that emerged in the 1990s was a far cry from its earlier incarnation. Neoconservatism dates back to the disillusionment of some important thinkers—mostly, former leftists—with Democratic Party thinking on domestic and foreign policy in the early 1970s and then the actual making of policy during the Carter years (Ehrman 1995). Many who joined the ranks, especially those concerned primarily with foreign policy, were disciples of Senator Henry M. "Scoop" Jackson, a Democrat from Washington. After his failed bid for the presidency in 1976, most then went on to support Ronald Reagan in the 1980 election and become permanently wedded to the Republican Party.

The central foreign-policy tenet of neoconservatism in those years reflected Jackson's top priority: strong, uncompromising opposition to communism and the Soviet Union. This position was set out repeatedly by two of neoconservatism's founders, Norman Podhoretz and Irving Kristol, in their magazines *Commentary* and *The Public Interest*, respectively. Indeed, as early as the first year of the Reagan presidency, Podhoretz expressed disappointment even with Reagan himself for being too soft with the Soviets. Later, others joined that chorus, excoriating the Reagan administration over negotiations with the Soviet Union—and compromises offered to it—especially during Reagan's second term, when Mikhail Gorbachev put forth a new face for the Soviet Union. But once Reagan left office, all was forgiven, and he became—and remains—a kind of demigod among the neoconservatives, the person who won the Cold War.

In any case, with the fall of the Soviet Union, neoconservatives found that the issue and cause that united them had disappeared. Like most others thinking about international affairs, they found themselves utterly adrift. They lacked a clear compass for assessing America's place in the world, the threats it confronted, and what its foreign policy should be. Some critics felt that with the demise of the USSR, the neoconservative mission was now complete and its raison d'être had disappeared (Fischel 1996).

Neoconservatism, though, proved much more resilient and adaptable than that. These now-loyal Republicans knew, not surprisingly, that they did not like the way Clinton was conducting foreign policy. James Ceaser (2006, 26) put it in no uncertain terms at the end of the Clinton presidency: liberals' failures "remain strikingly evident in the half measures, the fecklessness, and the unwillingness to assert decisive American leadership that have characterized foreign policy in this decade." But some conservatives, too, expressed frustration with policy even when Republican George H. W. Bush was in power, from 1989 to 1993. Grumbling came both, quietly, from within the administration and, more loudly, from outside. Criticism was especially sharp after the Bush administration's failure to topple Saddam Hussein and occupy Baghdad at the conclusion of the Gulf War in 1991. One neoconservative later called the Bush reluctance to overthrow Saddam Hussein a "squandered" opportunity (Wurmser 1999, 1).

The most notable implicit critique came from within the senior Bush's administration, in a remarkable classified document, the "Defense Policy Guidance," written in March 1992 and then leaked to the *New York Times*. This document would eventually have a gargantuan effect in defining America's place in the world and in explaining the sharp turn the Bush administration took in Washington's role in the Middle East.

The document's principal author was Paul Wolfowitz, who was undersecretary of defense for policy at the time, working for Defense Secretary Dick Cheney. Wolfowitz had a storied career in government and academia. Unlike many other neoconservatives, who had undergone a kind of born-again experience, Wolfowitz seemed to have developed his conservative orientation in the womb. His studies at the University of Chicago brought him under the wings of the leading conservative thinkers of the time, including Allan Bloom; Albert Wohlstetter, Wolfowitz's principal mentor; and Leo Strauss, who, more than being politically conservative himself, tended to attract legions of conservative disciples. Wolfowitz began his government career assisting Fred Iklé, Nixon's head of the U.S. Arms Control and Disarmament Agency, and served early on under Senator

Henry Jackson. He eventually would end up during George W. Bush's administration as deputy secretary of defense and, then, as president of the World Bank, before bowing out of public service after a much ballyhooed ethical impropriety at the bank.

Also contributing to the "Defense Policy Guidance" document was Wolfowitz's own deputy, I. Lewis "Scooter" Libby. Libby later became an infamous figure because of his criminal conviction in 2007 for his role in the disclosure of the identity of a CIA undercover agent, Valerie Plame, and the subsequent cover-up surrounding that event. President Bush eventually commuted his prison sentence. Libby had worked under Wolfowitz during the Reagan administration and the first Bush administration, and in 2001 he became Vice President Cheney's chief of staff.

In Washington, the 1992 "Defense Policy Guidance" caused a stir. The paper was the first concrete attempt to move conservatives from carping about what they did not like in foreign policy to laying out their own agenda. It advocated important major shifts in the way the United States should conduct itself internationally, most of which were not looked upon kindly by the Democratic-majority Congress and even by some prominent Republicans. In fact, after the leak of the document, the paper was rewritten and toned down considerably. The original document is well worth looking at, however, because its themes crop up later in papers on foreign and military policy written by conservatives—and because of the principals involved with it, Wolfowitz, Libby, and Cheney.

The implicit target of the document's aggressive tone was what Ceaser had termed America's fecklessness, particularly the penchant to engage in international power sharing. Such power sharing could be in international organizations, especially the United Nations; strategic partners such as Britain and a handful of other countries; and military alliances like NATO. Wolfowitz's attack on power sharing is reminiscent of the debate between the Roosevelt internationalists promoting a 51 percent American share in the new postwar world order and the Truman officials who sought 80 percent. The "Defense Policy Guidance" emphasis was on using all means—in fact, there was a strong emphasis on using military force—to maintain U.S. global leadership, blunting potential pretenders to superpower status. Russia was singled out as possibly reemerging to such a position and, ominously, as a threatening force to U.S. global leadership.

Pushing aside the well-established tenets of multilateralism and the UN Charter's notion of collective security, the draft argued for what would later be called unilateralism. There must be "the sense that the world order is ultimately backed by the U.S. . . . and the United States should be postured to act independently when collective action cannot be orchestrated" or when a quick response is needed. The United States, the document went on, would have to intervene selectively where it saw threats emerging. It pointed to the Middle East as an area of special concern, where the United States had to preserve "access to the region's oil."

The implications of the paper were momentous. Its authors were breaking with the key principles and tactics of the last half century, the search for strategic partners and the sharing of international responsibility through military-treaty organizations. The complexity of the Middle East and the recent transformation of its regional dynamics were reduced to America's access to its oil.

If the "Defense Policy Guidance" came from within the halls of government, most of the subsequent new neoconservative ideas were generated outside it, mostly in think tanks. Throughout the Clinton years, the disgruntled lot of neoconservative thinkers fielded multiple seminars and wrote numerous papers, aiming to forge a new way of thinking about foreign policy. During Clinton's second term, they began to focus these activities. Kristol and the well-known foreign-policy pundit Robert Kagan founded a new think tank in 1997, the Project for the New American Century (PNAC). It quickly became the locus for new conservative ideas on international affairs.

The PNAC introduced itself by issuing a "Statement of Principles." Its message was simple: in the post–Cold War environment, the United States needed to be *the* world leader, protecting the existing world order, which is conducive to the country's security, prosperity, and principles. "We aim to make the case and rally support," the statement emphasized, "for American global leadership" (Golan 2007). That meant policy makers had to recognize that hostile forces bent on undoing the United States still lurked in various corners of the globe, even after the collapse of the communist bloc. The government, according to the statement, needed to increase defense spending significantly, confront hostile regimes, support others already committed to freedom, and promote democracy and freedom in places were they were currently suppressed.

The signatories were a veritable who's who of American conservative policy making and thinking. Among them were Jeb Bush, Dick Cheney, Steve Forbes, Francis Fukuyama, Dan Quayle, Donald Rumsfeld, and, not surprisingly, Paul Wolfowitz. Another key figure was Elliott Abrams, who had served as assistant secretary of state for Reagan and later became George W. Bush's deputy national security advisor for global democracy strategy. Two other signers were Gary Bauer and George Weigel, connected to Christian evangelicals and conservative Catholics, respectively, both of which were emerging at the time as political forces in foreign affairs. William Bennett, a leading conservative thinker who had been secretary of education for Reagan and drug czar for the first Bush, also signed on.

Wolfowitz had been a mentor to several other signers, including Zalmay Khalilzad. In the administrations of Reagan and George H. W. Bush, Khalilzad had served in a variety of posts before becoming America's ambassador to Afghanistan, Iraq, and the United Nations under George W. Bush. Another Wolfowitz disciple who signed on was Scooter Libby, the same Libby who had written the 1992 "Defense Policy Guidance" with Wolfowitz. Later, during George W. Bush's term of office, Libby was identified so closely with the vice president that he was sometimes called "Dick Cheney's Dick Cheney," a phrase that had, I suppose, several meanings.

Subsequent reports, papers, and seminars sponsored by the PNAC remained faithful to the initial agenda established in its statement of principles. At the time, the project's members were swimming against the current of American thought and policy. Defense budgets in the 1990s were flat or shrinking. Most policy makers and politicians did not see a global threat that might be nearly as daunting as that posed earlier by the Soviet Union. The most important of the reports to come out of the projects and seminars of the PNAC, *Rebuilding America's Defenses: Strategy, Forces, and Resources for a New Century,* acknowledged "the relatively peaceful, prosperous and free condition the world enjoys today." The report continued, "At no time in history has the international security order been as conducive to American interests and ideals" (Donnelly 2000, i, iv). Under these conditions, it was no easy task to paint a foreboding picture that would succeed in prying free huge new resources for defense. Yet that is precisely what the report tried to do. Resonating strongly with the ideas and themes set out in the 1992 "Defense Policy Guidance," it demanded a major commitment to defense, simply to maintain the peace and prosperity that already existed: "The challenge for the coming century is to preserve and enhance this 'American peace'" (Donnelly 2000, iv).

The report argued that the United States had had the relative luxury during the Cold War of "wholesale" security policy through the global deterrence of the Soviets. Now, it needed to secure itself at the retail level, deterring or fighting, if necessary, multiple foes. And the United States was ill-equipped and poorly positioned to play that retail game. Threats were global—from a rising China; from adversaries like Iran, Iraq, and North Korea; and from other nations in the oil-rich, volatile Middle East. Also singled out were "terrorists, organized crime, and other 'non-state actors,'" who threatened "the international system of nation-states" (Donnelly 2000, 4). While the United States had to remain vigilant in now peaceful Central and Western Europe and in East Asia, where China's emergence might be of future concern, the immediate threats were elsewhere. The Iraqi invasion of Kuwait, the mission in Somalia, and the 1990s wars in the Balkans after the dissolution of Yugoslavia were all examples of the sorts of complex political and military challenges that the United States now faced and of the new kinds of threats to its own national security.

Certainly, there was also emphasis in the report on some familiar Republican themes, such as reviving the old Star Wars policy, the Strategic Defense Initiative missile-defense system advocated by the Reagan administration. The report predictably called, too, for increases in the size of the military. But it sounded new themes, as well, including the rebuilding, reorganizing, and repositioning of American armed forces to reflect and defend against the new sorts of global threats. The most novel dimension came in elevating the perception of the importance of threat not only from superpower pretenders like Russia and China but from seemingly insignificant figures and forces. "Neglect or withdrawal from constabulary missions will increase the likelihood of larger wars breaking out and encourage petty tyrants to defy American interests and ideals" (Donnelly 2000, 13).

The PNAC members clearly feared a retreat into what they called "Fortress America." Reorganized armed forces must be deployed widely to face the multiple Lilliputian threats: these forces "are the cavalry on the new American frontier" (Donnelly 2000, 15). And like the cavalry, they had to be poised and used for offensive military action (again recalling Wolfowitz's theme in the 1992 leaked document). America could not simply wait to respond to the initiatives of those who could threaten its security. The project promoted an activist, aggressive, mobile, and unilateral (when necessary) foreign policy. Referring to these conservative thinkers, including himself, as "internationalists," Ceaser (2000, 27) wrote that their thinking was not designed to see the military simply as a deterrent or "for being placed in a storehouse. Internationalists regard military force as an instrument of foreign policy to be called upon when necessary to achieve our goals. . . . It allows America to pursue a noble purpose on the stage of world history, one that our Founders intended it should serve."[1]

The new thinking eschewed the tools that had marked American foreign policy since World War II. Diplomacy and mediation were nowhere to be found. Multilateralism was not part of the vocabulary. Collective defense and military alliances were downplayed in their accounts. The strategic relationships that American officials had nurtured for decades seemed to be of little concern. In short, the pillars of American security policies around the word, not least in the Middle East, were now being pushed aside in the new thinking in favor of a new set of proposed tools and structures.

Bush Adopts a New Foreign-Policy Orientation

George W. Bush was not a participant in the Project for the New American Century discussions, nor did he seem to be a target for conversion in the 1990s by the project's core participants. Other senior Republicans—George Bush's brother Jeb, Steve Forbes, Donald Rumsfeld, Dick Cheney—were the ones selected as possible proselytes to the new ideas being generated. And all of them did indeed sign onto the initial "Statement of Principles." When George W. Bush was elected president, then, it was not clear that his presidency would go down the road that the PNAC was blazing. Other well-worn paths existed in the Republican Party, including isolationism and realism (or neorealism, as it was often called), which might have attracted the new president more (Ceaser 2000).

During the campaign, Bush had famously expressed opposition to American involvement in nation building abroad. At the time, nation building was largely a code word alluding to the possibility of a quagmire for the United States in establishing working states in the former Yugoslavia. As Robbins (2007, 92) commented, "Nothing from his presidential bid even hinted at an ambition to remake the post-cold war world." This cautious position seemed to put him at odds with PNAC thinkers. Their foreign-policy ideas dictated, as Bennett (2000, 29) put it in evoking no one less than George Washington, that once the country was secure Americans "could think and act [internationally] not only in pursuit of 'interest' but also in pursuit of 'justice.'" Bush seemed disinclined to pursue a strategy with a strong stake in pushing international justice—a foreign policy with a strong moralistic flavor.

But no one knew for sure which direction his foreign policy would take once he entered office. Even on the eve of his inauguration, an interview with Bush on international affairs seemed to indicate a realist's wariness of an aggressive foreign policy and of a proselytizing internationalism. He showed little regard for the sorts of issues that were vexing the PNAC thinkers (Sanger 2007, 75).

Bush was unlikely to pursue isolationism, what the PNAC participants called a retreat to Fortress America. Isolationism did find some lonely voices in the Republican Party, but they never gained resonance after the Cold War ended. Globalization was the watchword at the turn of the millennium, and the only serious currents to resist aspects of globalization were found within the Democratic Party, mostly in opposing the World Trade Organization (WTO) and unregulated free trade.

But realism did seem a more likely bet for the Bush foreign policy than the sorts of notions coming out of the PNAC. It was, after all, the long-time standby approach of Republicans and presented a familiar palette to the new president, one that his father had adopted during his own administration. Like the ideas developed by the PNAC, realism viewed the world as threatening and dangerous. But there the two approaches parted ways. Most realists (although there was significant variation among them on this point) tended to be cautious in exercising power and much less offensively minded in military affairs than the PNAC thinkers were. They worried about overreach for the United States, operating abroad beyond its resources and capacities. It was precisely the approach taken by Eisenhower and subsequent presidents in looking for ways to limit American commitments and expenditures by sharing international power with select partners.

Also, realists shied away from the PNAC's moral emphasis and its proposals to export American principles of democracy and freedom to the rest of the world. Realism tended to eschew high-minded idealism and stick to gritty issues of national interests and national security. It framed international relations as a game largely consisting of state actors, each with its own clear set of national priorities and interests. And realism's adherents supported multilateral institutions and collective-security measures. They especially encouraged military alliances for the United States, such as NATO, but also military actions under the aegis of the

United Nations. They shied away from trumpeting America's status as the unquestioned global leader and advocating that the United States go it alone.

The tenor of Bush's appointments to senior posts did not tip off whether he would lean toward wary realism or the more aggressive and offensively minded approach advocated by the PNAC. The new secretary of state, Colin Powell, seemed to be a cautious realist, at least from what people could tell from his limited political role until that point. Likewise, the president's national security advisor, Condoleezza Rice, was an academic who presented herself as a realist and seemed in her writings to fit the mode.

But across the table were Defense Secretary Rumsfeld and Vice President Cheney, longtime politicos, whose conservative credentials reached back to the Nixon era. Both had been realists (of the more aggressive stripe) for most of their careers but had become involved with the PNAC. Rumsfeld, in particular, was now expounding the kind of reorganization of American armed forces put forth in the project's working paper, *Rebuilding America's Defenses*. He echoed Wolfowitz's ideas written into the "Defense Policy Guidance" draft, which had been repeated and developed by Wolfowitz throughout the rest of the 1990s. Once in office, Rumsfeld's selection of Wolfowitz as deputy secretary of defense indicated that Rumsfeld's realism had given way to the more aggressive mode of the PNAC. As the number-two man in the Pentagon, Wolfowitz opened the door for multiple appointments in the administration—particularly but not exclusively in the Pentagon—of those who had participated in the PNAC or lower aides who bought into the project's principles.

Struggles between Powell in the State Department and Rumsfeld at the Pentagon were widely reported during the first Bush term. It is difficult to know which way the new president leaned at first, but the attacks of September 11, 2001, were decisive. They provided an opportunity for PNAC ideas to gain the acceptance, inside government and in the broader public, that had eluded them throughout the 1990s and even during the first year of the Bush administration. The 9/11 attacks moved Bush firmly into the PNAC circle. Rumsfeld and Cheney prevailed over Powell in gaining the ear of the president and shaping the overall direction of foreign policy.

Bush's conversion became clear in a series of speeches he gave following 9/11, including to a joint session of Congress on September 20. He followed that with an address abroad, at the Warsaw Conference on

Combating Terrorism, less than two months after the attacks. Later, in his State of the Union Address in January 2002, Bush introduced the notion of the "axis of evil," singling out Iraq, Iran, and North Korea as global troublemakers. His conversion to the foreign policy of Wolfowitz and the other PNAC thinkers became most evident in his commencement speech at West Point on June 1, 2002, where he noted famously, "if we wait for threats to fully materialize, we will have waited too long."

Those speeches became the basis for what came to be known as the Bush Doctrine. How different Bush's second inaugural speech was from his interview before his first inauguration! In January 2001, he had wistfully spoken of a foreign policy that would provide respite to the United States. He stressed the need to steer clear of entanglements that come through nation building and to avoid foreign adventures that would divert America from the urgent changes needed at home. In 2005, in contrast, he spoke of the worldwide spread of freedom as "the calling of our time" and committed America's support for democratic forces "in every nation and culture, with the ultimate goal of ending tyranny in our world." Although his aides later retreated from the audacious agenda set out in that 2005 inaugural speech, the tone pointed to a president who had come a long, long way since 2001. The months following the 2001 al-Qaeda attacks on the World Trade Center and Pentagon were a gestation period for the new president: it was then that his orientation to foreign policy took shape. In that time, the Middle East—and America's role in it—rose to the top of the emerging agenda, although the new administration was notably lacking in Middle East experts who knew the region intimately. As it would turn out, this mixture of making the Middle East the focus of policy yet not having much expertise on the area would prove to be a lethal combination, especially in dealing with a region that had been so fundamentally transformed in recent years.

The National Security Strategy of the United States of America

The period after 9/11 was one in which broad ideas of how the United States might change the world and spread freedom and democracy were seriously contemplated. The Bush Doctrine was most fully expressed in "The National Security Strategy of the United States of America," a document posted on the White House website a year after the terrorist attacks. It had all the markings of earlier ideas expressed in the Project for the New American Century seminars and papers. Two elements, which could be found as far back as Wolfowitz and Libby's "Defense Policy Guidance" paper a decade earlier, at least in embryonic form, were unilateralism and preemption.

Unilateralism expressed, in part, disappointment, even disgust, with what came to be called by administration officials the Old Europe. In the terms of Bush aides, the *Old* Europe was the Western European allies, including NATO members, who had been the bedrock of America's postwar multilateral policies. Now, key officials, including Rumsfeld and Marc Grossman, who had been Clinton's assistant secretary of state for European affairs and was now Bush's undersecretary of state for political affairs, displayed open disdain for European views and preferences on international affairs.

Lip service was paid to international institutions, multilateralism, and the need for foreign states to help themselves. And to be sure, in certain realms, such as the War on Terror, international cooperation did remain paramount for the United States (Mendelsohn 2009). But the shift from past multilateralism was marked. The United States was not a partner but a dominant leader. Its leadership meant that where others demurred America would be ready to play an imperial role in regions important to its national security. The bedrock of previous American foreign policy— the emphasis on military alliances and shared leadership with key strategic partners—was now discarded, even ridiculed, by Bush officials.

Even in combating international terrorism, where international coordination was often crucial, the message was the same: "While the United States will constantly strive to enlist support of the international community, we will not hesitate to act alone, if necessary." The document added, "Our best defense is a good offense." These sentiments were not expressed simply in theoretical terms. Project thinkers considered the Europeans to be pusillanimous and did not expect them to come through when the going got tough. The United States would inevitably have to act on its own. And that approach would be carried from Europe to the most dangerous areas threatening American security, most notably the all-important Middle East.

Preemption in the Bush Doctrine was the idea that the United States had the right and responsibility to strike first against any states or non-state actors that might threaten the country's security, even if an attack by them was not imminent. Or, as Bush put it in discussing Iraq before the 2003 invasion, "Facing clear evidence of peril, we cannot wait for the final proof, the smoking gun that could come in the form of a mushroom cloud" (Sanger 2007, 79). The strong focus on fighting terrorists after the 9/11 attacks meant "acting preemptively against such terrorists, to prevent them from doing harm against our people and our country." "The National Security Strategy of the United States of America" recognized that it was changing long-held norms of international relations, moving beyond international law's tolerance of preemption in the case of imminent attack only:

> For centuries, international law recognized that nations need not suffer an attack before they can lawfully take action to defend themselves against forces that present an imminent danger of attack. Legal scholars and international jurists often conditioned the legitimacy of preemption on the existence of an imminent threat—most often a visible mobilization of armies, navies, and air forces preparing to attack.
>
> We must adapt the concept of imminent threat to the capabilities and objectives of today's adversaries. . . . In an age where the enemies of civilization openly and actively seek the world's most destructive technologies, the United States cannot remain idle while dangers gather.

The radical connotations of unilateralism and preemption—their sharp turn from accepted practices of international relations and from the way the United States had conducted its foreign policy up until the Bush administration—attracted most of the attention among those in Washington and the press. What is of equal interest, however, is the broader picture of the world that that lay behind "The National Security Strategy of the United States of America" and the PNAC's and other think tanks' papers. Underlying the public documents was a coherent view of the overall architecture of contemporary international relations—and how it presented a series of interrelated threats and opportunities to the United States. In a word, all the thinking of the 1990s had resulted in a new way of understanding how the world works and the possibilities for the United States in it. It meant discarding the old caution, alliances, and partners in favor of a new set of aggressive tools. And those tools, so confidently trumpeted by neoconservatives, led to inattention to the intricacies of particular regions of the world—most portentously, to the dynamics of the Middle East, which had changed dramatically by the end of the twentieth century.

The Coming Dangers

That architecture began with the by now familiar refrain that neoconservatives had hammered home since the mid-1990s: the preeminence of the United States as *the* global leader. That said, the thinking turned to the question of what might upend U.S. supremacy—where did the threats reside? From the documents, one can derive two spheres of threats to America's position in the near- and medium-term future. First were the pretenders to world power, particularly China and Russia, which preoccupied many of the neoconservative thinkers, especially in the 1990s. From Wolfowitz's 1992 leaked document on, conservative thinkers were concerned with Russia. That document stated, "Our first objective is to prevent the reemergence of a new rival, either on the territory of the former Soviet Union or elsewhere, that poses a threat on the order of that posed formerly by the Soviet Union."

And that concern, along with the growing recognition of China's expanding power, continued as a focus throughout the 1990s and beyond. For example, after the general overview, the first two countries to be discussed in detail in the important neoconservative book *Present Dangers*, edited by Robert Kagan and William Kristol and published in 2000, were Ross Munro's "China: The Challenge of a Rising Power" and Peter Rodman's "Russia: The Challenge of a Failing Power." Russia and China, of course, were primary subjects among all sorts of thinkers, not only the neoconservatives, and the neoconservative ideas on these subjects did not seem especially innovative. Munro, for instance, castigated Clinton for becoming too cozy with China and suggested treating it with more wariness and building ties with democratic forces on China's periphery. And in the case of Russia, Rodman simply cautioned that America not underestimate it. These were hardly original—or radical—critiques.

The innovative thinking among the neoconservatives came in conceptualizing the second sphere of threats that they identified, the "petty tyrants" and "terrorists." Again, the "Defense Policy Guidance" document of 1992 had singled out this sphere, if somewhat obliquely:

The second objective is to address sources of regional conflict and instability. . . . Various types of US interests may be involved in such instances [where the U.S. would assume the responsibility for addressing wrongs]: access to vital raw materials, primarily Persian gulf oil; proliferation of weapons of mass destruction and ballistic missiles; threats to US citizens from terrorism or regional or local conflicts; and threats to US society from narcotics trafficking.

Petty tyrants, terrorists, and regional conflict were elevated to central importance in the new conservative architecture of international relations. Dictators like Saddam Hussein and groups like al-Qaeda posed a new and very different sort of challenge to the United States. These perils led to novel sorts of conceptions by conservative thinkers about the locus of threats to U.S. national security. The identification of the lurking dangers also hinted at what sorts of options existed for the United States to minimize or eliminate them.

Neoconservative thinking about the architecture of international relations can be captured through the concept of the "arc of instability." The territorial swathe of the arc stretched from West Africa through the Balkans, the Caucasus, and the Middle East to Afghanistan and Pakistan. Inside the arc was a concentration of malevolent forces, beliefs, and trends—including those petty tyrants and terrorists as well as an increasingly popular radical form of political Islam, all of which directly threatened the national security of the United States, in the minds of conservative authors.

A key writer in identifying the arc and the dark forces bubbling within it was Robert D. Kaplan, who emerged in the 1990s as a celebrated journalist and travel author. After writing a couple of books that barely made a blip on the radar screen, Kaplan published *Balkan Ghosts* in 1993, just as the wars sparked by the collapse of Yugoslavia flared up. The book not only sold well; it was also read by government officials, including President Clinton, and by opinion makers. It catapulted Kaplan to instant renown, and he went on to become a regular contributor to the *Atlantic* magazine.

But more important, he became a crucial source of ideas about the threats the United States faced and the country's place in the world to neoconservatives, and to others as well. Kaplan too has been described as a neoconservative (e.g., McGowan 2007), although he has not identified himself that way, nor was he part of the Republican, conservative thinking that went on in the PNAC and other think tanks. Still, some of his sentiments were very much along the lines that Wolfowitz and others were setting out at the time. A *New York Times* piece captured Kaplan's worldview:

> The world is a threat. Anarchy is waiting at the arrivals gate; tribal and cultural grudges crowd the borders. The present is the past traveling under a pseudonym. Humanitarian idealists always muff it; realists count on power politics, cooperative dictators and imperialism. Years before the invasion of Iraq would make his words prescient, Kaplan urged a clenched foreign policy: "We will initiate hostilities . . . whenever it is absolutely necessary and we see a clear advantage in doing so, and we will justify it morally after the fact." He added, "Nor is that cynical." (Lipsky 2005)

It is impossible to know whether Kaplan's ideas directly affected neo-conservative thinkers, but his writings were widely disseminated, and the ideas became part of Washington's policy discourse. The Kaplan ideas that became so important in the neoconservative lexicon of how the world was constructed and where threats lay emerged in two publications that appeared after *Balkan Ghosts*—an article in the *Atlantic*, "The Coming Anarchy" (1994), which he later expanded into a book, and a sort of companion book, *The Ends of the Earth* (1996). The article is more political in tone; *The Ends of the Earth* is more a travel book, but with an emphasis more on festering sores than on tourist beaches. Kaplan introduced *The Ends of the Earth* as a volume in which he "tried to see the present in terms of the future. . . . Think of it as a brief romp through a swath of the globe"; it is a "book, which folds international studies into a travelogue" (Kaplan 1996, xi–xii). The descriptions in the book complemented the more explicit analytic categories in the article "The Coming Anarchy."

The article projected what Kaplan believed the political character of the world would be in the twenty-first century. His account started in West Africa, which he believed held a mirror up to the future in many other parts of the world:

> Disease, overpopulation, unprovoked crime, scarcity of resources, refugee migrations, the increasing erosion of nation-states and international borders, and the empowerment of private armies, se-

curity firms, and international drug cartels are now most tellingly demonstrated through a West African prism.

In the developing world, the future holds "the withering away of central governments, the rise of tribal and regional domains, the unchecked spread of disease, and the growing pervasiveness of war." Resource scarcities and environmental stress will fuel the emergence of the "Saddam Husseins of the future." This was not a pretty picture of how the future will unfold.

What Kaplan witnessed, he believed, would change international relations and the very nature of war. He commented that the Cold War as a "world of one adversary seems as distant as the world of Herodotus." Here he anticipated the neoconservatives' refrain that the United States was moving from securing itself at the wholesale level to doing that now at the retail level. Kaplan underscored that point by quoting Malraux: " 'Oh, what a relief to fight, to fight enemies who defend themselves, enemies who are awake!' Andre Malraux wrote in *Man's Fate*. I cannot think of a more suitable battle cry for many combatants in the early decades of the twenty-first century" (Kaplan 1994).

He repeatedly cited the same places as breeding the coming dangers— West Africa (particularly Liberia and Sierra Leone), the Balkans (Bosnia, especially), the Caucasus, Central Asia, and the Middle East (referring to failing Arab states and societies, Turkey, and the threats posed by the Kurds, most notably in Turkey). In fact, in *The Ends of the Earth* Kaplan structured his travelogue along nearly the same axis, or arc: Part I, "West Africa"; Part II, "The Nile Valley"; Part III, "Anatolia and the Caucasus"; Part IV, "The Iranian Plateau"; Part V, "Central Asia"; Part VI, "The Indian Subcontinent and Indochina." And if there is a thread through many of these, it is that "Islam's very militancy makes it attractive to the downtrodden. It is the one religion that is prepared to fight."

The Arc of Instability

Neoconservatives, including Kaplan, were influenced by another recent article that had appeared, Samuel Huntington's "The Clash of Civilizations?" (1993). Like "The Coming Anarchy," Huntington's article caused a considerable stir in the 1990s and was expanded into a book widely read by government officials, opinion makers, undergraduates, and the broader public (Huntington 1996). Even more than Kaplan's,

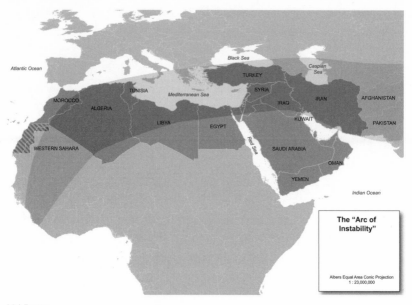

The "Arc of Instability"

Albers Equal Area Conic Projection
1 : 23,000,000

MAP 10.1

Huntington's ideas became part of the Washington policy discourse, including among those who did not take the time to read him.

Huntington, a renowned professor at Harvard, was also trying to decipher the post–Cold War character of global politics, specifically the coming sources of conflict. And his vision, while not quite as gloomy as Kaplan's, foresaw ongoing tension generated by incompatible cultures rubbing up against one another. The interactions among seven or eight principal civilizations will shape global relations, he predicted, especially conflicts along the boundaries between these civilizations. "The fault lines between civilizations," Huntington wrote, "are replacing the political and ideological boundaries of the Cold War as the flash points for crisis and bloodshed" (1993, 29). Western power will only exacerbate tensions, as other civilizations react by seeking their own indigenous way of shaping the world.

Huntington pointed to the already existing hotspots in global politics as signs of the future. "On the Eurasian continent . . . the proliferation of ethnic conflict, epitomized at the extreme in 'ethnic cleansing,' has not been totally random. It has been the most frequent and most violent between groups belonging to different civilizations." And, he added in a rhetorical flourish, "Islam has bloody borders" (1993, 34–35). For Huntington, the emerging clashes would demand extreme vigilance. But he was not a neoconservative. While he, like a number of key neoconservatives, had been tied to Henry Jackson and his tough-minded stance toward the Soviet Union, Huntington was extremely wary of attempts by the United States to shape this world of multiple civilizations—through nation building, the export of democracy, or ending ethnic clashes. He departed from realism by arguing that states were no longer the key element of international relations, but he retained a realist's caution about what the United States could accomplish in the world.

The neoconservative thinkers of the 1990s and, later, the policy makers of the Bush administration cherry-picked from Kaplan and Huntington. They abandoned an outlook that looked exclusively at relations among big powers, although they certainly did not dismiss the likes of Russia and China, which constituted their first sphere of threats to America. But they saw a second sphere, too: the perils for the United States of diffuse scattered threats. These sorts of dangers could be found almost anywhere in the world, but they were concentrated in the arc of instability stretching from West Africa to South Asia. It was in this arc that malignant forces fed off one another, it was here that the fault lines between cultures were concentrated, it was here that radical Islam most actively preyed on peoples' vulnerabilities and achieved its greatest successes, and it was within the arc that the most critical resources necessary for American prosperity lay. In an op-ed in 2004, Kaplan likened the challenges the United States confronted to those faced in fighting Indians in the nineteenth century: the warring ethnic and religious militias that the United States now faces are no less varied than "the range of Indian groups, numbering in the hundreds, that the U.S. Cavalry and Dragoons had to confront" (2004, 22). Again, the cavalry image.

In one important way, though, the Bush policy makers and other neoconservatives departed from both Huntington and Kaplan. They were much more sanguine than both these writers about the possibility for initiating reform and instituting calm in these turbulent regions. Huntington had a much more cautious, even jaundiced, view of what the United States could accomplish, especially in such dysfunctional areas. He saw the business of American policy makers as acting largely to protect U.S. interests, especially its security. But he shied away from the kind of imperial role for the United States—a role of control and transformation—that the neoconservatives touted. Kaplan did tend toward a more activist, imperial role for the United States, but he also was skeptical of what could be achieved as it tried to shape the world. Control, yes. Genuine transformation, probably not. Indeed, Kaplan (2002, 4–6) envisioned in-creases in freedom actually unleashing more violence and mayhem, as populist groups would take advantage of increased democracy.

The Bush team, on the other hand, had a more Pollyannaish view. It believed that what was good for America in these areas was also good for the people living there. The United States could secure not only its own interests but also freedom and democracy for the people of these regions. Freedom would not bring Kaplan's imagined havoc but stability and pros-perity. The neoconservatives conceived of an arc of instability that was currently rife with dark forces—the petty tyrants and terrorists that they repeatedly conjured up—but that was ultimately open to reform. They es-chewed Huntington's caution and Kaplan's ever-grim scenarios. They be-lieved that democracy could triumph almost anywhere, unleashing the public's pent-up frustration against authoritarianism and repression. In-deed, years later, neoconservatives saw the 2011 Arab Spring as a vindica-tion—if somewhat delayed—of the policies undertaken by them during the Bush years. Back in the 1990s, their upbeat view of the future of freedom and democracy was reinforced by yet another important article (which later became a book) published in *The National Interest* in 1989, "The End of History?," written by one of their own, Francis Fukuyama. In it, Fukuyama made the case

> that a remarkable consensus concerning the legitimacy of liberal democracy as a system of government had emerged throughout the world over the past few years, as it conquered rival ideologies like hereditary monarchy, fascism, and most recently communism. More than that, however, I argued that liberal democracy may con-stitute the "end point of mankind's ideological evolution" and the "final form of human government," and as such constituted the "end of history." (Fukuyama 1989, xi)

The Reverse Domino Theory

What did these analysts and officials see as the central dynam-ics in the arc of instability? How might those dynamics, which were now generating violence and chaos, be reversed to encourage freedom and democracy, as they believed was possible? For these thinkers, the arc was not an undifferentiated black hole or a mass of random events. Occurrences, networks, and regimes within the areas of instability were related, feeding off one another and creating a vicious cycle of descent. The triumph of one brutal dictator made it easier for another to emerge next door. Petty tyrants invited in nasty terrorists.

Moreover, from two perspectives, not all the places in the arc held equal value. First, some places were simply more important to U.S. interests than others. What happened in Sierra Leone, for example, was regrettable but of scant importance to America's achieving its international goals. At the same time, Iraq—with its massive oil reserves, its penchant for attacking neighbors that were also oil rich, and its aspiration to secure a larger share of the Persian Gulf coastline—was seen as very much in the crosshairs of American concerns abroad. Second, American interests aside, some parts of the arc, these analysts surmised, had a much greater influence, or spillover effect, than others in propelling the vicious cycle of violence, authoritarianism, and corruption throughout the arc.

Admittedly, neoconservative thinkers did not publish a list of trouble spots ranked from most to least important. During the 1990s, though, their papers, reports, and books demonstrated a clear focus on the Middle East, which trumped West Africa, the Caucasus, and other regions in the arc. And during the Bush administration, even before the invasion of Iraq in 2003, that preoccupation with the region continued and intensified. For foreign-policy makers, the Middle East was the beating heart of the arc of instability. From both of the perspectives mentioned above—direct relevance to U.S. security interests and the spillover effect—Bush officials viewed the Middle East as the critical lever in the arc.

At least in one important respect, then, the Bush foreign policy followed along the lines of the policies of previous administrations. The Middle East was central to American national security concerns for Bush officials, just as it had been for earlier policy makers. If anything, the Bush administration moved the region even higher up the list of priorities. But the interpretation of the role that the area played in America's place in the world and, conversely, the place that America should play in the region differed markedly from that of prior presidencies.

Some speculation surfaced that the preoccupation of neoconservatives inside and outside the administration with the Middle East was rooted in their strong support of Israel. Many of them, after all, were American Jews with close ties to Israel and to Israeli right-wing politicians. And a number of them, including one of the leading neoconservative figures and advocates for regime change in Iraq, Richard Perle (one of Henry

Jackson's protégés), did lead the writing of a provocative paper for Benjamin Netanyahu when he became prime minister of Israel in 1996. The paper reflected neoconservatives' jaundiced view of the Middle East and how Israel should negotiate the "bad neighborhood" in which it found itself (Study Group on a New Israeli Strategy Toward 2000 1996). ("Negotiate," perhaps, is not the best word for me to use, since the principal message for Netanyahu was actually to scrap the Oslo Peace Process and ditch negotiations based on land for peace altogether as part of his diplomatic repertoire.)

In any case, my review of neoconservative writings in the 1990s and 2000s found no evidence that Israeli security concerns were the primary motivation for singling out the Middle East as the region for direct U.S. action. Their analyses pointed repeatedly and unmistakably to their underlying belief that it was in this region principally that the dominant threats to *America* lay and that it was here that the United States could find the fulcrum for reshaping the arc of instability. For them, increased stability for America's close ally Israel would be a collateral benefit of such a transformation, not the motivating cause.

For the neoconservatives, the Middle East was brimming with direct threats to the United States. Two of the three charter members of Bush's "axis of evil"—Iraq and Iran—were Middle East countries. Only North Korea was outside the region. Later, the interim American ambassador to the United Nations, John R. Bolton, amplified Bush's axis. Bolton was another of the neoconservatives (although he seemed not to like the label very much) associated with the PNAC. In a speech several months after Bush's State of the Union address introducing the "axis of evil," Bolton added three additional members to the club—Cuba, Libya, and Syria. Again, two of these three were in the Middle East. All of these, he asserted, were "state sponsors of terrorism that are pursuing or who have the potential to pursue weapons of mass destruction (WMD) or have the capability to do so in violation of their treaty obligations." Important members of the administration believed at the time that "military action was the best way to democratize the Mideast and end its days as an incubation ward for terrorists" (Sanger 2007, 71).

Four of the six members of the expanded "axis" were Middle East regimes, but one of them drew particular attention from the neoconservative thinkers in the 1990s and then from the Bush team in the 2000s: Iraq (Sanger 2007, 77–80). It was the center of the center of the arc of instability—the jewel in the crown. As early as 1996, in the paper for

Netanyahu, neoconservative thinkers wrote of how "Iraq's future could affect the strategic balance in the Middle East profoundly." They pointed to the need for regime change in Iraq, hoping, of all things, for a return to pre-1958 Hashemite rule (Study Group on a New Israeli Strategy Toward 2000 1996).[2] The Hashemites, it will be recalled, were the Arab dynasty, supported by tribal alliances in the Arabian Peninsula, which turned out to be the early leaders of Arab independence in the post–World War I period. But with the fall of the Hashemite kingdom in Iraq in 1958 only a remnant of the dynasty's power remained, in the weak Kingdom of Jordan.

The preoccupation of Bush administration neoconservatives with overthrowing Iraq was even more explicit in a letter sent from the PNAC in early 1998 to President Clinton. It grew out of a study group assembled at another conservative think tank in Washington, the American Enterprise Institute. The letter was signed by eighteen neoconservative thinkers, including the usual suspects: Francis Fukuyama, Robert Kagan, Zalmay Khalilzad, William Kristol, Elliott Abrams, Richard Armitage, Richard Perle, William Bennett, John Bolton, and, of course, Paul Wolfowitz.

> We are writing you because we are convinced that current American policy toward Iraq is not succeeding, and that we may soon face a threat in the Middle East more serious than any we have known since the end of the Cold War. . . . We urge you to act decisively. If you act now to end the threat of weapons of mass destruction against the U.S. or its allies, you will be acting in the most fundamental national security interests of the country. If we accept a course of weakness and drift, we put our interests and our future at risk. . . . We urge you . . . to turn your Administration's attention to implementing a strategy for removing Saddam's regime from power. (Iraq Watch 1998)

How did the Middle East, and Iraq specifically, fit into the new foreign policy being fashioned in Washington before and during the Bush administration? If the vicious cycle could be reversed in Iraq, the thinking went, that would have an ameliorative effect on neighboring regions and beyond. "Regime change" became the byword for effecting a fundamental transformation not only in Iraq but more broadly in the Middle East and beyond.

Embedded in their thinking was an economy of scale. The United States could not and need not take on every nefarious dictator in the arc.

Direct U.S. military action resulting in regime change and the elimination of all the despots was simply not feasible. But if America invested its efforts wisely, focusing them on key regimes, those investments would have far-reaching payoffs beyond the particular dictatorships that had been singled out. Wurmser (1999, 8) put it this way in describing the likely spillover effect if Saddam Hussein were overthrown, an operation he advocated:

> The problem is not restricted to the monstrosity of Saddam's character. Rather, it is the inherent threat and violence of tyrannical government itself. . . . Not the tyrant alone, but tyranny itself must be challenged. . . . Iraq presents an urgent opportunity for the United States to signal a new policy message to the Middle East region: that despotism, the greatest, most irreconcilable threat the West can face, is unacceptable to us.

In short, the Bush administration was doing more than establishing a doctrine of unilateralism and preemption. It was developing a new portrait of where threats to American well-being reside (the arc of instability) and a theory of action that renounced the old tools of diplomacy and posited that carefully selected military action could have a positive, reverberating effect. At the heart of its interpretation was the importance and centrality of the Middle East as well as the key to the reverberating effect: regime change in Iraq.

The thinking that evolved among those advocating regime change in Iraq has been termed a reverse domino theory. The original domino theory of a generation ago, of course, raised the specter of a vicious cycle: the fall of South Vietnam to the communist North could unleash the toppling of the other Southeast Asian states, falling like a row of dominos. In the "reverse" theory case, a virtuous cycle would be generated in which the fall of Saddam Hussein and his regime would have a domino effect, bringing the demise of other despots in the region and beyond.

After 9/11, President Bush ramped up the threats to attack Iraq. In his 2003 State of the Union address, in particular, he listed multiple ways in which Iraq endangered the United States and others. The president laid the groundwork for the publicity blitz for going to war in which administration officials engaged in the early months of 2003. During that speech, Bush also hinted that regime change in Iraq could have far wider repercussions than in that country alone, as "all people have a right to choose their own government, and determine their own destiny—and the United states supports their aspirations to live in freedom."

It was left to others in the administration to tease out the reverse domino theory beyond Bush's oblique statements and the slightly more explicit declarations by Wolfowitz and Cheney. Some of that elaboration came in a telling article by Nicolas Lemann in the *New Yorker* on the eve of the American invasion of Iraq. In it, he interviewed, among others, the neoconservative Douglas Feith, one of the authors of the earlier paper for Netanyahu and now Wolfowitz's undersecretary of defense for policy. Feith spoke of the possible spillover if Iraq fell. He observed that the Middle East (and, he might have added, the rest of the arc of instability) had missed out on the spread of democracy in Latin America and Asia in the last two decades of the twentieth century, what Huntington had called the "Third Wave" of democracy (Huntington 1991). Feith then noted that members of the Bush administration believed that no inherent incompatibility existed between Middle East cultures and democracy. "If Iraq had a government like that," he said, "and if that government could create some of the institutions of democracy, that might be inspirational for people throughout the Middle East to try to increase the amount of freedom that they have, and they would benefit both politically and economically by doing so."

Beyond undoing dictators in the region, regime change in Iraq would undermine terrorist networks. Feith went on:

> One of the principal reasons that we are focused on Iraq as a threat to us and to our interests is because we are focused on this connection between three things: terrorist organizations, state sponsors, and weapons of mass destruction. If we were to take military action and vindicate our principles, in the war on terrorism, against Iraq, I think it would *register* with other countries around the world that are sponsoring terrorism, and would perhaps change their own cost-benefit calculations about their role in connection with terrorist networks. . . . This can't be done solely by military means, but it is interesting how military action sometimes reinforces philosophical messages. (Lemann 2003)

He emphasized that any U.S. military action would be primarily to achieve the immediate goals in Iraq itself, namely regime change. But once the United States succeeds and "the Iraqis show an ability to create a humane representative government for themselves—will that have beneficial spillover effects on the politics of the whole region? The answer, I think, is yes."

Perhaps the most detailed rendering of the idea of reverse dominos came in David Wurmser's 1999 book, *Tyranny's Ally: America's Failure to Defeat Saddam Hussein*. Wurmser was another of the authors of the paper for Netanyahu and was active in a variety of conservative organizations during the 1990s, including the American Enterprise Institute, which published his book. He later would serve in a number of posts during the administration of George W. Bush, including in a small intelligence unit in the Pentagon organized by Feith and in the State Department, assisting UN Ambassador Bolton. Wurmser also was Middle East adviser to Cheney. The book was an expansion of the ideas that underlay the letter on Iraq to President Clinton in 1998.

Tyranny's Ally foresaw a kind of Age of Aquarius in the Middle East once Saddam Hussein was driven from power. In the foreword of the book, Perle argued that the then current Clinton policy tolerated tyranny. He castigated Middle East regional experts as well. These area specialists, Perle wrote, "believe that a strong, resolute, and unapologetic American defense of its interests would be regarded regionally as provocative and insensitive, and would therefore thwart our influence and foster anti-Americanism." Such beliefs were dead wrong, he insisted. They have led the United States consistently into defeat in the Middle East (Wurmser 1999, xiv). The correct palliative, as Wurmser asserted, actually should start with stalwart U.S. leadership, which would be demonstrated through the overthrow of Saddam Hussein. "Any serious display of American determination will cause the resolve, prestige, and confidence of our regional enemies [he is alluding here to Iran] to wilt, just as it will bolster the prestige of those who choose to ally themselves with the West" (Wurmser 1999, 72).

At the heart of the Middle East's problems, Wurmser (1999, 133–136) argued, have been radical Arab nationalists who have distorted the region into a haven for despots. They have displaced a populace and leadership that had been positively disposed to Western ideas and democracy. "The traditional leadership of the Middle East rebelled against the Ottoman Empire but welcomed and cooperated with the British and even the Zionists, whom they viewed as a brotherly national movement." This was a bizarre rendering of Middle East history, to say the least, but Wurmser used the premise to assert that American leadership, in toppling the Iraqi regime, will cause similarly despotic regimes to "wilt." Middle East tyrannies have robbed their societies of their true nature: "Values such as patriotism, honor, and virtue, which must come from the population itself in a healthy society, have been arrogated by the state and its tyrannical leaders." Once the despotic regimes have wilted, the United States must encourage a "conservative restoration," the rise of traditional leadership, such as the Hashemites, which can reconstitute "the sense of community from which a solid and eventually free, liberal nation can emerge." Indeed, Wurmser spends a surprisingly large portion of the book pushing the Hashemites, whose star in the Middle East had "wilted" markedly since World War I.

A Flawed Theory

The reverse domino theory voiced by Wurmser in the 1990s and echoed from within the Bush administration by Cheney, Wolfowitz, Feith, and others drove the administration's policy after 9/11. The gathering storm clouds in 2002 and early 2003 were swept forward by the deep animus toward Saddam Hussein. That hatred simmered partly because he had survived the 1991 American attack and subsequently thumbed his nose repeatedly at the United States and partly because of his failed plot to assassinate the first President Bush after the 1991 Gulf War. At home, Americans heard a variety of justifications for going to war, including the existence of weapons of mass destruction in Iraq and the promotion of international terrorism by Saddam Hussein. Additionally, Wolfowitz, Feith, and other administration officials floated the view that unseating the current Iraqi regime would transform not only Iraq but the larger Middle East and adjacent regions, as well. The realpolitik soundings about the threat posed by Saddam were complemented by moral claims of the broader repercussions of unleashing freedom and democracy in Iraq.

The war in Iraq started on March 20, 2003, and eventually became the second-longest running war in U.S. history, after its sister war in Afghanistan. Many of the administration claims promoting and justifying the war turned out not to be true, as is well known. The Bush administration failed to find any evidence of programs for the weapons of mass destruction after 1991 or of ties to terrorist networks. As to the reverse domino theory, some signs actually seemed to support it. In December 2003, the Libyan government indicated its willingness to dismantle its own nuclear program, at a time when the country was purportedly close to producing a nuclear device. And in the Middle East, Central Asia, and the Caucasus, a wave of popular demonstrations in and around 2005 seemed to presage the democratic wave that had so far eluded countries in the arc of instability. In a speech in Slovakia in February 2005, President Bush gushed, "In recent times, we have witnessed landmark events in the history of liberty, a Rose Revolution in Georgia, an Orange Revolution in Ukraine, and now, a Purple Revolution in Iraq." Later, the Tulip Revolution in Kyrgyzstan and the Cedar Revolution in Lebanon could be added to the list.

But all these colorful "Revolutions" turned out to be far from revolutionary; the wave was anemic and short lived. Iraq failed to generate the spillover results that Feith and others had anticipated. Indeed, the toppling of Saddam did not even have the outcome in Iraq itself that they had expected. On the contrary, Iraq's politics, while operating within a framework of formally democratic institutions, descended into violent internecine religious and ethnic struggles.

Some neoconservatives have not given up on the reverse domino theory. Finger pointing among administration officials and other neocons suggested other reasons to account for the failure to reshape Iraq and the rest of the arc of instability. It was not the theory that was at fault but the management (or lack of it) by the administration of the victory in Iraq. Robert Kagan (2008), for example, complained about "the misapplication and poor execution of an otherwise sound strategy." Fukuyama, an early defector, stated that "it was evident from the beginning that the Bush administration wasn't preparing the American people for that kind of a mission [i.e., one long and complex enough actually to bring democracy to Iraq]" (*Spiegel Online* 2006).

The quagmire that Iraq became for the United States, however, cannot be accounted for by poor execution alone. Neoconservative thinking and the Bush policies propelled by it rested on a couple of untenable assumptions and a serious misreading of the Middle East region. The first assumption had to do with the word "region" itself. In all the 1990s writings and in official government documents during the Bush administration, the word appeared repeatedly. Its meaning, though, was limited. It referred, quite simply and directly, to the familiar specific territorial areas of the globe, most of which became ossified during the Cold War. What was absent from their thinking was the insight provided by the political scientist Peter Katzenstein (2005, 1) that "regions differ in their institutional form, type of identity, and internal structure."

Both in the seminars of the 1990s and the policy making of the 2000s, few Middle East regional specialists participated. Conservative academics seemed to have only limited influence on the burgeoning neo-conservative agenda. Bernard Lewis, the elder statesman of Middle East studies, became something of an icon among the neoconservatives, but there is not much evidence that his ideas were read or absorbed by them. From the days of his friendship with Henry Jackson, dating back to the 1970s, Lewis provided a cloak of academic respectability to tough-minded foreign-policy makers. Little that appears in his books, though, seems to have made its way into their analyses of the Middle East.

Much the same could be said of Fouad Ajami, who was the director of the Middle Eastern Studies Program at the Paul H. Nitze School of Advanced International Studies in Washington and a frequent contribu-tor to popular magazines and newspapers. Ajami served on a Wolfowitz-inspired group at the American Enterprise Institute shortly after 9/11 to provide ideas on the War on Terror, and he defended the Bush adminis-tration's positions. But as with his mentor Lewis, there is little evidence that Ajami's writing contributed to neoconservative thinking. Wurmser was put forward as a Middle East expert, as was Elliott Abrams at times, but neither of them had contributed any serious work to the understand-ing of the region or been recognized by other area specialists. Their ideas, though, did make it into the neoconservative platform.

When a person with deep linguistic and historical knowledge of the area, such as Noah Feldman, was actually appointed in the Bush years, he did not last long. Feldman, now a well-known law professor at Har-vard with expertise in Islam, Arabic, and Hebrew, had joined the Bush team following the invasion of Iraq in 2003. He had been tapped by Paul Bremer, Bush's head of reconstruction of Iraq, to help fashion the new Iraqi constitution. But Feldman's role quickly and mysteriously ended be-fore the constitution was ever drafted.

The absence or brief shelf life of Middle East specialists in the Bush ad-ministration, Lewis's and Ajami's aura notwithstanding, was not happen-stance. The internal workings of the region and individual countries—their distinct qualities—did not matter much to the neoconservatives. Their thinking rested on an understanding of the world as being led and shaped by the United States. What America was transforming was a set of phenomena that, in their analysis, did not look very different in West Africa, the Balkans, South Asia, or the Middle East. To them, the world was composed of similar checkers, not distinct chess pieces. In fact, the various regions of the world, as Katzenstein suggests, are porous and susceptible to America's penetration of them, just as the neoconservatives assumed. At the same time, however, they are complex and different—and just as likely to shape the United States as to be shaped by it. A one-size-fits-all set of policies was bound to run up against the distinguishing qualities of each region. Like other regions, the Middle East is a difficult ball of twine to untangle, and the changes detailed in the previous three chapters made it all the more difficult to comprehend. Ignoring those complexities and changes could—and did—have disastrous results.

A second faulty assumption involved the neoconservatives' understanding of how change could take place. Here, a mechanistic view of social and political change held sway among the Bush team. There was a deus ex machina quality to their thinking, in which America would set a string of changes in motion that would ripple out from Iraq to the far reaches of Africa and Asia—those dominos, again. As Fukuyama distanced himself from the neoconservative cohort of which he had been such a central part, he attributed this sort of "ripple" thinking to the neoconservatives' drawing the wrong lessons from the demise of the Soviet Union: "They generalized from that event that all totalitarian regimes are basically hollow at the core and if you give them a little push from the outside, they're going to collapse" (*Spiegel Online* 2006).

Neoconservatives gave little thought to unpredictable contingencies. They avoided "what-if" scenarios. Their thinking was linear: one action induces change, which, in turn, creates additional change, and so on down the line. Feedback loops in which those being changed come back to bite the changer, altering the entire process, did not enter into their calculations. The absence of detailed postconquest plans for Iraq in 2003 stemmed not so much from poor planning or mismanagement but from an understanding of the process of change in which such meticulous planning was simply not needed.

The misreading of the Middle East was built on these mistaken assumptions. The thinkers who contributed to the Bush administration's approach to the Middle East had little grasp of the changing dynamics in the region. In chapter 7, I highlighted the changing roster of primary powers in the region, from Arab core states, led by Egypt, to non-Arab states on the territorial periphery, led by Iran. The thinkers and officials pushing an Iraq-first strategy before and during the administration of George W. Bush failed to account for its slipping relative status as the Middle East changed around it.

Iraq, even more starkly than the other Arab core states, Egypt and Syria, had been declining dramatically relative to the non-Arab states. Take literacy, a prime measure of human capital, for example. In 1970, both Iraq and Iran had very high illiteracy rates for those fifteen-years-old and above. In fact, their respective rates were within shouting distance of each other—72.9 percent for Iraq and 65.7 percent for Iran. By 2000, Iraq still had an astronomic 60.7 percent illiteracy rate; Iran, in contrast, was down to only 24 percent. Turkey's decreased in that period from 43.5 percent to 15 percent. More than three-quarters of Iraq's women were still illiterate in 2000. In short, even as Iraq slipped badly relative to non-Arab Iran and Turkey in maintaining the social requisites for regional power, the neoconservatives continued to focus their attention on Saddam Hussein and his regime as the major dangerous power in the region.

Similarly, they were consumed with Arab nationalism, or pan-Arabism, as the threat to U.S. national strategic interests. But this preoccupation came at a time when Arab nationalism, as discussed in chapter 9, was a spent force—and that had been recognized as the case in Arab and academic writings at the time. Lemann's (2003) statement on Wurmser captures how Arab nationalism was uppermost in neoconservatives' minds long after it ceased playing a serious role in the region: "For Wurmser, the larger enemy is the ideology of Pan-Arabism, which he presents as the Middle East's version of the various forms of totalitarianism that swept across Europe in the twentieth century." Wurmser, the person who closest resembled a Middle East expert[3] among active participants in neoconservative circles, believed that "pan-Arabic nationalist orthodoxy dominating Arab politics since the 1950s" still prevailed (Wurmser 1999, 129). This analysis simply missed the drastic decline of Arab nationalism as a potent force in the Middle East by the 1990s. The continuing focus on Arab nationalism led Wurmser to the far-fetched belief that Saddam and his nationalist agenda could be displaced by "an indigenous, traditional leadership that included the Shi'ites, to operate eventually under the Hashemite umbrella" (Wurmser 1999, 129). Shiites under the (Sunni) Hashemite umbrella? Not likely.

Along with the other neoconservatives who penned the letter to Clinton in 1998, Wurmser mistakenly believed that "all roads have led to Iraq" (Wurmser 1999, 129). Their calculations on how to orient American foreign policy rested on the assumption, as Perle (2000, 100) put it, of "the increasing strength of Saddam's position and the accelerating decline of our own. . . . Current [Clinton] policy fails to comprehend the fundamental nature of Saddam Hussein's regime as well as the likely consequences of his removal from power." Perle badly misjudged Saddam's ability to exert regional power. And, likewise, he underestimated Iran's improving position. He argued that Iran would not benefit by America's deposing Saddam and enabling Shiites to share in power in Iraq, since Iran's "influence over the affairs of Iraqi Shi'ites remains marginal. . . . If an Iraq without Saddam Hussein would best serve our interests, efforts to remove him should not be affected by fear of Iran's influence" (Perle 2000, 102). It was not simply that Perle and other neoconservatives failed to predict the future accurately—a future in which Iran benefited mightily from America's overthrow of Saddam Hussein and in which it strongly influenced Iraqi Shiites—it was that they were ignorant of the transformation that had *already* occurred in the Middle East, which made their assumptions bogus.

The misreading of the region—overstating the primacy of Iraq, its influence on the rest of the Middle East and beyond, and the power of Arab nationalist ideology, as well as understating the increase in Iranian regional power—has been a tragedy for both the United States and the Middle East. It propelled the United States into an ill-advised war that, besides the obvious and cataclysmic human and material loss it has caused, distorted a proper grasp of the critical problems in the region and what the American role there might be. As political Islam grew in importance, nonstate actors gained as key players, and Shiite activism grew, "Iran's regional position . . . ironically improved under the Bush administration's tenure and war on terror, however unintended" (Shannon 2007, 171). It was Iran, not Iraq, that emerged as the leading regional power.

The Bush Doctrine minimized the importance of strategic partners for the United States. Previously, U.S. policies in the Cold War and the 1991 Gulf War had relied heavily on the participation of allies to shoulder burdens, both military and economic, that the United States could not or would not undertake alone. The Bush policies in the 2000s, in contrast, stressed singular American global leadership. To be sure, administration officials sought out participation of countries such as the United Kingdom, Italy, and Poland in the Iraq and Afghanistan wars. But their involvement was much more limited than the participation of allies in the 1991 Gulf War. Multilateralism under the second President Bush took on a symbolic rather than strategic flavor. Strategic concerns tended to be dealt with unilaterally.

America's relationship to Israel under George W. Bush reflected his administration's overall tendency to spurn strategic relationships and become self-reliant instead. To be sure, the United States and Israel had close ties during Bush's two terms. Gone were the tensions that had marked the presidency of his father's administration in 1989–1993. Back then, the strategic relationship between Israel and the United States, which had become so evident in the Black September War and which had held until the end of the Cold War, ruptured in the new postbipolar environment. The 1991 Gulf War and the subsequent U.S. pressure on Israel to join the Madrid Peace Process in that same year badly strained relations between the two countries. Those ties improved significantly during the Clinton years, especially in light of the close personal bond between Clinton and Israeli Prime Minister Yitzhak Rabin. And they became even stronger during George W. Bush's terms, as U.S. senior aides up and down the line in the State Department and Pentagon held a soft spot for Israel.

Even with all those warm feelings, though, no strategic relationship between the United States and Israel was actually restored. To the neoconservative mind, there was little that Israel could do for the United States, although there was much that the United States could do for Israel. In other words, Israel was a friend—indeed, the special relationship was stronger than ever—but not a strategic partner. In the paper that the neoconservatives had prepared for Netanyahu back in 1996, "A Clean Break," there was some hectoring of Israel to attack Syrian forces and proxies in Lebanon and even bomb Syria itself. But, for the most part, the advice was for Israel to scrap its ambitious peace talks with the Palestinians and wait for the United States to transform the "bad neighborhood" in which Israel found itself, starting with the overthrow of Saddam Hussein.

That message became even stronger during the first Bush term, in which America's deposing Saddam would have supposedly substantially improved Israel's security and acceptance into the region. While the Bush administration did propose, together with the European Union, the Russians, and the United Nations (the Quartet), the so-called Road Map, including negotiations for a final Israeli-Palestinian peace, Ariel Sharon understood that to be the smokescreen that it was.[4] In fact, for the first seven years of Bush's presidency, his administration put minimal time and effort into advancing Israeli-Palestinian peace talks, certainly compared to past administrations.

For some in Israel, the message that Israel could sit back and wait for the United States to transform the Middle East was reassuring. I recall listening to an Israeli radio call-in show just before the U.S. attack on Iraq in March 2003. One enterprising Israeli talked about the new business he had created to take Israeli tourists to visit the sites of ancient Babylonia as soon as the United States disposed of Saddam. But for others concerned about Israel's long-term security, the dependence on the United States in an asymmetrical relationship seemed emasculating to Israel and also dangerous. The memory of Israelis sitting on their hands and absorbing blows during the 1990–1991 Gulf War was still fresh. American forces had indeed defeated Saddam Hussein, but the damage to Israeli deterrent power was considerable, according to most Israeli officials. U.S. goodwill was a real asset, to be sure, but Israeli policy makers worried about the solidity of support in the absence of a strategic partnership in which Israel could provide critical services for the United States that might not be otherwise available to it.

When Bush's 2003 Iraq War failed to transform the Middle East—the Israeli's tour business to Babylonia, alas, never did get off the ground—a gaping hole was left. For Israel, there was no longer a clear path to increased security in the volatile region. Negotiations had been spurned. Unilateral withdrawal (from Gaza) was tried and failed to deliver increased security. Israel waged wars in 2006 and 2008–2009 against members of the Iran-led bloc, Hezbollah and Hamas, without eliminating either or weakening the bloc as a whole. Those wars only further shook the Bush administration's confidence in Israel as a possible strategic ally. Israel, quite simply, had failed to do for the United States what it could not do for itself—deliver a body blow to those the Bush administration labeled as terrorists. The failure of negotiations, unilateralism, and brutal blows on the enemy led Israel in a couple of directions. The first was a desperate attempt, at the tail end of the Bush years, by Prime Minister Ehud Olmert to close a deal with the Palestinians, which failed. And the second was to simply accept inertia—and do nothing to change Israel's security dilemmas.

For other U.S. allies in the region, such as the regimes in Egypt, the Gulf states, Jordan, and Saudi Arabia, the Iraq War led to deteriorating regional security and made them even more vulnerable to Iran's active machinations in the region, to homegrown political Islam, and to their own restive populations. And for the United States itself, the Iraq War, together with the war in Afghanistan and the War on Terror, left it over-extended and ill-equipped to address any of those conflicts adequately. It no longer had strategic partners that could relieve some of the burden in the region. And it was focused on unwinnable wars rather than on the eye of the storm—the powerful Iran-led coalition that had emerged from the transformed Middle East and the shaky autocratic regimes that regarded Iran with increasing terror. In short, the Bush administration bequeathed the next administration a regional strategy in shambles.

11   Obama: Engaging the Middle East on Multiple Fronts

As Deep and Wide a Mess as Ever

If ever a makeover in American foreign policy was needed, it was at the end of George W. Bush's term—and nowhere more so than in the Middle East. Global and regional forces of the last decades of the twentieth century had precipitated a major transformation of Mideast dynamics: the advent of new leading powers as Arab dictatorships stagnated and decayed, the fall of Arab nationalism and the rise of political Islam as the reigning ideology, the emergence of nonstate players, and the push by the area's Shiites to upend the area's religious-social pecking order. But the Bush administration's analytic lenses—its overarching global perspective on U.S. leadership, its indifference and inattention to regional detail, its focus globally on the arc of instability and faith in the reverse domino theory—made its policy makers miss the import of this region's specific transformation, both for the United States and for the Middle East itself.

After 9/11, Bush had forsaken the "chastened doctrine" of previous administrations for the region, including their array of built-in hedges: spreading risk through multilateral institutions, playing the role of mediator and facilitator, and seeking regional strategic partners to help shoulder some of the leadership burden. The new Bush policies substituting for the chastened doctrine were not simply aggressive—that recurring image of the cavalry—but also rested on faulty assumptions of mechanistic change through a reverse domino theory. The specific institutional details of countries and their processes of change—and, indeed, of processes of change of whole region's—were not all that important in officials' calculations. As Bush's eight years in office went on, his Mideast policies and their ill-fated outcomes saddled his administration with flagging domestic support, resources stretched to the limit, ballooning national debt, and soldiers returning in body bags, with few palpable gains to show for any of it.

The combative Bush practices—unilateralism, turning his nose up at negotiations and mediation, disregard of regional experts, and a quick trigger—had taken their toll. America had become the imperial power of the Middle East, shaking the area in fundamental ways. The 2000s became a decade of war for America. But it found itself flailing as it tried to direct change in the region or even simply meet the challenges the area posed. It felt unprecedented hostility from the peoples of the area. Middle East politics continued to be volatile, but Washington was ill-equipped to help the region find some tranquility. The United States in the region was like a boulder dropped into a pond, making big waves but unable to catch a fish.

Whoever became the new president would have to reconsider the Bush approach to the Middle East. The new president and his advisors, like the Bush team at the outset of his presidency, would have to determine what the United States wanted in the Middle East, now that the old Cold War rationales had evaporated. They would have to sort out American goals in the shadow of 9/11. But they would also have to depart from the illusion, so prominent during the Bush years, that the United States could fix everything on its own, especially in light of the massive economic crisis that started during Bush's final year in office. And they would also have to figure all this out in the context of three ongoing wars—Iraq, Afghanistan, and the nebulous War on Terror—which were fast losing support of the American population. Once those goals were clear, the new president would also have to assess if any of the old pre-Bush tactics, including special relationships and military alliances, made sense in the new environment. How could Washington achieve its aims? Whatever the answer to that question, this time around the new administration would have to take into account the complexity of the region—its new institutional realities, the power distribution, the complex relations between rulers and subjects, and the area's key fault lines.

As it would turn out, the few years following the Bush presidency would be the most eventful and momentous in the Middle East since, perhaps, the last half of the Carter administration and first half of the Reagan presidency. Back then, in a compressed amount of time, the United States dealt with, among other events, the Iranian Revolution and the ensuing hostage crisis, the Islamic rebel takeover of Mecca's Grand Mosque, the Israel-Egypt peace treaty, the Iran-Iraq War, Israel's attack on Iraq's purported nuclear-weapons facility, the Lebanese Civil War, and Israel's invasion of Lebanon. The volatility of the region back then pointed to the areawide transformation that was beginning and that would ensue for the rest of the twentieth century.

In the transition from Bush to Obama, just as in the late 1970s and early 1980s, a host of disruptions signaled yet another regionwide transformation. With the tail end of the 2009–2010 Gaza War and its aftermath, continuing crises in Israel-Palestine, a major crackdown in Iran, continuing turmoil in Lebanon, and, what was most important, the upheavals of the Arab Spring, the Obama administration faced the dual difficulty of forging an areawide shift in U.S. policy away from the Bush approach while dealing with a surfeit of day-to-day Mideast crises, managing three wars, and witnessing a major shift in the relationship between the region's rulers and ruled. Like it or not, it was on the Obama administration's watch that the Mideast region underwent its once-in-a-generation metamorphosis.

On the eve of the 2008 presidential election, the seasoned diplomat Richard Holbrooke wrote about the foreign-policy challenges that the new president would face. He focused on a kind of truncated arc of instability, what he called the "arc of crisis." Whoever turned out to be the president, Holbrooke claimed, would inevitably face this arc, which "directly threatens the United States' national security—Turkey, Iraq, Iran, Afghanistan, and Pakistan" (Holbrooke 2008). While I might have substituted Israel-Palestine for Turkey on his list, the message was clear: the daunting foreign-policy agenda of the new president would center on the Middle East and two adjoining countries, Afghanistan and Pakistan. The area had never before been in quite as deep and wide a mess at the beginning of a new president's tenure—and that is saying a lot for the Middle East. Indeed, Holbrooke was right: the only other foreign-policy issue garnering the kind of attention that the Middle East and neighboring

Afghanistan and Pakistan received in the first year of the new presidency was the international financial crisis. And through his entire first term, the Middle East remained the number-one region preoccupying Obama.

Once he took office, Obama immediately battled the Mideast crises on multiple fronts. He quickly moved toward a U.S. drawdown of troops in Iraq. His aides dangled carrots in front of Iran and Syria. The president gave his first major speech abroad in the Middle East. In his remarks, he thrust the United States into the tangle of state-society relations in the region: the growing divide between rulers and ruled, the yearning for freedom and democracy, and the stagnation of countries in the region. And he did not waste a day in throwing his administration into the to-date intractable Israeli-Palestinian conflict. The headlong dive into the thicket of Mideast crises and conflicts both helped define Obama's presidency and, eventually, indicated the limitations of his approach.

Bush and Obama: Similarities and Differences

George W. Bush and Barack Obama actually agreed on a number of important tenets of foreign policy, believe it or not. Like the neoconservatives, Obama, while still a candidate, made the importance of American world leadership a central refrain. "The mission of the United States is to provide global leadership," he wrote (Obama 2007). Additionally, he reproduced Rumsfeld's and Wolfowitz's emphasis on the need to revitalize the military. Obama also cited the same sorts of international perils that Bush aides had; indeed, the following quote (Obama 2007) sounds as if was lifted from the Bush-era "National Security Strategy of the United States of America 2002":

> [Threats come] from weapons that can kill on a mass scale and from global terrorists who respond to alienation or perceived injustice with murderous nihilism. [Threats] come from rogue states allied to terrorists and from rising powers that could challenge both America and the international foundation of liberal democracy. They come from weak states that cannot control their territory or provide for their people.

These statements echoed the principal fears of the neoconservatives: foreign powers that could challenge American global leadership (i.e., China and Russia), failed states, terrorists, and weapons of mass destruction. Obama's primary goals followed directly from his expressed concerns and proved not to be a radical departure. His presidency would aim to maintain American global predominance as an antidote to world disorder and fragmentation. His administration followed almost all others in the postwar era in tying security to economics: emphasizing the protection of markets, the preservation of freedom of navigation by patrolling sea lanes, the enhancement of trade by promoting global shipping, and the like. It also committed to foiling rising powers and so-called rogue states that were poised to disrupt the liberal world order. And there would be a special emphasis on thwarting terrorists and weapons of mass destruction landing in the wrong hands. It would be hard to imagine Bush officials taking much exception to Obama's goals.

Also in line with Bush, Obama stressed the need to foster freedom and democracy abroad. "Our global engagement cannot be defined by what we are against; it must be guided by a clear sense of what we stand for" (Obama 2007). His rhetoric carried the same moralistic overtones as his predecessor's; both Obama's and Bush's rhetoric fell into the mode of Woodrow Wilson, who stressed the international promotion of democracy (Eikenberry et al. 2009), and departed from the language of the neorealists, who disdained and feared moral missions. And, like Bush, Obama insisted on the primacy of the Middle East for the United States—for America's economic and military security and for defining its larger place in the world. In his preelection *Foreign Affairs* article, among all the international tests the country might face in his term, Obama turned first to the challenges of the Middle East.

The continuity in some aspects of American foreign policy from Bush to Obama is understandable, even if Obama made a point of trying to differentiate himself from his predecessor (Lynch and Singh 2008). Both were coming to terms with a world in which bipolarity had given way to unipolarity, in which 9/11 and the threat of terrorism at home had become an integral part of America's story about itself, and in which many of the same security dangers abroad continued to haunt the United States.

Moreover, the steps that the Bush administration had taken—its tactics to achieve its strategic goals—were not so easily reversed. They forced any possible successor into commitments he or she might not have otherwise chosen, willy-nilly following a path that Bush had blazed. At the very least, the top of Obama's agenda included the wars that Bush had begun. The undeniable continuities in foreign policy between the two administrations prompted some to argue at the time that Obama "will not augur any significant changes in US foreign policy" (Parmar 2009, 178; see also Lynch and Singh 2008).

But that has not been the case. For all the continuity between the two, Obama parted dramatically from the Bush foreign policy in both perspective and tactics. Obama started with the issue that would dominate the campaign, bringing the Iraq War to a close and withdrawing American troops from that country. His reasoning, though, did not focus on Iraq itself—freeing it from Saddam's oppressive rule and bringing Iraqis freedom or simply extricating the United States from the morass there. Nor did his thinking indicate a withdrawal of interest for the United States from the Middle East altogether.

Obama's statements as a candidate were by no means a detailed agenda, and some of his goals would change once he was in office. But he was clear about where he wanted to pave new roads. Beneath his words was a view of the Middle East very different from that of the Bush administration. For Obama, Iraq was a tragedy and a nuisance for the United States—and, now, a responsibility, as well—but it was not America's central worry.

It was far from clear from Obama's early statements, however, what he felt the central concern in the Middle East actually was; his statements were more of a laundry list than a coherent understanding of the dynamics of the region—where the linchpin lay, how the multiple fault lines intersected. He did not make evident what he understood the national-security interests of the United States to be in the area nor what the dynamics of the region were—or how the two meshed. What *was* clear was that he thought the Middle East would be very important in his presidency and that it was necessary for the United States to develop new ways of dealing with the region.

The New Middle East Team

Even during the transition period between the election and inauguration, Obama signaled through the Middle East transition team that he was assembling how much care he was taking to get that part of the world right and that Middle East policy was to be one of the highest priorities of his administration. He called on experienced Middle East hands—all with previous ties to the Clinton administration—to forge the outlines of a set of policies and suggest possible appointees. Among them were Daniel Kurtzer and Dennis Ross. Kurtzer had been a wunderkind in the State Department, rising from the ranks to the post of ambassador to Egypt and, then, Israel. He was a major player in the peace process from the 1980s on. Having recently coauthored a new book on Arab-Israeli talks, representing the ideas of a U.S. Institute for Peace study group (Kurtzer and Lasensky 2008), Kurtzer saw the no-negotiations approach of the Bush administration as deeply flawed. Bush had advocated, mistakenly to Kurtzer's mind, "broader social and political change [as] a necessary precondition to resolving the Arab-Israeli conflict" (Kurtzer and Lasensky 2008, 27). Ross served as the point man for both George H. W. Bush and Clinton on Israeli-Palestinian negotiations. He, too, had written a recent book on Middle East negotiations (Ross 2007). Ross and Kurtzer had aired their differences in the past, indicating that Obama was willing to entertain a variety of views, itself a departure from the previous president.[1]

Obama's principal aides and advisers for the region would not be limited to the regular slots in the State Department, such as undersecretary for political affairs (who oversees the Middle East among other regions) or the principal deputy assistant secretary of state for the Near Eastern affairs. Obama's key personnel for the Middle East included a number of job titles with the word "special" at the beginning of them. And he did not go after bright young faces but appointed a roster of all-stars with considerable diplomatic experience. He looked not only for smart aides but also ones wise and wizened. Perhaps his own thin background in foreign affairs made him all the more eager to have a seasoned team to fall back on.

Even while facing the biggest economic and financial crisis since the Great Depression, the new president spent a good part of his first days in office filling out his entirely new Middle East lineup card. Indeed, the 100 percent turnover in the Middle East team from the outgoing administration was a novelty in its own right. George H. W. Bush and Clinton had both kept on a good part of the previous president's team, lending considerable stability, across partisan lines, to Middle East policy from the second Reagan administration on. George W. Bush had initially maintained some of that roster, too, but then radically changed directions and personnel, in effect cleaning house and breaking the continuity of American policy in the region. Obama's own housecleaning signaled that there would be a major break in Mideast policy from the last eight years, but his team would have clear connections to how the region had been handled in the halls of government in the 1990s. It quickly became evident that the new president's aides for the area would each carry considerable weight; this was not a crew of yes men.

On the first morning of his presidency, Obama telephoned Israeli and Arab leaders, demonstrating his seriousness in making the Palestinian-Israeli conflict a top priority. It is true that almost all post–World War II presidents had ended up tackling the Arab-Israeli conflict. But there was a difference here. Some of Obama's predecessors had delayed entering this particular fray in a deep and sustained way for at least a year into their terms (such as George H. W. Bush) or, more commonly, even waited until their second terms (think of Reagan). Others became involved earlier but only because the Arab-Israeli issue was thrust upon them: Ford, who inherited Nixon's initiative in separation-of-forces agreements between Israel and Egypt in the wake of the 1973 War; Carter, who was put on the line in the first year of his presidency by Egyptian President Anwar Sadat's unexpected trip to Israel and his famous speech in the Israeli Knesset; and Clinton, who inherited the ongoing Madrid negotiations (begun in the latter half of George H. W. Bush's term) and was then taken by surprise in his first year by the secret Oslo talks between Israel and the PLO that opened a new era of negotiations. Obama's voluntary entry into the epicenter of the conflict from the outset of his term was a departure for a new president. It was not as if he did not have a shortage of other issues to address, from the downward spiral of the economy to healthcare.

On Obama's second day in office, George Mitchell was named as special envoy for the Middle East, specifically to pave the way for a Palestinian-Israeli peace agreement. During the Clinton administration, he already had played an important role on this same issue, writing the Mitchell Report (officially, "The Mitchell Report on the Al-Aqsa Intifadeh") based on his fact-finding mission. He was indeed a luminary. After his Senate career, in which he had risen to Senate majority leader, he hopped among American institutions at the highest levels, from diplomacy to sports to private business.

Mitchell's most remarkable achievement in his post-Senate career had been brokering the Good Friday Agreement, which brought the long, brutal conflict in Northern Ireland to an end in 1998. Mitchell quipped about how the Northern Ireland conflict, based on "only" eight hundred years of animosity, might have seemed easy to solve compared to the Israeli-Arab conflict. He referred to one elderly Middle Easterner who told him after hearing the figure of eight hundred years, "Uh, such a recent argument.

No wonder you settled it." And indeed, Mitchell would eventually find the Northern Ireland conflict a cakewalk compared to the Mideast one. He also went on to head the Disney Company and then to write another Mitchell Report, this one based on his investigation into the use of steroids in major-league baseball. Obama could not have selected a more prestigious statesman.

On the same day, the new president also announced the appointment of Holbrooke as special representative for Afghanistan and Pakistan. Along with the Middle East, these two countries, with clear connections between them and to the neighboring Middle East, were to be the primary focus of the new administration. Holbrooke was another heavy hitter. He had served in as many diplomatic posts as one could imagine, starting his storied U.S. Foreign Service career in 1962, almost half a century earlier. His shining moment was the brokering of the Dayton Peace Accords in 1995, which ended the savage war in Bosnia, a feat coming in as a close second to Mitchell's Good Friday Agreement. When Holbrooke died suddenly in 2010, he was lauded widely in the press as a modern hero of foreign policy, although some on the left held a much more negative view of his exploits (e.g., Zunes 2010). Both Holbrooke and Mitchell were men who had achieved great successes in diplomacy, emphasizing Obama's concern with hands-on statesmanship and with people bringing a record of tangible results.

Other big names followed, although not quite at the level of Mitchell and Holbrooke. Christopher Hill became ambassador to Iraq. Hill had had more than thirty years of experience in the State Department. His crowning moments came in working on the Dayton Peace Accords under Holbrooke and then, in Korea, after he was appointed head of the U.S. delegation to the six-party talks on the North Korean nuclear program in 2005. Opening negotiations with the North Koreans had marked a sharp break for the Bush administration from its early, no-negotiations policies on North Korea.

The new policy on North Korea, in fact, had reflected a larger shift in Bush's second term, as his approval rating plummeted in large part because of the Iraq War. Not only did Bush change course on North Korea; the president also sacked Rumsfeld as secretary of defense in 2006, engaged in tentative direct contacts with the Iranians in 2008 for the first time in nearly thirty years, and hosted the Annapolis Conference in 2007, nudging Israelis and Palestinians toward direct negotiations and a two-state solution to their conflict. Of all the new negotiations Bush aides engaged in, only the North Korean ones headed by Hill enjoyed a modicum of success. The Hill-led negotiations achieved the closing down of the nuclear reactor at Yongbyon by the North Koreans, their granting permission to an international inspection team to enter the country, and, finally, the outline of an agreement in the last year of Bush's tenure that included the shutdown of North Korea's nuclear-weapons plant along with America's lifting sanctions against it. Hill's appointment by Obama to be ambassador to Iraq again indicated a preference for experienced hands who had a track record of achieving tangible results.

Another appointee carried over from Obama's transition team was Ross, the long-time lead negotiator for Israeli-Palestinian talks. He was given the role of special adviser for the Persian Gulf and Southwest Asia (mainly, Iran) to Secretary of State Hillary Clinton. While he had not had the weighty diplomatic successes of Mitchell and Holbrooke or even Hill, he far outweighed them all in Middle East experience. Under the first President Bush and continuing on with Clinton, Ross had been the lead diplomat in convening the Madrid Peace Conference in 1991 (working under Secretary of State James Baker, who took the main hands-on role) and in U.S. mediation during the prolonged Oslo Peace Process.

The strength of the team, it turns out, was also its weakness. As with any all-star roster, it was impossible to tell if the players would actually mesh as a team. Every appointee held fervent views on what the central problems of the Middle East were, how they related to U.S. concerns, and what the United States should do about them. Some, like Holbrooke, built their positions into fiefdoms of foreign policy in the government, with multiple hands (serfs) working for them. These offices were largely outside the traditional lines of government control and supervision.

Several of the new aides, including Ross and Obama's chief of staff, Rahm Emanuel, had strong ties to the established leadership of the American Jewish community, which historically weighed in heavily on any policies that directly or indirectly affected Israel. Others, such as Mitchell, were studious in their evenhandedness on Israeli-Palestinian issues. And still others, like General David Petraeus, who played a major military-diplomatic role under Obama as he had under Bush—the major exception to Obama's housecleaning—expressed skepticism on Israel. Obama had gone to great pains to reassure American Jews about his commitment to Israel, but questions about which way the administration would tilt would continue to dog the president throughout his term, right into his reelection campaign.

Doubts about the team's ability to devise and carry out a coherent, areawide set of policies stemmed not only from the strong personalities and divergent orientations of the aides; blurred lines of command also cropped up as an issue. Some aides reported directly to the president; others were under Secretary of State Hillary Clinton, who maintained her own forceful views on Israel, peace negotiations, and other Middle East issues. Ross, for example, started out in the State Department as special advisor for the Persian Gulf and Southwest Asia under Secretary of State Clinton. Within four months, his position was switched to the NSC, where he became special assistant to the president and senior director for the Central Region. The Central Region referred to the Middle East, Afghanistan, Pakistan, and, presumably, India, which meant overlap (and possible conflict) with other forceful personalities, such as Holbrooke.

The positions of Mitchell, as special envoy for Middle East peace, and Holbrooke, as special representative for Afghanistan and Pakistan, were technically within the State Department, and it was Clinton who made the formal announcements of their appointments. But both had that word "special" in front of their titles, indicating extraordinary powers and autonomy. Unclear was their relationship to those holding the regular organizational positions in the department, including the ambassadors to the various countries in the region, the head of the Near Eastern desk, the undersecretary for political affairs, and the secretary of state herself. In fact, it was not transparent if Mitchell and Holbrooke reported directly to the president or through the secretary of state.

In short, President Obama early on identified his toolkit for dealing with the turbulent region of the Middle East. His stress was on diplomacy, negotiations, and regional partnerships. He chose a team of high-profile figures with wide-ranging diplomatic experience, who were well equipped to employ the president's toolkit to best advantage. It is worth adding, too, that serving under these diplomatic stars were often younger, lesser-known aides with significant Middle East knowledge and background, complementing their bosses, who had broad knowledge and clout in world affairs but not necessarily deep knowledge of the region (with the clear exception of Ross).

What was still missing from this mix of archers and arrows was a clear target. There was no comprehensive understanding of how the various hotspots, wars, and other challenges that the United States faced in the area intersected with one another, so that a coherent regionwide policy could be devised. The Bush administration had had such a strategy, based on a broad understanding of global threats, especially the arc of instability. It simply was not one that worked.

But Obama had not articulated an overall strategy. The means were in hand but still not the ends. The appointment of a stellar cast of envoys and aides dealing with the individual aspects of the Middle East, Afghanistan, and Pakistan exacerbated the difficulty in achieving an overarching approach to the region. At the same time, a return to some of the hedges used during the Cold War, such as offloading some responsibility to local partners, and a clearer understanding of how the Middle East had changed in recent decades laid a foundation for a possible future comprehensive strategy linking a number of the Middle East puzzle pieces together.

The proliferation of personages as Obama's Mideast aides and the vagueness of the organizational chart in the new Obama administration held several dangers. One was that the administration would speak with multiple, perhaps conflicting voices on priorities, policies, and perspectives. Another was that a Holbrooke or a Mitchell (more likely Holbrooke than Mitchell) could aspire to be a policy czar, overseeing a sizeable staff, in his own domain, with little coordination (and increasing friction) with others.

As it turned out, remarkably little backbiting among the foreign-policy team was evident during Obama's first term, at least to the public. National Security Adviser General Jim Jones and Secretary of State Clinton tripped over each other when Jones asked General Anthony Zinni to be ambassador to Iraq; Clinton had tabbed Christopher Hill for the job. Reports surfaced, too, that Ross and Mitchell were engaged in a turf war. Ross assumed a growing role in the Israel-Palestine issue "as the White House . . . felt a need to repair frayed ties with American officials and Israeli officials disturbed over perceptions that the administration was pressuring Israel" (Guttman 2011).

Perhaps the most notable tiff was on the area adjacent to the Middle East, when Commander Stanley McChrystal, heading the U.S. forces in Afghanistan, and Ambassador to Afghanistan Karl Eikenberry, himself a retired general, locked horns. McChrystal initiated the call to Obama to beef up U.S. combat troops in order to reverse the flagging effort in Afghanistan, while Eikenberry argued against a U.S. "surge" there. Some commentators, such as Adam Garfinkle (2009), saw the split as evidence of "too many Chiefs, not enough Indians," but, in fact, it was noteworthy that these three instances seemed to be more exceptions than the rule.

The larger questions, though, involved the possibility, given the existence of so many chiefs, for developing an overall understanding of what the American role in the Middle East should be. Could an umbrella concept linking challenges in the region be crafted by the president under these circumstances? Could the administration develop an understanding of how issues and crises related to one another, and could it put into practice its goals of creating key partnerships to pursue what it considered to be the central U.S. interests? And what were those central interests? If the United States was not to be the imperial power in the region that Bush envisioned, what would its new role be?

Current Wars Notwithstanding: Iraq and Afghanistan Would Not Be the Center of U.S. Mideast Policy

Both in the months before and after his election, Obama indicated that he saw the Middle East as multiple burning fires, ranging from the ongoing wars, to the political uncertainties and upheaval in Lebanon, to transformed relations with Syria, to the ongoing Israeli-Palestinian conflict. What he did not do, either as a candidate or after the election, is explicitly grapple with the questions above on how to order priorities among the burning fires and how the various crises related to one another.

What he did do, both as a candidate and as president is affirm how central the Middle East would be to his presidency. The high priority he afforded Middle East issues was already indicated in his *Foreign Affairs* article before his election. After he became president, his determination to put the Middle East at the center of his administration's foreign policy became all the more evident in a highly touted speech that he delivered on June 4, 2009, less than half a year into his presidency. The speech, his first presidential foreign-policy address and his first major address abroad, was delivered in Cairo, Egypt. It followed on the president's first formal TV interview, which was granted to the Arabic cable TV network *Al Arabiya*. The interview and then the speech highlighted how important he considered the Middle East to be both for the well-being of the United States and for his presidency. Like many of Obama's speeches, it was a rhetorical tour de force. At the outset, the president set out his ambitious overall goal while separating himself from his predecessor: "I've come here to Cairo to seek a new beginning between the United States

FIGURE 11.1   Barack Obama speaks in Cairo, Egypt, June 4, 2009.
Source: Courtesy White House Photograph.

FIGURE 11.2   Youth listening.
Source: Courtesy White House Photograph.

and Muslims around the world. . . . America is not—and never will be— at war with Islam" (Obama 2009b).

If Obama did not set out initially what was so critical about the Middle East, he did convey what was *not* America's central concern in the region. Iraq, he made clear, would *not* be the touchstone of the American role in the Middle East. Nor would it be at the center of American security concerns in the region, as it had been for the Bush administration. In his preelection article, Obama (2007) alluded to the misplaced priority of the Bush administration in focusing so heavily on Iraq—both materially and conceptually—at the expense of other ominous trends in the region. Obama stressed the need to disentangle the country from Iraq in order to "refocus our attention on the broader Middle East."

His message in that article was that Iraq was not, as Bush officials had argued, the linchpin to the Middle East (and, by implication, to the entire arc of instability) but a distraction. Obama noted that Iraq diverted America from the fight against those who had perpetrated 9/11; from solving the Israeli-Palestinian conflict; from the growing strength of Iran; and from the rising power of the principal nonstate actors al-Qaeda, Hamas, and Hezbollah. (Interestingly, nowhere did he cite the Middle East's oil as an issue of concern, the issue that had risen repeatedly in neoconservatives' writings.)

The downgrading of the Iraq issue took shape after Obama's election. Iraq, which had been the primary U.S. foreign-policy focus for six years, now became a secondary issue. This marginalization was especially surprising because it had occupied such a central place not only in the Bush administration's conception of national interests and Bush policy but in the 2008 electoral campaign. The conflict that continued to rage there was, still, after all, far and away the major war that the United States was currently fighting and among the most prolonged in American history.

Iraq's centrality prior to Obama's downgrading of it was reflected in the human and material resources that the United States had invested in it from the beginning of the war there in 2003. The resources committed to Iraq exceeded those it had expended on all other Mideast issues combined since World War II. By the time that the United States withdrew all troops in 2011, it had spent on the order of a trillion dollars by the administration's calculations and as much as $3 to $5 trillion by the reckoning of others. Whatever the precise figure, these were incredibly large expenditures, which had run up worrisome government deficits in the United States. These war costs had become magnified at the end of the Bush presidency and the beginning of the Obama tenure by the Great Recession and the crossing of the $1 trillion barrier for the Iraq and Afghanistan wars combined. Indeed, a 2007 Congressional Budget Office report figured the cost of those two conflicts alone could total $2.4 trillion by 2017. Another report by the Eisenhower Research Project at Brown University's Watson Institute (2011) estimated the costs for Iraq and Afghanistan-Pakistan to run $3.2 to $4 trillion (in addition to 225,000 lives lost).

Even with the centrality that these war costs gave to Iraq, events there quickly receded into the background in the first year of the Obama's presidency. In fact, what was notable about the Iraq issue was how unnotable it quickly became after Obama took office. Quite suddenly it became the "forgotten war," as one commentator put it (Guzansky 2009). Multiple newspaper columnists in Obama's first year in office used the ironic lead, "Remember Iraq?" And although deadly, massive suicide bombings could and did grab the headlines from time to time in 2009 and subsequent years, the policy side of the Iraq War and even the continued fighting there quietly slipped beneath the public radar.

The slide down the priority list was not happenstance. Despite the continued volatility of the situation in Iraq, the Obama administration moved toward an American drawdown in the country and a shift in policy focus to elsewhere in the region. From a peak of 160,000 American soldiers fighting during Bush's "surge," in the last stage of his presidency, the numbers fell to 115,000 by the end of 2009, a nearly 30 percent decrease, and to well under 50,000 in 2010 and, finally, to an end to American troop presence in the country in 2011.

Following his promises during the campaign, Obama used his first year to implement the Status of Forces Agreement, approved by the American and Iraqi governments in the last month of the Bush administration. The agreement was another of Bush's retreats under duress, generated by an unpopular war and his own plummeting approval rates. U.S. combat forces were to pull out of Iraqi cities by the end of June 2009, under the terms of the accord, and leave Iraq entirely at the end of 2011. Indeed, the United States did end its direct combat role in the summer of 2010 and withdraw its troops on schedule (although by 2011 members of the administration hoped that they could negotiate leaving a residual force in Iraq, which did not happen).

Rapid withdrawal of American troops was accompanied by efforts to stabilize the political situation in the country. These moves were taken with the aim of handing responsibility for governing and securing the country to Iraqis themselves and refocusing America's attention elsewhere in the region. The grand nation-building projects of the Bush era were mostly downgraded or discarded.

The shift away from the Bush administration's preoccupation with Iraq and the centrality accorded it as the linchpin for U.S. security globally generated many challenges for Obama. Moving Iraq from the center of the government's worldview to the sidelines was fraught with danger because of the extreme fragility of the situation there:

1. Still ill-prepared Iraqi troops had to assume responsibility for maintaining domestic order and securing the borders in place of American soldiers.
2. Al-Qaeda cells had purportedly established a presence in some parts of the country, threatening domestic peace and the survival of any agreements among the major population groups—Sunni Arabs, Shiite Arabs, and Kurds.
3. The agreement between Iraqi Kurds and largely Sunni Arabs on control of the city of Kirkuk and income from its plentiful oil reserves, which was in part brokered by Obama aides, was a fragile one, threatening ethnic conflict if it blew up.
4. Many Sunni Arabs, despite increasing participation in civic life, still simmered with resentment over their displacement by Shiites as the country's principal leaders, and Shiite leaders did not seem disposed to real power sharing with Sunnis.
5. Sunnis begrudged, too, the American occupation regime's de-Ba'athification policy, which excluded key, experienced figures from Saddam Hussein's period from future political positions.
6. Government corruption was rampant.
7. Suicide bombers repeatedly rocked domestic peace.
8. Certain militias rejected the new political order altogether.

Underlying all these challenges that the Obama administration encountered in Iraq was the question of the long-term viability of the country itself. Could Kurds, Sunnis, and Shiites hold together in the semblance of a national society, and could a unified Iraqi state survive intact? The long-term prospects for an integrated Iraqi state and society were shaky, at best. Already the Kurds had established their own highly autonomous region in the north of the country, which looked and acted like an independent state, even if its leaders did not officially declare it to be one. They negotiated multiple oil deals with international companies, for example, despite an explicit agreement that all such deals would be signed only by the national Iraqi government in Baghdad. The problem was not only the Kurds. Among the Arabs, many Sunnis balked at the idea of Shiites as the dominant leaders of the state. And Shiite leaders seemed bent on bypassing Sunnis. Also, violent Sunni and Shiite militias fought against one another and the government.

A disintegration of Iraq held dire prospects for the United States. At the very least, it could have derailed the administration's plan to refocus U.S. attention to what it considered issues more central to its security interests in the region. What was even more threatening was that the failure of the Iraqi state could precipitate widespread instability in the area, possibly even a general Mideast War, which could draw the United States into new fighting in the region. A declaration of formal Iraqi Kurdish independence, for example, could risk an invasion from Turkey, as Turkish leaders might see such a development as a provocation to Turkey's own restive Kurdish population.

And the Turks were not the only problem if the Kurds seceded from Iraq. Kurdish independence—including exclusive control of oil revenues in Kurdish territory—could prompt intervention by other Iraqi groups. Vulnerable Shiite and Sunni forces in what was left of Iraq or in their own rump states could invite active outside intervention—even military in nature—from their respective protectors, Iran and, possibly, Saudi Arabia or Egypt. The Iranian and Syrian regimes also faced restive Kurds and might also see an independent Kurdistan as dangerous for them. Israel (and others) could view an Iranian foothold in an Iraqi Shiite state as undermining their own security. And so on. Iraq's future integrity was far from assured, and the scenarios following a possible breakup were bleak both for the country and the region as a whole.

The Obama administration was certainly committed to keeping the country intact (despite comments by Vice President Biden, back in his days in the Senate, advocating its split-up). Obama spoke of the United States supporting "a secure and united Iraq." He emphasized in the Cairo speech that "America has a dual responsibility to help Iraq forge a better future—and to leave Iraq to Iraqis" (Obama 2009b). He went on to repeat that refrain time and again. The image the administration seemed to hold was of a relatively weak, federated Iraq that would neither be a threat nor a prize to its neighbors. It would have minimal effect on broader regional dynamics.

The administration adopted a two-pronged policy to meet its goals of maintaining the integrity of the country, even while aiming to leave Iraq to the Iraqis. First, like the Bush administration before it, the Obama team put great stakes in the success of parliamentary elections in 2010. The key was finding an election formula that Kurds, Shiites, and Sunnis could all live with, which was painstakingly achieved in the fall of 2009. Agreement on the parameters for elections came only after hard bargaining and significant pressure put on the parties by the United States, raising questions about the agreement's long-term durability. Even after the election deal was struck, no comprehensive power-sharing agreement emerged in the run-up to the elections.

After the voting, it took the better part of a year to form a government and divide up the spoils of the state among the various sects and subsect factions. The result was less a cohesive government than an attempt to have multiple power brokers on board, in a ship that seemed hopelessly adrift. Intrasectarian infighting was intense, and the prospects for effective governance to emerge from the process was iffy, at best. Many questions among the three Iraqi groups and factions within each group, especially the Sunnis and Shiites, were left to future negotiations (or, in a worst-case scenario, to fighting). After the exit of American troops, Shiites seemed intent on a power grab that would marginalize Sunni politicians. In the most notorious case, Prime Minister al-Maliki accused the country's Sunni vice president, Tariq al-Hashemi, of having engaged in bombings and assassinations. Al-Hashemi was later sentenced to death by hanging, after he fled the country. Also in 2011, Iraq was not immune to the protests sweeping across the region. The demonstrations there, while nowhere nearly as big as in other Mideast states, nonetheless signaled a dissatisfaction with a largely paralyzed and sometimes high-handed regime.

U.S. officials since the invasion of Iraq in 2003 had tended to see the building of institutions and the forging of institutional agreements as sufficient conditions for achieving democracy and stability. But time and again they found that while a constitution and parliament and other such institutions might be a necessary condition, they were far from sufficient to insure stability and democracy. Still, the Obama administration proceeded full steam ahead with the second prong of its Iraq policy strategy, the withdrawal of military forces—all combat troops from major cities only months after the scheduled 2010 election (which had to be postponed beyond its originally planned date in January, to March) and all troops out in late 2011.

In brief, for Obama, Iraq was not in his presidency (nor had it been in 2003, when he opposed the impending war) the linchpin to American security interests in the Middle East. In part, Bush's surge had improved the security situation so that Obama could contemplate moving Iraq down his list of priorities. But high risks still prevailed there. Even with all those risks and the challenges for the United States to withdraw without precipitating a Mideast apocalypse, the Obama administration was committed to focus more on other issues as it tried to develop a Middle East strategy. Even if all went well in Iraq, the administration seemed to regard Iraq's future to be one as a relatively emasculated state somewhat peripheral to larger U.S. concerns in the region—certainly not the beacon of democracy and stable anchor that the Bush administration had envisioned on the eve of the American invasion. The United States, if the administration had its way, would have an active hand in keeping the country afloat, but the Iraqi leadership did not seem interested in a continued American presence. Certainly, Iraq would not and could not be a strategic partner for influencing larger regional dynamics. Although its stability and oil were important concerns for America, the efforts of the new administration were to reduce its role in the country severely; there were bigger fish to fry elsewhere.

It is worth noting that in the second war that the United States was fighting at the outset of Obama's term, in Afghanistan, his administration took much the same tack as with Iraq. Initially, like the Bush administration, Obama's team had aimed at nation building in Afghanistan, creating democratic institutions and good governance that could serve as the basis for a unified national community. In his Cairo speech, the president said, "We also know that military power alone is not going to solve the problems in Afghanistan and Pakistan. . . . And that is why we are providing more than $2.8 billion to help Afghans develop their economy and deliver services that people depend upon." Obama sought to have a U.S. hand in constructing viable institutions that could win over the population, with the hope that the process would inoculate the country against al-Qaeda and the Taliban.

But the Americans found Afghanistan to be the same sinkhole that, historically, the British and Soviets had before them. Obama's high hopes for institution building and moving Afghanistan toward democracy notwithstanding, actual American efforts on this front foundered during the Bush years and in the first eighteen months of the Obama administration. Corruption was rampant, President Hamid Karzai drove American officials to distraction, and those beneath him inspired little confidence.

Meanwhile, the Taliban, whose regime had been quickly dispatched when the United States invaded the country less than a month after 9/11, experienced a major resurgence. Their now potent insurgency exercised control over as much as 80 percent of Afghan territory by the end of the Bush years and continued to thrive during the Obama presidency. The Taliban's growing strength precipitated a prolonged policy review in Washington in mid-2010 about how to proceed—what *The Atlantic* called the "Afghanistan Policy Wars" (Clemons 2011).

One group inside the administration argued for beefing up America's fighting force there; others wanted to combine increased troops with intensified nation building. Advocates for both these positions aimed, ultimately, at defeating both al-Qaeda and the Taliban. Still others (led by Vice President Biden) saw that kind of victory as yet another chimera. Instead, they aimed to tamp down both military and political assistance, with the aim of defeating al-Qaeda (or at least making Afghanistan inhospitable to it) but probably incorporating the Taliban into the rule of the country instead of pursuing its total elimination.

Obama's decision seemed to be modeled after the Iraq experience: a surge of forty thousand troops for the U.S.-NATO force in the country to reverse the deteriorating military situation followed by a planned drawdown of American troops. Serious efforts at nation building were scrapped. Whether stability would be won by defeating the Taliban insurgents, simply containing them, or joining forces with them, the Obama administration seemed to be indicating that as long as al-Qaeda is defeated or at least checked, Afghanistan would not be key to the dynamics of the Middle East or South Asia. The assassination of Osama bin Laden in May 2011, while heightening tensions with Pakistan, served in Afghanistan as a sort of fig leaf for the Obama administration to portray al-Qaeda as severely weakened and now largely contained.

In the end, Obama followed those advisors who argued that Afghanistan, like Iraq, would not be the center of U.S. regional strategy, nor a possible strategic partner to secure vital American interests, nor a viable candidate for prolonged American investments in nation building. The assassination of bin Laden reinforced the administration's belief that it could disable al-Qaeda and then seek some arrangement with the Taliban that would allow the United States to exit from Afghanistan. For the Obama administration, it was neither in Iraq nor Afghanistan that central, long-term American interests lay.

Sorting out Priorities and America's Place in the Middle East

Obama's policies regarding Iraq—as well as Afghanistan—demonstrated quite clearly where he felt America's long-term Mideast concerns did *not* reside. Neither Iraq nor Afghanistan was regarded by the Obama officials as a linchpin for a future American role in the region. Both were unruly problems, to be sure. But their weak social and political institutions meant that those states were unlikely to exert significant influence on a regionwide basis. Neither was going to be transformed easily into a beacon of democracy and freedom—or even into a cohesive, integrated state and society. In the minds of administration officials, Iraq would not be the center point of the Mideast dynamic or the focal point for U.S. national-security interests. The hope was that neither Iraq nor Afghanistan would be so vulnerable so as to force a recurring American role to rescue them.

If the Obama team did not see Iraq or Afghanistan as the fulcrum for defining America's place in the Middle East, what would? Some answers to that question began to be articulated in Obama's major Mideast address in Cairo, in June 2009. The speech sounded four principal themes, three of which signaled his emerging foreign-policy concerns. These themes can serve as lenses through which to see what, if any, overall strategic plan, what comprehensive vision of American security interests, the Obama administration held for the future American role in the Middle East. How both the speech and the administration's actual actions in the years following dealt with these themes provide a glimpse into how the Obama team did—and did not—sort out priorities in the Middle East as it dealt with the complex problems of the region.

"Violent Extremism"

Obama's first theme in Cairo signaled where he stood on the issues that had consumed the Bush presidency after 9/11: the wars in

Iraq and Afghanistan and the War on Terror. Although Obama carefully avoided using the words "terror" or "terrorism" in the speech, they were very much on his mind. Instead of terrorists, he spoke of "violent extremists," but the intent was the same. Carefully, he sought to separate the overwhelming majority of Muslims from such militants, relegating the extremists to a fringe element. Implicitly, the president was attacking Huntington's notion of Islam's bloody borders, the idea of an American war against Islam generally, and American Islamophobia. His language was aimed at winning over Muslims, but he left no doubt that a key priority of his administration would be thwarting terrorism or, as he put it, violent extremism. "We will," he stated, "relentlessly confront violent extremists who pose a grave threat to our security." In that regard, at least, he did not depart from Bush or from the post-9/11 dominant national sentiment. Nor did he depart from that view as his administration proceeded; in a debate with his challenger Mitt Romney in the 2012 campaign, Obama reiterated that terrorism remained America's number-one national-security threat. (Romney, in contrast, said it was the looming possibility of Iran possessing nuclear arms.)

Two elements of note were embedded in Obama's Cairo remarks in 2009: he spent almost half the speech on this theme. The first was that of the three wars the United States was then fighting in and around the Middle East—in Iraq, in Afghanistan (and spilling over into Pakistan), and the War on Terror—only the last, the war against the "violent extremists," was embraced as representing a continuing central national-security concern for the country. In this sense, he broke sharply with Bush.

And the second was that the central purpose of the other two wars, to his mind, was embedded in the problem at the head of his list in the Cairo speech: violent extremism. Iraq, as noted above, would not be the linchpin for the U.S. role in the Middle East, as the Bush administration had intended. But it (and Afghanistan) were still of importance to Obama's overall understanding of the region; in fact, both countries, though barely able to hold together as states and societies, were emblematic for the president. The menace to the United States, in Obama's thinking, was that those countries, as divided and weak as they were, served as attractive bases for nonstate militant forces such as al-Qaeda, who were intent on changing the area's dynamics. Later, he developed the same mindset for Yemen, Somalia, and Mali—all, in his eyes, of direct concern to the United States because their porcelain-like fragility provided succor to anti-American terrorists.

In that sense, at least, Iraq and Afghanistan did hold a broader regional significance: they represented a larger cohort of Mideast and nearby states that were favored by violent extremists. The absence or weakness of state political authority in Iraq, Afghanistan, and these other states opened broad areas for alternative sources of authority. Of particular concern to Obama were nonstate actors bent on establishing political Islamic rule, what were popularly called Jihadists, most notably al-Qaeda. In Yemen, for example, even before the upheavals that came in the Arab Spring, the state's rule in the south was tenuous, at best. Once the war of the state against society began in the 2011 uprising, the state, in its practice if not in its rhetoric, abandoned altogether trying to govern the south (and parts of the north, as well). In the south, political Islamic groups, including ones identified with al-Qaeda, stepped into the breach. Washington officials saw such areas as potential breeding grounds for terrorist attacks against the United States.

The Cairo speech indicated clearly that Obama's preoccupation with the Middle East lay, in great part, in the threat it posed in producing terrorists who could strike America. He used all his rhetorical skills to isolate these violent extremists from the overwhelming majority of Muslims, but he left no doubt that America's place in the Middle East, in good part, was geared to thwart these nonstate actors.

Israel-Palestine

The president also singled out the Israeli-Palestinian conflict as his second deep source of concern. Here, he was reiterating what had become clear in the months before his Middle East address: this conflict would be near the top of the president's priority list. In Cairo, already beginning to sense how difficult it would be to move the parties toward negotiations, let alone a solution, he scolded Israelis, Palestinians, and other Arabs for not doing enough to move toward a solution to the conflict. But he did not back away from committing the United States to facilitate a fix for the problem.

From day one of his presidency, Obama had hammered home the mantra that the Israeli-Palestinian conflict posed grave threats to American interests and that the United States was in a position finally to solve the problem. Attempting to resume direct negotiations between Palestinians and Israelis immediately became a major focus of the Obama team, led by the administration's special envoy Mitchell.

Throughout his tenure, though, Mitchell ran into walls. Part of the difficulty was that the president, at least in some of his early pronouncements, set the bar much too high for such a complex issue. Additionally, he established unrealistic benchmarks that the parties would have to meet so that the long-stalled talks could resume. For all the energy and determination that the Obama team demonstrated on this single issue, nothing of substance was accomplished in the months leading up to the Cairo speech or, for that matter, in the ensuing years of his first term.

By the end of his first year in office, even some of the hopefulness expressed in Cairo began to fade. The president, for the first time, used the word "intractable" to describe the conflict. In one interview (Klein 2010), he sounded almost contrite—his great self-confidence tempered: "The Middle East peace process has not moved forward," he lamented.

And I think it's fair to say that for all our efforts at early engagement, it is not where I want it to be. . . . I think we overestimated our ability to persuade [the Israeli and Palestinian leaders to engage in a meaningful conversation] when their politics ran contrary to that. . . . I think it is absolutely true that what we did this year didn't produce the kind of breakthrough that we wanted, and if we had anticipated some of these political problems on both sides earlier, we might not have raised expectations as high.

It is not surprising that even before the end of that first year in office the former Bush aide Elliott Abrams called the administration's Middle East policy an "abject failure" (Abrams 2009). To be fair to Obama, Abrams's criticism seemed extraordinarily self-serving, especially from such a prominent figure in the Mideast policy making of the Bush administration, which had not managed to make headway at all in eight years in dampening the ongoing Israeli-Palestinian conflict. Still, the fact remained that nothing the Obama administration did seemed to crack the nut of the Israeli-Palestinian conflict. If anything, years into his presidency, the situation looked more bleak than it had in the six months before Obama's inauguration.

What approach did the administration take to the Palestine-Israel conflict? Did the path it chose hint at an overall strategic view by the Obama team in the Middle East? Like previous administrations that pushed for negotiations in the conflict and for an American role as broker or mediator—think of Nixon and Kissinger in the wake of the 1973 War—the

Obama administration had to walk a fine line. It sought to build its image among both Israeli leaders and the pro-Israel American public, especially the Jewish community, as a hardcore supporter of Israel—in the face of some outspoken skepticism about the new president. (I should add parenthetically here that Obama officials were well aware that the American Jewish community was much more heterogeneous in its views on Israel in 2009 than it was in, say, 1973.) Indeed, one of Romney's recurring themes as he battled Obama for the presidency in 2012 was how the administration had distanced itself from Israel (or, as some of the campaign literature put it, "threw Israel under the bus").

At the same time that the president expressed his unswerving support of Israel, he wanted the United States to carve out a role as a fair broker. He also felt it important to signal to the Palestinian leadership that it could trust the Obama team to help secure an agreement, including a Palestinian state, that would satisfy fundamental Arab demands. In the Cairo speech, Obama reflected America's delicate position—its steadfast support for Israel and its concern with Palestinian suffering.

In numerous other speeches, too, Obama seemed to be walking a tightrope. Here is how he handled the situation in a town hall meeting he held on January 28, 2010. The quote is his response to a pro-Palestinian question in front of a largely pro-Israeli crowd:

> Okay, now, everybody has got to be courteous, everybody is answering the question.
>
> Let me just talk about the Middle East generally. Look—all right, everybody, come on, come on, hold on. Hold on one second, I've got to answer my question first, sir. Okay. . . .
>
> Look, look, look, the [Palestinian-Israeli conflict] is obviously an issue that has plagued the region for centuries. And it's an issue that elicits a lot of passions, as you heard.
>
> Here's my view. Israel is one of our strongest allies. It has—(applause.) Let me just play this out. It is a vibrant democracy. It shares links with us in all sorts of ways. It is critical for us and I will never waver from ensuring Israel's security and helping them secure themselves in what is a very hostile region. (Applause.) So I make no apologies for that.
>
> What is also true is that the plight of the Palestinians is something that we have to pay attention to, because it is not good for our security and it is not good for Israel's security if you've got millions

of individuals who feel hopeless, who don't have an opportunity to get an education or get a job or what have you.   (Malcolm 2010)

And while they walked the line, administration officials had to make certain that they were clear as to what *American* interests were in the peace process and that they were securing those interests. They had to do this even as Mitchell and others shuttled between the two parties trying to mesh *their* distinct interests. To accomplish all that, the administration put pressure on both parties.

On the Israeli side, the pressure involved formal acceptance of a future Palestinian state and a freeze on settlement building in the West Bank. These issues were complicated by the elections that occurred in Israel shortly after Obama took office, which resulted in a new right-wing government coming to power at the end of March 2009, with Binyamin Netanyahu at the helm. Netanyahu entered office with a shaky mandate. His party actually came in second in the balloting, although he was the only candidate who could stitch together a majority coalition.

The coalition that he managed to assemble was heavy with prosettlement, antinegotiation nationalist and religious parties. His coalition partners aside, dealing with Netanyahu, who had managed to alienate personally the highest echelons of two previous presidential administrations, those of George H. W. Bush (when Netanyahu was opposition leader) and Bill Clinton (when Netanyahu served his first stint as prime minister), could not have brought much joy to the White House. Holdovers from those two previous American administrations, including Secretary of Defense Robert Gates, Secretary of State Clinton, and Chief of Staff Emanuel, had vivid negative memories of what members of those administrations had called Netanyahu's arrogance. They did not hold him in high regard.

These obstacles notwithstanding, Obama aides moved forward on the administration's two demands, or benchmarks, which, if met, could facilitate the resumption of direct Palestinian-Israeli negotiations. He made clear to Netanyahu that he wanted him publicly to accept the idea of a future independent Palestinian state alongside Israel. Even more strongly, Obama pushed the Israeli prime minister to announce and enforce a freeze in building Jewish settlements in the occupied West Bank—incorporating East Jerusalem, as well.

Previous Israeli prime ministers, including Netanyahu's two right-wing predecessors Ariel Sharon and Ehud Olmert, had accepted the goal

FIGURE 11.3   Barack Obama with Benjamin Netanyahu in the Oval Office, May 18, 2009.
Source: Courtesy White House Photograph.

of creating a Palestinian state, but Netanyahu had never signed on to this concept. Surprisingly, though, in a much ballyhooed speech at Bar-Ilan University, two and a half months after he entered office, Netanyahu did just that. "In my vision of peace, there are two free peoples living side by side in this small land, with good neighborly relations and mutual respect, each with its flag, anthem and government, with neither one threatening its neighbor's security and existence. . . . We are ready to agree to a real peace agreement, a demilitarized Palestinian state side by side with the Jewish state."

Netanyahu attached two important caveats to his acquiescence to a Palestinian state, which watered down his embrace of the concept. As stated in his last sentence above, the new state would have to be demilitarized, a condition that made Palestinians bristle. Beyond that, the Palestinians would have to recognize Israel as the *Jewish* state, an idea that had been percolating in recent years among right-wing politicians in Israel.

There was grumbling by Palestinian and American officials, as well as Israelis on the left, about Netanyahu's conditions. Mahmoud Abbas, the Palestinian president, for example, asked what business it was of the Palestinians to define the character of the Israeli state. That was the job of the Israeli people themselves. Behind Abbas's refusal was a concern for the 20 percent Arab minority in Israel. The rights of Israeli Palestinians,

Abbas feared, could be compromised were Israel defined exclusively as a *Jewish* state rather than a state of all its citizens.

Despite all the grousing, though, Netanyahu's speech seemed to remove a key stumbling block for Mitchell in reconvening talks. Issues like whether the new state fielded an army or if the Palestinians would explicitly recognize the Jewish character of Israel could be deftly deferred to the negotiations themselves, should they ever actually resume.

Obama's demand for a settlement freeze, however, proved to be much more contentious and remained an obstacle to moving forward. Mitchell had long been associated with the notion that Jewish settlements in the occupied territories flouted international law and Israelis' continued building of them was a major obstruction to any possible peace process. In fact, his stance had been the official American position for years.

U.S. officials in the past had (mostly privately) complained that the growing population of Israeli settlers in the occupied territories, now numbering in the hundreds of thousands and edging up toward half a million, was an impediment to finding a peaceful solution to the conflict and flew in the face of international law. Publicly, most past administrations looked the other way at what they considered to be illegal Jewish settlement. Periodically, the United States and Israel had tussled publicly about settlements, but only once before had they risen to the central issue in relations between the two countries—during the presidency of George H. W. Bush. Now, Obama and Mitchell were prepared again to make settlements a deal breaker.

Not surprisingly, much of the entire first year and well into the second year of the Obama presidency, from Netanyahu's election on, was fruitlessly consumed by this issue. The Israeli prime minister repeatedly rejected the call for an end to all settlement construction. Finally, clearly concerned about long-term relations with Washington, he acceded to a ten-month freeze, excluding East Jerusalem. This was hardly enough time to make serious headway on resolving the conflict.

The difficulty became that the United States had taken a sensitive issue and elevated it to a highly public all-or-nothing question. Once public, it became nearly impossible for the Palestinians to accept anything less than a full, openly announced freeze by the Israeli government, including East Jerusalem. And, once public, it became highly problematical for a right-wing Israeli government, with an unsteady coalition and a core of prosettlement constituents, to agree to such an all-out freeze. When Netanyahu's freeze expired, U.S. officials at first tried, unsuccessfully, to entice him to add on yet another three months and then finally threw up their hands and took the issue off the table.

On the Arab side, the pressure involved benchmarks that the Obama team set out involving confidence-building measures by Arab states, principally Saudi Arabia and the Gulf emirates. The thinking was that moves toward normalization of relations with Israel by Arab states would lend assurance to Israeli leaders as they were pressured to make concessions of their own. But these benchmarks, too, fell on deaf ears, especially on the part of Saudi Arabia, further impeding Mitchell's progress. Saudi officials may have felt that, in the Arab Peace Initiative that they had proffered in 2002, they had offered an acceptable tit-for-tat that could lead to an overall solution of Israel's conflicts with the Palestinians and, also, with Syria. Unilateral confidence-building measures, they may have felt, undermined their own proposal.

Again, as in the case of the demand for a halt to settlement construction, the public nature of the request and the refusal to accede served only to complicate and prolong the stage of prenegotiations. Privately, Obama aides began to talk of ways to back down from the demands that they had set. The dithering caused both Palestinians and Israelis to question the ability of the Obama administration to broker a deal between the parties.

With the failure to overcome the settlement-freeze issue and to initiate meaningful negotiations, Obama found his policies on the Israel-Palestine conflict in tatters. Mitchell resigned in 2011 having achieved almost nothing. He did manage to steer U.S. resources to Abbas and Prime Minister Salam Fayyad to build Palestine Authority institutions on the West Bank. And even Israeli officials acknowledged that American aid and training had made Palestinian police forces better equipped to assume security responsibilities should a Palestinian state materialize. But that did little to move the parties toward practical negotiations.

U.S. officials were saddled with an Israeli prime minister who talked the talk but was simply unwilling to walk the walk. And on the Palestinian side, they had no answers to the divide between Hamas and the Palestine Authority. An absence of reconciliation between Hamas and the leadership of the Palestine Authority (mostly coming from Fatah) would mean that no agreement on all of Palestine was possible, and a successful reconciliation would mean that Israel would refuse to deal with the reconciled leadership, since it included parties (Hamas) unwilling to accept its existence. There seemed to be no winning formula on the Palestinian side. Each time a reconciliation agreement was signed, it predictably led Israel only to dig in its heels, and in any case, none of those agreements held.

Even with all the setbacks and with the sense of hopefulness that Obama expressed in Cairo now drained, the president did not back away from the issue, clearly conveying the importance for the United States that he attached to a settlement. In 2011, Obama made another valiant try to jumpstart negotiations. The initiative came in the midst of the second major speech of his presidency on the Middle East, this one delivered at the State Department, on May 19, 2011, almost exactly two years after the Cairo address.

The speech's principal theme, which I will return to below, was the Arab Spring. But he took the opportunity to push forward on the Israel-Palestine conflict, as well. The president admitted that on the conflict, "expectations have gone unmet. Israeli settlement activity continues. Palestinians have walked away from talks." Again, despite the odds, he expressed hopefulness and determination, although less resolutely than in his Cairo speech. His new approach was to give priority in negotiations to more manageable issues (territory and security) and defer talks on more difficult matters (Jerusalem and the possibility of the return of Palestinian refugees to their original homes in Israel). A tiered approach, he argued, could provide a foundation for resuming talks. He recognized this would not be easy, especially in light of another recently announced reconciliation of the PLO and Hamas, echoing the question many Israelis repeatedly asked: "How can one negotiate with a party that has shown itself unwilling to recognize your right to exist?"

Still, he insisted a solution was possible. Reiterating the two-state ideal, the president noted, "We believe the borders of Israel and Palestine should be based on the 1967 lines with mutually agreed swaps, so that secure and recognized borders are established for both states." While this formulation was one that had been accepted by Obama's predecessors for years, none had used this precise formulation, "the 1967 lines with mutually agreed swaps."

In the aftermath of the speech, in a finger-wagging session with Obama and in a strident address to Congress, Netanyahu was able to raise a brouhaha about the indefensibility of these 1967 lines. And he steadfastly commented that Israel would never negotiate on that basis (although that is precisely what two of his predecessors, Barak and Olmert, had done). It is worth noting that only a couple of months later, on August 2, 2011, when Netanyahu was relying on the United States to counter (unsuccessfully) the Palestine Authority's bid for UN recognition of a Palestinian state, Netanyahu shifted gears and expressed a willingness to negotiate on the basis of the 1967 borders. But by then, all the momentum the president's speech had created toward resuming talks had been lost. As the 2012 election neared, Obama lost his taste for diving further into this "intractable" issue and abandoned any hope of resuming negotiations before the election.

Why did the Obama administration select such a complex, contentious problem as the Israel-Palestine conflict as one of the highest priorities of his administration from the outset? Why did he embrace an issue that had repeatedly turned out to be a graveyard for past presidential efforts? One answer may be that his top two advisors, Emanuel and David Axelrod, American Jews who held deep commitments to finding a solution, helped push the issue up the president's priority list. Another more likely answer may be that an energetic young president, with little experience in foreign affairs but with tremendous self-confidence, both underestimated the difficulty of moving ahead on the issue and overestimated his own powers. Like Bush before him, Obama miscalculated the degree to which the United States could shape the Middle East.

On the Palestine-Israel issue specifically, Obama actually might not have been so different from most of his post–World War II predecessors. They, too, at one point or another in their terms, jumped into the icy waters of Israeli-Palestinian relations, believing that they had the competence and ideas necessary to end the conflict. What drew Obama and his predecessors to this issue? No president has held to the illusion that solving the Israeli-Palestinian conflict would repair all U.S. relations with Arab and other Muslim states. Settling the conflict would not prove to be a panacea for American relations in the Middle East and the Muslim world.

Still, Obama and previous presidents saw gains to be reaped in strengthening America's place in the region and beyond if this contentious issue were put to rest. The president made this point explicitly in his May 2011 speech: "This conflict has come with a larger cost to the Middle East, as it impedes partnerships that could bring greater security and prosperity and empowerment to ordinary people." His understanding was that the Israeli-Palestinian dispute has been so destabilizing to the region and to U.S. relations there (those "impeded partnerships") that it seems intuitive that the United States must press on.

But there were no indications in the speech or in other messages emanating from the administration about what kinds of "partnerships" the president had in mind and what the role of the United States in such partnerships would be. He did not address in the speech or elsewhere why the conflict remains so central to Washington's perception of its place in the region and the world. Instead, there seemed to be a vague sense that Obama's goal of improving American ties with Muslims worldwide, expressed early in his presidency in the Cairo speech, could come that much closer to being achieved if "The Conflict" could only be swept away.

Just as the United States had gained handily by brokering the Egyptian-Israeli peace during the Carter years, the Obama foreign-policy aides hoped to secure American interests in facilitating a Palestinian-Israeli agreement, even if they were hazy as to just how this would come about. What was left unclear was how a solution to the Israeli-Palestinian conflict would help the administration establish a clear role for the United States in the Middle East. To what sorts of partnerships was Obama alluding? In particular, the administration did not articulate how an Israeli-Palestinian peace would relate to the other long-term problem with which it had been grappling: Iran.

Iran

Besides the threats of violent extremism and the Israeli-Palestinian conflict, Obama's Cairo address in 2009 sounded a third concern of his for the Middle East. The conundrum over what to do about a recalcitrant Iran occupied the administration from the outset. Obama aides faced two primary, linked challenges. First was the general issue of that country's increasing regional power over the previous two decades, including throwing around its weight so as to undermine U.S. aims and allies: support for Hezbollah and Hamas against Israel, aid to Shiite militias attacking the government and Sunnis in Iraq, attempts at destabilization through support of Shiite forces in several Arab countries, and more. Second was the country's steady move toward a capability to produce and fire ("deliver," as the security experts say) nuclear weapons. It was the nuclear issue, in particular, that Obama voiced in Cairo, and this issue only grew in importance as Obama's presidency moved forward.

While the Bush team had been slow to recognize the centrality of Iran to the entire region, the Obama administration immediately paid the highest regard to Iran, its nuclear program, the emerging regional bloc it led, and complaints by neighboring states that it was meddling in their affairs and fostering instability. In an interview days after his inauguration, Obama (2009a) encapsulated these concerns: "Iran has acted in ways that's not conducive to peace and prosperity in the region: their threats against Israel; their pursuit of a nuclear weapon which could potentially set off an arms race in the region that would make everybody less safe; their support of terrorist organizations in the past—none of these things have been helpful."

In the Cairo speech, Obama (2009b) put Iran's actions into the context of its stance toward the United States. "Iran," he noted, "has defined itself in part by its opposition to my country." The president knew, too, that the anxiety and enmity felt by U.S. policy makers was shared by key officials in the Middle East. In fact, Iran's growing power and nuclear ambitions had created near hysteria among many of America's allies in the Middle East, including three of the most important pro-American regimes, Egypt, Israel, and Saudi Arabia.

During the last throes of the Bush administration, as the original neoconservative ideas receded in importance, U.S. aides had already begun to acknowledge the centrality of Iran to the region and the deep concern that other Mideast states harbored about its intentions. In response to the fears of Iran's neighbors, Bush announced a massive arms deal with Gulf states worth tens of billions of dollars during his July 2007 visit to the region. Contracts were signed a year later, opening the way for new or improved air-defense systems for Saudi Arabia, the United Arab Emirates, and Kuwait.

Egypt and Israel also received large weapons commitments for the next decade. Abu Dhabi was promised an advanced antiballistic-missile system that, to date, had been procured only by the American military (and was not yet operational!). Additionally, Commander of the Central Command General David Petraeus stated that two U.S. cruisers with advanced antiballistic systems on board were now in the Persian Gulf at all times (Shapir 2010). In short, in its end years, the Bush administration put increasing emphasis on an Iranian threat to the region and to U.S. interests. It addressed that threat almost exclusively through a military buildup.

As in the case of the Israeli-Palestinian conflict, the Obama team early on placed great stock in the *diplomatic process* of addressing the challenges that Iran posed, moving beyond straight-out military means. The president believed that engagement with Iran, sitting down at the negotiating table, could achieve results—the point that he had first made during the campaign. Indeed, in June 2009 officials of the United States and Iran did sit down, if not to address the central question of the Iranian nuclear program, then at least to talk about the two sides' mutual interest in stabilizing Iraq. Later, in October 2009, more comprehensive negotiations involving the United States and Iran (plus the other UN Security Council members and Germany) opened in Geneva. Again, in January 2011, officials from these six major powers participated in talks with counterparts in Iran, attempting to persuade them to freeze uranium enrichment. But the talks collapsed ignominiously. And in 2012, newspapers reported secret direct Iranian-U.S. talks, but the administration denied these were taking place.

While Obama officials were interested principally in addressing Iran's weapons program in all those talks, they believed that the United States and Iran also shared important broader aims, which could create a platform for possible cooperation between them. Both wanted, the thinking went, to stabilize not only Iraq but also Afghanistan, Iran's other troubled neighbor. Throughout Obama's term, the Afghani regime faced a dire threat from the Taliban. What was key in the Iranian-American context was the Shiite-hating quality of the Taliban, which provided a possible shared interest, a basis for Iran to help in thwarting the Taliban's bid for a return to power.

Those common goals, Obama aides hoped, could be the underpinning for progress in the 2009 Geneva negotiations, especially on the nuclear issue. To sweeten the pot, the United States offered Iran a nuclear fuel–exchange program with the West, which would be brokered through the United Nations. Basically, through such an exchange, Iran would ship its uranium to another country, possibly Russia, which would enrich it and then return it to Iran as rods. The enriched rods, presumably, would not be able to used to make nuclear bombs (although some experts found that premise dubious).

While initially the talks seemed to be heading toward some sort of resolution, ultimately they faltered, just as the effort to jumpstart Palestinian-Israeli negotiations had gone awry. Face-to-face talks and the U.S. nuclear fuel–exchange proposal seemed to do little more than afford Iran more time to enrich uranium successfully itself and presumably move toward an operable nuclear-weapons system. At first, Iran accepted the American fuel-exchange idea, then rejected it, and finally said that it had not turned it down definitively. It turned out to be a nonstarter again in 2011, when the United States and the other powers revived the idea.

After the failure of the Geneva talks, a clearly frustrated Obama set a deadline of the end of 2009 for some solution to the nuclear issue. When the end-of-year deadline came and went, Obama stated that the rejection of the fuel exchange by Iran demonstrated that country's determination to build nuclear weapons. The international community, he emphasized, would now move toward harder-hitting sanctions. The new tougher approach reflected a chastened Obama's emphasis on the "dual-track approach," which he described as, "if they don't accept the open hand, we've got to make sure they understand there are consequences for breaking international rules" (Klein 2010). Obama had at first parted from his predecessor's aversion to face-to-face talks with Iran. But by the end of his first year in office, he ended up continuing the Bush policies, deploying antiballistic missiles, both on U.S. ships and through sales to Iran's neighbors, to counter the powerful Iranian presence in the region. And that approach continued in following years. In 2010, the administration announced accelerating the sales of antimissile systems to Bahrain, Kuwait, Saudi Arabia, and Qatar and moving Aegis cruisers, with their limited antimissile capability, into the Gulf.

Other nondiplomatic means may have also come into play, although none could be confirmed. In November 2010, for example, one Iranian nuclear scientist was killed and another injured when motorcyclists attached bombs to their cars as they were driving. This attack followed the murder of yet another nuclear researcher earlier in the year, when a motorcycle exploded near his car. Iran's interior minister pointed the finger at the CIA and Israeli intelligence as the culprits. Then another scientist was assassinated by passing motorcyclists in the summer of 2011.

Additionally, in 2010, an extremely complex computer worm dubbed Stuxnet appears to have destroyed 20 percent of Iran's centrifuges, key components in uranium enrichment. Strong clues exist, the *New York Times* reported, "suggesting that the virus was designed as an American-Israeli project to sabotage the Iranian program" (Broad, Markoff, and Sanger 2011). Indeed, some American and Israeli officials have hinted, although not stated outright, that the virus was devised by their two countries. Initial assessments were that the computer attack had set the Iranian nuclear-weapons program back as much as three years, although some analysts later expressed doubt that all these efforts did much to slow down the program (Zetter 2011).

Partly, the administration's frustration with diplomacy as a primary tactic stemmed from Iran's inconsistency—or stall tactics. In part, Iran's stonewalling may have been related to its domestic upheaval. As I will discuss in part 5, the June 12, 2009, elections there led to months of protest and brutal repression by the regime, with significant effects on larger regional dynamics. Those extraordinary domestic upheavals seem to have deeply influenced the possibilities for Obama to engage the Iranian regime. One scholar on nuclear-nonproliferation issues put it this way at the time: "The leadership in Iran must now contend with domestic instability, which leaves little room for nuclear negotiations with the international community. . . . The chance for direct engagement with the re-elected Ahmadinejad is thus much less likely now that his own legitimacy in Iran has been questioned" (Humphrey 2009).

It became clear to the Obama administration that, like the Palestinian-Israeli issue, no quick fixes would present themselves in the case of Iran. The hope that the president expressed in Cairo—"we are willing to move forward without preconditions on the basis of mutual respect"—dissipated during his term, just as his hope for movement forward on the Israel-Palestine issue had. Increasingly, the Obama administration relied on stronger and stronger international sanctions against Iran. It also danced around rumors of an American or Israeli military strike against Iran's nuclear facilities and parried Netanyahu's jabs trying to goad the United States into bombing Iran's reactors.

For Iran, an open hand did not yield much, and the turmoil in that country after its elections only further complicated an already complex issue. The failed talks in early 2011 reinforced the thinking in Washington that means other than direct diplomatic engagement with Iran would have to be used. And through all the stillborn diplomatic initiatives the worry grew that lost time only served to give the regime more opportunity to reach the threshold for producing nuclear weapons and guidance systems.

State-Society Issues in the Middle East

In his 2009 Cairo speech, Obama addressed one last set of Mideast concerns for the United States—democracy, religious freedom, women's rights, and economic development and opportunity. Unlike the other issues he sounded in Cairo—violent extremism, Israel-Palestine, and Iran—these were all principally domestic matters, involving the relationships between rulers and those they governed in the region. But these domestic concerns did not move much beyond the rhetorical level;

they had little resonance in administration decision making, at least until the upheavals of the Arab Spring in 2011, which I will address in the final chapter.

Rather, as the new administration turned away from the Bush perspectives and policies and tried to set out a new understanding of America's role in the area, it was the other issues raised in his Cairo speech that preoccupied his aides and lent shape to his overall Middle East policy: the region's nurturing of nonstate actors that could carry out terrorist attacks against the United States, the powder keg of the Israel-Palestine conflict that could spark broader conflict and prevent the United States from forging partnerships with Arabs and Muslims, and Iran's actions that could undermine U.S. allies and destabilize the entire region.

New Assumptions for the United States in the Middle East

What did the Obama administration's handling of these key issues on the international relations of the region indicate about its vision of the future American role in the Middle East? Where did it see the major threats to the United States? What did officials now see as U.S. goals and priorities in the region, after a decade of American frustration and futility? Did the administration's policies and actions on the themes of his Cairo speech reflect a set of new assumptions about the region and a comprehensive take on what longer-term U.S. interests in the Middle East were?

To the degree that the Obama administration addressed these questions, it did so through its actions rather than through an elaborated comprehensive doctrine (although in the press and popular websites an "Obama Doctrine" was inferred to emphasize negotiation over Bush's interventionism). The Obama team signaled the direction in which it was going by abandoning two key Bush administration foreign-policy assumptions: (1) that in the international relations of the area America could singlehandedly reshape Mideast regional dynamics in intended ways, and (2) that inside individual Mideast countries America could reconstitute state and society.

I will address the Obama administration's rejection of the second assumption in part 5. Here I want to underline its strategic perspective that the United States could not reshape the region alone. From the beginning, Obama saw America's role in the Middle East to be that of one player—a very big and important player, to be sure—among others. The president rejected the creation of an American imperium while accepting a continuing, active role for the United States in the region. Of course, as the world's sole superpower, it would bring special attributes to its regional role. Secretary of State Hillary Clinton (2011), talking about East and Southeast Asia, described a model of the United States as the first among equals in a region, an underwriter. It appears that the administration was aiming for much the same role in the Middle East:

> And though [Asia's] progress is largely due to the hard work and ingenuity of the people of Asia themselves, we in the United States are proud of the role we have played in promoting prosperity. Of course, we helped Japan and South Korea rebuild, patrolled Asia's sea lanes to preserve freedom of navigation, promoted global shipping, and supported China's membership in the WTO. Along with our treaty allies—Japan, South Korea, Australia, Thailand and Philippines, and other key partners like New Zealand and Singapore—we have underwritten regional security for decades, and that in turn has helped create the conditions for growth.

Obama judged the possibilities for America to be less those of transforming a "bad neighborhood" and more of countering and checking "bad neighbors." To deter unwelcomed and unfriendly power in the Middle East credibly (read, Iran, for the Obama administration), Washington would need regional partners. Indeed, it is striking how often the words "partners" and "partnerships" turned up in Obama's discourses on the Middle East. Such partnerships would be a portion of the "symbolic and practical steps to return the United States to multilateral engagement" (Patrick 2009). Policies now followed the dictum that Montesquieu and modern-day realists, or neorealists, propounded: peace is assured when power is checked by power. That was a dictum largely rejected by the previous administration, which had taken on a more imperial stance, aiming to transform those with whom America engaged (think of "regime change") rather than serve as a counterweight to existing powers (McGowan 2007).

For Obama officials, the key was to form coalitions with like-minded states, rejecting Bush's unilateralism. Some observers saw in the administration's global search for partners a reflection of America's declining role in the world—no longer the hegemon it was in the wake of World War II (Calleo 2009). But it seems more likely that the shift toward finding partners cleaved to the traditional realist intuitions of the president and a return to the glory days of multilateralism after World War II. In his preelection *Foreign Affairs* article, he made his preferences clear, hammering home multilateralism and diplomacy as the cornerstones of American foreign policy. "America cannot meet the threats of this century alone," he wrote in rebuke of the neoconservative cavalry image, "and the world cannot meet them without America. . . . To renew American leadership in the world, I intend to rebuild the alliances, partnerships, and institutions necessary to confront common threats and enhance common security."

In a region where the United States would be one of many players and in which the sort of regional transformation that Bush had in mind would be unattainable, a different set of foreign-policy tools would be needed. Statesmanship and diplomacy, Obama argued, would have to be returned to their proper place in the foreign-policy toolkit. By diplomacy, he meant above all the use of negotiations, bilateral and multilateral, involving concessions by the United States in return for desired action by others, especially hostile regimes.

For Bush aides, especially in the heady days of his first term, almost all negotiations—for example, directly with North Korea or Iran or as mediator between Israelis and various Arab parties—had spelled weakness and concessions to evil. Indeed, when Bush actually did pursue negotiations in all those realms later, in his second term, it was with a sense of resignation that his slipping approval rate and the straits in which the United States found itself internationally forced him into these unsavory policy shifts. For his administration, at least during his first term, avoiding negotiations had taken on a positive moral quality.

Obama assumed an entirely different stance. Citing one key Mideast example prior to his election, he wrote, "Diplomacy combined with pressure," he wrote, "could also reorient Syria away from its radical agenda to a more moderate stance—which could, in turn, help stabilize Iraq, isolate Iran, free Lebanon from Damascus' grip, and better secure Israel" (Obama 2007). His undue optimism not withstanding, Obama was sending clear messages about the tools his team would use. Even over the course of his campaign for the presidency, he expressed willingness to sit down with Iranian officials, at the highest levels, as well. His position famously drew derision from his Democratic opponent, Hillary Clinton, in a debate during the primaries and then from his Republican adversary, John McCain, but he stuck with it.

Once Clinton shifted gears and became Obama's secretary of state, she echoed his views on restoring diplomacy to the American toolkit, including negotiations with Iran. She also touted multilateralism and the still prominent, but nonimperial, role the United States would play in various regions, including the Middle East. In her Asia speech in 2011, for example, she used that region to reflect a broader understanding of America's place in regions around the world: "The Obama Administration has made a comprehensive commitment to reinvigorate our engagement as a Pacific power—shoring up alliances and friendships, reaching out to emerging partners, and strengthening multilateral institutions" (Clinton 2011). The same thinking applied to the Middle East inside the administration.

At the outset, Clinton stressed another theme Obama would pursue, the types of people working on foreign policy. Two days after the inauguration, she said, "The President is committed to making diplomacy and development the partners in our foreign policy along with defense, and we must be smarter about how we exercise our power. But as I said this morning upon entering the building, the heart of smart power— are smart people" (Clinton 2009). By smart she meant not only intelligent but also people who were experienced and skilled in the ways of diplomacy.

At the same ceremony where Clinton spoke, Vice President Joe Biden, who would himself turn out to be a key figure in the administration's foreign-policy making, especially in trying to extricate the United States from Iraq and Afghanistan, underlined the high priority the administration would put on diplomacy. "We've come here today to the State Department," he noted, "to send a very clear message, a clear message at home as well as abroad, that we are going to reinvigorate America's commitment to diplomacy" (Clinton 2009).

Both in terms of securing allies and engaging unfriendly regimes, give and take would be the first path taken. Even with all the difficulties the administration faced in Israel-Palestine, it persisted in plodding toward negotiations brokered by the United States. Even with the utter failure to woo Syria, Obama emissaries continued to trek to Damascus until civil war overtook that country. And the president proceeded to emphasize the *dual* track with Iran, keeping the door to talks open even as he moved toward stronger sanctions, militarization of Iran's neighbors, and stepped-up covert activity.

The Obama team rejected the Bush-era assumptions that both the region and individual states and societies could be transformed by the United States. It put forward a different model—one that recognized the limitations of U.S. power and that relied on diplomacy and partnerships. He saw his model as creating a new beginning for the United States in the Middle East. That model, to his mind, dealt with an area of multiple crises but in which a thread ran through these crises. In his interview with *Al Arabiya* in his first year in office, for example, Obama emphasized "that it is impossible for us to think only in terms of the Palestinian-Israeli conflict and not think in terms of what's happening with Syria or Iran or Lebanon or Afghanistan and Pakistan. These things are interrelated. . . . We are looking at the region as a whole" (Obama 2009a).

But as time went on, no blueprint could be discerned for how to achieve the goal of what he had expressed in his Cairo speech: creating "a new beginning" for the United States in the region. Neither his speeches nor his administration's policies made clear the thread that ties the issues of the region together—how all these "things are interrelated." No priorities were set out, nor was there a sense of whether solutions were independent of one another or, instead, if some solutions rested on prior successes of other problems. On the Palestinian-Israeli conflict, Obama stressed that a two-state solution would be in the interests of the Palestinians, Israelis, and Americans. While one could see the clear interests in this particular solution—or any solution, for that matter—for Palestinians and Israelis, Obama did not clarify why such a solution was in the U.S. interest, that is, how it fit into America's larger role in the region and the world. What did it want in the Middle East, and how would a solution of the conflict help it achieve its goals?

After the Cairo speech, the issues that remained on the front burner were terrorism, Iran, and Israel-Palestine. It was around these issues, administration officials felt, that America's role in the region would be shaped. If the administration had rejected the Bush belief that all roads run through Baghdad, it did appear to act as if many, if not all, roads run through Tehran. The new administration seemed attuned to the transformations that had overtaken the Middle East at the end of the twentieth century, which put Iran at the center of regional dynamics: the atrophy of the leading Arab states, the displacement of Arab nationalism by political Islam as the leading ideology, the emergence of nonstate actors, and the resurgence of Shiites. But it seemed uncertain where to find the sorts of partners in the region that could serve as a counterweight to Iran and its allies.

Likewise, it poured resources and its attention into preventing the Middle East from becoming a breeding ground for terrorism, but, again, it was not clear where it would find viable partners. It grounded its hopes on the cracked foundation of dictators such as Yemen's Ali Abdullah Saleh, who was soon to be at war not only with violent extremists but with his own population—and who would soon be unceremoniously dumped from office.

Israel-Palestine also drew the administration's attention, but it was unclear what, if any, connection the conflict had to the issue of engaging Iran or to fighting terrorism. While Obama did not display the same overt affection for Israel that Bush had, he did repeatedly profess its unbreakable bonds with the United States, reaffirmed by a visit to the country early in his second term. What was left unstated—and undeveloped—by the administration was the broader importance for the United States if Israel could move beyond affection, if it could reemerge as a strategic partner for the United States, one that the United States could lean on to enhance its role and security in the region. The question of whether a solution to its conflict with Palestinians could change Israel's status from an object of American policy to a key strategic partner remained unanswered. I will suggest my own answer to it in chapter 13.

The Obama Administration and the Arab Spring

The agenda that the Obama team had set for itself in the Middle East—headed by the issues of Iran, the Palestinian-Israeli conflict, and lingering pockets of terrorism—simply imploded after two years in office. It was not only that Palestinian-Israeli enmity defied the efforts of even the brightest of the administration's stars, that every effort to engage Iran or slow down its move toward becoming a nuclear power foundered, or that the War on Terror proved interminable and unwinnable. Nor was it that the Obama administration failed in its first two years to stitch together a comprehensive strategy for dealing with this difficult region.

Beyond all that, the events in Egypt, Libya, and Syria and, less so, in Tunisia, Bahrain, and Yemen in 2011 and 2012 left the administration chasing after events for which its policies were understandably unprepared. If ever the phrase "seat-of-the-pants" foreign policy applied, it was to Obama's reactions to the events of the Arab Spring. Just as in the period following the fall of the Berlin Wall, Washington again found itself saddled with policies geared to the past and irrelevant to the future.

As the Middle East lurched from uprising to uprising, any thought about a comprehensive Mideast strategy for the United States took a decided back seat. In important ways, the revolutionary changes that seemed to be ushering in yet another fundamental transformation in Mideast dynamics were immune to clear doctrines and preplanned policies. The president acknowledged as much when he indicated that the events in each Middle East country differed and would have to be approached on an individual basis. Also, the United States could not escape entirely the legacy of its past policies, especially its unwavering support for Mubarak and some of the other Arab autocrats.

To its credit, in one uprising after another, the administration's instincts led it to take the calls for democracy seriously. It tempered and then withheld support from most (but not all) of the autocrats to whom it had been previously tied and who were now under fire—Ben Ali in Tunisia, Mubarak in Egypt, Saleh in Yemen. In the very first series of demonstrations, in Tunisia, for example, Washington did not follow France's lead in reflexively lining up behind Ben Ali. Rather, it initially took more of a wait-and-see stance and later threw its support firmly behind the protestors.

It was Egypt, though, that provided the first serious test for Obama in the new circumstances, and not surprisingly his response was cautious and grew bolder only as events moved toward the January 25 mass demonstrations and beyond. To the clear benefit of Washington, the Tahrir Square demonstrators in January and February 2011 barely acknowledged the United States in their cries for change beyond alluding to the American-supplied rubber bullets the security forces aimed at the protestors. In contrast to many demonstrations in the past, the wrath of the public was directed inward, to Mubarak and his repressive, sclerotic regime, rather than the Western bogeyman.

The discipline and single-mindedness of the protestors in focusing on Mubarak and his cronies gave Washington a bit of breathing room to find its footing. In the early stage of protest, the Obama team avoided action or even clear commentary on the events, but it did withhold from Mubarak the backing he expected. As the demonstrations grew, the administration became increasingly pointed with Mubarak and in public comments, finally making it clear to the Egyptian president that his refusal to resign only made matters worse. As the pace of events picked up dramatically, Obama officials finally threw their support behind the demonstrators in the street (much to the dismay not only of those surrounding Mubarak but also American allies like Saudi Arabia and Israel). By the time Mubarak ignominiously left office on February 11, Washington had aligned itself fully with the revolutionary forces.

The fateful shift in American policy away from Mubarak over the course of Egypt's most important three weeks in the previous sixty years was crucial for Washington. It enabled the Obama administration later to continue close, if sometimes tense, relations with Egypt's new leaders after Mubarak's fall. Cooperation continued even after the Muslim Brotherhood, long reviled and shunned by Washington, dominated the first free parliamentary elections after the revolution and Mohammed Morsi, who came from the Brotherhood, won the first postrevolution election for president.

On a variety of issues, including the continuing brutal strife in Syria, Egypt and the United States acted in tandem after Mubarak's exit. In the brief Gaza War of 2012 between Hamas and Israel, Washington stood firmly with Cairo as it brokered a ceasefire. Certainly relations were not free of friction. Morsi's steamrolling of a new constitution on Egyptian society, including his neutering of the judiciary in late 2012, met with significant murmuring in Washington (if not public condemnation). Still, Obama's policy toward Egypt in January and February 2011 put Washington in a position to maintain solid relations with the successor regime.

In short, the Obama administration created policy on an ad hoc basis through the Egyptian upheaval, which led to some lurching back and forth and some uncertainty. All in all, though, the mixture of early caution and later open support for the revolution, as well as the decision to back away from Mubarak fairly early in the course of events, enabled Washington to be in a position to continue working with the still most powerful Arab state.

Obama's improvisation, wobbling, and reliance on instincts in his administration's Mideast policy in the new era of the Arab Spring could be seen in its policies toward Bahrain, Yemen, Libya, and Syria, as well. The Sunni-dominated government in Bahrain lashed out violently against protestors from its largely Shiite population. And when the battering of its own citizens failed to quell the protests, the regime turned to Saudi Arabia, which rolled its troops into the country under the aegis of the GCC and quashed the people's uprising. Unlike its support, even if cautious at first, for the demonstrators in Tunisia and Egypt earlier, Washington was nearly mute as the uprising in Bahrain was violently put down. For one, the United States was reluctant to further antagonize Saudi Arabia after the two ended up on opposite sides of the Egyptian uprising. Also, Bahrain had important strategic significance, harboring America's Fifth Fleet. Finally, the Shiite-dominated uprising was seen as possibly working in Iran's favor.

Yemen's Arab Spring, which started concurrently with the Egyptian protests, elicited similar ambivalence from the Obama administration. President Saleh had been a key figure for the United States in the War on Terror, cooperating with the administration in attacking al-Qaeda cells in the country. That cooperation had been tempered by Saleh's penchant to work out all sorts of arrangements with various tribal leaders in the mountainous, often nearly inaccessible parts of the country, including arrangements that provided sanctuary for al-Qaeda operatives. Still, Obama officials saw Saleh as mostly an asset, particularly his willingness to sanction American bombing and drone strikes of targets in the country. Sympathy with demonstrators demanding an end to dictatorship was mitigated by reliance on Saleh in what the administration considered the all-important War on Terror.

The sheer complexity of the events in Yemen made Washington's policy making even more problematic. The demonstrations that began in January 2011 seemed to fit the Arab Spring template as seen in Tunisia and Egypt. As the violence dragged on, however, it was difficult to sort out calls for democracy from tribal and family rivalries. The GCC tried to broker a solution and failed after multiple attempts. Saleh combined brutal attacks on his population with a variety of delaying tactics to make the situation even more complicated. He signed the GCC agreements and then ignored them.

Saleh was gravely wounded in an attack on June 3 and left the country for Saudi Arabia, which seemed to provide the conditions necessary to end the fighting and find a solution. But even from Saudi Arabia Saleh continued to use delaying tactics, and to nearly everyone's surprise he returned to Yemen in September. Protests and international pressure finally led him to accept the final GCC plan, paving the way for him to leave office. Once again, he dallied. More than a year after the protests began, a new president was elected, although even then it was not clear that Yemen had seen the last of Saleh.

Even in the early stages of the Yemeni uprising, Obama officials did not remain silent, as they had in Bahrain, whose protests started a month or so after than those in Yemen. Reacting to the violence that Saleh unleashed against his own people, Obama, Clinton, and others expressed support for the demonstrators. They supported the GCC peace initiative and eventually left no doubt that Saleh had to resign and leave the country. Saudi Arabia's distancing itself from Saleh and the absence of a potential major Iranian role in the events opened the door for the United States to take a much stronger position in favor of the uprising than it had in Bahrain.

Bahrain and Yemen, though, paled as crises for the United States next to the events that unfolded in Libya and Syria, two countries in which the United States had not been allied with the longtime strongmen ruling the country. Mere days after the ouster of Mubarak in Egypt, protests erupted in the city of Benghazi demanding the ouster of Colonel Muammar Qaddafi. Qaddafi had headed the country for nearly half a century without facing a major challenge to his rule. Now, the uprisings to his west in Tunisia and to his east in Egypt were closing in on him like a vise.

In a short time, the Benghazi demonstrations engulfed most cities in the country and elicited a vicious response from the regime, with security forces firing indiscriminately on protestors and bystanders in Benghazi from the outset and on other demonstrations soon after. The protests quickly turned into an all-out civil war, with Qaddafi bombarding dissident forces and the protestors' creating a ragtag fighting force of their own and a provisional government, the National Transitional Council.

Working with the United Nations, NATO, and an informal coalition of states (including Qatar and, later, other Mideast states), Washington led the way in a series of actions designed to protect the Libyan population from its government. These included a no-fly zone, arms embargo, and naval blockade. Within a month of the first demonstrations, the international coalition unleashed barrages of missiles on Libyan forces, fired at first by the United States and the United Kingdom. The United States quickly moved away from direct military action—that was left largely to the French and British—and instead assumed command functions. By the end of March, NATO took control of the bombings, again with the United States playing key command and logistical roles. The actual war dragged on through the spring and summer, eventually killing as many as fifty thousand Libyans (exact numbers will probably never be known). It ended only in October with the killing of Qaddafi and the assumption of control by the National Transitional Council.

In the entire tumult of 2011 in the Arab world, it was in Libya that Washington displayed the most forceful and decisive responses. The U.S. military deployed eleven ships (including aircraft carriers, nuclear submarines, and cruise missile–firing submarines), a variety of aircraft (including stealth bombers, F-15 and F-16 fighter planes, and U-2 reconnaissance planes), and CIA operatives on the ground (which were not acknowledged by the administration). Although the justification for the military intervention was to protect defenseless Libyan citizens, there was little doubt that the underlying purpose was to eliminate Qaddafi's regime and enable Libya's dissidents to triumph.

In what struck many observers as strikingly similar circumstances— the Syrian civil war—the Obama administration's response was almost the polar opposite of its bold actions in Libya, which undid Qaddafi. The Syrian protests started later and unfolded more slowly than in Libya, and the civil war there lasted much longer. Demonstrations began in March 2011, as protestors for the first time demanded an end to the rule of the Ba'ath Party and the Asad dynasty. Within a month, the Syrian army was employed to quell the riots, firing on protestors and uninvolved citizens indiscriminately.

The demonstrations slowly transformed into pitched battles between the Syrian armed forces and dissidents, and by the end of the year, with 5,000 already dead (a number that would grow to well over 100,000 by the end of 2012, with most of those being noncombatant civilians), a full-scale civil war was underway. The destruction and brutality of the war, particularly the willingness of Asad's forces to bombard and raze neighborhoods and kill huge numbers of defenseless citizens, were without precedent in the modern Middle East.

If in Libya Obama exhibited boldness, in Syria he demonstrated hesitancy and caution. He was slow to call for Asad's ouster, lagged in recognizing the Syrian National Coalition formed in November 2012 (Syria's version of Libya's National Transitional Council), blocked direct U.S. military action to protect the Syrian population or counter the Syrian forces, and prevented even indirect involvement by supplying rebel forces with arms or logistical support. Eventually, the administration did condemn the government's use of force against civilians, called for an end to Asad's rule, and agreed to supply nonlethal aid to the rebels. It lagged behind other countries in recognizing the Syrian National Coalition as the legitimate representative of the Syrian people but did come on board in December 2012, a month after the coalition was assembled (with strong pressure put on the constituent Syrian members by Western powers).

Obama's reluctance to dive into the Syrian crisis was not difficult to understand. The patchwork nature of Syrian society—Arabs and Kurds, Muslims and Christians, Sunnis and Alawites, among numerous other divisions—heightened the threat of a breakup of the country and the possibility of regional war as various Mideast powers sided with internal factions. Certainly, the civil war served Washington's purposes by weakening Iran's sea-to-sea bloc. The weakening of Asad also negatively affected Washington's longtime nemesis Hezbollah. Still, the growing power of militant Islamic groups among the fighters and the feeling among many fighting rebel groups that the Syrian National Council was foisted on them gave the Obama administration pause as to what a rebel victory might mean.

In the end, the administration simply did not believe there could be the kind of decisive termination to the Syrian crisis that Western military intervention had helped bring about in Libya. Military intervention in a state holding chemical weapons, in a highly fractured society, and in a country backed by Russia and China did not seem like a safe bet. With memories of the long, bitter experience in Iraq, where the United States suffered mightily after its intervention to create a semblance of unity and stability in a badly fragmented society, the administration had little appetite for another long and draining intervention in Syria.

Obama brought the vision of a "new beginning" to the region, which held multiple meanings: a turn from the soured relationships with the Muslim and Arab worlds, new and renewed partnerships, a fresh start with adversaries through shared interests and frank dialogue, an end to nettlesome conflicts, and more. To achieve such broad ends, the president fired on all cylinders simultaneously at the beginning of his presidency, attacking multiple problems with his own persuasive rhetoric and cracker-jack foreign-policy aides. But the region was not necessarily amenable to such an approach.

What the former policy maker, now turned analyst Aaron David Miller (2011) said of the Israel-Palestine issue alone is true for the region as a whole. "This issue is a perfect storm of headaches—one giant root-canal operation that can bring sustained pain to any administration even under the best of circumstances." He went onto comment about the different foci of power inside the Obama White House: "It's not that these centers of influence are in ferocious competition; everybody—or almost everybody—seems to get along. It's just that there appears to have been no adult supervision to differentiate what might work from what absolutely wouldn't." Once the Arab Spring erupted, policy making became all the more difficult.

The outcomes of the Arab Spring are still far from clear. But in some of the countries, the dust has begun to settle. It is necessary now for Washington to recalibrate its strategy for the Middle East. I take up the issue of what sort of model the United States might employ as it goes forward in chapter 13. What can be said here is that the region has simply not been amenable to the kind of multifocal, all-out assault that Obama put forward in the first couple of years of his presidency. As the Obama team learned, problems have been individually complex and linked in mysterious ways. A clearer sense is needed now of what might be possible, what role the United States could carve out for itself, which interests should have the highest priority, how addressing one issue might affect others, and how the administration might achieve its national-security goals.

PART V

Conclusion: Looking Back and Looking Forward

12   Ups and Downs of an Everyday Player, on the Cheap

The United States as a Permanent Mideast Player

Whether they cared to be or not, American presidents found themselves drawn into Mideast regional affairs from the 1940s on. Indeed, a significant chapter of modern Middle East history consists of a parade of American presidents, each with his own float garlanded with programs and policies for dealing with this nettlesome region. Doctrines abounded—the Truman Doctrine, the Eisenhower Doctrine, the Nixon Doctrine, the Carter Doctrine, the Reagan Doctrine, the Bush Doctrine, the Obama Doctrine—most of them designed to deal with (or inspired by) events in the Middle East. Perhaps the most explicit in its Middle East focus was the Eisenhower Doctrine, which stemmed from a presidential speech to Congress at the beginning of 1957 entitled "Special Message to the Congress on the Situation in the Middle East." But other presidents' doctrines were similarly inspired by events in that troubled part of the world.

Truman took the first sustained steps toward making the United States a permanent player in the area. He saw the Soviet Union as a grave threat to the stability of the region at the very moment that America was trying to make sense of the new postwar world and decide on the international role it would play. Truman was alarmed at domestic unrest in Greece and Turkey, which he saw as fomented by the Soviets. Soviet threats against Turkey and the USSR's slowness in removing its troops from Iran in 1946, as had been agreed to in the Great Power meetings in the waning days of the war, also provoked Truman. And on the heels of all that came Israel's declaration of independence and the regional war that ensued.

Following Truman, Eisenhower, with no great enthusiasm on his part, was drawn into the 1956 Suez crisis. Then in 1958, his recently proclaimed doctrine was tested by the revolution in Iraq and by domestic unrest threatening to unseat friendly regimes in Lebanon and Jordan. A decade later, Johnson too was reluctantly pulled into the Mideast maelstrom. While he would have rather focused his attention on the deteriorating situation in Vietnam (Spiegel 1985, 124–127), he found the lead-up to and the fallout from the 1967 Arab-Israeli War planting the seeds for fundamental changes in the international relations of the region and beyond.

Like Johnson, Nixon also wanted to attend to Southeast Asia and leave the Middle East to its own devices. Robert Dallek (2007, 172) put Nixon's feelings about the Middle East this way: "Two considerations shaped Nixon's initial response to Middle East problems: their hopeless complexity and lesser urgency than Vietnam." But like other presidents, no matter how much he preferred to stay clear of the region, Nixon was pulled into its turbulence. He felt the shockwaves of one Mideast crisis after another—the War of Attrition in 1970 between Israel and Egypt, the daring hijackings and the Black September War, the October 1973 War, with its nuclear saber rattling and its aftermath of U.S. mediated separation of forces—and they inevitably drew his attention. The Nixon Doctrine, which led to major military aid to Saudi Arabia and Iran, was aimed in part to shore up America's shaky position in the Persian Gulf and the rest of the Middle East.

And so it went: Ford and the Egypt-Israel and Syria-Israel disengagement talks and his infamous "reconsideration" of relations with Israel; Carter and his doctrine to save the Persian Gulf (yet again) following the Soviet invasion of neighboring Afghanistan, as well as his misadventures with the Iranian Revolution and his signature accomplishment at Camp David; Reagan and the Iran-Contra scandal, as well as American misadventures in the Lebanese civil war. All the way through to Obama, no president could escape the volatility and centrality of the Middle East. The area was a black hole sucking the United States in, whether its leaders wanted to be or not. The Middle East proved to be less the object of American foreign policy than it was a complex game into which the United States was absorbed willy-nilly as an ongoing major player.

Working on the model established only four years after World War II, when NATO was created, American presidents attempted globally to build multilateral security alliances from region to region to blunt the forces that they felt jeopardized the United States. In the Middle East, as in other areas, they sought out local strategic partners that could shoulder some of the security burden for the United States and face off against the radical forces of that region. Administration after administration ended up allying with an assortment of Mideast regimes—the shah's Iran, Hashemite-ruled Iraq, Saudi Arabia, the Gulf states, Jordan, Turkey, Sadat's and Mubarak's Egypt, and Israel, among others. But most of these allies were far from the sorts of states that were allied with the United States in NATO. Whether confronting an Egypt-led Arab nationalist bloc supported by the Soviet Union, as in the 1950s and 1960s, or Iraq in the 1990s and 2000s, or an Iran-led coalition of states and nonstates with strong Islamic and Shiite flavors, in the 2000s, Bush and then Obama found slim pickings among Middle East states for constructing their own countercoalitions.

If one central theme of the last sixty-plus years has been the establishment of the United States as a permanent, everyday player in the Mideast regional system, seeking out strategic partners to aid in playing that role, another has been the efforts by administration after administration somehow to do all this cheaply. In this regard, presidents' concerns about the Middle East were part of a larger anxiety they harbored about America: as the world's greatest power, it might be overreaching in its ambitions. Other critical regions—first Europe and Northeast Asia and then Southeast Asia in the 1960s and 1970s—had been veritable sinkholes for American resources. As a result, one administration after another attempted to limit severely the commitment of resources to other critical areas, not least of all the Middle East.

Even as the United States was establishing itself as a global power under Roosevelt during World War II, with tentacles that would reach every nook and cranny of the world, the president feared that the United States would bleed resources as it established itself in region after region. He worried that, ultimately, the United States would find that its unparalleled status as preeminent world power would eventually turn on America and sap its strength.

A significant dimension of Roosevelt's grand strategy involved limiting the outlay of U.S. resources by sharing responsibilities with, and inevitably ceding some power to, the other major world powers, including the dark Soviet Union. It also included actually foregoing some sovereign power by shifting management and even some rulemaking and executive power to international organizations. His ideas for the Four Policemen, the United Nations, the IMF, and other international organizations reflected his cautious approach to America's preeminent world leadership. His notion was hegemony with an asterisk.

As the Cold War unfolded, Truman jettisoned much of Roosevelt's blueprint. Still, Truman's commitments to the reconstruction of Europe and creation of NATO were not only ways to demonstrate U.S. power but also to put limits on its global role. A key aim was to restore Europe so it could serve as an active partner in containing the dreaded communism. Truman's secretary of state, Dean Acheson, spoke also of strategic "redlines," which would limit U.S. commitments in some areas of the world. But his and others' soundings about the limits of power were lost in the aftermath of the adoption of the National Security Act of 1947 and the 1950 NSC-68, which rushed to create the sprawling, bureaucratic security/intelligence state. The first test of a crisis outside Acheson's redlines, the North Korean attack on South Korea in 1950, had the United States diving in headfirst to an area that the secretary had defined as outside the U.S. security perimeter, not only to defend South Korea but to take the war to the North.

Truman's ironic experience—looking for ways to limit, share, or offload aspects of America's world-leadership role while finding that the sprawling security/intelligence state generated its own momentum for expansion of that very role, especially in the context of a heated-up Cold War—became the paradigm for almost every president that followed him. Indeed, an ongoing paradox throughout the postwar period was the recurring expressions of concern by administrations about how much the United States could or should do globally—fear of overreach—at the same time that the momentum of the security state drew them into ever-expanding commitments globally. The building of hundreds of military bases abroad, the maintenance of a huge standing army, the procurement of ever more sophisticated weapons, and the construction of a global intelligence network all made the goal of limiting American commitments highly elusive.

The Korean War had Eisenhower and others again looking carefully at the limits the United States needed to confront as a global power. At the beginning of his presidency, with the war still raging, Eisenhower sounded the first clear alarm in the Cold War era of the danger of the United States actually bankrupting itself if it tried to do too much in too many places. But, as in the Truman era, the momentum of the newly created Pentagon, CIA, and other security and intelligence agencies, as well as the establishment of all those military bases around the world, drowned out Eisenhower's warning at the time and, then again, as he exited the White House, in his famous concerns about the emerging military-industrial complex.

The Vietnam War's outlandish price tag of nearly a trillion dollars in today's terms confirmed many of Eisenhower's worst fears. At its height, it consumed as much as 2.3 percent of the U.S. GDP. The war drained the United States economically, not to speak of the lives it took and the harm it did to the fabric of American (and Vietnamese) society. In some ways, the economy never fully recovered from the Vietnam War, although by the 1990s much of the damage to the economy inflicted by America's Vietnam adventure had dissipated. Over the course of the fighting in Southeast Asia, the United States went from having a recurring positive balance of payments to chronic and worsening deficits, and these were never reversed. Steadily increasing inflation during the war eroded confidence in American global economic leadership and in the dollar, the world's reserve currency. It was not until nearly a decade after the war that inflation was finally tamed.

As the fighting dragged on, a weakening dollar eventually forced Nixon to devalue the American currency, up until then an unthinkable act. He did this first by the sleight of hand of forcing other states to revalue their currencies upward and finally by abandoning the gold standard altogether, the so-called death of Bretton Woods. The new post–World War II gold standard, adopted at the famous international conference in 1944 in Bretton Woods, New Hampshire, had been one of the few foundational pieces of Roosevelt's vision for a stable postwar world that had survived into the 1970s, until it became a victim of America's overreach globally and, particularly, in Southeast Asia.

The Nixon Doctrine, issued in the midst of the fighting in Vietnam, was one of several plans by the United States to find a way to limit outlays.

It called on allies to contribute to their own defense, especially in terms of their own ground troops instead of American troops—even as the United States continued to play an assertive global role. Nixon, like Carter later in the 1970s, geared his doctrine, in large measure, to the Persian Gulf.

Seeking "regional influentials" that could share America's burden, Nixon set out to center the U.S. presence in the Middle East in a grand strategic alliance with the traditional monarchies of the Gulf and the Arabian Peninsula. The aim was to counter Soviet influence and Arab nationalism through a set of ties to the shah's Iran, Saudi Arabia, and the Arab Gulf states (Petersen 2009). Henry Kissinger, Nixon's national security adviser and, later, secretary of state, went on at some length in his memoirs about the importance of Iran as the cornerstone of this grand alliance. He wrote of how "the Shah absorbed the energies of radical Arab neighbors to prevent them from threatening the moderate regimes in Saudi Arabia, Jordan, and the Persian Gulf" and how "Iran was a vital ally carrying burdens which otherwise we would have had to assume" (Kissinger 1979, 1262). Iran did serve until 1979 as America's most dedicated ally in the eastern reaches of the Middle East. Still, Kissinger greatly exaggerated Iran's role in protecting America's Arab friends, most likely as a posthumous elegy to his old, disgraced friend, the shah.

Through the 1980s, the Middle East played an outsized role in American strategic thinking, but Nixon and other presidents still managed to

U.S. Troops in the Middle East and North Africa

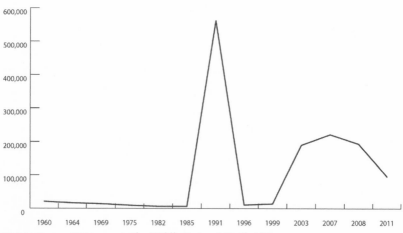

FIGURE 12.1   U.S troops in the Middle East and North Africa.

TABLE 12.1 Number of U.S. Troops Deployed in the Middle East and North Africa, 1960–2011

	1960	1969	1982	1985	1991	1999	2003	2007	2008	2011
Egypt	67	31	1,490	1,390	1,135	892	385	250	284	273
Iran	639	699								
Iraq	24		8	8	540,000		183,002	218,500	190,400	91,700
Saudi Arabia	1,518	153	610	438	14,617	5,552	953	243	284	435
Turkey	7,454	9,652	5,162	5,268	6,342	2,312	2,021	1,594	1,575	1,511
Morocco	8,031	1,668	56	52	40	12	14	15	13	17
Libya	3,942	2,847								1
MENA Total	21,876	15,140	7,644	7,643	562,991	15,206	191,108	222,779	194,793	96,839

Note: MENA (Middle East and North Africa) totals include numbers of troops deployed in Bahrain, Egypt, Iran, Iraq, Israel, Jordan, Kuwait, Lebanon, Oman, Qatar, Saudi Arabia, Syria, Turkey, United Arab Emirates, Yemen, Algeria, Libya, Morocco, Sudan, and Tunisia for the year indicated.

Source: All numbers are taken from the Department of Defense's Personnel and Procurement Reports with the exception of 1991 numbers for Iraq. The 1991 numbers for troops deployed in Iraq are taken from the United States Central Command's Executive Summary on Operation Desert Shield/Storm.

keep the costs of being a permanent player in this region relatively low. With hundreds of thousands of troops sitting in Europe, Northeast Asia, and Southeast Asia (for the decade plus of the Vietnam War), American policy makers looked to the Middle East as an arena of clear strategic importance but one in which they could use a strategy of "economy of force": to put it bluntly, playing an everyday role as a major power in the region on the cheap.

Writing specifically of the Persian Gulf through the 1970s (although his words apply to the Middle East more generally), Andrew Bacevich (2005, 180) saw the continuing commitment to Saudi Arabia, initiated by Roosevelt, as critical but as one that would be played out without outlandish expenditures:

> In implementing this commitment, the United States opted whenever possible to keep its forces over the horizon and out of sight. For religious reasons, the Saudis considered this essential. As huge wartime U.S. troop deployments in Europe and the Pacific gave way after 1945 to onerous Cold War–mandated requirements to continue garrisoning Europe and the Pacific, the limitation suited Washington as well. . . . Roosevelt's successors sought to achieve their objectives in ways that entailed a minimal expenditure of American resources and especially of U.S. military power. . . . The clear preference was for a low profile and a hidden hand.

The Gulf War of 1990–1991 put an end to limited U.S. troop deployments in the Middle East (see figure 12.1 and table 12.1). The U.S.-led coalition placed nearly three-quarters of a million armed forces in the region during the war, including more than half a million American soldiers, hardly a "hidden hand." Even in that case, though, the United States aimed to limit the expenditure of its own resources. Besides the troops from other coalition countries, Secretary of State James Baker's Tin Cup Trip (see chapter 6) netted billions of dollars to help the United States wage the war. Indeed, coalition partners absorbed most of the costs, leaving the United States with a bill of $4.7 billion (in 2008 dollars), which in relative terms was a bargain. The next war in Iraq would cost about a thousand times that amount.

Once the fighting ended in 1991, the Bush and Clinton administrations again reverted to the earlier policy of keeping most of America's "forces over the horizon and out of sight." With no-fly zones and more troops over the horizon than during the Cold War, the American profile was not as low as it had been in the 1980s. Still, the final years of the twentieth century, with much talk in the United States of a peace dividend following the collapse of the Soviet Union, largely continued along the path the United States had walked for the previous four decades: act as a heavyweight everyday player in the Middle East but limit expenditure of resources, especially by forging productive strategic alliances.

Indeed, of all the techniques that the United States employed to cap its own commitments and costs in the Middle East during the twentieth century, the one it fell back on repeatedly was seeking out strategic partners. Those partners, American policy makers hoped, could provide a physical presence in the region that would further American ends, even as U.S. troops remained over the horizon. Partner states' troops could deter U.S. opponents and do some of the dirty work that American administrations did not want to do—or could not do—themselves, as occurred in the Black September War (see chapter 4).

The Lows and Highs of America's Role in the Region

But Washington's success in finding reliable strategic partners fluctuated greatly in the half century after World War II. Indeed, playing the Mideast game was like riding a wild bronco, with the United States fighting to hold on as it sought to find reliable partners that would allow it to exert significant influence and power while limiting outlays. At times, the United States was thrown badly, suffering a variety of humiliations; at other times, the ride was much smoother, with stable allies and palpable successes in the region. The ups and downs of American participation in the area (or, more accurately, the downs and ups and downs) were evident in two distinct periods before 9/11, 1945–1970 and 1970–2001, and in the decade after 2001.

The Rocky Period: 1945–1970

The first quarter-century after World War II was very turbulent for Washington in the region, with the United States suffering numerous setbacks. Some of its targeted strategic partners became overtly anti-American, as in the case of Egypt in the mid-1950s and Iraq in 1958. Others, like Saudi Arabia, proved of far less value to Roosevelt and his successors than they had hoped, as the monarchy there kept a relatively low regional profile during the heyday of Arab nationalism (although there were exceptions, as in the Saudis' participation in Yemen's civil war in 1962). The two major non-Arab Muslim states, Iran and Turkey, which were closely linked to the United States in a variety of ways, both largely turned their backs on most of the power plays in the Arab Middle East and shunned deep engagement on a day-to-day basis (Kissinger's panegyric on the shah's friendship notwithstanding). Thus neither Turkey nor Iran fit the bill as a strategic partner, one that would do for the United States in the core of the region what Washington could not or would not do itself.

Regional dynamics during the first generation after World War II came to be influenced most by the new nationalist regimes in Egypt, Iraq, and Syria, in addition to the ever-present local machinations of the two superpowers in the Cold War. To Washington's dismay, each of these nationalist regimes—the cutting edges of Middle East trends—spurned the United States in favor of friendship treaties with the Soviet Union, which was the big winner during this period. Washington seemed to be on the wrong side of history. U.S. policy, first under Eisenhower and then in the 1960s, was "to secure the support of nationalist forces in the region in its struggle against the Soviet Union" (Takeyh 2000, ix). It failed entirely in achieving this primary goal. The United States was left buttressing shaky non-Arab nationalist regimes in Lebanon and Jordan and repeatedly scrambling to find some credible umbrella to defend the highly vulnerable, seemingly anachronistic Gulf states.

All in all, then, Washington's first foray into being an everyday actor in the Middle East did not go well at all. Policy makers found themselves straining to keep up with the transformations that were reshaping the region—starting in 1948 with the birth of Israel and the opposition it engendered in the area, the emergence of a hostile Egypt as the Mideast fulcrum, and the flowering of Arab nationalism. Washington's ability to mold the area was very limited, and attempts to find reliable partners and effective military-treaty organizations that would help the United States wield power while keeping costs down foundered time and again.

Smoother Sailing: 1970–2001

U.S. fortunes rose, however, in the second postwar period, the final three decades of the twentieth century. In these years, which included the last decades of the Cold War and its aftermath, the United States found itself in effective strategic partnerships with both Israel and the leading Arab state, Egypt, a state of affairs that had seemed inconceivable before 1970. With a bit of added luck, U.S. policy makers achieved many of their goals in the region, albeit with some notable bumps in the road.

The biggest break came when Egypt expelled Soviet advisors and edged into a close relationship with the United States in the early 1970s. This was no longer the Egypt with the swagger and power it had held before its 1967 war with Israel, especially with the charismatic Nasser now gone. Nonetheless, it was still the most powerful Arab country. With America's key role in shaping peace between Egypt and Israel after the 1973 War, the U.S.-Egypt partnership could now coexist with the U.S.-Israel strategic relationship.

The latter tie between Washington and Israel had been forged in the Black September War and, with its own ups and downs, remained in force until the Gulf War of 1990–1991 (see chapters 4–6). Moreover, the United States was able to create the new Egyptian-U.S. relationship while also maintaining close ties with the Arab monarchies (which earlier had been anathema to Egypt). These ties to the Gulf were increasingly valuable as Saudi Arabia came out of its shell and took a more active regional role in the 1980s, following the Iranian Revolution, especially with the creation of the Gulf Cooperation Council in 1981.

The biggest speed bump for the United States during this period, of course, was the fall of the shah and the establishment of the virulently anti-American Islamic Republic in Iran in 1979. Indeed, "bump" badly understates the blow that revolution was to Washington as it sought to solidify its role in the Middle East. Still, regarding America's ability to secure its interests in the Middle East without huge expenditures, William Quandt (2004, 60) wrote, "At century's end, the scorecard does not look so bad." In fact, he went on, "no other country has gained more influence and succeeded better in protecting its interests in the region—certainly not the old colonial powers of Britain and France, and not the Soviet Union (and now Russia)." Quandt's striking assessment was in stark contrast to Kissinger's gloomy account of American fortunes in the region at the beginning of the 1970s, thirty years earlier.

A Period of Universal Opprobrium: Post-2001

However, fortunes can change quickly in this turbulent region. The highs of the previous three decades did not carry into the twenty-first century. On the contrary, the first decade after 9/11 yielded a series of disasters for the United States in the Middle East. These misadventures not only hurt the country's influence in the region but also sapped its economic strength and undercut its global role.

Almost like an echo of the 1950s and 1960s, alarmingly, almost nothing seemed to go well for the United States in the Middle East in the 2000s. Lightning wars turned into decade-long slogs. High-profile terrorists targeted by the military and CIA thumbed their noses at Washington on YouTube videos. The leaders of Afghanistan, Iraq, and Pakistan— all recipients of American largesse—openly distanced themselves from the United States and on occasion derided Washington openly. Societies and governments targeted for nation building and a variety of "hearts-and-minds" projects, particularly Iraq and Afghanistan, proved immune to reform or seduction: in 2011, Iraq ranked 175 out of 183 countries and Afghanistan, 180, on a government corruption index (*Corruption Perceptions Index 2011*). The United States sank like a stone in popularity polls in almost every country in the region. And America's war bills and debts rose ominously.

The United States appeared to be walking through a morass after the turn of the century. The historian Rashid Khalidi (2009, 232) characterized the fall from the heady days of the late twentieth century to the mire of the twenty-first as "the precipitate decline in the influence and standing of the United States in the Middle East . . . , from a position of unparalleled worldwide power, influence, and popularity at the end of the Cold War, to one of nearly universal opprobrium with public opinion in the Middle East."

What accounted for this decline? It stemmed most directly from a basic change in the first decade of the twenty-first century in how Washington played its role as a permanent, everyday player in the region—a stark departure from the policies of all eleven presidential administrations from Roosevelt through Clinton. Following 9/11, the administration of George W. Bush altered the fundamental parameters of American engagement in the Middle East. It jettisoned the idea of keeping "its forces over the horizon and out of sight." It ignored the previous ways that Washington tried to put caps and limits on U.S. participation in the region. It raised America's profile in the area substantially. It disregarded the network of Middle East experts whose knowledge had long guided Washington policy makers.[1] In changing America's approach to the region so radically, the Bush administration fell into the trap that Eisenhower had warned against, in the process bankrupting America.

The Bush team did maintain existing regional alliances and even pieced together an international coalition, as Bush's father had, to fight its wars in Iraq and Afghanistan. But those alliances were no longer the same sort of *strategic* relationships as earlier, in which the partners had done for America what it could not or chose not to do itself. The new Bush strategic doctrine of preemption and unilateralism raised the profile of the United States in the region while lowering those of its allies. Allies were now dependents rather than partners. Far from being "out of sight," American troops were now called upon as a cavalry to come over the horizon and plant themselves indefinitely on Mideast soil.

This new level of commitment did not mean that the Bush administration had abandoned all hopes of limiting U.S. outlays. Secretary of Defense Donald Rumsfeld and his deputy secretary of defense, Paul Wolfowitz, aimed to reorganize the American military into a leaner, meaner fighting machine. The centerpiece was a plan to break up the armed forces' large divisions (15,000 soldiers), designed to fight one (or, at most, two) large wars, into smaller (1,800–4,000 soldiers) modular units that could be called upon quickly to fight multiple small wars. Those efforts ran into various sorts of opposition as well as huge troop demands when it became clear that the 2003 invasion of Iraq would not be a surgical operation. In any case, the reorganization did not result in any overall savings.

The other way that Bush strategists hoped costs would be contained was through their misguided theory of the effect of regime change in Iraq. As discussed in chapter 10, that theory posited that with the fall of the Iraqi dictatorship the reverse domino effect would lead to democracy and stability elsewhere in the dangerous arc of instability. And these results would materialize without the need for costly U.S. intervention in country after country. Even if one argues, as some neoconservatives have, that the Arab Spring was indeed the playing out of the reverse domino theory, eight years after the fact—a highly dubious claim, in any case, with no evidence from any of the cases that the events in Iraq emboldened dissidents in other countries—it came far too late to save the United States from buckling under the costs of the ambition of empire in the Middle East. The *New York Times* columnist Thomas Friedman (2011) commented that in terms of Iraq, "the price America paid was huge. Iraq may still have a decent outcome—I hope so, and it would be important—but even if it becomes Switzerland, we overpaid for it." Overpaid grossly. And I don't see any signs of a new Switzerland.

The shift in foreign policy toward unilateralism and aggressive preemption, the blind faith in the regionwide reverberations that regime change in Iraq would have, and the absence of influential Middle East hands who could warn the administration off foolhardy missions all had far-reaching effects. They led the United States into a quagmire of fighting multiple, unwinnable wars. Indeed, under Bush, a vicious cycle eroded U.S. influence in the region: the length and cost of the Iraq War (compounded by the even longer Afghanistan War and the limitless War on Terror) steadily chipped away at America's global power, which had been celebrated by the neoconservatives (and others) at the end of the Cold War. The slipping status of the United States, in turn, further undermined its ability to influence regional events.

By the end of Bush's eight years in the White House, the United States was in dire straits. It was fighting three wars simultaneously—in Iraq, Afghanistan, and worldwide through the War on Terror. Until the last stage of Bush's presidency, when a date was created for the withdrawal of American troops in Iraq, all three wars were open-ended conflicts that seemed to have no discernible concluding point, at least in the near term. The U.S. economy was in shambles. Although these wars consumed much less a share of GDP than the Vietnam War had (1.2 percent of GDP in 2008 versus 2.3 percent in 1968), the economy in the twenty-first century was on far less steady ground and less able to weather such sustained costs. Recurring government operating-budget deficits and balance-of-payment deficits since the 1960s, in no small part because of the Vietnam War, and exacerbated in the 2000s, again by drawn-out wars, have made the United States a permanent debtor nation.

The proximate causes of the financial crisis and the Great Recession in Bush's last year in office lay in the U.S. housing market and profligate and predatory bank lending, especially through subprime mortgages. But the severity and depth of the crisis were tied to the chronic weakness of the American economy, related in great measure to the escalating costs that Bush's three wars imposed. Slowly but surely, the costs of those drawn-out conflicts wore away at the economy. Nonproductive military spending meant that job creation lagged. The wars also exacerbated the problem of a huge trade deficit and balance of payments that were constantly in the red. As much as an additional trillion dollars in the country's foreign debt

FIGURE 12.2
George W. Bush walks
with Ryan Philips to
Navy One.
*Source: Courtesy White
House Photograph.*

could be attributed to those wars in the first decade of the twenty-first
century. Stiglitz and Bilmes (2008, 7) put it this way:

> The price [of the Iraq War] in treasure has, in a sense, been financed
> entirely by borrowing. Taxes have not been raised to pay for it—in
> fact, taxes on the rich have actually fallen. Deficit spending gives
> the illusion that the laws of economics can be repealed, that we can
> have both guns and butter. But of course the laws are not repealed.
> The costs of the war are real even if they have been deferred, pos-
> sibly to another generation.

The wars were not the straw that broke the camel's back, bringing on
the Great Recession beginning in 2007–2008. But they did play a huge
role in the severity of the economic crisis, having redirected capital from

productive investments, increased debt, and made the country less prepared to deal with the acute economic crisis when it hit. The stimulus proposed first by Bush and then by Obama to combat the recession was underfunded, in part, because so many congressmen feared the effects of taking on even greater debt as these wars raged on.

Bush officials had first predicted the Iraq War to be a $1.7 billion war, less than half the costs his father had incurred in the 1991 war with Iraq. Later, when that figure proved totally fantastical, Bush officials predicted it would be the $50 billion war, as well as a war that would pay for itself through Iraqi oil revenues. In fact, it turned into the one-*trillion*-dollar war—or the three-trillion-dollar war, if one takes into account factors such as the costs of disability care for veterans and replenishing armaments—or the *five*-trillion-dollar war, if one adds in interest on the money borrowed to wage the fight (Stiglitz and Bilmes 2008, 31).

Since 9/11, the United States has been on a permanent war footing. In a decade, the Pentagon's budget doubled to $700 million a year. The extraordinary outlays, which were not compensated for by generating new revenue or slashing other programs, created a chronic drain on the U.S. economy. They led to a weakened dollar, outsized national debt, and a weaker America worldwide. Even outside the actual war zones in the area, America became a diminished player. Disregarding Eisenhower's cautionary statements on how an overly ambitious foreign policy could bankrupt the United States and departing from the precedent of limiting expenditures in the Middle East set by every president since Roosevelt, the Bush administration's policies undercut America's power in the region and worldwide.

Misreading the Middle East

The Bush administration's mishandling of the Middle East in the 2000s, then, was the primary factor in "the precipitate decline in the influence and standing of the United States in the Middle East" in the twenty-first century. But even before Bush, in the earlier relatively successful final decades of the twentieth century, American policy makers were laying the basis for the difficulties that were to follow 9/11.

Perhaps because their successes were so palpable, earlier administrations were slow to apprehend the significance of transformation in the region. In the 1980s, the period of smoothest sailing in the area for the

United States, the Reagan administration continued to be preoccupied with possible Soviet threats in the Middle East. Washington feared especially that the Soviets' invasion of Afghanistan would spill over into their aggression in the Middle East, particularly the Gulf states (again). This fixation persisted even as Soviet power in the region was in clear decline, and Afghanistan was more quicksand for the USSR than it was a jumping-off point for other adventures in the area.

The administrations of George H. W. Bush and Bill Clinton did not fare much better in reading the changing region. They kept the Arab nationalist regime in Iraq at the top of their list of security threats even after the 1990–1991 Gulf War, at a time when Saddam's regime was already in disarray and its regional influence had dwindled considerably. For too long, Washington saw Saddam-led Iraq as its principal bogeyman, even as regional power shifted away from the Arab nationalist states, like Iraq, to the non-Arab states and as Saddam Hussein trimmed Iraq's sails after the double debacles of the invasions of Iran in 1980 and Kuwait in 1990.

Those same administrations were slow to grasp Iran's increasing regional influence, especially after its war with Iraq, and the beginnings of its formation in the 1980s and 1990s of what would become a contiguous northern-tier coalition. Washington wasted precious years and resources before understanding how Iran's emergence had changed the dynamics of the region, from the Gulf to the Mediterranean and into North Africa.

These administrations also interpreted the strengthening ideology of political Islam and the nonstate actors pushing these ideas largely as terrorist threats rather than as parts of a complex movement with multiple political faces. The foreign-policy establishment's slowness in recognizing how differentiated political Islamic groups were is reminiscent of how long it took policy makers to recognize the different faces of communism during the Cold War.

Perhaps most ominously, Washington also shut its eyes to the ossification of Arab regimes by the 1990s (and the slipping position globally of the Arab Middle East on standard development indicators). U.S. policy makers threw their hats in with aging dictators who were increasingly removed from the dynamic changes and frustration in the societies they ruled. The administrations of George H. W. Bush and Bill Clinton, like practically every other previous administration since World War II, tended to overlook ambiguous events and complex trends in Mideast societies in favor of dealing with strongmen, who were less complicated and more predictable.

Indeed, for better or for worse, one component of America's presence in the region did not change from Roosevelt/Truman in the 1940s to Bush in the 2000s. In the periods following the two major transformations in regional dynamics initiated in 1948–1952 and then in 1979, all American administrations ended up pitting the United States against popular, radical, or revolutionary forces that were intent on changing the status quo.

One administration after another felt the shockwaves that rocked the region over the two-thirds of a century after World War II: the end of European imperialism, an ambitious President Nasser, rising Arab nationalism, socialism, political Islam, a belligerent Saddam Hussein, an aggressive Iran, and more. The reaction of U.S. officials to these convulsions was reflexively to oppose transformative, sometimes revolutionary, forces in the Middle East and to ally with strongmen intent on preserving the status quo.

The word that appears repeatedly in policy makers' statements is "stability." Over the years, the United States reduced the multiple components that go into trying to create "a benign international environment," in the words of John Eickenberry and Ann-Marie Slaughter (2006, 6), into the single value of "stability." More often than not, that meant lining up with autocratic leaders and against the popular sentiments of Mideast populations. There were exceptions, as in Eisenhower's opposition to the attempt of the United Kingdom and France to reassert imperial control over the Suez Canal in 1956. But in most cases, Washington took little heed of popular sentiment in the Middle East. Over the decades, America's role in the Middle East came to be increasingly tied to Arab dictatorships, particularly what the United States saw as strategic relationships with Sadat's and, then, Mubarak's Egypt and with the Saudi dynasty.

The Fall of the Arab Middle East

But this kind of connection for the United States to the Middle East turned out to be increasingly problematic after the turn of the century. The Mideast transformation that started in late 1979 not only eventually pushed the nationalist Arab states from the pedestal of regional leadership; it also coincided with the early stages of the domestic corrosion of state-society relations in countries across the Arab world. Slowly but surely, Arab state leaders, including the ones that Washington came to rely on so heavily, found it difficult to excite citizens' passions, extract revenues from them, mobilize them for action, or promote economic development that incorporated the bulk of their populations. And in turn, they were able to exercise much less influence on the region.

The tired, nasty regimes that ran Arab states quashed their populations' ingenuity and originality. As the twentieth century drew to a close, economies sputtered; science flagged. New ideas were greeted with suspicion, or worse. There was widespread resentment of crony capitalism, which benefited a miniscule portion of the population. The impressive statistics on economic growth in Egypt and a number of other Arab states in the 2000s, for example, involved the gobbling up of the lion's share of the new wealth by an exceedingly thin slice of society. Public disgust with the cozy relationships among tycoons, the Arab regimes, and, often, the military grew in the shadow of so-called neoliberal reforms. New laws, often encouraged by the United States through the "Washington Consensus," transferred valuable state assets, through privatization and other means, into the hands of a privileged few, both civilian capitalists and military entrepreneurs. Inequality grew. Public pique simmered just below the surface.

More than that, these regimes feared their populations. They did not want their citizens moving around the country freely or exchanging ideas without supervision. Washington's closest ally, the Egyptian regime, for example, throttled economic and social life in Cairo by ensuring that there was a wholly inadequate public-transportation system in a city that was growing explosively and in dire need of an infrastructure that could move people from their slum housing to areas where jobs existed. (The Syrian regime topped that by regulating who could make Xerox copies.) Such inane policies not only choked the flowering of vibrant civil societies in the Arab world; they also further stifled the economy and choked the dissemination of new ideas. The journalist Mohammad Ali Atassi, the son of a former president of Syria, wrote in 2011 of the strangulation of that country under the Asad dynasty. What he wrote could have applied to practically any Arab country. Even as Syrian society changed dramatically, political repression closed the door to serious reform:

> All through the past four decades, the regime refused to introduce
> any serious political reform. But meanwhile Syria witnessed great
> demographic, economic and social transformation. The population
> became larger and younger; today, more than half of all Syrians are

not yet 20 years old. Enormous rural migration to the cities fueled a population explosion at the outskirts of Damascus and Aleppo. With unemployment widespread, wealth became concentrated more tightly in the hands of a small class of regime members and their cronies.

Once the Cold War ended, Washington was the sole world power to play an ongoing role in the Middle East. But it found its policy tethered, in good part, to these autocrats who hung onto power, even as the substance of that power steadily eroded. In the Arab world, political turnover disappeared almost entirely. And without a changing of the guard at the top, the emergence of new social and economic forces was stymied. Loyal cronies occupied leading positions not only in the economy but in a variety of other social, political, educational, and cultural institutions. They gained handsomely from the economic growth spurt of the 2000s. But innovation was suppressed. Immovable dictators and their aging confidants slowly squeezed out the possibilities of any sort of institutional breakthroughs from their societies.

Three core Arab countries—Egypt, Iraq, and Syria—had been the heartbeat of the Middle East as Arab nationalism had spread like wildfire during the 1950s and 1960s. But in the last couple of decades of the twentieth century, each experienced political paralysis that resulted in social and economic immobility into the twenty-first century. In 1979—the year the major transformation of the region was set in motion—Saddam Hussein began his twenty-three-year-long chokehold as Iraq's new president. In that year, Hafez al-Asad was already a decade into his heavy-handed, sometimes brutal thirty-year rule of Syria. And Hosni Mubarak would shortly begin his own three-decade reign in Egypt. His reign was not nearly as brutish as Saddam's or Asad's, who killed their own citizens en masse, but it was still highly repressive, especially in his later years. These were men who came to dinner and never left.

The same pattern prevailed in the rest of the Arab world, where other American allies, besides Mubarak, held onto power for inordinately long terms. In 1979, some Arab leaders were already well into their remarkable runs, including Sultan Qaboos bin Said Al Said of Oman, who eventually lasted over forty years; King Hassan II of Morocco, thirty-eight years; King Hussein of Jordan, an astounding forty-seven years; Emir Isa ibn Salman Al Khalifa of Bahrain, a mere twenty-eight years; and President

Ali Abdullah Saleh of Yemen, thirty-three years (starting in North Yemen, even before the country's unification).

Others joined the ranks of frozen Arab politics later: Zine El Abidine Ben Ali, twenty-three years in Tunisia; Saudi King Fahd, also twenty-three years; Emir Jaber III Al-Ahmad Al-Jaber Al-Sabah in Kuwait, twenty-eight years. The absence of turnover in an environment of immovable and often megalomaniacal heads of state made institutional innovation in society, economy, and culture nearly impossible. As it played out its role in the Middle East, Washington enjoyed the stability and predictability these long-lasting rulers and their accomplices provided, even as their power slowly ebbed. Its Mideast partners were often unsavory, widely abusing their own publics; diffident about playing a regionwide leadership role; or downright shaky (Ulrichsen 2009). All in all, they offered an unsteady foundation for American partnerships in the region.

The absence of reasonable political turnover in the Arab world did not mean that the straightjackets that political leaders fitted onto Arab societies actually prevented major social changes. In fact, all these societies were rapidly being transfigured, as Atassi noted for Syria in the excerpt above. They grew enormously. From 1970 to 2005, the total Arab population soared from 122 million to more than 300 million, with a UN forecast of nearly 400 million by 2015. In Egypt alone, during the Mubarak era, the population soared from around 47 million to about 84 million. Arab societies became younger, more urban, and better educated. The percentage of children completing primary school in Mubarak's Egypt, for example, rose from about 45 percent in 1980 to over 95 percent when he resigned under pressure in 2011.

The Arab world's working-age population climbed dramatically as well, from 64 million in 1970 to a projected 240 million in 2015. Jobs, especially high-skill jobs, though, did not keep pace. Unemployment and underemployment increased. People exited their countries, both temporarily and permanently, and they sent more and more money back to the societies they had left. These remittances, like oil profits, are what economists call "rents," meaning that they do not stem from the establishment of productive enterprises in these societies.

Religiosity increased rapidly, especially public displays. Personal communication was transformed, as cell phones became ubiquitous. And the Internet penetrated rapidly, especially in the 2000s, allowing new forms of contact among citizens, including online social networks. It also exposed populations to all sorts of outside sources, from websites of Islamic imams to those of Western fashion. Blogs abounded. All these changes occurred in an environment not only of stifling political repression but also of one in which the adaptation of old institutions and the creation of new solutions to address and accommodate all the social changes lagged badly.

The United States did not tie itself to all the Arab strongmen who had clung to power for so long—Muammar Qaddafi (in power for forty-two years) and the Asad dynasty in Syria (now going on forty-three years) were notable exceptions. But it did forge ties with most of them—in Bahrain, Jordan, Kuwait, Morocco, Oman, Saudi Arabia, Tunisia, Yemen, and, most important, Egypt. It even flirted with the likes of Saddam Hussein (as described in chapter 5), the Asads, and Qaddafi at one time or another. Certainly, all these dictators provided Washington with continuity and a clear address for where decisions were made. But their regimes and states were falling stars in the Middle East, frail reeds on which to base America's presence in the region.

The Rise of the Non-Arab Middle East

The period of 1979–2009 was not without any institutional breakthroughs in the Middle East. Although institutional renewal and creativity were rare commodities in the Arab world, non-Arab Mideast countries underwent a kind of institutional renaissance. Iran, Turkey, and Israel all experienced major changes in both state and society during the last two decades of the twentieth century. In each case, the institutional flowering followed a watershed event—the Iranian Revolution in 1979; the Turkish military coup d'état in 1980; and the 1977 Israeli election, what Israelis called the "political earthquake."

In Iran and Israel, the forces at the helm after these milestone events were self-consciously revisionist, determined to undo the old order. In Turkey, the military leaders and the civilians who succeeded them desperately sought to preserve the old order. But for all three, those initiating these key events effected a reordering of state and society, of the relationship of the populace to the forces that ruled them. All three societies jettisoned moribund institutions—social, economic, educational, cultural, and political—which had remained in force far too long. They undercut the cronyism that had come to dominate these societies, in which the political elites—the shah's men, the Kemalists, and the Mapai-niks (the well-connected in Israel's Labor Party)—had insinuated themselves into every nook and cranny of economic, social, and cultural life. Each society fashioned daring new institutional arrangements that reshaped how people related to one another and to those who ruled them.

These new institutional arrangements in the non-Arab countries opened the door, for better or worse, to the inclusion of younger cohorts, formerly shut-out social classes, groups from the periphery, and emerging religious forces. All three societies experienced a lashing out against the secularism that had dominated public life previously. New vibrant groups began to innovate in business, religious life, cultural affairs, and politics. In Israel and Turkey, the reordering of society and state-society relations led to a refashioned economy and unprecedented economic prosperity. New social forces in all three countries reshaped the public square as much as (or even more than) they did formal political life. And the new institutional arrangements recast how these societies related to those beyond their borders, especially in the Middle East itself.

Their renewal led to a turnaround in who set the tone for the region. One newspaper article focusing on the most important Arab state, Egypt, captured the reversal of the positions of Arab and non-Arab states: Egypt, the author wrote, "can no longer claim automatic primacy as the foremost political, economic and cultural country in the Middle East. Non-Arab Turkey, Iran and Israel all arguably pack a bigger punch than Egypt these days" (Lyon 2010).

Despite several major bumps in the road, Iran's revolutionary regime raised the country to the rank of the most politically important state in the region by the end of the twentieth century. After its revolution, both the country's political elite and ordinary Iranians addressed and engaged citizens of other countries across the Middle East and put untold pressure on other regimes in the area. Aided by the Soviet invasion of Afghanistan, which occurred the same year as Iran's Islamic Revolution, Iranians succeeded in reinserting Islam into the center of Mideast political discourse and practice. And they empowered Shiites across the region.

By no means were state-society relations in Iran uncomplicated after the creation of the Islamic Republic. But there is no doubt that the takedown of the shah unleashed a tremendous surge of new energy from society. Shah Mohammad Reza Pahlavi had been on the throne for nearly thirty-eight years—and in firm control as an autocrat for more than a quarter of a century—when he was finally deposed. The heavy hand of the shah's state, especially his secret service, Savak, was lifted. Also significant in unseating the old arrangements was the "reign of terror" in the immediate aftermath of the revolution, which was directed not only at the old elites but at the religious forces' erstwhile leftist comrades in the struggle against the shah. These changes opened the door for a new, young generation of innovation—often, ironically, religious innovation—and a new engagement of state and society.

The country's domestic transformation at every level of life, from the political organization of the state to the way men and women appeared and acted in public space, was the most thoroughgoing of any country in the area. The revolution precipitated changes across Iranian society—in religion, family life, the economy, and much more. It catapulted Iran to the rank of the most important country in setting the region's dynamics. And that ranking lasted at least through the first term of Mahmoud Ahmadinejad, who was elected in 2005. Only the repression that followed the fraud in his reelection in 2009—and the Green Movement that it provoked—threatened to unseat Iran from its regional pedestal.

Iran's institutional transformation after 1979 contained an additional dimension: the regime and important segments of the population supporting it came to define themselves, in key ways, through their anti-Americanism. The legacy of the Mossadeq affair, which had unfolded a generation before the revolution, remained vivid for many Iranians. And the hostage crisis that dragged on for 444 days crystallized many Iranians' understanding of their own new place in the Middle East. Ironically, then, at the very moment that the United States was most successfully establishing itself in the Middle East, a transformation was underway in Iran that would catapult it into the position as the most formidable state in the region—one whose worldview was rooted in political Islam and anti-Americanism.

While the changes in Turkey and Israel were less dramatic than the social-political revolution in Iran, they were still substantial and, within a couple of decades, led to new social-political orders in each. For Turkey, the turning point was the harsh 1980 military coup d'état and the return to civilian rule that followed. The military's political intervention was meant to bolster the flagging Kemalists, who had dominated all aspects of political and social life since Mustafa Kemal founded the republic in 1923. In fact, its actions had quite the opposite effect, although it would take almost three decades to break the grip of the Kemalists entirely.

The army's takeover in 1980 brought a period of social clashes and vitriol to an abrupt, brutal end. The fighting, particularly between leftists and nationalists, had resulted in more than a thousand deaths in each of the two years leading up to the coup. Once in power, the military moved with great force to quell the violence and to break the back of what it considered to be the social forces responsible for the collapse of social peace. It arrested more than 120,000 people in the year after the coup, many of them leftists. "In addition to suppressing democracy," wrote Reşat Kasaba (2010), "the coup established a plethora of new laws, regulations and institutions designed to give enduring power to the military-bureaucratic elite and its ideological supporters, even after the formal end of the military regime."

Three years after the coup, the military stepped aside, although it retained an oversight function over the new civilian government that lasted for the rest of the century. In the ensuing election, the officers' handpicked candidates lost in favor of the party of Turgut Özal, who became the prime minister for the next decade. While himself a Kemalist, Özal used the eerie social peace created by the military to initiate a period of economic and political liberalization. The new neoliberal policies had the effect of opening the door for new social groups to participate actively in civil society and the state in ways that did not pit them against one another violently. Even after his death in 1993, when the military again tried to dominate politics, participation by new civic groups made the old military-Kemalist monopoly impossible to sustain. The most notable of the new groups entering into the public square were political, social, and economic provincial forces, many of whom were deeply grounded in Islam.

The fruits of the new, postcoup constitution and renewed civilian rule did not all come at once—it took years for a party with an Islamic orientation to be elected. And additional years passed before such a party could withstand the military (and its allies) to remain in power and still longer finally to subdue the military leadership politically. Political Islamists weathered the military's challenges to their first attempts at creating broad political parties—the Welfare Party (founded in 1983, elected to power in 1996, and forced out by the military in 1997) and then the Virtue Party (founded in 1998 and banned in 2001).

A key moment came in 1992; at that time, the Welfare Party won the mayoralty elections in both Istanbul and Ankara. More key changes followed after the Kemalists' last stand in 2001. Islamic-leaning party leaders were finally able to sustain control through the Justice and Development Party (AKP), founded in 2001 and elected to power in 2002. Under the leadership of Recep Tayyip Erdoğan, it slowly but decisively broke the hold of the Kemalists on Turkey's central institutions, including the vaunted military.

By no means have all the old issues that ripped society apart or that sustained a top-heavy state that choked social innovation disappeared. Still, in the wake of the 1980 coup, especially once the political breakthrough came in 2002, Turkish businesses, universities, and other social institutions showed a growing vibrancy and ability to take part in civil and political society. The Turkish economy has taken off, and Turkey has become a major player in the regional dynamics of the Middle East.

In Israel, there was no revolution or coup. But the final decades of the twentieth century, especially after the 1977 elections, saw a marked change away from a society where all initiative seemed to come from the state—specifically, the state dominated by the Labor Party, or Mapai, establishment. Israeli occupation of the territories captured in the 1967 War had eventually led to the mobilization of civic groups, both those opposed to the occupation and those taking advantage of it to create new settlements. The 1967 War also had driven wild economic growth, at least until the next war in 1973. That growth, coupled with the role that Jews whose families had immigrated from Mideast countries played in earning Israel's amazing victory in the 1967, allowed these Mizrahi Jews to play a much more active role in the state's economy and politics. Their growing political participation helped unseat the Israel Labor Party in 1977, after more than half a century of dominance in Zionist politics.

Once Labor was out of political power, cracks appeared in dominant social and economic organizations (mostly controlled by Labor Party elites) as well, allowing the infusion of new social forces. In addition, neoliberal economic reforms in the mid-1980s, combating runaway inflation, began to open new spaces for economic innovation outside the control of the slow-footed state. The Israeli economy flourished in the last part of the twentieth century and into the twenty-first, fed partly by the wave of post-Soviet immigrants to the country, including large numbers of scientists and engineers. Israel became a world leader in high-tech industries.

At the same time, the number of NGOs increased by leaps and bounds. The vibrancy of society grew even as it was beset by a bevy of difficult issues—deep social and religious divisions, continuing occupation of the

West Bank and Gaza Strip, growing income inequality, and formidable foreign threats. For a time in the 1990s, Israel seemed on the cusp of playing a major, permanent diplomatic role in the region—beyond its already daunting military presence. That opportunity slipped away in the 2000s, but I will discuss in the next chapter how it may still find a key place in regional diplomatic and security affairs, building on its relationship with the United States.

After 1979, Iran, Turkey, and Israel steadily moved to become the pacesetters for the region. The institutional renaissance they experienced in the 1980s and 1990s, as the old cronyism in their politics and economy was shattered, created states and societies that were now in a position to dominate Mideast regional dynamics. Washington, though, basking in vanquishing the Soviet Union in the Cold War and, then, Iraq in 1991 and in nailing down partnerships with practically all other Arab regimes, somehow missed the tectonic shift that was occurring, as the non-Arab states rose to be the preeminent regional players. In the final decades of the twentieth century, the United States failed to respond to a refashioned Middle East, one in which the non-Arab states were moving to change regional dynamics radically.

Transforming the Middle East (Again)

American presidents in the halcyon days of the last three decades of the twentieth century overlooked the bubbling social pot in the Arab world. Their attention was directed at propitiating the aging autocrats who still managed to keep a lid on that pot. But in the twenty-first century, the social-political crisis in the Arab world could no longer be overlooked so easily. George W. Bush and Barack Obama both advocated for a reordering of state and society in the Arab countries, a change that would have inevitably undercut Arab dictators. Both presidents, filled with the hubris of heading what was now the world's sole superpower, believed that the United States could reverse the corrosion of state-society relations in Arab countries, bring democracy to the region, and induce a flowering of civil society and the economy—all while protecting American interests in the region.

Democracy promotion in countries like Egypt was seen as a key facet of American foreign policy during the Bush administration. But much of the practical focus initially was on reshaping countries opposing the

United States, especially (but certainly not exclusively) Iraq. America's imperial presence in the Middle East, Bush aides believed, could set a process of democratic reform and societal renewal in motion. Once the thumbs of strongmen like Saddam Hussein were lifted from the societies they repressed, in the administration's scenario, democracy would flourish, and anti-American policies would disappear. Obama's goal in reshaping state-society relations was different. He aimed at a reform of flagging American allies, particularly (but not solely) Egypt (as well as Afghanistan, on the periphery of the region), in the hopes of making them more vibrant and powerful and more trustworthy partners for the United States.

Bush did not presume initially that the United States could succeed at "nation building." But during his first term he did an about face. He came to believe that, given a reasonable investment of resources and time, the United States could forge functioning, cohesive democracies in the Middle East.

For Obama, it was just the opposite. He started by regarding nation building as entirely feasible (although, like Bush, he fled from the term itself). Early on, he stressed the need for the government to export what Americans stand for. Here, he shared some of the neoconservative agenda.[2] The echoes of Woodrow Wilson's democratizing mission, however, became fainter as his first term progressed. Obama's Mideast foreign policy increasingly came to be grounded in realism, jettisoning the earlier hopes of reconstituting Mideast states and societies.

Discarding the nation-building assumption was a sharp move away from Obama's previous moralistic statements. But eventually he came to the conclusion that U.S. efforts to reconstitute other states and societies was a fool's errand. Actually, the assumption that nation building was something that Washington could or should do was dropped fairly rapidly by Obama in the case of the now-friendly regime in Iraq, but it took the lengthy policy review in his second year to move the administration to conclude that Afghanistan, too, could not be remodeled.

Obama's Cairo speech at the outset of his presidency had reverberated with the conviction that Egypt and other Arab countries could develop robust civil societies, just as Bush had painted the picture of a reformed, democratic Middle East crystallizing as a result of American intervention. For both presidents, though, their recurring, chimerical goal of "stability" overrode their hopes of institutionally refashioning state and society in the Arab world. Chasing stability translated into standing behind those autocrats whose crony capitalism and inability to let go of the reins of power squelched major social and political change. That meant that supporting Mubarak and other Arab dictators, even as they repressed their populations, trumped nation building, in practice if not in rhetoric. Obama, like Bush, gave Mubarak and other Arab dictators plenty of slack, and those Mideast rulers continued their autocratic, repressive ways.

By 2010, America's position was tenuous indeed. The Iraq War had badly undercut popular support for it in the region. Outlays of U.S. resources in the area were still sky high (although they were falling as American troops left Iraq). The country had been badly wounded by the financial crisis and Great Recession, which affected the perception of its actual power in the region and worldwide. And there were no full-blown strategic allies to which Washington could outsource regional responsibilities. Turkey seemed to be edging away from the United States. Israel still presented the conundrum that had been expressed long ago in Truman's office in 1948, as Clark Clifford and the Wise Men faced off on whether to support the creation of the Jewish state. Finally, the Arab world consisted of hollow shells, hardly capable of serving as reliable strategic partners—regimes that appeared menacing but were highly vulnerable as they ignored and repressed their own societies.

13   Toward a New Strategic Partnership?

The longstanding ties of American administrations to Mubarak of Egypt, Ben Ali of Tunisia, Saleh of Yemen, and Shaikh Hamad bin Isa Al Khalifa of Bahrain complicated policy making for Washington when the citizens in those countries took it upon themselves to overturn the old order. The upheaval in the Middle East that began at the tail end of 2010 surprised everyone, including Washington policy makers.

Its immediate spark was the self-immolation of a single person, Mohamed Bouazizi, a fruit vendor in Tunisia. His act electrified the Tunisian public and then, improbably, reverberated through the entire region and beyond. Hundreds of thousands, if not millions, of people took to the streets. Besides Tunisia, the regimes in Egypt, Yemen, Libya, Syria, Bahrain, and Morocco all were roiled by large-scale protests. Even Israel experienced mass demonstrations and tent-city protests that summer. Other countries, Jordan, Iraq, and Saudi Arabia, felt the sting of smaller protests.

The story of Bouazizi's suicide rippled through the entire Middle East, leading to "jasmine revolutions"—the toppling of once-mighty dictators. By the end of 2011, the old autocrats had been routed in Tunisia, Egypt, Libya, and Yemen. The blast that Bouazizi sounded reverberated in less benign ways, too: civil wars, brutal repression, and countless deaths rocked the Middle East in 2011. In Syria, nearly five thousand people died that year and that number skyrocketed in the next two years—mostly protestors killed by Asad's security forces. The National Transition Council claimed that around thirty thousand people were killed in Libya's vicious six-month civil war that led to Qaddafi's demise, with at least another fifty thousand wounded.

A fruit seller's individual act may have been the immediate catalyst for the Arab Spring, but the remarkable regionwide turmoil had both medium- and long-term roots, as well. In the medium term, the Green Movement in Iran, in the summer of 2009, provided succor to Arab populations. Arabs intently watched the Iranian people's public anger over blatant political fraud. They saw, too, how Iranian citizens' use of new technological tools, including social media sites and cell-phone photos and videos posted on YouTube, could break down their own social isolation and challenge the regime's framing of events.

Another medium-term factor playing into the uprisings was the preparatory activities undertaken at great risk, and often under the nose of the autocrats' security services, by small groups in the Arab countries themselves. In Egypt, for example, at least four groups laid the groundwork in the previous decade for the startling events of January and February 2011. Around the year 2000, a small group of activists, led by an indomitable figure, the sociologist Saad Eddin Ibrahim, began demanding accountability from the regime for its ongoing human-rights abuses. Several years later, in 2004, a second group added its voice. These activists, who were demanding a major political restructuring that would lead to true democracy, included public intellectuals, university professors, and students who were more overtly political than those in the human-rights groups. Calling themselves Kefaya (Enough), or the Egyptian Movement for Change, their numbers began to grow as Mubarak rammed through constitutional amendments in 2005 and 2007 to strengthen his already iron grip and as he maneuvered to designate his son, Gamal, as his successor. A third set of activists came from the labor movement, which grew—and became politicized—in the wake of a major industrial strike in 2008. Finally, thousands of Egyptians mobilized online to support the strikers. These citizens created the April 6 Movement, a Facebook group. April 6 was the date the strike was set to begin. The online movement quickly combined with other smaller activist sites on the Internet, as well as with the activities of thousands of bloggers, to make this a mass movement with over seventy thousand members by 2009.

Beyond the medium-term effects of the events in Iran and the work of small but growing groups of organizers in the Arab counties, the longer-term causes of the Arab Spring lay in the vise that had been created over the previous thirty years. As I noted earlier, in the period since the last regional transformation began in 1979, Arab autocrats had choked off institutional adaptation and innovation even as the societies they ruled were growing and changing in a myriad of ways. The rot that had set into Arab states over the previous thirty years created the environment in which millions of people now began to follow the lead of small organizing groups and came into the streets following the self-immolation of the owner of a fruit cart. The rumbling that started at the lowest level of one of the most peripheral Middle East states, Tunisia, quickly reached to the very top of Arab politics, from North Africa to the Persian Gulf.

The New Regional Dynamics?

It is far too soon, at this writing, to predict with any precision how the region will be revamped by the latest precipitating events, which continue the Middle East's thirty-year cycle of major transmutations in regional dynamics. I (nor anyone else) can say with confidence now what the ongoing tensions and conflicts, persistent cleavages and alliances, state-society relations, and pivotal regional powers—all of which constitute the substance of regional dynamics—will be. In particular, it will take some time to see how Arab state organizations will develop: whether they will build strong, stable institutions; move toward democracy, transparency, and accountability; serve as arenas for resolving and managing social differences; and turn inward or outward (and in which direction they will face).

Even at the very outset of this transfiguring of the region, though, it is possible to point to and speculate about four emerging patterns of the new Mideast dynamics:

Civil and Uncivil Society

The Arab Spring opened the way for a much more politically involved and participatory citizenry. But these increases in citizen action seem to be headed in two opposing directions simultaneously: the creation of vibrant civil organizations bridging sectarian, ethnic, and other differences, on one side, and, on the other, a spike in social violence between various religious, kinship, and ethnic groups—communities that had often (but not always) coexisted relatively peaceably, even if uneasily, under the thumb of autocrats. How state institutions develop, of course, will be one of the key factors determining which sorts of intrasocietal relations predominate. One can expect, though, that even as civil society expands, with new cross-cutting groups creating a broad public voice for the first time, fragmented patterns of religious and ethnic violence will etch themselves into the daily lives of many Arab societies. It will be difficult to avoid persistent intercommunal turbulence.

A Fractured Religious Front Versus a Fractured Secular Front

Arab societies, too, will likely experience a breach between a host of secular forces, on one side, and multiple political Islamic groups, on the other. Both the secular and religious sides of the divide, however, will have multiple, diverse faces, with major differences (and tensions) on each side revolving around what sorts of state and society various groups hope to build. Still, the major fault line domestically will be between those who want to create political institutions in which Islam plays a major or dominating role, granting some privileged role to sharia, or Islamic law, and those seeking to assign religion largely to the private sphere—or even the public sphere as long as Islam is not overly privileged in the political/legal realm.

Already, in the post–Ben Ali and Mubarak era, Tunisia and Egypt have shown clear signs of an emerging political Islamic-secular divide, with a clear advantage to religious forces, that will last well into the future. They have demonstrated splintering on both sides of that divide, as well. In some countries, both the religious-secular cleavage and the fracturing on either side may follow the Turkish experience in which the state's institutions have fairly successfully served as the arenas in which most of these differences have played out. In others, though, the fragmentation may be far more deadly. The secular-Islamic fault line means continuing turmoil in creating an overarching sense of national belonging—a consensus as to what it means to be a citizen of a particular country—as well as ongoing uncertainty and insecurity for religious and ethnic minorities.

The Arab Prize

Even with all the upheaval that can be expected in the Arab world in the coming years, it will remain the center of the Middle East, literally and figuratively. Its strategic location, resources, and population, especially if coupled with continuing unrest and consequent social-political weakness, will make it the prize for other powers in the region. The ongoing upheaval that the Arab world can expect as battles rage over how state and society will be organized will invite other powers to try to direct the massive changes that will be taking place and to blunt the influence of rival powers also attempting to influence the process of change in the Arab world. In other words, the Arab world will continue to be a prime playing field for non-Arab powers.

The Region's Primary Powers

The non-Arab states in the area—Iran, Israel, and Turkey—and the United States will remain the principal Mideast regional powers, but their relative standing will change, as will the levels of cooperation and conflict among them. That is not to say that other outside powers will not also be involved in the area—Russia, China, the European Union—or that countries like Egypt and Saudi Arabia will not be playing important roles. But it is doubtful that any of these others will be serious contenders for power status in shaping regional dynamics; the other foreign powers will not be everyday players, and the Arab states will be limited, too.

Among the non-Arab states, Iran seems headed for the most tumultuous changes. The large-scale, postelection demonstrations in 2009 and the creation of the Green Movement demonstrated that significant segments of society no longer have confidence in the regime. And the regime's brutal repression after the voting only further alienated key social sectors.

Since 2009, the Islamic Republic has faltered. Sanctions have taken their toll, and after an attack by Iranians on the British embassy in 2011, Europeans and the United States only tightened the noose. The sanctions have had a severely detrimental effect on Iran's economy. Its currency, the rial, entered a freefall, depreciating rapidly starting in 2009. Iran's vaunted northern-tier bloc of state and nonstate allies in the region was damaged badly by the brutal civil war in Syria and the continuing political uncertainties in Iraq, especially after the withdrawal of the remaining

American troops in 2011. Even Hamas's statements in its reconciliation talks with Fatah at the end of 2011, in which some factions seemed to take the first baby steps away from armed resistance and toward popular (non-violent) resistance to Israel, was a rebuke to Iran. Hamas's unwillingness to back Asad during the Syrian upheaval and its politburo's abandonment of Damascus further distanced it from Iran. Hamas's move toward Egypt in the post-Mubarak period and its acceptance of Egyptian mediation in the brief war with Israel at the end of 2012 also pointed toward its exit from what was left of the Iranian bloc.

In early 2011, Iranian regime spokesmen attempted to present the country as the inspiration for, and regional benefactor of, the Arab Spring. But a closer look indicates that Iran may have been a big loser in the Arab uprisings. The 2009 large-scale antigovernment demonstrations in Iran not only called the regime's domestic legitimacy into question; they also badly tarnished the Iranian model in the Arab world. Prior to 2009, the Iranian regime had served as a beacon for repressed and dissatisfied Arab populations, even including many Sunnis. Iran represented a Middle East state able and willing to stand up to the United States as it played out its imperial role in Iraq. Iran also reflected the possibility of creating a working Islamic republic and opposing the dictators that the United States underwrote.

But after the fraud and trauma associated with the 2009 elections, it was the opposition Green Movement that now offered a model for Arab populations. Iranian resistance, rather than the established regime, provided a blueprint for the Arab future. For many in the Arab world, not to mention those in Iran itself, the Islamic Republic became just another Mideast government waging war against its own citizens. Islamic political models abounded in the Arab Spring, but in practically no instance was the Iranian model cited as an inspiration.

Tremendous uncertainty surrounds Iran—its political future, the very existence and possible role of the Green Movement, its nascent nuclear-weapons program, the continued survival of its contiguous bloc (especially with Iraq and, especially, Syria in turmoil and Hamas' inching away from Iran), the possibility of a military strike by the United States or Israel, the effects of sustained sanctions and sabotage on the part of the West and Israel, and more. Iran's unpredictable domestic future makes it impossible to speculate how it will affect Mideast dynamics in coming years. At least for the near term, though, both the United States and Israel will continue to see Iran as their principal nemesis in the region. Key fault lines, then, will continue to exist between Iran and the United States and between Iran and Israel. For the United States, Israel, and the Sunni Arab states that have so feared Iran, this is now a weakened Iran with an aging regime—still troublesome but not as fearsome.

Israel's opposition is tied to the Iranian regime's refusal to accept the legitimacy of Israel's very existence; its willingness to advocate Israel's destruction; its support for and alliance with Israel's immediate archenemy, Hezbollah (and Hamas before it moved away from the Iranian embrace); and its continuing development of nuclear weapons and delivery systems in a region where Israel has held a nuclear-weapons monopoly. U.S. hostility stems from its recurring concern with Iranian meddling in the Arab Gulf states (including Saudi Arabia); the Islamic Republic's standing behind the brutal Asad regime in Syria; its support for groups that the State Department lists as "terrorist"; Washington's concern with protection of oil production in the Gulf and shipping through the Hormuz Strait; Iran's nuclear program; and, more generally, Iranian efforts to undermine Washington's own vision for what American policy makers consider "a benign international environment," including encouraging the building of democratic, nonsectarian governments in the Arab world.

Washington's ambitions of blunting Iranian influence and helping create the kind of Middle East states American policy makers would like to see, however, must be tempered by its own reduced status as a global and regional power. America's foreign-policy fiascos in the first decade of the century, the alarming fall in popular support for it in the Middle East, the crippling effect of the Great Recession, and the continuing effects of mounting debt all have made America far less a formidable power in the region than it was at the end of the Cold War or even during the Cold War—although it still is certainly not a power to be taken too lightly. If ever there were a time and need for Washington to find a cheap way to remain an everyday player in the region, it is now. America's place in today's Middle East is at a crossroads, much as the dynamics for the entire region are.

A New Strategic Blueprint for the United States in the Middle East?

Since the end of World War II, the United States has used, with variable success, two principal models to exert influence in the Middle

East. Beginning with Roosevelt's vision for America's role in the postwar world and continuing through most of the rest of the twentieth century, particularly the Cold War era, the United States followed the "chastened doctrine." In that blueprint, Washington ambitiously tried to shape the overall dynamics of the region and the internal politics of many Mideast countries. Those efforts, though, were undertaken without a huge commitment of U.S. resources or military personnel. Instead, American presidents looked for regional partners to help contain the Soviet Union and shape the region, using foreign military and economic aid to secure those partnerships.

The second blueprint—the imperial model—came on the heels of two triumphs, the collapse of the Soviet Union and nearly a decade of economic growth and innovation at home, and in the context of the trauma of September 11. The imperial model shared the earlier model's ambitions, trying to shape Mideast regional dynamics and the politics of individual countries. But now those ambitions were unleashed without the limits that partnerships with local powers impose and backed by an immense military presence in the area. In this model, Washington eschewed traditional partnerships and committed massive material resources and personnel to the region, embarking on what President Obama would later call a decade of war.

Washington's illusions, or delusions, of nation building and acting unilaterally as an imperial power in the Middle East were largely put to rest by the end of the first decade of the twenty-first century. That said, the United States will assuredly remain a permanent player in the region. It continues to have a huge stake in what happens in a nuclear-armed, tumultuous Middle East. The extraction of oil and its passage through the narrow waterways of the Middle East continue to inform both the popular imagination and the calculations of policy makers. The United States cannot turn its back on the question of how Arab states and societies that have been rocked by the Arab Spring will turn out, even if it has exorcized the fantasy of orchestrating full-blown nation building. It is deeply invested in Israel's security and the furthering of a peace process with the Palestinians. Even given its reduced power status, the United States still will have a significant and deep influence on the ongoing transformation in these countries and conflicts and in the Middle East as a whole.

To my mind, the continued smooth functioning of a highly interactive world means that the United States will have to play a role as a major Mideast power. The United States remains the sole world power able to backstop the global economy, including the movement of goods and people, and the geostrategic location of the Middle East means that regional order there is of prime interest to the United States. But Washington will need to overcome the paranoia and single-mindedness that came to dominate its policies in the region during the Cold War, the run-ins with Saddam Hussein, and the post-9/11 decade. Instead, it will need to play a much more sophisticated role, one in which it gently nudges events and players in the area toward peaceful solutions to conflicts between states and to democratic and pluralistic states and societies that can deal with internal divisions peaceably. It needs now a third model—a new blueprint that can avoid some of the pitfalls of the past and take into account both the diminished status of the United States and the changing dynamics of the Middle East itself. What should the parameters of this new model be?

The answer to that question begins with two negatives—what the United States should not do, or two illusions it must abandon. Washington needs to jettison the limitless War on Terror. Without an end date, that war threatens to do far more harm to the United States than good. It gobbles up huge and growing shares of national wealth; it at times creates the opposite effect from what policy makers intended by giving credibility to existing extremists and breeding an endless stream of new ones; and, like emergency rule elsewhere in the world, it threatens citizen rights and the fabric of American society.

Here is not the place to do a full-blown critique of the War on Terror, the Patriot Act, and the practices of the Department of Homeland Security, but I do concur with the conclusions of the political scientist Ian Lustick. He demonstrated how the War on Terror has taken on a life of its own, how it has grown far beyond anyone's original intentions, and how it has escaped "the self-correcting forces which normally operate on American politics" (Lustick 2006, 114). All this is not to say that the United States should not be thwarting and striking terrorists who would do harm to the country and its citizens. That is the job of any government.

It is a call, though, to move away from Bush's and Obama's elevation of the fight to a central plank of American domestic and foreign policy and one of the pillars of its strategy in the Middle East. The campaign against terror, as Lustick intimates, should be seen as a chronic law-enforcement problem, one with international dimensions, but it should not be upgraded to an all-out war. All too often, America elevates recurrent problems that need ongoing attention—immigration, drugs, terrorism—into national crusades that end up absorbing inordinate shares of national attention and resources. They become primary goals, but goals that are unattainable. As such, they erode confidence in government and push out more attainable aims.

A second negative for a new model for the United States in the Middle East is to dispose of the illusion that the United States can shape the region. Even in the heyday of American power, Washington could not actually mold state-society relations in the region or the fault lines of conflict. In an era in which the United States is dealing with the aftermath of the Iraq War, both in its effect on Mideast populations and on the will and capability of the American people to undertake an imperial role in the region, success in shaping the region is even more unlikely. That means that the United States cannot be an 80 percent shareholder (as Truman envisioned) in the Mideast regional system, nor even a 51 percent shareholder (as in Roosevelt's plan).

The model must begin, then, with the premise that the United States will continue to be an everyday player in the Middle East but now as the first among equals. Washington—as much as at any time since World War II—will need strategic partners. America's continuing global commitments coupled with its huge debts and deficits mean that, more than ever, the United States must find partners to shoulder the burden if it is to remain a permanent player in the area.

What should these partnerships move to accomplish in the region? They should aim to (1) create regional security by using diplomacy and multilateral deterrence, cajoling others to participate in containing and managing conflicts and mediating between protagonists where possible; (2) maintain navigation through the crucial straits, using similar methods as well as its overwhelming naval advantage; (3) assist in the economic reconfiguration of the region, especially the stagnant Arab areas, through partnerships with Mideast states and civil-society groups as well as other outside states and international organizations; (4) defuse Iran's ability to bully other states in the region through a combination of deterrence and diplomatic engagement; (5) lend support to Arabs as they reconfigure their states and societies in the wake of their long run of autocracy and repression; and (6) progress toward a settlement of the Palestinian-Israeli conflict.

For at least three reasons, administrations since the end of the Cold War have managed to sidestep the question of if and where the United States would find partners to help secure what they designated as America's core national interests in the Middle East. First, the global transformation of international relations—the end of bipolarity—made it unclear, at least during the 1990s and the early 2000s, whether the United States even needed the same sorts of strategic partners as before. Certainly, they did not need them to stare down a rival superpower or deter a superpower's client states.

Second, if the new *global* power configuration did not push the United States to seek out strategic partners in the area, neither did policy makers' perception of the Mideast *regional* system. The transformation in that system since 1979—decline of the Arab powers and the rise of the non-Arab powers, the weakening of Arab nationalism, the resurgence of Shiites, and the emergence of nonstate players—were not recognized by Washington officials and analysts in the 1990s as a new regional configuration of power that demanded local strategic partners. Experts in the administrations of George H. W. Bush, Bill Clinton, and George W. Bush had only a tenuous grasp on how all these changes in the area added up to totally transformed regional dynamics.

At least for the first President Bush and for President Clinton, the lack of clarity about the overall regional system change can be explained by the freshness of all that was happening. Moreover, their own seat-of-the-pants foreign policies did not dovetail with grand analyses of systemic change in the area. Without a clear sense of how regional dynamics affected the United States in the area and globally, there was little urgency to forge new strategic partnerships. The misunderstandings of the regional dynamics of 1979–2009 cannot be repeated in the new dynamics that are emerging in the era following the Arab Spring.

Third, in the 2000s, the Bush administration's take on international relations axiomatically precluded looking for strategic allies. In fact, the fantasy of an American imperium made the question of such allies moot. Asserting America's global dominance, the Bush Doctrine eschewed U.S. dependency on others, and the administration opted to reshape the troublesome Middle East independently. As in the Cold War, Middle East states were crudely divided into friends and foes, but, unlike that earlier period, friends were not selected on the basis of what they could do for the United States. The search was for a coalition of the willing, not a coalition of the able.

Now, with its grand visions behind it and, one hopes, the single-mindedness that reduced regional dynamics to a single source of evil, Washington needs to reverse America's plummeting fortunes in the region. And, improbably, it has to achieve that reversal while reducing the

burden that the Middle East has put on American resources and its economy. The reduced status of the United States and the new transformation
of the region triggered by the 2009 demonstrations in Iran and especially
the 2011 upheavals in the Arab world demand a new course. Finding a way
out of the morass of the last decade will entail taking a step back from
the individual issues—the surge in regional violence, the Iranian threat,
the Arab Spring and the fracturing and reconstitution of Arab societies,
the Israeli-Palestinian conflict—and assuming a broader view of the region through a new overall strategic model. That will certainly mean pay-
ing heed to the perspectives and concerns of other regional powers and to
the ongoing turmoil in Arab countries.

Three different sets of possible partnerships will define the new model
of America's place in the Middle East in the next decade—with Turkey,
selected Arab countries (most notably Egypt and Saudi Arabia), and Israel. Of these, the lynchpin, I maintain below, will be Israel. In each instance Washington will have to redefine its relations with those partners,
and it will have to work hard to ensure that relations with each one of
those complement, rather than conflict with, ties to the others.

Turkey

In the coming years, the United States will need to reconfigure
its alliance with Turkey, engaging it in a different sort of relationship
from the one that has prevailed in the decades after World War II. Those
earlier ties centered on NATO and the containment of the Soviet Union.
The Cold War is now a distant memory, and Turkey has twice refashioned
its foreign policy in the twenty-first century. The first reconstitution was
described by Foreign Minister Ahmet Davutoğlu (2008) as Turkey's moving to deepen its participation in regional affairs and facilitate order and
security in the tumultuous area, maintaining good relations with all its
neighbors.

Even in the first decade of the twenty-first century, that goal was more
aspired to than achieved. It was largely put to rest, though, at the start of
the second decade of the century. The turmoil in Syria, which heightened
the regional divide between Sunnis and Shiites, pitted Turkey against Syria's Alawite regime (a signal to its own restive Alevi population). And the
Syrian conflict led to increased cooperation with Arab Sunni regimes, including Saudi Arabia, against Syria's Shiite backers, notably Iran. In short,
Turkey has moved from stalwart U.S. ally in the Cold War to a heightened

role in the Middle East, first as facilitator and mediator and then as a leading power taking clear stands on regional issues. Over the course of the last decade, it cooled its relationship with Iran, supported the dissident forces against Asad's Syrian regime, aligned itself with Hamas and Egypt under the Muslim Brotherhood's rule, and all but ended its previously close relationship with Israel before a partial reconciliation in 2013.

Whether acting as conciliator or protagonist in an increasingly polarized Middle East, Turkey has moved from its disinterest in Middle East regional dynamics during the Cold War to its new role as a key player in the region. Turkey has not totally turned its back on Europe and Russia, but its focus has narrowed, most notably, to the Middle East. As it pivoted toward the Middle East, Turkey has found itself at times on the same side as the United States, as in its opposition to the Asad regime in Syria, and at times on the opposite side of the line, as in its relationships with Israel and Hamas. And that divergence has heightened tensions between the Turkey and the United States.

The distance that policy makers in Turkey put between themselves and Washington, though, could work in America's favor. A more prosperous and powerful Turkey is poised to serve as a bridge for the United States to parties like Hamas, which Washington will need to engage but with whom direct contacts may not always be possible or advisable. Turkey can no longer be the wholly loyal ally Washington once had. It will not be a strategic partner. But the two countries' many common aims and the long history of Turkish-American relations make it imperative for American policy makers to sustain a reconfigured alliance with Turkey. Turkey may act as an effective intermediary in dampening tensions precisely because it is no longer perceived to be a U.S. agent. American policy makers will have to adjust to a different sort of partnership with Turkey from what they enjoyed in the past. Turkey also may further America's interest in fostering democratic regimes in the Arab world. But the model may be one that weds Islamic politics and democracy.

Tensions between the United States and Turkey will likely be more prominent in the future. Ankara will undoubtedly take more autonomous positions. But these ties can still be mutually beneficial. As one Turkish writer put it, the shift in Turkish foreign policy "should not be attributed to Turkey's departure from its Western ties to be replaced by those with the East but rather, a shift of power as the inevitable outcome of the end of the Cold War and a fact of the new millennium" (Çandar 2009, 10).

The Arab World

The United States will need more than good relations with Turkey if it is to have a sustained and positive effect on the region—protecting world oil production, ensuring shipping, and, most of all, helping create an environment where Arab societies can create participatory institutions and deal with their gargantuan social and economic problems. Even if Arab states have lost their shine in recent decades, and even if the prognosis for the future is continuing social and political turbulence, it is hard to imagine a viable U.S. presence in the Middle East without a strong connection to key Arab states and societies, most notably Egypt, but Saudi Arabia and others as well. Egypt alone is now larger than any European power. The resource-rich, strategically located, and populous Arab world will be impossible for the United States to sidestep.

Redefining relations with Arab countries will constitute a long, difficult process. Both U.S. policy makers and American NGOs will need to pay more direct attention to Arab civil society, even if that is fraught with risks, including accusations of meddling. Washington will have to learn to appreciate the diversity of political Islamic groups and, as in Turkey, engage those with which it can forge positive connections. It will have to use its resources quietly and wisely to help create a regional environment facilitating the building of indigenous institutions that can deal with fractured, desperately poor societies.

It is still too early to tell what sorts of coalitions American policy makers will be able to forge in the Arab world. Will Iraq join forces with Iran? What regional role will Egypt play? What will the outcome of Syria's and Egypt's ferment be? How will the changes stemming from the Arab Spring affect states' foreign policies? How will emerging political Islamists regard the United States?

No matter how these questions will be answered, what will probably remain true is that like the United States, many Arab regimes, especially those with largely Sunni populations, will continue to be very wary of Iran. And those regimes likely will include both those, like Saudi Arabia, that have not so far undergone regime change and those, like Egypt, that have. Iran's penchant for supporting dissident Shiite groups in other countries, its meddling in the internal affairs of neighbors, its ties to nonstate actors like Hezbollah, its own internal upheavals, its continuing commitment to the model of an Islamic state in the Muslim world, and its nuclear ambitions will probably send shivers down the spine of even many post–Arab Spring regimes. That fear was certainly evident prior to the Arab Spring, as seen in various U.S. documents made public by Wikileaks. Arab leaders, the documents revealed, labeled the Iranians as "liars," the "greatest long-term threat," and "adventurous in the negative sense." They openly feared Iran's "growing strategic influence" (*Guardian* 2010a, 2010b).

A basic conundrum that Arab regimes faced in the decade leading up to the Arab Spring may continue to haunt even new regimes, especially where their countries' internal turmoil makes them now more susceptible to foreign penetration and adventurism. And that quandary is related to one the United States faces, as well. The difficulty for shaky Arab regimes begins with the question of how to counter such foreign meddling, especially if it comes from Iran. A partnership with the United States may help rickety Arab regimes, but for both Arab states and the United States such a partnership would be incomplete.

From the Arab point of view, declining American power and its diminishing role in the Middle East have increased anxiety about its steadfastness—not to speak of lingering resentment over the war in Iraq, Abu Ghraib, and more. Moreover, many have feared that overly close ties with Washington carry the double threat of public backlash and manipulation by an America that has not shed all its imperial feathers.

From the American perspective, the Arab states cannot be true strategic partners; their current weakness does not put them in a position to do for the United States in the region what it cannot do for itself. The prize that the Arab world represents will assuredly prevent Washington policy makers from developing the kind of disinterest in the region that they have demonstrated time and again for, say, Central America or sub-Saharan Africa (except in times of crisis, sometimes). Washington will continue to play an ongoing role in the Arab world, but it will not find there the sorts of strategic partners on whom it can lean heavily.

How, then, will the Arab states meet their regional security needs, and where will the United States find the kind of partner it needs to play an effective role as an everyday player in the region?

Israel

For both the Arab states and Washington, Israel is the only Mideast-based regional power that shares anxieties about Iran, has the muscle to deter or stand up to Iran, and could serve as a strategic partner. But throwing Israel into the mix simply deepens the conundrum. The basic quandary is that Israel's ongoing conflict with the Palestinians makes it anathema to Arab societies and states. And that enmity, in turn, diminishes Israel's utility for the United States, which is eager to be in a position to influence the direction of the momentous changes in the Arab world.

In the 1990s, changes in the Middle East opened the door for a sustained Israeli diplomatic role—for it to become one of the shapers of regional dynamics. Many of those changes were in the Arab world. Arab leaders at that time, struck by changes in the global and regional arenas, engaged in some new thinking about their own states and questions of regional security, which had important repercussions for how they regarded Israel. Their longstanding notion of *general* Arab security (theoretically, if not practically) had been that each state should subordinate its own concerns to collective Arab interests. This doctrine had been a product of the pan-Arab nationalist ideology that had held sway in the decades after World War II. Now, in the 1990s, the doctrine gave way to one of *individual state* security and interests.

Michael Barnett (1996–1997, 603) noted two far-reaching elements coming out of this shift in thinking. First was an openness to consider the creation of new interstate security agreements among sovereign Arab states, with each making its own decisions based on its particular needs. Second was that, reversing their longstanding position, "many Arab states indicated their willingness to reconcile themselves to, if not recognize, Israel's legitimate presence in the region." Indeed, Barnett went on to argue that these changes actually created the opportunity for "the comparatively rapid integration of Israel into the region." Israel's ability, in Barnett's words, to be "more fully recognized as a legitimate member of the region" allowed it to become, along with Iran and Turkey, one of the new non-Arab dominant regional players. The Arab states' willingness to reconsider their view of Israel was also enhanced by the PLO's steady move toward the acceptance of a two-state solution, recognizing Israel's existence and its long-term future in the region.

The 1990s saw Israel engage with Arab states in multiple arenas for the first time. Together, under an American aegis, they participated in the five working groups established by the 1991 Madrid Conference—on the environment, refugees, arms control, water, and economic development. Other groups established by NATO and the European Union also brought Israel into ongoing contact with Arab states and societies at a variety of levels—meetings of ministers, bureaucrats, civil-society leaders, and various sorts of experts.

Toward the turn of the century, when the threat of Iran loomed ever larger in the minds of Arab state leaders, they began to worry even more profoundly about their own ability to constitute a viable counterweight and deterrent to the coalescing Iranian bloc. The idea of incorporating Israel, with its powerful military and nuclear weapons, into new arrangements that would offset Iranian power bubbled just beneath the surface. And in some cases, explicit security coordination with Israel began to take root.

Some of these frameworks and arrangements lasted into the 2000s, but for the most part, Israel's promising start in engaging the Arab Middle East through multiple contacts fizzled out after the turn of the century. The failure of the Oslo Peace Process in 2000 and the harsh Israeli military responses in the Al-Aqsa intifada, the Lebanon War of 2006, and the Gaza War of 2008–2009 had the effect of killing off most of the direct and backdoor contacts at the governmental and societal level between Israel and the Arab world, including a myriad of Palestinian-Israeli working groups that had been spurred by the 1993 Oslo Accords.

The principal roadblock for Israel in sustaining engagement with the Arab world was the festering conflict with the Palestinians, which somehow seemed to defy solution. The peace treaties with Egypt and Jordan remained intact, but the promising headway Israel had made in establishing relations with Arab states and societies stalled as the peace process of the 1990s gave way to vicious armed conflict between Israel and Palestinians in the 2000s. As a former ambassador to both Egypt and Israel put it, "The Arab-Israeli conflict is not the most violent or dangerous conflict globally, perhaps not even in the top tier of dangerous conflicts. But it has become a chronic, enduring and open wound, susceptible to dangerous infection that generates fever throughout the region" (Kurtzer 2012, 41).

The renewed enmity for Israel in the twenty-first century simply increased the Arab states' conundrum. The answer to the question of who would ensure state security, Arab leaders increasingly felt, would not be found among the Arab states themselves. As a *New York Times* commentator put it, even leaders of Egypt and Saudi Arabia themselves, let alone those of weaker Arab states, saw those two states "as diminished actors whose influence is on the wane. . . . They have been challenged by Iran, opposed by much smaller Arab neighbors, mocked by Syria and defied by influential nonstate groups like Hamas and Hezbollah. . . . Officials in

Saudi Arabia and Egypt acknowledge all this; they admit that they are no longer masters of their universe" (Slackman 2009). The conundrum did not disappear after the Arab Spring.

For the United States, Israel had since its inception been an attractive candidate as a strategic partner. And, as laid out in chapters 4 and 5, the two decades after 1970 were the heyday of such an alliance. But the nettlesome issue for Washington from the outset was how to retain influence in the Arab world while maintaining close ties to Israel. As the historian Rashid Khalidi (2009, 14–15) wrote, "Starting with Truman's presidency, the issue of Palestine became a continuing irritant to . . . virtually every single Arab regime, democratic or autocratic, ever since. It remains so down to the present day." Indeed, the predicament has become even more acute for the United States, with Washington's dual goal of maintaining its historically close relationship with Israel while also identifying with the popular forces behind the Arab Spring. For Arab populations from Morocco to the Persian Gulf, Israel's perceived mistreatment of the Palestinians remains the most heartfelt of issues. Close association between the United States and Israel blunts Washington's efforts to influence Arab societies, although many other factors go into shaping U.S.-Arab relations, as well.

One interpretation of how Washington has dealt with this predicament has come in the much ballyhooed series of works by John Mearsheimer and Steven Walt (2006a, 2006b, 2007). They argued that the United States has sacrificed its own national interests under the relentless pressure of the pro-Israel lobby. Israel has not been a strategic asset for America, they maintained; on the contrary, the pro-Israel path the United States has taken has made America only more vulnerable in the region.

Their analysis, however, fails on multiple accounts. It assumes that the United States does indeed have a set of "true," singular national interests, rather than these interests being constructed by the precise struggle of social and political groups that the analysis excoriates. The "special relationship" of the United States and Israel, first articulated by President John F. Kennedy, rests on very high popular American support for Israel, which itself helps define the "national interest." Also, Mearsheimer and Walt, realists *par excellence*, posit in their theoretical writings that national interests inevitably trump domestic politics. But they then fall into the very trap that realism aims to avoid: a domestic-politics interpretation (the power of the pro-Israel lobby) to explain the deviation by the United States from what they consider its actual national interests to be.

Most strikingly, their analysis misapprehends the two-pronged nature of American-Israeli ties: the "special relationship" and the "strategic relationship." The special relationship—the deep American-Israeli friendship on multiple societal and state levels—has grown steadily over time. As Klieman (1990, 188) wrote, "Ideologically, Israel is often held up as a mirror image by Americans." But the strategic relationship has been much more up and down, with extended periods—including the recent decades after the Cold War—where Israel's strategic value was questioned in the White House.

In the post–Arab Spring environment, the question is not whether the special relationship will last. It inevitably will; it involves a unique friendship by the U.S. government and the American people with Israel, which has transcended day-to-day tensions, moments of crisis, and inevitable ups and downs. Mearsheimer and Walt's simple prescription for the United States is to rid itself of the Israeli millstone so that it can pursue its *true* national interests in the Middle East. But Israel's popularity in the United States makes that an illusory goal. And even if an administration could distance itself from Israel, American alliances with states in an Arab world in turmoil will leave the United States overcommitted and underserved in the region.

The question for Washington is whether the United States and Israel can build on their special relationship to recreate their strategic relationship, in which Israel can do for the United States what it cannot do itself and without impeding the United States from building effective relationships in the Arab world. Can the United States maintain positive relationships with Israel *and* the Arab world? Can Israel help enhance security in the Arab world? Can it be an asset in helping create an environment in which the United States can have a positive effect in the reconstruction of states and societies following the Arab Spring?

Certainly, events since the turn of the century—the al-Aqsa intifada, the 2006 Lebanon War, the 2009 Gaza War, the 2012 Gaza War—all have made it much harder to imagine future Israeli cooperation with the Arab world and America's maintaining strong relationships with Israel and Arab states simultaneously. The path for Israel to serve the strategic interests of Arab states and the United States is one strewn with obstacles. There may be one way, though, to clear that path. The Arab Peace Initiative, adopted by the Arab League back in 2002, may provide the win-win-win situation for the United States, Israel, and Arab nations to address their respective security needs along with the rebuilding of Arab states and societies.

The Arab Peace Initiative: Opening the Door to New Strategic Partnerships?

Remarkably, at the height of the al-Aqsa intifada, Arab leaders moved forward, adopting one of the most daring Mideast political initiatives in recent memory, one that has been underappreciated and misunderstood. At its heart was a formula to cut through the Gordian knot involving the Arab world, Israel, and the United States. Saudi Arabia—long the most insular Arab power and the one most resistant to any sort of interaction with Israel—put forth a peace plan at the Arab League summit meeting in Beirut in 2002.

As it turns out, the plan was adopted at the summit on one of the worst days of violence during the Palestinian intifada, March 27, 2002. On that date, a Hamas suicide bomber killed thirty mostly elderly Israelis and wounded well over one hundred others who had gathered for a Passover seder in the Park Hotel in the coastal town of Netanya. Indeed, the bombing may have occurred then precisely because it was intended to undermine the Arab peace plan.

King Abdullah of Saudi Arabia, who was at the time the crown prince but still the effective ruler of the country, presented the proposal, which came to be known as the Arab Peace Initiative. He skillfully pushed it through the Beirut Summit, managing to overcome significant disinterest and opposition to it. A number of heads of state did not even bother showing up for the meeting, including President Mubarak of Egypt and Jordan's King Abdullah. Syria and Lebanon both expressed dissatisfaction with parts of the text. Still, the initiative eventually won unanimous, if not universally enthusiastic, endorsement from League members.

The initiative built on what Barnett had already detected in the 1990s: the Arabs' acceptance of Israel's legitimate presence and its growing integration into the region. One of Riyadh's aims was to bring Israel's conflict with Syria to an end, opening the door for Syria to move away from the Iranian-led axis and closer to other Arab states. What was even more important to the Saudis was eliminating the Palestinian issue from the Arab agenda by securing a state and Palestinian rights. Even in pre–Arab

Spring era, popular opinion on the Palestinian issue put roadblocks in front of Arab autocrats who hoped for any security cooperation with Israel. The removal of these barriers could open the way to the integration of Israel into regional affairs and the formation of an at least informal security coalition.

The Saudi leadership held no special fondness for Israel; over the years, in fact, its rhetoric was vitriolic and among the most anti-Israeli and anti-Jewish in the Arab world. But by the turn of the century, its fears of Iran had grown. It was those anxieties that lay behind this plan, which could pave the way for Israeli participation in explicit or implicit security arrangements. The proposal for creating "normal relations" suggested the possibility of ties beyond diplomatic missions, tourism, and trade; they insinuated that common national interests, particularly regarding Iran, could open the door for security cooperation. But for all that it offered, the initiative mostly languished (but never died) in the decade following its adoption, as violence, disinterest, and domestic politics shoved it to the back burner.

The columnist Thomas Friedman of the *New York Times* published the initiative's essence in the month prior to its adoption at the Beirut summit, based on an exchange he had with Abdullah (Friedman 2002). The reaction of key parties to Friedman's column and the response to the plan after its actual adoption in Beirut could have only frustrated the Saudis and other Arab leaders supporting the plan. Some of those who took notice of what the Arabs had done groused about the initiative's deficiencies; other key players greeted it with a deafening silence. Some of the carping by analysts, for example, noted that the wording adopted in Beirut appeared not to be quite as generous as what the Saudi leader had earlier conveyed to Friedman.

Many Israeli and American leaders simply did not remark on the plan at all, while others commented that it offered nothing new. Henry Siegman (2002) of the Council on Foreign Relations noted after the plan was first divulged by Friedman that it "seems to have been greeted with a yawn by the Israeli government." In Israel, as time went on, some spoke for the record and, for the most part, dismissed the initiative in terms similar to the following, articulated by an adviser to then Foreign Secretary Tzipi Livni:

The initiative speaks specifically about [Palestinian refugees'] return to Israel, whereas Israel's position on this is clear. Therefore,

there is no revolutionary proposal here, but rather a slight change
in the semantics, only a blurring of the intentions. . . . A more profound analysis would see in this proposal the negation of the existence of the State of Israel: There is an attempt here to create two
states with a Palestinian majority.   (Eldar 2007)

To be sure, the years after the initiative was passed by the Arab League
were not ones conducive to nurturing Arab-Israeli reconciliation. In the
decade after the Arab plan was adopted, time and again events squelched
opportunities to move forward on negotiations. The al-Aqsa intifada
raged on. Yasser Arafat continued to be held hostage by the Israelis in
Ramallah until his death in 2004. Spurning talks and cooperative action with the Palestine Authority, Israel unilaterally withdrew from Gaza
in 2005. Israel and Hezbollah fought an intense and destructive war in
2006. And Palestinian solidarity shattered. Hamas won elections in
Gaza in 2006, leading to a brief Palestinian civil war in 2007 and a lingering deep split between Hamas-run Gaza and the West Bank, which
continued to be administered (albeit under Israeli occupation) by the Palestine Authority. The Bush administration, while making some polite
comments about the initiative, did little to promote Syrian-Israeli or Palestinian-Israeli negotiations. Israel and Hamas fought brief, bitter wars
in 2008–2009 and 2012. All the while, the Arab Peace Initiative sat on
the shelf, gathering dust.

The 2002 initiative was presented with the axiom in mind that Barnett had written about five years before: "Israel's prospective ties to its
Arab neighbors are dependent on progress in the peace process" with
the Palestinians (Barnett 1996–1997, 606). In other words, a mutually
acceptable deal with the Palestinians would be a sine qua non for Arab
recognition of Israel and integration of it into any future regional security
arrangements. The absence of a Palestine-Israel peace agreement would
be a deal breaker for the formation of a counterbloc to the Iran-led coalition. After the Arab Spring, the more prominent role of the Arab public,
with its deep investment in the Palestinian issue, made this point even
more salient.

Both the temptations—and barriers—to an Israel-Arab axis were evident in the Arab reaction to Israel's fighting in Lebanon in 2006 and
again in Gaza in 2008–2009. At the outset of each war, heads of U.S.-
backed Arab regimes did not shy away from pointing fingers at their
fellow Arabs in Hezbollah and Hamas. Criticism came even in the face

of the norm for Arabs not to air their dirty laundry in public. After the outbreak of the Lebanon War, for example, an emergency Arab League meeting on July 15, 2006, singled out the "unexpected, inappropriate and irresponsible acts" of Hezbollah (*Israel-Hamas-Hezbollah: The Current Conflict* 2006, 14). The statement referred largely to the July 12 Hezbollah attack in Israel, which resulted in the deaths of three Israeli soldiers and the apparent kidnapping of two others (who actually were killed, as well, it turned out later, but whose remains were kept at the time by Hezbollah).

That kidnapping sparked the war. Arab states lambasted Hezbollah as engaging in acts that were unhelpful to the pursuit of regional peace and stability (*BBC News* 2006, 23). Saudi officials labeled Hezbollah's attack as "uncalculated adventures," as opposed to "legitimate resistance" to Israeli occupation, and pointed to Hezbollah and those "behind its back" (read: Iran) as precipitating the war (*Israel-Hamas-Hezbollah: The Current Conflict* 2006, 14). The well-known Jordanian commentator Adnan Abu Odeh critically described the dissatisfaction with Hezbollah at the outbreak of the war: "There is a school of thought, led by Saudi Arabia, that believes that Hezbollah is a source of trouble, a protégé of Iran, but also a political instrument in the hands of Iran. This school says we should not play into the hands of Iran, which has its own agenda, by sympathizing or supporting Hezbollah fighting against the Israelis" (Fattah 2006). Egypt's President Mubarak and Jordan's King Abdullah were members of that same school. The two issued a joint statement that took a swipe at Hezbollah, saying that "the region is being dragged along by an adventurism that does not serve the interests of Arab affairs" (*Israel-Hamas-Hezbollah: The Current Conflict* 2006, 23).

Similar soundings of Arab against Arab could be heard early in the 2008–2009 Gaza War. As Israel pounded Gaza, even Mahmoud Abbas, the Palestine Authority president, seemed to indicate that Hamas was receiving its just desserts. A Congressional Research Service (2009) report cited the Arab media's allegation "that the relative restraint of Abbas's remarks [in criticizing Israel] during the conflict signaled his passive acceptance of the Israeli offensive." Similar toleration for Israel's Gaza offensive could be found in Saudi Arabia and Egypt during the initial stages of the war. Cairo criticized Hamas openly and, in an act that sparked popular demonstrations against the Egyptian regime in Syria, Lebanon, Libya, Algeria, Yemen, and Egypt itself, it kept the Rafah border crossing between Egypt and Gaza closed during the war, accentuating Hamas and

Palestinian isolation and desperation. Mubarak's National Democratic Party (NDP) issued a strongly worded statement:

> The leadership of Hamas is responsible for the turn that events have taken [in Gaza]. . . . The Hamas movement has thwarted all attempts to achieve Palestinian national unity and has not accepted repeated Egyptian advice on the importance of maintaining the truce [with Israel]. Instead, it has dealt with the situation in a spirit of adventurism and irresponsibility, without taking into account the consequences of its positions. The Hamas leadership has been dragged behind delusional promises by parties and quarters [again, read: Iran] who have contributed to the Palestinian cause only words and slogans.   (Quoted in Wright 2008)

The Qatar leadership, a lone voice in the Gulf that was cautioning other Arab states about their unrepentant hostility to Iran, was highly critical of the muted response of fellow Arab governments to Israel's attack. After the war, Qatar's emir implicitly criticized other Arab states for tolerating Israel's actions because of their opposition to Iran and Hamas's close ties to Iran. "We will not . . . stand with America against Iran. For sure. Iran never bothered us, it never created a problem for us" (*Israel-Hamas-Hezbollah: The Current Conflict* 2006, 8). But Qatar was an outlier and, factually, was quite right in citing other Arab regimes' indulgence, at least at first, of Israel's offensive. Other Gulf states, especially the United Arab Emirates, which has had a forty-year dispute with Iran over three strategically located Gulf islands that Iran has occupied, stood with other Arab states that saw Iran, not Israel, as their primary nemesis.

The surprising tolerance of Israeli attacks on Hezbollah in 2006 and Hamas at the end of 2008 by officials in many Arab states did not last long. What Arab leaders could accept at the outset of these wars as a justifiable reaction to these troublemaking nonstate actors quickly turned to deep antipathy toward Israel for its attacks on Arab *populations*. The expressed sentiments of Arab leaders closely followed the growing outrage of Arab publics over Israel's attacks. A statement by Egypt's foreign minister, Abul Gheit, during the Lebanon War typified the repulsion toward Israel as the war progressed: "Targeting civilians under the pretext of fighting terrorism is unacceptable and unjustified. Israeli practices violate international law. We condemn any military action that targets civilians. We consider it a terrorist act, regardless of who the civilians are or its source" (*BBC News* 2006).

Arab leaders moved loudly and pointedly toward lambasting Israel for its onslaught against the Lebanese population as the Israeli military tried to dislodge Hezbollah and stop the rain of missiles that Hezbollah fighters fired into Israel. Even so, once the war was over, as Iran's nuclear program became a growing cause for concern, Arab leaders quietly put their criticisms of Israel aside and tried to revive the Arab Peace Initiative. At the Riyadh Summit in 2007, they officially renewed support for the plan.

And this time the league's endorsement prompted a flurry of positive reactions by Israeli leaders. Prime Minister Ehud Olmert, while reaffirming his doubts, stated a week after the initiative's renewal at Riyadh, "I think this new way of thinking, the willingness to recognize Israel as an established fact and to debate the conditions of the future solution, is a step that I can't help but appreciate" (Laub 2007). Later that year, at the Annapolis Peace Talks organized by the Bush administration in November 2007, Olmert spoke directly to the Arab state leaders, saying, "I am familiar with the Arab peace initiative, which was born in Riyadh, affirmed in Beirut and recently reaffirmed by you in Riyadh. I value this initiative, acknowledge its importance and highly appreciate its contribution" (Olmert 2007).

Likewise, in that same year, Ehud Barak, hoping (in vain) to become prime minister once again in the next elections, also regularly referred to the initiative while on the stump. He claimed that even if Israel could not accept the plan as it stands, it should at least offer a counterproposal. Others took note that the plan did not actually use the term that made Israelis shudder: the Palestinian refugees' "right of return." Indeed, they argued, the initiative implicitly called for Israel's agreement to the solution of the refugee problem. Specifically, the initiative called on Israel "to accept to find an agreed, just solution to the problem of Palestinian refugees in conformity with Resolution 194." The wording, they felt, mitigated fears widely expressed in Israel that the plan was a smokescreen for undoing the Jewish majority in the country or, in the words of the earlier quotation, was "an attempt here to create two states with a Palestinian majority." Writing in 2008, one Israeli commentator noted that Israel was driven to reconsider the initiative for precisely the reasons that had led the Saudis to offer it in the first place.

The promise of normalization with all Arab countries has gradually become increasingly attractive to the Israeli security community as it comes to grips with the difficult strategic challenges posed by Iran and nonstate militant Islamist actors like Hezbollah and Hamas. Israel has sought ways to cooperate with those Arab states in the Gulf and elsewhere that share its security concerns. Over the past few years, Israel has been moving steadily toward ever greater readiness to involve its neighbors and the international community in solutions to its problems with belligerent nonstate neighbors and with Iran (Alpher 2010).

For that fleeting moment in 2007–2008 when the initiative was resurrected, at least, conditions did seem riper for it. The al-Aqsa intifada had petered out. In its last two years in office, the Bush administration was much more encouraging of a negotiated settlement to the Palestine-Israel conflict than it had been earlier. The appointment of Salaam Fayyad as prime minister of the Palestine Authority in that year of 2007 initiated a period of institution building and increased security in the West Bank, which even Israeli officials openly applauded. Hamas and Fatah signed a Saudi-brokered unity plan, the Mecca Agreement, on February 8, 2007. They agreed to stop their fighting and form a government of national unity, and, even when that agreement faltered, Egypt continued to broker talks between the rival Palestinian parties. In Israel, Ehud Olmert's succession of Ariel Sharon as prime minister put a person at the helm much more disposed to a negotiated settlement of the Israel-Palestine conflict by way of a two-state solution. Indeed, secret talks in 2008 between Olmert and Abbas came close to hammering out a solution to the Israeli-Palestinian conflict.

Unfortunately, again the moment of interest in the initiative did not last long. Arab leaders had extended slack to Israel after the Lebanon War to try again to bring it into a possible security arrangement that could deter Iran. But they were not able or willing to look the other way during the later stages of the Gaza War in January 2009 and after. The same Arab leaders who had singled out Hamas for instigating the conflict soon turned on Israel. They felt the sting of criticism in the Arab press accusing them of aligning with Israel (and America) at the expense of the Palestinian people's rights, and they were highly sensitive to their restive populations.

Their belief that joining with Israel could protect their own regimes and, possibly, the interests of Arabs more generally ran up against that steel barrier of the Israel-Palestine conflict. The intensity of the Israeli attack against Palestinians in Gaza coupled with the highly charged symbolic importance of Palestinian rights among Arab societies throughout the Middle East poured cold water on the idea of an Arab-American-Israel axis. In the aftermath of the Gaza War, the election of Netanyahu, who had spoken out sharply against the initiative, put another nail in the coffin of the hopes to revive the plan (Sofer 2007). Conservative Israeli organizations such as the Jerusalem Center for Public Affairs also raised red flags—actually, mostly red herrings—about it (Teitelbaum 2010).

During the first Obama administration, the Arab Peace Initiative returned to its somnolent state. Rumors even surfaced that it might be rescinded by the Arab Summit in Sirte, Libya, in 2010, although that did not occur. The Obama team, as described in chapter 11, took an entirely different tack in trying to solve the Israeli-Palestinian conflict, sidestepping the Arab peace plan almost altogether. And once the turmoil of the Arab Spring overtook the Arab world in 2011, including the destructive civil wars in Libya and Syria, the initiative seemed all but forgotten. Indeed, at an Arab League Ministerial Council meeting in 2012, Qatar's prime minister warned that the initiative would not be on the table indefinitely.

Nonetheless, as the prospect of Iran's developing nuclear weapons has grown, the importance of popular opinion on foreign-policy issues in the Arab world has increased dramatically, and the inner turmoil in Iraq and especially Syria has ground on, the Arab Peace Initiative has become all the more timely. The plan offers important payoffs for all those who would be party to it.

Arab States

For Arab states, the Arab Peace Initiative would allow them finally to put the Palestinian issue to rest. It would give Arabs what they have longed for during the last two-thirds of a century: a measure of justice for the Palestinian people—a measure with which most Arabs could live.

Beyond that important achievement, the plan promises a counterweight to Iranian power to states with largely Sunni populations and Sunni-dominated regimes. In their weakened and vulnerable condition stemming from the turbulence of the Arab Spring and its aftermath, Arab regimes' need for a non-Arab partner to stand up to Iran seems more important than ever. Both those Sunni countries that underwent change in the Arab Spring and those that did not have leaders who seem to be aware of that need. Qatar's cautionary statements in 2012 that the initiative would not "be an offer forever" received little support from other

Arab regimes, which seemed to still hold hope for the plan. In fact, Palestine Authority President Mahmoud Abbas countered the Qatari statement, saying that the Arabs could not speak of sidelining the plan.

The Arab states' desire not to alienate Israel altogether, to maintain connections that might be the basis for negotiations based on the Arab Peace Initiative, could be seen during the brief Gaza War of 2012, where the motives of the Sunni Arab states were quite mixed. Rather than berating Hamas and treating it as little more than an arm of Iran, as Arab leaders had at the initiation of the Gaza War of 2008–2009, post–Arab Spring President Mohamed Morsi of Egypt and King Abdullah of Saudi Arabia were eager in 2012 to lure Hamas from the Iran-dominated bloc into their own Sunni coalition, of which now even Qatar was an active member. That process of moving Hamas away from Iran had been underway even before the Israeli-Hamas flare-up. The Hamas leadership had split with the Asad regime in the midst of Syria's bitter civil war, which effectively meant its distancing itself from Iran. But even with the seeming embrace of Hamas by Egypt and some other Sunni regimes, Arab leaders tempered their criticism of Israel during its 2012 bombardment of the Gaza Strip. Indeed, Egypt limited its support for Hamas during the fighting. Morsi even led the way for Egypt to maintain its treaty with Israel and eventually broker a ceasefire between Israel and Hamas.

If the Arab Peace Initiative were used as the lever toward developing a bloc that would include the United States, Israel, and a number of Arab states, including Egypt, a $64,000 question still remains. Would an Israeli-Palestinian agreement sufficiently propitiate the Arab public— now more influential than ever before—so as to make Israel's inclusion in a bloc that included Arab states actually feasible? Is Israel's acceptance by Arab states realistic in countries with popularly elected governments and particularly ones led by Islamic parties? Would continuing or lingering animosity to Israel on the part of Arab publics be insuperable obstacles?

There are no definitive answers to those questions, but my conversations with people from various walks of life in multiple Arab countries during the Oslo Peace Process in the 1990s point to a positive answer twenty years later. Back then, people repeatedly made two points to me. First, they did not leave a shred of doubt as to their concerns for Palestinians and their disgust with Israeli occupation and shabby, sometimes brutal, treatment of them. To a person, they wanted justice for the Palestinians. Second, they expressed strong hopes, especially in the wake of the signing of the Oslo Accords on the White House lawn in 1993, about finally putting the conflict with Israel behind them. Most of the people with whom I spoke openly championed the Oslo Process, despite severe criticisms of it by some intellectual elites. They saw it as a way to create a solution, even if imperfect, that would allow them to focus their energies elsewhere and prevent their leaders from using the Palestinian issue as a diversion from their own severe domestic problems.

That very same sentiment, I believe, would manifest itself today, too, if some plan for ending the conflict seemed viable. By no means will *all* Arabs consider a two-state solution—based on the pre-June 1967 borders (with some land swaps), a divided Jerusalem, and refugee resettlement and compensation—proper justice for Palestinians. But enough, I believe, will feel that it could suffice. The Arab Peace Initiative could provide the opportunity for many Arabs to let go of their longstanding animosities and focus their attention on the fascinating changes in their own countries.

United States

For the United States, the Arab Peace Initiative may provide the opportunity to reexamine not only how to deal with the Arab-Israeli conflict but America's larger role in the Middle East. From the perspective of the United States, the initiative may be the way to resolve the predicament that has fettered American policy in the Middle East since that fateful meeting in Truman's office in 1948, when Clark Clifford and George C. Marshall faced off: would Israel be an albatross around America's neck or a blessing for America's presence in the region?

The initiative holds out the promise for the United States of offloading responsibilities onto Israel while rebuilding its own presence in the Arab world. The plan provides a viable blueprint for creating a multilateral arrangement, even if informally organized, as it was in the 1970 and 1980s. It could create for the United States an avenue to participate positively in the unfolding events in the area while allowing Washington to reduce America's direct presence, especially militarily, in the region. Additionally, the plan enables a security coalition of Arab states and Israel to serve as a deterrent force against Iran, which can open possible new avenues of diplomatic engagement between Washington and Tehran, possibly using Turkey as a go-between.

Israel

For Israel, the initiative holds triple incentives. First, at long last it offers not only the prospect of normal relations with the Arab world but a workable solution to the Israel-Palestine conflict. The outline of such an agreement has already been hammered out. It can be found in the so-called Clinton Parameters, offered by President Bill Clinton in December 2000 and eventually accepted by both Israel and the PLO (Clinton 2000), as well as in the near-agreement between Ehud Olmert and Mahmoud Abbas in 2008, in that hopeful period between the 2006 Lebanon War and the 2008–2009 Gaza War (Benn 2009). It is not the content of a future peace agreement that stands in the way of Israeli leaders' moving toward meaningful negotiations. Rather the process is stuck in a mix of international and domestic factors that make the payoff for concessions seem inadequate to Israeli leaders compared to their assessment of the security and domestic costs. Achieving normal relations with Arab countries and a meaningful multilateral security arrangement to deal with the Iranian threat could break the logjam by making anticipated payoffs far more meaningful.

One formidable obstacle for Israel in the path of a Palestinian-Israeli peace agreement is the split between the Palestine Authority and Hamas. But the Arab Peace Initiative does provide some hope (although no certainty) for moderating Hamas's stance toward Israel and bringing it on board an Palestinian-Israeli peace agreement. Elevating the Palestine Authority into a genuine negotiating partner and increasing the prospects of true Palestinian sovereignty would put pressure on Hamas to agree to a reconciliation agreement with the Palestine Authority and accede to (or at least tolerate) an Israeli-Palestinian agreement (most likely in Hamas's support for a long-term truce with Israel, rather than actually signing onto a peace treaty). In fact, the Hamas leadership had run hot and cold on the issue of agreeing to a two-state solution even before the Arab Spring. Sometimes it railed against the very existence of Israel. It gave quite different signals, however, on a number of other occasions. One of its signed agreements with Abbas, for example, had indicated its willing to accept (if not be direct party to) a two-state peace plan. In the post–Arab Spring period, support by Sunni Arab states, especially Egypt, for such an agreement would only ramp up the pressure on Hamas to fall in line.

Besides the prospect of resolving the longstanding conflict with Palestinians and gaining normal relations with the rest of the Arab world, a second advantage for Israel of the plan, as mentioned, addresses Israeli anxieties about its nemesis Iran. The initiative would enhance Israeli clout through its integration into a regional security arrangement. Such a coalition would also spread Israel's risk in confronting Iran.

Finally, the plan would ground Israel's relationship with the United States—what it terms its greatest international asset—in a strategic partnership in which it can do for the United States what America cannot or will not do for itself. Washington's ties to Israel, rather than serving as an obstacle to meaningful influence in Arab states, could actually offer those states and societies a broad umbrella while they sort out internal differences and build enduring social and political institutions. Specifically, such a triangular relationship could provide vulnerable and rapidly changing Arab states and societies with a multistate bulwark, including Israel with its powerful army, navy, and nuclear arsenal, to serve as a check on Iranian opportunism and mischief-making (Podeh 2007). The counterbloc would provide an important deterrent to the Iran-led bloc and would be a stick designed to make the carrot of negotiations more inviting to the Iranian leaders.

By no means will such a solution be an easy sell in Israel. Indeed, it is unlikely to happen under a Likud government. But Washington and Arab leaders alike will have to convince the Israeli people and Israeli leaders of the great advantages of a Palestinian-Israeli agreement: that it would be accompanied by a game-changing transformation of Israel's place in the Middle East and in its relationship with the United States. Signs of understanding the importance of the Arab Peace Initiative and the need to place the Palestinian issue in the broader context of regional relations have appeared in Israel. In 2011, key figures presented a counterpart to the Arab Peace Initiative, what they pointedly called the Israeli Peace Initiative. The signatories included a former head of Mossad, a chief of staff of the military, two security chiefs, academic deans, CEOs, and labor leaders, among numerous other key figures. They called upon their "government to present a framework for the conclusion of the Israel-Arab conflict, as a comprehensive response to the 2002 Arab peace initiative."

Even a right-wing Israeli newspaper, *Ma'ariv*, recognized the link between an agreement with the Palestinians and regional security:

When the Palestinian issue has been wiped off the Arab world's agenda and when the map of genuine interests is spread on the table; Israel can open a direct dialogue with the Gulf States. Intelligent, but assertive management, and the creation of correct ties with the moderate leaderships, could fundamentally change the balance of alliances and threats against Israel for decades to come.

(Israel Ministry of Foreign Affairs 2012)

In the end, Israeli leaders and the population at large will need to see an active role by Arab and American diplomats in promoting the initiative. Neither the U.S. administration nor the Arab heads of state can afford simply to let it speak for itself, as Arab leaders did for the first ten years after it was proffered. Second-term American presidents have had a much freer hand in addressing the Israeli-Palestinian conflict. Although it was burned in its first four years, the Obama administration is in a position in its second term to ride the horse of the Arab Peace Initiative, selling its benefits to Israel and creating the foundation for a new role for the United States in the Middle East.

Underlying the advantages that individual states could reap from such a multilateral security arrangement has been the common anxiety about Iran, especially at a time of vying domestic ideas and forces in the Arab world. Indeed, Iran has taken center stage in the struggles that have defined the region in the last two decades. The Islamic Republic, after all, has led the clarion call against America's role in the region. It has been the driving force in the unrelenting pressure that political Islam has put on secular (and some religious) Arab regimes. From Morocco to Bahrain to Yemen, it has been deeply involved in the Shiite uprisings that have challenged Sunni-dominated regimes. It has insinuated itself deeply into the Palestinian-Israeli conflict and worked hard to delegitimize Israel. And it has promoted key nonstate players vying for influence in Lebanon, Palestine, and the region as a whole. But Iran, too, has been a loser in the Mideast turbulence in the current decade. Severe cracks have opened in its once tight bloc that stretched from the Gulf to the Mediterranean. Iranian support for Syria's repressive Asad regime has been countered by a number of key Arab states, who are concerned not only about the Syrian regime's brutality but also by the Shiite revival. At the same time, Iran's economy has been ravaged by sanctions. The Green Movement fractured its society and shattered its image as a beacon to other Mideast peoples.

Now, a strong counterbloc may provide just the incentive Iranian leaders need to negotiate meaningfully with the United States.

The United States in a Changing Middle East

Since the end of Ottoman rule almost a century ago, the history of the Middle East has been written in terms of powerful forces rushing across the region, seemingly sweeping away all in their path. After World War I, it was European colonization and imperialism and the establishment of new states (many of which existed only through inordinate Western influence). After World War II came the age of Arab nationalism and a dream of Arab unity, the assertiveness of new states, and the creation of Israel. The Iranian Revolution in 1979 set off another wave, this one marked by the Islamization of politics. Finally, the Green Movement and the Arab Spring ushered in the newest whirlwind, democratization and participatory politics alongside the multiple faces of political Islam.

There is no denying the importance of these forces—"-izations," if you like. U.S. leaders, not unlike the British before them, tended to see these giant forces in fairly undifferentiated forms and either tried to control them or oppose everything about them. But a close reading of Mideast history shows that these ideologies and movements did not sweep away everything in their path. The Middle East remained a complex region, one with many particularities—sects, tribes, localities, and more—resisting and indeed transforming the forces washing over them. The outcomes were multifaceted; the broad ideologies and movements looked different from place to place in the Middle East. Nor could global powers like the United States and Britain do much on a grand scale to further these forces or block them entirely.

Half a century ago, the Iraqi-born British historian Elie Kedourie (2004) cautioned against the penchant for great powers to believe they could control monumental forces and make things right in the Middle East:

Ever since the nineteenth century, when so-called reforms were initiated in the Ottoman empire, there have not been wanting western ministers and diplomats to look on middle eastern politics with hope and expectancy. It is quite common knowledge that in the last hundred years the middle east has seen no quiet, that disturbance has succeeded disturbance, and that violent, categorical men have followed each other to prescribe and apply drastic but unavailing remedies. It might therefore seem more prudent to assume that the distemper of the modern east is not a passing one, that its political instability is rather the outcome of a deep social and intellectual crisis which the schemes of the reformer and the goodwill of the philanthropist can scarcely assuage or modify. And yet the sober assumption that middle eastern instability is today endemic has found *little* favour either in Britain or in America. The prevalent fashion has been to proclaim the latest revolution as the herald of a new day, and the newest turbulence as the necessary and beneficent prelude to an epoch of orderliness and justice.

Kedourie stood against "missionary arguments," which claimed that the Middle East could be shaped by Western reformers. America's follies of the 2000s certainly speak to the enduring ambitions of great powers to overreach in the region.

The turbulence starting in 2009–2011 offers yet another revolution that seems the "herald of a new day." The temptation is there once again for the United States, as the world's strongest power, to try to usher in "an epoch of orderliness and justice." There is no doubt that the United States will continue to play a crucial everyday role in the Middle East. But Washington would be well advised to temper policy makers' grandiose dreams of transforming the region.

Still, it can do more than what the dyspeptic Kedourie saw as possible, when he proclaimed that the very best outside statesmen can hope for is to "keep disorder at bay." There is no reason to write off the region as suffering from "endemic" instability. In addition to dealing with the continuing turbulence in the region and helping ward off troublemakers, Washington can quietly and carefully nudge states toward more benign views of and behavior toward their own populations. It can model and encourage democratic institution building.

To achieve those ends will demand alliances with both Arabs and non-Arab Turkey and Israel. The Arab Peace Initiative offers an important means to forge some of these multiple ties. It is premised on another Kedourie insight: in the Arab Middle East, he wrote, "Israel is the immediate but not the most important factor" (2004, 6). The initiative offers the possibility of removing Israel as an immediate factor by bringing a measure of justice to Palestinians through a state of their own. It creates an opportunity for the United States, now that its power has been reduced by the events of the first decade of the twenty-first century, to create a new place for itself in the Middle East, one grounded in tempered ambitions and a multilateralism that stretches across both the Arab and non-Arab parts of the region.

Afterword

In the months since I finished writing this book and it went into production, dizzying changes have overtaken the Middle East. Deaths in Syria's full-blown civil war topped 100,000, with arms, money, and foot soldiers pouring in from other Mideast countries and beyond. The U.S. administration accused the Asad regime of killing more than 1,400 Syrian citizens in a nerve gas attack and threatened an armed response. Al-Qaeda in the Arabian Peninsula, based in Yemen, not only survived increased drone attacks but created a scare large enough for the United States to shut down its embassies throughout the region. The seemingly indestructible Turkish regime was shaken by the largest popular protests there in decades. Iran elected a new president whose rhetoric breathed new hope for avoiding a military confrontation over his country's nuclear program. Secretary of State John Kerry's indefatigable diplomacy improbably succeeded in restarting the long-dormant negotiations between Palestinians and Israelis. And, after the hopeful events of the Arab Spring, Egypt simply imploded. Its elected (but tone-deaf) regime headed by the Muslim Brotherhood faced massive public protests followed by a military takeover followed by other massive protests against the coup followed by severe repression against the protesters followed by yet more protests against the repression. And the story is far from over.

The one element in the Middle East that seems not to have changed is how the region has managed to continue insinuating itself into the center of international affairs. For the United States, the unfolding crises in the area kept it at the top of the foreign-policy agenda despite the administration's stated preference for a turn to Asia. There certainly was no shortage of reasons to deemphasize the Middle East in U.S. foreign policy making. American energy dependence on Mideast oilfields declined markedly. Continuing economic shakiness in the United States amplified worries about imperial overreach. Problems in the region were so complex as to seem beyond solution. The domestic fatigue in the United States from the wars in Iraq and Afghanistan eroded public support for an active, let alone interventionist, foreign policy in the Middle East. And the Obama administration was very attentive to that public fatigue, as seen in its zigzag decision making following the Syrian regime's poison-gas attack on its own population.

Still, despite all the forces pulling the United States away from the Middle East, Obama, like Nixon and other previous presidents, found that the United States could not seem to get up and walk away from that troubled area. The threats the region posed, its critical geostrategic position, its bountiful mineral resources, the penchant to produce crisis after crisis, and the now-substantial history of U.S. commitments to Mideast countries all point to the fact that the United States could not and will not turn its back on the Middle East. What is much less clear is what kind of role America will take in the region.

The legacy of the extended recession and the even more prolonged wars in Iraq and Afghanistan and the worldwide War on Terror dictates that the United States cannot be the sort of hegemonic power that many imagined it would be after World War II or again after the Cold War. Realists always worried about the United States operating abroad beyond its resources and capacities to influence events. If anything, the economic and security crises of the first decade of the twenty-first century heightened those worries and demanded a trimming of America's sails. The idea of an imperial America, of a superpower with an 80 percent or greater share of world leadership, if it ever had any merit, can now be assigned to the dustbin of history.

But a more limited United States does not mean withdrawing into its shell. It is still the world's leading power, and with that comes international responsibility. The abject failures in American foreign policy in this century's first decade demand now not a shirking of a key international role for the country but a rethinking of America's global responsibilities in making the international arena as peaceful and friction free as possible. At the center of that reassessment lies the volatile Middle East.

In that region, four key events in the spring and summer of 2013—another Obama foreign-policy speech, the coup in Egypt, the poison-gas attack in Syria, and the resumption of Palestinian-Israeli peace negotiations—pointed to the contours of such a new role for the United States as a world power and a continuing permanent player in the Middle East. That emerging role makes no grandiose claims to reshape entirely the dynamics of the region or state-society relations in Mideast countries; no defining war or grand military alliance or extravagant nation-building project is on the horizon. What *is* possible is a role that establishes the United States as an essential partner with other powers and a backstop against actions that could threaten the region as a whole or challenge key international norms essential for the functioning of the international system. America can help manage conflicts, if not solve them; facilitate and mediate wherever possible among conflicting parties; and join with others to deter mischief making.

The first event indicating the emergence of a new U.S. role was a major foreign-policy speech at the National Defense University by Obama in May 2013. In it, he sketched out some of his new thinking on America's place in the world. Much of it directly applied to the Middle East. He addressed both practical tactics, such as the use of drones, and broader strategy, including the announced end of the War on Terror. Citing the end of the Cold War and 9/11 as the two defining moments in the last generation for the United States internationally, the president set out the need for limits on fighting terror: "America is at the crossroads. We must define the nature and scope of this struggle, or else it will define us." Obama went on to state what I suggest in my conclusion, a move from a *War* on Terror to specific targeted actions against terrorists. To date, the speech seems to have had little resonance in actual policy making, but even the rhetorical statement limiting the parameters of U.S. action abroad, of moving from crusades to police actions, is important.

Second, the series of eruptions in Egypt in the summer of 2013 helped define the limits and possibilities for the United States during the birth pangs of the latest Mideast transformation. The limits of what the United States could do to influence the course of events became evident through the massive protests against President Mohamed Morsi, the usurpation of power by the military, the sit-ins by Morsi's backers, and the heavy-handed crushing of the Muslim Brotherhood and its supporters. For better or for worse, Egyptians will need to work out their deep divisions mostly by themselves. What Obama officials could do, at times with some effect and at other times with little or none, was cajole and keep lines of communication open. The U.S. position could not be determining, but it certainly could be one of several important factors as events played out.

The third event, still unfolding as I write, was the Syrian regime's nerve-gas attack in August 2013. As the conflict turned from a Syrian tragedy to a major threat to regional and international peace and as the Syrian regime violated one of the most widely held norms of warfare, the uncertainty of America's capacities bubbled to the surface. U.S. politicians' opinions ranged from calling for an all-out assault on the Asad regime along with ramped-up support for the rebels to opposition to any intervention at all by the United States in the conflict. Obama drew what he called a "redline," which the massive poison-gas attack crossed. The president's intent was to signal that when basic international norms are jeopardized, the United States will intervene with force. But with all the recent memories of the quagmires in Iraq and Afghanistan, intervention could not proceed as in the past. It had to be mediated through the caprices of flagging international support, the stalemate in the United Nations, a conflicted Congress, and wariness on the part of the American public. The United States was not paralyzed, but any decision to intervene directly faced a much higher bar than in the past.

Finally, Obama's second-term secretary of state, John Kerry, undertook a single-minded mission to restart Palestinian-Israeli peace negotiations. Improbably, he succeeded not only in sitting the parties down but in persuading them and Arab states to undertake some important confidence-building measures. The obstacles to achieving a bona fide peace agreement remain huge, and few analysts are sanguine about the near or medium future.

Nonetheless, Kerry's approach revealed some of the possibilities for a renewed U.S. role in the region. His doggedness sent clear signals to the Israelis and Palestinians, as well as to others, that the United States continues to have an abiding interest in the region's conflicts, that it has staying power in the area, and that it still has the clout to demand and win key concessions from the parties and neighboring states. Moreover, Kerry used precisely the frame that I recommended in my final chapter, the Arab Peace Initiative, moving the conflict from a strictly bilateral issue to a larger regional scaffolding.

The secretary brought Arab foreign ministers to the United States and persuaded them to once again reaffirm the initiative. This time, however, they agreed to the added element of the possibility of deviating from the exact pre–1967 War borders through land swaps between Israel and Palestine. The swaps would allow flexibility in setting the final borders, especially permitting Israel to retain the most populated settlement blocs. A number of important Israeli politicians also accepted the initiative as a framework for the future, including a key member of the ultra-Orthodox Shas party, a senior Israeli cabinet member from the Yesh Atid Party and former head of the Shin Bet security service, and the faction head of the Ha'Tnua party (another member of Netanyahu's coalition).

What Kerry did not do was explicitly tie the Arab Peace Initiative into a larger strategic vision as I suggest in chapter 13. Officials in the Obama administration often continue to talk about the Middle East as if it were a series of burning fires. The challenge is to fold issues into a broader U.S. role in the region. Even here, though, there were hints of the development of a larger strategic vision. In May, the British press reported that the Obama administration was pushing a new alliance, the so-called 4+1 plan. Its members would be Israel, Turkey, Saudi Arabia, and the United Arab Emirates plus Washington.

Several points regarding this purported plan are worth noting. First is the fact that such an alliance could not be possible without the Arab Peace Initiative and success in moving toward a final solution of the Israeli-Palestinian conflict. A second notable element is the absence of Egypt in the plan, which needs to be integrated into any regional coalition, whatever the outcome of its internal battles. Third is the centrality of the implied strategy of containing (rather than attacking) Iran. That country has been markedly weakened by the draining conflict in Syria, but it still poses some of the most vexing challenges for the Unites States internationally. A regionally based coalition that included Washington would ramp up pressure on Iran to engage diplomatically. And, last but certainly not least, such a plan would offer the now much more limited Washington a series of partners, including Israel as a strategic partner, not to remold the Middle East as a whole or individual countries in the region, but to help create "a benign international environment" in a currently highly explosive part of the world.

Joel S. Migdal
Seattle
September 9, 2013

Notes

Preface

1. Fawaz A. Gerges (1994, 1) opens his well-regarded book as follows: "One of the enduring features of the study of the Middle East has been the emphasis on the relations—socioeconomic, religious, and political—between the outside world and the region itself." See also Khalidi (2004, 2009), Friedman (1990), and Zunes (2003). Similarly, Salt (2008, 4) focuses on "the techniques of domination and control employed by distant governments [most recently, the United States], ranging from invasion and occupation to a more discreet exercise of power."

2. America's Place in the Middle East

1. The Middle East region (sometimes called the Near East) has had no clear boundaries. Its core area is Egypt (in Africa) and southwestern Asia (or Asia Minor), including today the countries of Bahrain, Iraq, Iran, Israel, Jordan, Kuwait, Lebanon, Oman, Qatar, Saudi Arabia, Syria, Turkey, United Arab Emirates, and Yemen. But the notion of this region has been constructed (and reconstructed) and is not a firm geographical unit. Depending on the time and issue at hand, some of the core countries have been omitted from the list. President Nixon, for example, definitively placed Iran outside the Middle East (Nixon 1970, 251). In contrast, sometimes the region expands to include such countries as Libya, Algeria, Tunisia, and Morocco in North Africa (sometimes labeled MENA, the

Middle East and North Africa); Greece and Cyprus; Sudan and Somalia; Afghanistan and even Pakistan (Halpern 1963). The administration of George W. Bush was intent on using a very broad definition of the Middle East, what Secretary of State Condoleezza Rice called "the arc of states that stretches from Morocco to Pakistan" (Rice 2008, 12). While issues relating to Afghanistan and Pakistan arise in the coming pages, my primary focus is on the core of the Middle East in southwestern Asia, plus the countries of North Africa, especially Egypt.

2. See, for example, Petersen's (2009, 1) discussion of the Nixon presidency.

3. I refer to these figures variously as "policy makers," "officials," "team," "administration," and "Washington."

3. Failed Partnerships and Fragile Partners

1. The Truman Doctrine came in the wake of the sending of the so-called Long Telegram by George Kennan, deputy head of the U.S. mission in Moscow, which urged "containment" as a strategy. The article appeared in 1947 under the pseudonym "X."

4. Finding a Place in the Middle East: A New Partnership Develops out of Black September

1. "The Israeli interpretation of the transaction was at variance from that of the Americans. . . . Israel did not view the sale as a one-time deal devoid of political meaning. . . . Israeli policy was to 'strive for a continued intensification of the existing U.S. commitment and the creation of sui generis strategic relations'" (Levey 2004, 274). Levey quotes the Israeli foreign minister Abba Eban.

2. The text of the resolution is as follows:

The Security Council,

Expressing its continuing concern with the grave situation in the Middle East, *Emphasizing* the inadmissibility of the acquisition of territory by war and the need to work for a just and lasting peace in which every State in the area can live in security, *Emphasizing further* that all Member States in their acceptance of the Charter of the United Nations have undertaken a commitment to act in accordance with Article 2 of the Charter, 1. *Affirms* that the fulfillment of Charter principles requires the establishment of a just and lasting peace in the Middle East which should include the application of both the following principles: (i) Withdrawal of Israel armed forces from territories occupied in the recent conflict; (ii) Termination of all claims or states of belligerency and respect for and acknowledgment of the sovereignty, territorial integrity and political independence of every State in the area and their right to live in peace within secure and recognized boundaries free from threats or acts of force; 2. *Affirms further* the necessity (a) For guaranteeing freedom of navigation through international waterways in the area; (b) For achieving a just settlement of the refugee problem; (c) For guaranteeing the territorial inviolability and political independence of every State in the area, through measures including the establishment of demilitarized zones; 3. *Requests* the Secretary-General to designate a Special Representative to proceed to the Middle East to establish and maintain contacts with the States concerned in order to promote agreement and assist efforts to achieve a peaceful and accepted settlement in accordance with the provisions and principles in this resolution; 4. *Requests* the Secretary-General to report to the Security Council on the progress of the efforts of the Special Representative as soon as possible.

5. The Strategic Partnership Faces Strains: The Yom Kippur War and the Changing Calculus of U.S. Foreign Policy

1. The text of Resolution 338 of October 22, 1973, is as follows:

1. The Security Council calls upon all parties to the present fighting to cease all firing and terminate all military activity immediately, no later than 12 hours after the moment of the adoption of this decision, in the positions they now occupy;

2. Calls upon the parties concerned to start immediately after the ceasefire the implementation of Security Council resolution 242 (1967) in all of its parts;

3. Decides that, immediately and concurrently with the ceasefire, negotiations shall start between the parties concerned under appropriate auspices aimed at establishing a just and durable peace in the Middle East.

It was passed unanimously, with China abstaining.

10. The Bush Administration and the Arc of Instability

1. It seems that Ceaser intended his article to have the subtitle "American Internationalism and Its Opponents," which is how it appears in the table of contents. But the heading of the article has the subtitle "American Interventionism and Its Opponents," a fitting irony of a misprint.

2. That was not the only reference to resurrecting Hashemite rule in Iraq. Another example is David Wurmser, a participant in the PNAC, who did a tendentious reading of Jordan's King Hussein to make the point that the Hashemites would and could revive their rule in Iraq (Wursmer 1999, 80–85).

3. Another possible neoconservative candidate as Middle East expert was Reuel Marc Gerecht, a CIA spy who went on to become director of the Project for the New American Century's Middle East Initiative.

4. The Israeli Cabinet officially accepted the Road Map, although with so many qualifications, fourteen of them, as to practically invalidate it. Subsequently, Sharon publicly disavowed the Road Map.

11. Obama: Engaging the Middle East on Multiple Fronts

1. Also on the team were Dan Shapiro and Toni Verstandig. Shapiro had earned a Masters in Middle East Studies from Harvard, worked under Lee Hamilton on the House Foreign Affairs Committee on Europe and the Middle East, and served for the State Department in the United Arab Emirates. Later he would serve in the administration as senior director in the NSC on the Middle East and, then, as ambassador to Israel. Verstandig also had been a House staff member and then became Clinton's deputy assistant secretary for Near Eastern affairs.

12. Ups and Downs of an Everyday Player, on the Cheap

1. For a critical account of the historical development of the Mideast knowledge network in Washington, see Jacobs 2011.

2. Joshua Muravchik (2009), a neoconservative thinker, took Obama to task for the deemphasis on exporting democracy, stating that the president valued moral equivalence over promoting freedom.

Works Cited

Aarts, Paul, and Michael Renner. 1991. "Oil and the Gulf War." *Middle East Report* 17, no. 1: 25–29, 47.

Abrams, Elliott. 2009. "Next, Locusts? The Abject Failure of the Obama Administration's Middle East Policy." *Weekly Standard* (November 16).

Abu-Amr, Ziad. 1993. "Hamas: A Historical and Political Background." *Journal of Palestine Studies* 22, no. 4: 5–19.

Alhomayed, Tariq. 2009. "Hamas: Extremism Breeds Extremism." *Asharq Alawsat* (August 18).

Alpher, Yossi. 2010. *Breathing New Life Into the Arab Peace Initiative—An Israeli Perspective from Yossi Alpher.* Council for Peace and Security: Association of National Security Experts in Israel.

Amos, Deborah. 2010. *Eclipse of the Sunnis: Power, Exile, and Upheaval in the Middle East.* New York: Public Affairs.

Arab Human Development Report: Creating Opportunities for Future Generations. 2002. New York: United Nations Development Programme and Arab Fund for Economic and Social Development.

Ashton, Nigel J. 2006. "Pulling the Strings: King Hussein's Role During the Crisis of 1970 in Jordan." *International History Review* 28, no. 1: 94–118.

Atassi, Mohammad A. 2011. "My Syria, Awake Again After 40 Years." *New York Times* (June 26).

Azimi, Fakhreddin. 2004. "Unseating Mosaddeq: The Configuration and Role of Domestic Forces." In *Mohammad Mosaddeq and the 1953 Coup in Iran*, ed.

Mark J. Gasiorowski and Malcolm Byrne, 27–101. Syracuse, N.Y.: Syracuse University Press.

Bacevich, Andrew J. 2005. *The New American Militarism: How Americans Are Seduced by War.* New York: Oxford University Press.

Baker, James A. III. 1995. *The Politics of Diplomacy: Revolution, War, and Peace.* New York: G. P. Putnam's Sons.

Barnett, Michael N. 1996–1997. "Regional Security After the Gulf War." *Political Science Quarterly* 111, no. 4: 597–618.

Baylouny, Anne Marie. 2008. "Ungoverned in the Middle East: Nonstate Actors and New Institutions." Presented at the Hilton San Francisco, California, March 26.

BBC News. 2006. "In Quotes: Lebanon Reaction." *BBC News* (July 13).

Behrooz, Maziar. 2004. "The 1953 Coup in Iran and the Legacy of the Tudeh." In *Mohammad Mosaddeq and the 1953 Coup in Iran*, ed. Mark J. Gasiorowski and Malcolm Byrne, 102–105. Syracuse, N.Y.: Syracuse University Press.

Ben-Zvi, Abraham. 2007. *The Origins of the American-Israeli Alliance: The Jordanian Factor.* New York: Routledge.

Benn, Aluf. 2009. "Olmert's Plan for Peace with the Palestinians." *Haaretz* (December 17). http://www.haaretz.com/print-edition/news/haaretz-exclusive -olmert-s-plan-for-peace-with-the-palestinians-1.1970.

Bennett, Andrew, Joseph Lepgold, and Danny Unger. 1994. "Burden-Sharing in the Persian Gulf War." *International Organization* 48, no. 1: 39–75.

Bennett, William J. 2000. "Morality, Character, and American Foreign Policy." In *Present Dangers: Crisis and Opportunity in American Foreign and Defense Policy*, ed. Robert Kagan and William Kristol. San Francisco: Encounter.

Benson, Michael T. 1997. *Harry S. Truman and the Founding of Israel.* Westport, Conn.: Praeger.

Broad, William J., John Markoff, and David E. Sanger. 2011. "Israeli Test on Worm Called Crucial in Iran Nuclear Delay." *New York Times* (January 15).

Calleo, David. 2009. "Closing Argument: A Change We Can Believe in?" *Survival* 51, no. 4: 193–200.

Çandar, Cengiz. 2009. *Turkey's "Soft Power" Strategy: A New Vision for a Multipolar World.* SETA Policy Brief 38. http://setadc.org/policy-briefs/185-turkeys -soft-power-strategy-a-new-vision-for-a-multi-polar-world.

Ceaser, James W. 2000. "The Great Divide: American Interventionism and Its Opponents." In *Present Dangers: Crisis and Opportunity in American Foreign Defense Policy*, ed. Robert Kagan and William Kristol, 25–43. San Francisco: Encounter.

Chomsky, Noam. 2006. *Failed States: The Abuse of Power and the Assault on Democracy.* New York: Metropolitan.

Clemons, Steve. 2011. "Biden's Burden: Last One Standing in Afghanistan Policy Wars." *The Atlantic* (July 21).

Clinton, Bill. 2000. The Clinton Parameters [guidelines for the Permanent Status Agreement].

Clinton, Hillary. 2009. "Secretary Clinton with Vice President Joe Biden Announce Appointment of Special Envoy for Middle East Peace George Mitchell and Special Representative for Afghanistan and Pakistan Richard Holbrooke." Washington, D.C.: U.S. Department of State.

———. 2011. "Remarks on Principles for Prosperity in the Asia-Pacific." Washington, D.C.: U.S. Department of State.

Congressional Research Service. 2009. *Israel and Hamas: Conflict in Gaza (2008–2009)*. Ed. Jim Zanotti. Vol. 7-5700 R40101. Washington, D.C.: Congressional Research Service.

Corruption Perceptions Index 2011. 2011.

Cumings, Bruce. 1981. *The Origins of the Korean War*. Princeton, N.J.: Princeton University Press.

Dallek, Robert. 2007. *Nixon and Kissinger: Partners in Power*. New York: Harper-Collins.

Davis, Forrest. 1943. "Roosevelt's World Blueprint." *Saturday Evening Post* (April 10): 20–21, 109–110.

Davutoğlu, Ahmet. 2008. "Turkey's Foreign Policy Vision: An Assessment of 2007." *Insight Turkey* 10, no. 1: 77–96.

Dawisha, Adeed. 2003. *Arab Nationalism in the Twentieth Century: From Triumph to Despair*. Princeton, N.J.: Princeton University Press.

Dobson, Christopher. 1974. *Black September: Its Short, Violent History*. New York: Macmillan.

Donnelly, Thomas. 2000. *Rebuilding America's Defenses: Strategy, Forces, and Resources for a New Century*. Washington, D.C.: Project for the New American Century.

Dowty, Alan. 1984. *Middle East Crisis: U.S. Decision Making in 1958, 1970, and 1973*. Berkeley: University of California Press.

Ehrman, John. 1995. *The Rise of Neoconservatism: Intellectuals and Foreign Affairs, 1945–1994*. New Haven, Conn.: Yale University Press.

Eickenberry, G. John, and Anne-Marie Slaughter. 2006. *Forging a World of Liberty Under Law: U.S. National Security in the Twenty-First Century*. Final Report of the Princeton Project on National Security. Princeton, N.J.: The Woodrow Wilson School of Public and International Affairs, Princeton University.

Eikenberry, G. John, et al. 2009. *The Crisis of American Foreign Policy: Wilsonianism in the Twenty-First Century*. Princeton, N.J.: Princeton University Press.

Eldar, Akiva. 2007. "What Arab Initiative?" *Haaretz* (March 6).

Fattah, Hassan M. 2006. "Militia Rebuked by Some Arab Countries." *New York Times* (July 17).

Fischel, Jack R. 1996. "The Rise of Neoconservatism." *Virginia Quarterly Review*: 367–370.

Friedman, Lawrence. 1990. *Republic of Choice*. Cambridge, Mass.: Harvard University Press.

Friedman, Thomas L. 2002. "An Intriguing Signal from the Saudi Crown Prince." *New York Times* (February 17).

———. 2011. "Barack Kissinger Obama." *New York Times* (October 26).

Fukuyama, Francis. 1989. "The End of History?" *National Interest* 16 (1989): 3–18.

———. 1992. *The End of History and the Last Man*. New York: The Free Press.

Garfinkle, Adam M. 1985. "U.S. Decision Making in the Jordan Crisis: Correcting the Record." *Political Science Quarterly* 100, no. 1: 117–138.

———. 2009. "Too Many Cooks." *AI: The American Interest Online* (November 12).

Gasiorowski, Mark J. 1987. "The 1953 Coup d'Etat in Iran." *International Journal of Middle East Studies* 19, no. 3: 261–286.

———. 2004 "Why Did Mosaddeq Fall?" In *Mohammad Mosaddeq and the 1953 Coup in Iran*, ed. Mark J. Gasiorowski and Malcolm Byrne, 261–277. Syracuse, N.Y.: Syracuse University Press.

Gerges, Fawaz A. 1994. *The Superpowers and the Middle East: Regional and International Politics, 1955–1967*. Boulder, Colo.: Westview.

Golan, Galia. 2007. *Israel and Palestine: Peace Plans and Proposals from Oslo to Disengagement*. Princeton, N.J.: Markus Wiener.

Guardian. 2010a. "U.S. Embassy Cables: Hillary Clinton Woos Prickly Egyptians." *Guardian* (November 28). http://www.guardian.co.uk/world/us-embassy -cables-documents/191130.

Guardian. 2010b. "U.S. Embassy Cables: Saudi King's Advice for Barack Obama." *Guardian* (November 28). http://www.guardian.co.uk/world/us-embassy -cables-documents/198178.

Gunning, Jeroen. 2008. *Hamas in Politics: Democracy, Religion, Violence*. New York: Columbia University Press.

Guttman, Nathan. 2011. "Latest Chapter in Mideast Tension is Dennis Ross vs. George Mitchell." *Forward* (January 21).

Guzansky, Yoel. 2009. " 'The Forgotten War': The U.S. Withdrawal from Iraq." *INSS Insight* 148.

Haass, Richard N. 2000. "The Squandered Presidency: Demanding More from the Commander-in-Chief." *Foreign Affairs* (May/June): 136.

Hahn, Peter. 2003. "National Security Concerns in U.S. Policy Toward Egypt, 1949–1956." In *The Middle East and the United States: A Historical and Political Reassessment*, ed. David W. Lesch, 89–99. Boulder, Colo.: Westview.

Halliday, Fred. 1991. "The Gulf War and Its Aftermath: First Reflections." *International Affairs* 67, no. 2.

Halpern, Manfred. 1963. *The Politics of Social Change in the Middle East and North Africa*. Princeton, N.J.: Princeton University Press.

Hiro, Dilip. 1992. *Desert Shield to Desert Storm: The Second Gulf War*. New York: Routledge.

Holbrooke, Richard. 2008. "The Next President: Mastering a Daunting Agenda." *Foreign Affairs* 87, no. 5.

Howard, Michael. 1998. "The Prudence Thing: George Bush's Class Act." *Foreign Affairs* (November/December).

Hroub, Khaled. 2004. "Hamas After Shaykh Yasin and Rantisi." *Journal of Palestine Studies* 33, no. 4: 21–38.

Humphrey, Paula. 2009. *Iran: June 2009 Elections and Nuclear Policy Implications*. NTI.

Huntington, Samuel P. 1991. *The Third Wave: Democratization in the Late Twentieth Century*. Norman: University of Oklahoma Press.

———. 1993. "The Clash of Civilizations?" *Foreign Affairs* 72, no. 3: 22–49.

———. 1996. *The Clash of Civilizations and the Remaking of World Order*. New York: Simon & Schuster.

Hussin, Iza. Forthcoming. *The Politics of Islamic Law: Local Elites, Colonial Authority, and the Making of the Muslim State*.

Iraq Watch. 1998. "Open Letter to the President." http://www.iraqwatch.org/perspectives/rumsfeld-openletter.htm.

Israel-Hamas-Hezbollah: The Current Conflict. 2006. Ed. Jeremy M. Sharp. CRS Report for Congress: Received through the CRS Web ed. Vol. Order Code RL33566. Washington, D.C.: Congressional Research Service, 2006.

Israel Ministry of Foreign Affairs. 2012. *Summary of Editorials from the Hebrew Press*.

Israeli Peace Initiative. 2011. http://israelipeaceinitiative.com/.

Jackson, Robert H. 1990. *Quasi-States: Sovereignty, International Relations, and the Third World*. New York: Cambridge University Press.

Jacobs, Matthew F. 2011. *Imagining the Middle East: The Building of an American Foreign Policy, 1918–1967*. Chapel Hill: University of North Carolina Press.

Johnson, Chalmers. 2004. *Blowback: The Costs and Consequences of American Empire*. 2nd ed. New York: Henry Holt.

Kagan, Robert. 2008. "Neocon Nation: Neoconservatism, c. 1776." *World Affairs Journal*.

Kagan, Robert, and William Kristol. 2000. *Present Dangers: Crisis and Opportunity in American Foreign and Defense Policy*. San Francisco: Encounter.

Kanan, Makiya. 1989. *Republic of Fear: The Inside Story of Saddam's Iraq*. New York: Pantheon.

Kaplan, Robert D. 1993. *Balkan Ghosts: A Journey Through History*. New York: St. Martin's.

———. 1994. "The Coming Anarchy: How Scarcity, Crime, Overpopulation, Tribalism, and Disease Are Rapidly Destroying the Social Fabric of Our Planet." *The Atlantic* (February).

———. 1996. *The Ends of the Earth: A Journey at the Dawn of the Twenty-First Century*. New York: Random House.

———. 2002. *Warrior Politics: Why Leadership Demands a Pagan Ethos*. New York: Random House.

———. 2004. "Indian Country." *Wall Street Journal* (September 21).

Kasaba, Reşat. 2010. "Turkey from the Rise of Atatürk." In *The Islamic Age of Western Dominance*, ed. Francis Robinson, 301–305. New York: Cambridge University Press.

Katzenstein, Peter J. 2005. *A World of Regions: Asia and Europe in the American Imperium*. Ithaca, N.Y.: Cornell University Press.

Kedourie, Elie. 2004. *The Chatham House Version and Other Middle Eastern Studies*. Chicago: Ivan Dee.

Khalidi, Rashid. 2004. *Resurrecting Empire: Western Footprints and America's Perilous Path in the Middle East*. Boston: Beacon.

——. 2009. *Sowing Crisis: The Cold War and American Dominance in the Middle East*. Boston: Beacon.

Khashan, Hilal. 2001. "The New Arab Cold War." *World Affairs* 159, no. 4: 158–169.

Khoury, Philip S., and Joseph Kostiner, eds. 1990. *Tribes and State Formation in the Middle East*. Berkeley: University of California Press.

Kimmerling, Baruch. 2004. *Immigrants, Settlers, Natives: The Israeli State and Society Between Cultural Pluralism and Cultural Wars*. Tel Aviv: Am Oved.

Kissinger, Henry. 1979. *White House Years*. Boston: Little, Brown.

Klein, Joe. 2010. "Q&A: Obama on His First Year in Office." *Time* (January 21).

Klieman, Aaron S. 1970. *Foundations of British Policy in the Arab World: The Cairo Conference of 1921*. Baltimore, Md.: Johns Hopkins University Press.

——. 1990. *Israel and the World After Forty Years*. Washington, D.C.: Pergamon-Brassey's International Defense.

Knudsen, Are. 2005. "Crescent and Sword: The Hamas Enigma." *Third World Quarterly* 26, no. 8: 1373–1388.

Korany, Bahgat. 2010. *The Changing Middle East: A New Look at Regional Dynamics*. Cairo: American University in Cairo Press.

Kristianasen, Wendy. 1999. "Challenge and Counterchallenge: Hamas's Response to Oslo." *Journal of Palestine Studies* 28, no. 3: 19–36.

Kurtz, S. 2003. "Democratic Imperialism: A Blueprint." *Policy Review*.

Kurtzer, Daniel. 2012. "Reviving the Peace Process." *The National Interest* 117: 38–46.

Kurtzer, Daniel C., and Scott B. Lasensky. 2008. *Negotiating Arab-Israeli Peace: American Leadership in the Middle East*. Washington, D.C.: United States Institute of Peace Press.

Kuru, Ahmet. 2003. "Fethullah Gülen's Search for a Middle Way Between Modernity and Muslim Tradition." In *Turkish Islam and the Secular State*, ed. M. Hakan Yavuz and John L. Esposito, 115–130. Syracuse, N.Y.: Syracuse University Press.

Laub, Karin. 2007. "Olmert Seeks Regional Peace Conference." *Washington Post* (April 2).

Lemann, Nicolas. 2003. "After Iraq: The Plan to Remake the Middle East." *New Yorker* (February 17).

Lesch, David W. 2003. "The 1957 American-Syrian Crisis: Globalist Policy in a Regional Reality." In *The Middle East and the United States: A Historical and Political Reassessment*, ed. David W. Lesch, 133–148. Boulder, Colo.: Westview.

Levey, Zach. 2004. "The United States' Skyhawk Sale to Israel, 1966: Strategic Exigencies of an Arms Deal." *Diplomatic History* 28, no. 2: 255–276.

Lewis, Samuel W. 1999. "The United States and Israel: Evolution of an Unwritten Alliance." *Middle East Journal* 53, no. 3: 364–378.

Lippmann, Walter. 1943. *The Four Policemen: What Will Hold them Together?* Speech for the Second War Conference of New England Council, November 18.

Lipsky, David. 2005. "Appropriating the Globe." *New York Times* (November 27).

Lustick, Ian. 2006. *Trapped in the War on Terror.* Philadelphia: University of Pennsylvania Press.

Lynch, Colum. 2006. "Security Council Seat Tied to Aid." *Washington Post* (November 1).

Lynch, Timothy J., and Robert S. Singh. 2008. *After Bush: The Case for Continuity in American Foreign Policy.* New York: Cambridge University Press.

Lyon, Alistair. 2010. "Why Egypt's Power Has Dimmed." *Reuters* (December 20).

MacArthur, John R. 2004. *Second Front: Censorship and Propaganda in the 1991 Gulf War.* Berkeley: University of California Press.

Macguire, Sean, and Khaled Owels. 2007. "Hamas Leader Says Israel's Existence Is a Reality." *Reuters* (January 10).

Maddy-Weitzman, Bruce. 2010a. "Amadinejad Goes to Lebanon." *Jerusalem Report* (November 22): 32.

———. 2010b. "The Impotent Summit." *Jerusalem Report* (May 10): 22.

Maghroori, Ray, and Stephen M. Gorman. 1981. *The Yom-Kippur War: A Case Study in Crisis Decision Making in American Foreign Policy.* Washington, D.C.: University Press of America.

Mahjar-Barducci, Anna. 2009. "New Best Friends: Iran and Egypt's Muslim Brotherhood." *Hudson New York* (May 13). http://www.hudsonny.org/2009/05/new-best-friends-iran-and-egypts-muslim-brotherhood.php.

Malcolm, Andrew. 2010. "Their Florida Town Hall: What Obama-Biden Said and Said and Said and . . ." *Los Angeles Times*, Top of the Ticket blog (January 27). http://latimesblogs.latimes.com/washington/2010/01/obama-biden-townhall-traqnscript.html.

Maoz, Moshe. 1988. *Asad, the Sphinx of Damascus: A Political Biography.* New York: Weidenfeld and Nicholson.

Maoz, Zeev. 2006. *Defending the Holy Land: A Critical Analysis of Israel's Security and Foreign Policy.* Ann Arbor: University of Michigan Press.

McAlister, Melani. 2001. *Epic Encounters: Culture, Media, and U.S. Interests in the Middle East, 1945–2000.* Berkeley: University of California Press.

McGowan, John. 2007. *American Liberalism: An Interpretation for our Time.* Chapel Hill: University of North Carolina Press.

Mearsheimer, John J., and Stephen M. Walt. 2006a. "The Israel Lobby." *London Review of Books* (March 23): 3–12.

———. 2006b. *The Israel Lobby and U.S. Foreign Policy.* Vol. RWP06-011. Cambridge, Mass.: Kennedy School of Government.

———. 2007. *The Israel Lobby and U.S. Foreign Policy.* New York: Farrar, Straus and Giroux.

Mendelsohn, Barak. 2009. *Combating Jihadism: American Hegemony and Interstate Cooperation in the War on Terrorism.* Chicago: University of Chicago Press.

Middle East Online. 2009. "Egypt Accuses Iran as Police Hunt 'Hezbollah Cell.'" *Middle East Online* (April 14).

Middle East Policy Council. 2011. "Amid Turmoil, GCC Extends Invitation to Jordan and Morocco." *MEPC.org* (May 16).

Migdal, Joel S. 1988. *Strong Societies and Weak States: State-Society Relations and State Capabilities in the Third World.* Princeton, N.J.: Princeton University Press.

Miller, Aaron David. 2011. "Wanted: Adult Supervision." *Foreign Policy.*

Minutes of a National Security Council Meeting. 2008. Vol. 24. Washington, D.C.: U.S. Government Printing Office.

Mishal, Shaul, and Avraham Sela. 1994. *Speaking Stones: Communiqués from the Intifada Underground.* Syracuse, N.Y.: Syracuse University Press.

———. 2006. *The Palestinian Hamas: Vision, Violence, and Coexistence.* New York: Columbia University Press.

Mottahedeh, Roy. 2009. *The Mantle of the Prophet: Religion and Politics in Iran.* Oxford: Oneworld.

Muravchik, Joshua. 2009. "The Abandonment of Democracy." *Commentary* (July/August): 21–26.

Nasr, Seyyed Vali Reza. 2001. *Islamic Leviathan: Islam and the Making of State Power.* New York: Oxford University Press.

Nevo, Joseph. 2008. "September 1970 in Jordan: A Civil War?" *Civil Wars* 10, no. 3: 217–230.

New York Times. 1953. "Text of Secretary Dulles' Report on Near East Trip." *New York Times* (June 2): 4.

Newhouse, John. 2003. *Imperial America: The Bush Assault on the World Order.* New York: Knopf.

Nixon, Richard M. 1970. "Off-the-Record Remarks by President Nixon, September 16, 1970." In U.S. Department of State, *Foreign Relations of the United States,* vol. 1, *Foreign Relations, 1969–1976,* 247–257. http://history.state.gov/historicaldocuments/frus1969-76vo1/comp1.

———. 1978. *The Memoirs of Richard Nixon.* New York: Grosset & Dunlap.

Obama, Barack. 2007. "Renewing American Leadership." *Foreign Affairs* 86, no. 4.

———. 2009a. Interview with *Al Arabiya. Al Arabiya* (January 27). http://www.alarabiya.net/articles/2009/01/27/65087.html.

———. 2009b. "Remarks by the President on a New Beginning." Speech in Cairo. http://www.whitehouse.gov/the_press_office/Remarks-by-the-President-at-Cairo-University-6-04-09.

Olmert, Ehud. 2007. *Address by PM Olmert at the Annapolis Conference.* Israel Ministry of Foreign Affairs.

Oren, Michael B. 2007. *Power, Faith, and Fantasy: America in the Middle East, 1776 to the Present.* New York: W. W. Norton.

Parmar, Inderjeet. 2009. "Foreign Policy Fusion: Liberal Interventionists, Conservative Nationalists, and Neoconservatives—the New Alliance Dominating the U.S. Foreign Policy Establishment." *International Politics* 46, nos. 2/3: 177–209.

Patrick, Stewart. 2009. "Prix Fixe *and* à la Carte: Avoiding False Multilateral Choices." *Washington Quarterly* 32, no. 4: 77–95.

Perle, Richard N. 2000. "Iraq: Saddam Unbound." In *Present Dangers: Crisis and Opportunity in American Foreign and Defense Policy*, ed. Robert Kagan and William Kristol, 99–110. San Francisco: Encounter.

Perlez, Jane, and Pir Z. Shah. 2008. "Power Rising, Taliban Besiege Pakistani Shiites." *New York Times* (July 26).

Petersen, Tore T. 2009. *Richard Nixon, Great Britain, and the Anglo-American Alignment in the Persian Gulf and Arabian Peninsula: Making Allies Out of Clients*. Portland, Ore.: Sussex Academic Press.

Podeh, Elie. 2003. "The Perils of Ambiguity: The United States and the Baghdad Pact." In *The Middle East and the United States: A Historical and Political Reassessment*, ed. David Lesch, 100–119. Boulder, Colo.: Westview.

——. 2007. "The Arab Peace Initiative: A Missed Opportunity." *Palestine-Israel Journal of Politics, Economics, and Culture* 14. no. 4.

Provence, Michael. 2005. *The Great Syrian Revolt and the Rise of Arab Nationalism*. Austin: University of Texas Press.

Quandt, William B. 2004. "America and the Middle East: A Fifty-Year Overview." In *Diplomacy in the Middle East: The International Relations of Regional and Outside Powers*, ed. L. Carl Brown. London: I. B. Tauris.

——. 2005. *Peace Process: American Diplomacy and the Arab-Israeli Conflict Since 1967*. 3rd ed. Washington, D.C.: Brookings Institution Press; Berkeley: University of California Press.

Rabin, Yitzhak. 1996. *The Rabin Memoirs*. Trans. Dov Goldstein. Expanded ed. Berkeley: University of California Press.

Rabinovich, Abraham. 2004. *Yom Kippur War: The Epic Encounter That Transformed the Middle East*. New York: Knopf.

Ramazani, R. K. 1986. *Revolutionary Iran: Challenge and Response in the Middle East*. Baltimore, Md.: Johns Hopkins University Press.

Reagan, Ronald. 1979. "Recognizing the Israeli Asset." *Washington Post* (August 15).

Rice, Condoleezza. 2008. "Rethinking the National Interest: American Realism for a New World." *Foreign Affairs* 87, no. 4: 2–26.

Robbins, Carla Anne. 2007. "Bush Foreign Policy: Grand Vision and Its Application." In *Second-Term Blues: How George W. Bush Has Governed*, ed. John C. Fortier and Norman J. Ornstein. Washington, D.C.: American Enteprise Institute/Brookings Institution Press.

Rodman, Peter W. 1991. "Middle East Diplomacy After the Gulf War." *Foreign Affairs* 70, no. 2: 1–18.

Ross, Dennis. 2007. *The Missing Piece: The Inside Story of the Fight for Middle East Peace*. New York: Farrar, Straus and Giroux.

Rotberg, Robert I. 2003. *State Failure and State Weakness in a Time of Terror*. Washington, D.C.: Brookings Institution Press.

————. 2004. *When States Fail: Causes and Consequences*. Princeton, N.J.: Princeton University Press.

Rubinovitz, Ziv. 2010. "Blue and White 'Black September': Israel's Role in the Jordan Crisis of 1970." *International History Review* 32, no. 4: 687–706.

Safran, Nadav. 1990. "Strike Supporters." *New Republic* (September 24): 24–26.

Sala-i-Martin, Xavier, and Elsa V. Artadi. 2002. *Economic Growth and Investment in the Arab World*. Vol. 0203-08. Columbia University, Department of Economics.

Salinger, Pierre. 1995. "The United States, the United Nations, and the Gulf War." *Middle East Journal* 49, no. 4: 595–613.

Salt, Jeremy. 2008. *The Unmaking of the Middle East: A History of Western Disorder in Arab Lands*. Berkeley: University of California Press.

Sanger, David E. 2007. "Bush Foreign Policy: First-Term Choices and Second-Term Consequences." In *Second-Term Blues: How George W. Bush Has Governed*, ed. John C. Fortier and Norman J. Ornstein, 71–87. Washington, D.C.: American Enterprise Institute/Brookings Institution Press.

Schalit, Joel. 2009. *Israel Vs. Utopia*. New York: Akashik.

Schiff, Ze'ev. 1991. "Israel After the War." *Foreign Affairs* 70, no. 2: 19–33.

Schoenbaum, David. 1993. *The United States and the State of Israel*. New York: Oxford University Press.

Seale, Patrick. 1986. *The Struggle for Syria: A Study of Postwar Arab Politics, 1945–1958*. London: I. B. Tauris.

Shadid, Anthony. 2011. "In Peril: The Arab Status." *New York Times* (January 16).

Shannon, Vaughn P. 2007. "Iran and the Middle East: The Pursuit of Security and Legitimacy in the American Age." In *Strategic Interests in the Middle East: Opposition and Support for US Foreign Policy*, ed. Jack Covarrubias and Tom Lansford, 171–193. Burlington, Vt.: Ashgate.

Shapir, Yiftah. 2010. "The United States and Buildup of Military Force in the Persian Gulf." *INSS Insight* 161.

Siegman, Henry. 2002. "Will Israel Take a Chance?" *New York Times* (February 21).

Simpson, Gerry J. 2004. *Great Powers and Outlaw States: Unequal Sovereigns in the International Legal Order*. New York: Cambridge University Press.

Siniver, Asaf. 2008. *Nixon, Kissinger, and U.S. Foreign Policy Making: The Machinery of Crisis*. New York: Cambridge University Press.

Slackman, Michael. 2009. "Influence of Egypt and Saudi Arabia Fades." *New York Times* (November 11).

Sofer, Ronny. 2007. "Jordanian, FMs: This Is a Time of Opportunity." *Ynetnews* (July 25).

Spiegel, Steven L. 1985. *The Other Arab-Israeli Conflict: Making America's Middle East Policy, from Truman to Reagan*. Chicago: University of Chicago Press.

Spiegel Online. 2006. "Interview with Ex-Neocon Francis Fukuyama: A Model Democracy Is Not Emerging in Iraq." *Spiegel Online International* (March 22). http://www.spiegel.de/international/interview-with-ex-neocon-francis-fukuyama-a-model-democracy-is-not-emerging-in-iraq-a-407315.html.

Stack, Liam. 2009. "Egypt's Peace Role—and Its Influence—Under Fire." *Christian Science Monitor* (July 31).

Stein, Janice Gross. 2003. "Flawed Strategies and Missed Signals: Crisis Bargaining Between the Superpowers, October 1973." In *The Middle East and the United States: A Historical and Political Reassessment*, ed. David W. Lesch, 211–232. Boulder, Colo.: Westview.

Stiglitz, Joseph E., and Linda J. Bilmes. 2008. *The Three Trillion Dollar War: The True Cost of the Iraq Conflict*. New York: W. W. Norton.

Study Group on a New Israeli Strategy Toward 2000. 1996. *A Clean Break: A New Strategy for Securing the Realm*. Institute for Advanced Strategic and Political Studies.

Tabler, Andrew. 2007. "Signs of Shiitization in Syria." April. http://www.andrewtabler.com/2007/04/signs-of-shiitization-in-syria.html.

Takeyh, Ray. 2000. *The Origins of the Eisenhower Doctrine: The U.S., Britain, and Nasser's Egypt, 1953–57*. New York: St. Martin's.

Tamimi, Azzam. 2007. *Hamas: A History from Within*. Northampton, Mass.: Olive Branch.

Teitelbaum, Joshua. 2010. "The Shiites of Saudi Arabia." *Current Trends in Islamist Ideology* 10.

Telhami, Shibley. 1994. "Between Theory and Fact: Explaining U.S. Behavior in the Gulf Crisis." In *The Gulf War and the New World Order: International Relations of the Middle East*, ed. Tareq Y. Ismael and Jacqueline S. Ismael. Gainesville: University of Florida Press.

Time. 1945. "Stassen's Creed." *Time* (March 12).

Tyler, Patrick. 2009. *A World of Trouble: The White House and the Middle East from the Cold War to the War on Terror*. New York: Farrar Straus Giroux.

Ulrichsen, Kristian Coates. 2009. "The Durability of Weak States in the Middle East." In *Persistent State Weakness in the Global Age*, ed.. Denisa Kostovicova and Vesna Bojicic-Dzelilovic, 83–96. Burlington, Vt.: Ashgate.

U.S. Department of State. 1947. *"The Pentagon Talks of 1947" Between the United States and the United Kingdom Concerning the Middle East and the Eastern Mediterranean*. Vol. 5.

U.S. Department of State, Office of the Historian. 1970. *Telegram from the Embassy in Jordan to the Department of State*. Vol. 24.

Vidal, Gore. 2004. *Imperial America: The United States of Amnesia*. New York: Nation Books.

Vitalis, Robert. 2007. *America's Kingdom: Mythmaking on the Saudi Oil Frontier*. Stanford, Calif.: Stanford University Press.

——. 2009. "How Imperial Oil Haunts the Present." Unpublished paper prepared for the Second Princeton–Sciences Po Conference on the State of Saudi Arabia.

Walt, Stephen M. 2000. "Two Cheers for Clinton's Foreign Policy." *Foreign Affairs* (March/April).

Watson Institute for International Studies. 2011. "Research Cites 225,000 Lives Lost and US$4 Trillion in Spending on Post-9/11 Wars." June 28. http://www.watsoninstitute.org/news_detail.cfm?id=1536.

Wedeen, Lisa. 1999. *Ambiguities of Domination: Politics, Rhetoric, and Symbols in Contemporary Syria*. Chicago: University of Chicago Press.

Wilber, Donald N. 1969. *Overthrow of Premier Mossadeq of Iran, November 1952–August 1953*. October. http://www.nytimes.com/library/world/mideast/041600 iran-cia-intro.html.

Woodhouse, C. M. 1982. *Something Ventured*. New York: Granada.

Wright, Jonathan. 2008. "Egypt's Ruling Party Attacks Hamas and Allies." *Reuters* (December 31).

Wright, Richard. 1945. "Introduction." In *Black Metropolis: A Study of Negro Life in a Northern City*, ed. St. Clair Drake and Horace R. Clayton. New York: Harcourt, Brace.

Wurmser, David. 1999. *Tyranny's Ally: America's Failure to Defeat Saddam Hussein*. Washington, D.C.: AEI.

Yeşilbursa, Behçt Kemal. 2005. *The Baghdad Pact: Anglo-American Defence Policies in the Middle East, 1950–1959*. New York: Frank Cass.

Zak, Moshe. 1996. "Israel and Jordan: Strategically Bound." *Israel Affairs* 3, no. 1: 39–60.

Zartman, I. William. 1995. *Collapsed States: The Disintegration and Restoration of Legitimate Authority*. Boulder, Colo.: Lynne Rienner.

Zetter, Kim. 2011. "How Digital Detectives Deciphered Stuxnet, the Most Menacing Malware in History." *Wired* (July 11).

Zuhur, Sherifa. 2008. *Hamas and Israel: Conflicting Strategies of Group-Based Politics*. Strategic Studies Institute, United States Army War College.

Zunes, Stephen. 2010. "Richard Holbrooke Represented the Worst of the Foreign Policy Establishment." *Truthout*.

———. 2003. *Tinderbox: U.S. Middle East Policy and the Roots of Terrorism*. Monroe, Me.: Common Courage Press.

Index